COMMUNICATION AND CRITIQUE

COMMUNICATION AND RACE

A Structural Perspective

OSCAR H. GANDY, JR.

A member of the Hodder Headline Group
LONDON • SYDNEY • AUCKLAND

Co-published in the United States of America
by Oxford University Press, Inc., New York

First published in Great Britain in 1998 by
Arnold, a member of the Hodder Headline Group
338 Euston Road, London NW1 3BH
http://www.arnoldpublishers.com

Co-published in the United States of America by
Oxford University Press, Inc.,
198 Madison Avenue, New York, NY 10016

British Library Cataloguing in Publication Data
A catalogue entry for this book is available from the British Library

Library of Congress Cataloging-in-Publication Data
A catalog record for this book is available from the Library of Congress

ISBN 0 340 67689 2 (pb)
ISBN 0 340 67690 6 (hb)

Production editor: Rada Radojicic
Production controller: Priya Gohil
Cover designer: Stefan Brazzo

Typeset in 10/12 pt Sabon by
Photoprint, Torquay, Devon
Printed and bound in Great Britain by
J W Arrowsmith Ltd, Bristol

Contents

Preface

These are troubling times. They are troubling for obvious reasons. Among the most troubling reasons are those which suggest that the smartest among us have either given up hope or haven't a clue about where to begin again. Derek Bell, legal scholar and civil rights activist, speaks in measured tones about the permanence of racism and the futility of action pursued under the agenda of civil rights. At the same time, an American president, who has helped to legitimate the most substantial retreat from the mission of equality and affirmative action since the emergence of segregationist Jim Crow legislation a century ago, has called on the nation to join him in his initiative on race. No wonder we are confused. Scholars within the academy can no longer be relied upon to provide guidance and direction because of the internecine struggles and turf wars that only seem to be about theory and method.

For most of my academic career, my attention to matters of race was always subordinate to my more general concern about the ways in which communication and information were resources that were linked to the exercise of power. During a critically important period in my career, when I taught at Howard University, students and colleagues like Jannette Dates, William Barlow, Paula Matabane, John Barber, and Larry Coleman helped to turn my attention more explicitly towards the ways in which the mass media's treatment of African independence struggles, Black politicians, and various challenges to the health and well being of African Americans influenced the ways in which these issues and concerns were understood.

The groundbreaking scholarship of colleagues and friends like Felix Gutiérrez, Clint Wilson, and Carolyn Martindale helped to make the point that both the news media and the entertainment industry shared responsibility for the ways in which ethnic minorities were understood as objects of ridicule as well as of fear. Understandably, this work focused on the ways in which the misrepresentation of race reflected the influence of historic barriers to minority ownership and employment in media. Jan Dates and

Bill Barlow helped us to understand more of the complexity in representation as a reflection of African American efforts to provide an alternative view. The resulting 'Split Image' and its varied refractions has been detailed over the years in the pages of a resource that we have all come to depend upon, William Starosta's gemstone, *The Howard Journal of Communications*.

For my own part, it was not until 1994, when Everette Dennis and the Freedom Forum provided me with the opportunity to devote my full attention to matters of communication and race. While most in the field were concerned with the ways in which the media represented minorities to the mainstream, I thought it was also important to examine the ways in which the press failed to perform responsibly as an agent of its minority consumers. My sense was that the mass media largely considered minority readers and viewers as an accidental audience, and that editors and producers were largely unconcerned about the impact that the habitual construction of African Americans as either criminals or victims would have on its readers of color. At the same time, I was interested to discover the ways in which variations in the presence and political power of African Americans in media markets and on newspaper editorial staffs were reflected as structural constraints in the way certain stories were framed.

As I worked to document the ways in which the news media covered stories of discrimination and risk, and then to study the ways in which Whites and African Americans differed in their assessment of their own vulnerability, I was approached by Vincent Mosco with an opportunity and a challenge. I saw Vinny's invitation to participate in the new series that he and Peter Golding were preparing for Arnold as providing an opportunity for me to write the book that I thought the times required. The perception of opportunity and risk is just one part of the larger process we understand as the social construction of race. I saw this book as providing an opportunity for me to explore the ways in which perception, media content, and the media industries themselves were all implicated in a social structure which governs the distribution of life chances. Consciousness, media content, and social relations are all structured in identifiable ways. It is the challenge of discovering and describing the ways in which these structures interact that I have added to the opportunity to comment on the problems of race.

In preparing a book that I hope will inform the thinking of advanced undergraduates, graduate students and their professors, as well as those outside the academy who are interested in the role that communication plays in the reproduction of racism and relations of power, I have been aided by two outstanding research assistants. Linus Abraham's assistance in the early stages of my review of the literature helped me to believe that the task could actually be accomplished. Jessica Davis's critical eye, and broad exposure to the literature within cultural studies, at times made me doubt that I would be the one to achieve it. But, as always, her generosity and boundless energy made it essential for me to try. The series editors, Peter Golding and Vinny Mosco, pulled and pushed just enough to bring my vision into line with theirs. I appreciate their confidence as well as their concern that we get it right. Production editor, Rada Radojicic, was always responsive to my questions and concerns and a joy to work with. I am sure I have that, and much more that I don't know about, to thank Lesley Riddle for.

For my wife, Judy, who has suffered through the sleepless nights and tense moments that seem to accompany each of these projects, I wish I could say it was over. Instead, I am afraid it is as I say to my readers, time to begin again.

Oscar H. Gandy, Jr.
Winter, 1997

1

Introduction

The purpose of this book is the development of a way of understanding the relationships between communication and race as they have evolved over time. Much has changed, and the pace of change seems to be accelerating. Some of these changes may be understood in the context of still other changes taking place in the ways we understand the world. These are changes in social theory.

Theory is a way of knowing. Theory provides a way of making sense of the great complexity in the world around us. The scope of any theory is necessarily limited, and therefore an assessment of any particular theory is most useful when it is organized in terms of that which the theory allows you to see or understand by means of its points of entry and its organizing principles (Resnick and Wolff, 1987).

No single theory or theoretical perspective could possibly serve *all* of our interests in knowing about the world. Some of our interests are conceptual, reflecting a curiosity about our environment. Other theoretical interests are more utilitarian or pragmatic, driven perhaps by the desire to avoid risk, and to realize individual or collective advantage. Other interests are more broadly social and political, reflecting an axiom of critical theory that the reason for understanding the world is to change it.

The purpose of critical social theory ought to be the active engagement of those systems of power that limit the realization of the human potential. This book and its engagement with theory is directed toward that critical goal of understanding the ways in which the relations between communication and race can be transformed in ways that are enabling, rather than limiting.

The approaches to critical scholarship in communication are many and varied. They include: (1) attempts to demystify the ways in which power and culture interact; (2) efforts to expose the different languages of manipulation and repression; (3) the pursuit of insights into the dynamic interdependence between industrial, social, and cognitive structures; (4) the

cultivation of competence in resisting persuasion and the search for alternative points of view; and, more generally, (5) the elaboration of theoretical
insights that support the empowerment of those traditionally excluded
(Gerbner, 1983a, p. 359).

The perspective which is used throughout this book is one which
emphasizes the theoretical value of notions of structure. The orientation
that I have taken toward structure in this book is primarily conceptual, in
that I have tried to avoid making claims about the underlying *reality* of
structures but, instead, talk about the ways in which we might usefully
think about social reality in structural terms. In pursuing the development
of the structural models we will use in exploring communication and race,
I will argue that structural models represent a very useful way of talking
about social relations.

The use of structural perspectives has a long, and occasionally troubled,
history in the human sciences. Fairly recently, structural linguistics has
served as a leading source for the metaphorical framework through which
to understand complex social systems and practices. The contributions of
Ferdinand de Saussure (1966), Claude Lévi-Strauss, and Louis Althusser
(1971) have been combined in ways which have challenged our assumptions about the behavior of autonomous rational actors (Best and Kellner,
1991). However, it is not representations of formal linguistic structures that
will be our primary guide in understanding the role of structure in our
lives.

Structure will be discussed as a feature of social systems, and this use of
structure is perhaps its most familiar use within social theory. We will also
use the concept of structure as a point of entry through which to understand the nature of the changing relationship between social structure and
individual agency in the complex of social relations. Continuing debates
among social theorists about the nature of structural features, structural
influence, and structural change reflect the high degree of theoretical
uncertainty about the nature of causality and determination within social
systems.

Structure is also a useful concept within the sphere of social psychology
and the engagement with the problem of meaning or cognition. Social
theorists differ in the emphasis they place on psychology and reason, and
assumptions they make regarding the nature of rationality. Mental structures, such as cognitive schema, provide a way to think about the influence
of information and ideas on the relationships that make up our day-to-day
existence. The ways in which cognitive structures are formed, and the ways
in which existing cognitive structures influence the ways in which new
information is processed, and decision making enabled, will be discussed
below, and in greater detail in the chapter on the social construction of
race.

Because of the relatively limited focus on communication and race within
communications studies, many of the insights discussed in this book will

have been adapted from social research not explicitly concerned with race, and from studies of race relations not generally focused on communications. For example, Jürgen Habermas's (1989) discussion of the bourgeois 'public sphere' emphasizes the ways in which public relations, marketing research, and other strategic communications threaten the realization of the fundamental social goal of communication – the enhancement of understanding. When these insights are applied to the subject of race, it seems clear that a complex of inequalities has resulted in the substantial inability of racial and ethnic minorities to voice their opinions in ways that can overcome the constraints inherent in a structure of race- and class-based privilege (Gandy, 1988). Because of the exclusion or subordination of minority perspectives, the press has been unable to overcome, and may have, in fact, tended to widen and reinforce the gap between White and Black perceptions of the social and economic status of African Americans (Hacker, 1992). We will discuss theories of the public sphere, communications competence, and the difficulties that individuals and groups in society experience in attempting to create an 'atmosphere of shared knowledge, values and trust' that an 'ideal speech situation' is presumed to support (Hardt, 1993).

While success in achieving the goals of critical scholarship are by no means assured, it should be clear that success is the product of effort rather than chance. Effort, understood as social practice, succeeds to the extent that it is guided by theory. Because the problems we understand as having a basis in communication about race must be engaged by theory if they are to be overcome, those postmodern theories which celebrate the indeterminancy of social practice (Ang, 1996b; McRobbie, 1994), and even question the value of high-level theory, will not win much praise within these pages (Best and Kellner, 1991). In contrast, that scholarship which critically engages media systems and audiences in an attempt to understand the ways in which the consequences of media consumption reflect the structures of power that surround it will command the center stage (Hardt, 1992; Morley, 1992).

Communication and race

The study of communication and race must of necessity take into account the contemporary uncertainty about the meaning of racial categories and the distinctions that are implied by racial classifications. These will be discussed in detail in the next chapter. However, no amount of uncertainty about the scientific status or validity of racial and ethnic categories is likely to displace the very powerful impression we share that social relations and the distribution of life chances are influenced mightily by such classifications (Dahrendorf, 1979). There is also little doubt that it is through communication that the structural influence of racism is maintained.

It is through language and communication that we develop and share the multidimensional impressions of ourselves and others that become part of the structures of meaning we rely upon to guide us through our day-to-day routines. To the degree that these impressions are broadly shared, they exist as a framework or structure of meaning within the culture that we also rely upon to guide us through interactions that may be outside our normal routines.

These commonsense impressions include a great many abstractions or distillations of complexity that we have come to recognize as stereotypes. Racial stereotypes are reinforced, enhanced, and then integrated into even broader systems of meaning by our own direct experience. However, as we will emphasize throughout this book, different forms of communication provide a kind of indirect experience that makes many of these stereotypes extremely resistant to change. While interpersonal communications will not be ignored, our primary emphasis will be on the racial and ethnic stereotypes which are reproduced and distributed by the mass media.

While stereotypes are a central focus within the study of communication and race, there are a number of other aspects of the communicative process which have to be understood if the goal of critical engagement is to be realized. A critical understanding of communication and race requires us to make sense of that complex of factors which influences the production, distribution, and reception of communications about race. Thus, because we recognize that the symbolic content of social communications are at some level the product of human labor, and therefore reflect some degree of individual agency, intent, purpose and choice, it becomes important for us to determine which of the sources of influence weigh most heavily on those decisions. Why do communicators rely upon hurtful stereotypes? What explains their longevity?

Because the mass media are to a great extent influenced by the logic of capitalist markets, a concern for profitability will be seen to play a dominant role in the reproduction of racial stereotypes. However, while there is a stable core of misrepresentation, there are also changes at the margin that are important for us to take note of and explain. We will explore the ways in which changes in technology, media ownership, and finance, as well as market demographics and audience preferences, have combined to influence the ways in which the representations of particular groups, such as African Americans, have varied over time.

Because we recognize that the process of communication is far more complicated than a simple transmission model would imply, it will also be necessary for us to examine the complex of factors that helps to determine the ways in which a member of the audience incorporates aspects of racialized content into his or her cognitive structure. The influence of social location, including those aspects determined by racial group membership, identification, and social class position on the reception and processing of media content will be examined from a variety of social science perspectives.

Critical theory and race

Engaging communication and race from a critical perspective requires an understanding of the ways in which changes in the material reality of social life and social theory tend to interact and influence each other.

Changes in understanding are the product of two interacting sources of influence: (1) actual changes in phenomena, as in (a) the readily identifiable changes in the character of communications media, and (b) changes that are not so readily observed in the changing character of those aspects of social reality that we refer to when we talk about race; and (2) changes in the theoretical systems that we use to assign importance and meaning to different aspects of phenomena and the relations between them. The attempt to understand the ways in which social theory affects our 'commonsense' understanding of reality is best understood as a problem in the sociology of knowledge (Berger and Luckmann, 1966). We will examine the ways in which changes in important concepts like power, determination, and influence have affected what we know, or at least what we believe, about communications, and the relations between communications and race.

Contemporary social theorists tend to believe that there is, in fact, a real world. We understand this world with the aid of systems of well-ordered and not so well-ordered concepts, or perhaps, more precisely, *theoretical constructs*. These constructs enjoy a strong, but evolving consensus within the community of knowers that share a commitment to the paradigms of normative and empirical social science that continue to modify, adjust, and adapt traditions of inquiry inherited from the leaders of the Enlightenment (Garnham, 1990; Popper, 1968).

Among all the aspects of relations between people that we might choose to explore, critical scholars of communication have tended to emphasize *power* and *influence* as being most worthy of our attention. Our concern within this book will be focused on the ways in which communication about race influences the distribution of power. As we will see, this concept of power within social theory is quite different from the construct as it has developed within the physical and natural sciences. Indeed, the ways in which we think about power, and the things that power affects, may ironically get in the way of our efforts to control its abuse.

The ways we think about power, and the ways in which we understand the consequences that flow from the use of power, have been influenced by the theoretical models which make sense, and have been put to good use in the work of scientists and engineers. However, some social theorists believe that we are not at all well served by our reliance on such conceptualizations of power. They argue that we might even be better off if we banished the concept of power from the discourse of communication theory (Krippendorff, 1995). Others suggest that what is needed is a 'rethinking' of power, rather than its abandonment (Wartenberg, 1992). Wartenberg suggests that

> power is one of the fundamental realities of human social existence, a reality that explains the oppressive and demeaning nature of the conditions of human life. Power remains an important concept for explaining those conditions and for thinking of possible means of ameliorating them. (1992, p. xi)

The study of power, influence, and determination will play a central role in our critical examination of communication and race.

In the same way that different conceptualizations of power and influence have affected the ways in which we understand communication, competing and complementary theoretical models have also affected the ways in which we have understood race. A biological orientation toward race has emphasized concepts of genetically determined *capacity*. Racial groups have been characterized in terms of what was believed about innate differences in their capacity for reasoning. When applied to the study of subordinate racial groups the emphasis on capacity tended to be focused on only one end of the scale, that of *deficit*, or limited capacity.

In the same ways that the concept of power is controversial, the concept of *intelligence* and the ways it might be measured, as well as the ways in which it might be understood to determine the behavior of individuals and members of racialized groups, continues to be a highly unsettled area of scholarship (Jacoby and Glauberman, 1995). Some theories of race that reflected a biological orientation understood cognitive deficits as having their origins in nature, such as in evolutionary processes of natural selection. While competing views may have emphasized the *social* origins of apparent differences in capacity, the primary focus tended to be on the deficiencies of subordinate groups. Changes in the dominant conceptualization of race have accompanied changes in the character and role of science within the public sphere. These changes will be discussed in the next chapter.

The scholarly approach to race has also been focused on the relations between the races. Concepts of status and class that had been developed as aspects of more general social theory also affected the ways in which conceptions about the nature of *race relations* developed. Theories about social structure, including those that linked social class with employment and wealth, as well as status and authority, have influenced the ways in which theories about race relations developed. The indicators of social status that had traditionally been associated with the nature of one's employment or relations with capital eventually proved to be unreliable when comparisons were made across and within particular racial groups.

Racial classification on the basis of *skin color* has been a powerful influence on the determination of individual and group status in different cultures. It is of particular theoretical interest that these biological or physical differences both reflect and influence social relations of power.

Variations in the skin color of children born to African slaves in the United States depended in part upon whether the mother was performing agricultural or household labor. Ways of talking about the relationships that produced these children reflect the structural relations of power that defined a critical epoch in the development of the peculiar racial character of the United States (Gutman, 1975).

We might note, for example, that the terms 'rape' and 'miscegenation' have been used by different observers to refer to the identical sexual act. The use of these terms can be seen to vary as a function of the social status and position of one party in relation to another. Such relations are reflected in systems of law such that historical records create some most improbable facts: 'if one looks at the record in 250 years of US history, no white man ever committed the crime of rape on a black woman in twelve southern states' (Duster, 1990, p. 97).

Racial discrimination and *prejudice* have also emerged as key concepts in the explanation of differential social status, and in the orientation of actions taken within the legal system toward the mitigation of social problems. The definitions of these concepts have changed over time, and their meanings have varied quite substantially within different expert communities. Although it was quite a while before W. E. B. Du Bois' emphasis on the social origins of Black poverty would come to dominate social theory in this area, racial discrimination soon became an aspect of race relations around which experts would argue and debate. The definitions of racial discrimination within the social sciences differed from, and changed in response to, the definitions that were continually being negotiated within the law, the press, and in the other social locales in which public opinion is thought to be formed.

Discrimination has been thought of as the product of an irrational preference, or of a set of beliefs that we call racist, and believe to be reflective of racial prejudice. Yet Critical Race Theorists (Crits) within the American legal academy (Delgado, 1995) have produced an impressive volume of studies which demonstrate that racism and racial discrimination are normal and quite commonplace features of American society that have been shaped, rather than discouraged, by the rule of law. We will explore the ways in which laws, social theory, dominant cultural views, and popular media have been implicated in the changing importance of racial identity to the quality of life chances that people enjoy.

Social science and cultural studies

There are distinctions to be made between the various approaches to the study of communication and race. Some distinctions may be profitably made on the basis of the questions, issues, or areas of knowledge which are the focus of scholars who identify with, or are identified as belonging to, a particular epistemic community. Distinctions may also be drawn on the basis of the methods and rules of evidence which are most commonly relied upon to make sense of critical aspects of a common phenomenon. Distinctions may also be drawn on the basis of the historical origins and deference to epistemic authority which is revealed in the works and authors that are cited most often as evidence in support of a particular claim or interpretation.

In the now classic issue of the *Journal of Communication* entitled 'Ferment in the Field' (Summer, 1983), several authors attempted to draw distinctions between 'critical' and 'administrative' research. Dallas Smythe and Tran Van Dinh (1983) suggested that, in addition to problems chosen and methods used, the ideological orientation of the researcher provided a basis for distinguishing between these camps because of the ways in which this orientation helps to determine both problems and methods. The evidence in support of this assumption about ideology and method or even problem focus is not particularly strong.

Indeed, in the view of one observer of communications scholarship in the 1980s, 'the split between theorized and relatively untheorized research, between a holistic and discrete approach, between concern for macro- and micro-issues, that once characterized the radical and liberal research traditions has largely disappeared' (Curran, 1990, p. 141). Curran's view reflects the fact that one can find ready examples of scholars who are pursuing similar questions with similar methods within schools that at an earlier time eschewed such work.

For example, it seems beyond question that the long-term research project of George Gerbner and Larry Gross identified as the Cultural Indicators Project, is at once both critical and empiricist. A theory of cultural reproduction that reflects Gerbner's historical connections to the Frankfurt School is used to generate a quantitative analysis of the manifest content observed in a relatively large sample of a year's prime-time television. The analytical traditions more common to the version of American social psychology that Gross learned at Columbia University form the core of the survey-based assessments of the consequences of exposure to television. The purpose is political and critical, but the methods are empirical and dependent upon large samples and statistical power (Gerbner, Gross, Morgan, and Signorielli, 1994). In this example, and in many more, it seems that the boundaries around the critical camp are not so easily drawn.

The distinctions within and between epistemic communities cannot be drawn very easily because identifiable subdivisions within any primary set will have markedly different foci, traditions, and historical trajectories that diverge and converge at different moments in time. This is as true of the social and behavioral sciences as it is of cultural studies.

Karl Erik Rosengren has provided us with a fourfold typology of communications studies, which he relates to a similar typology of sociological

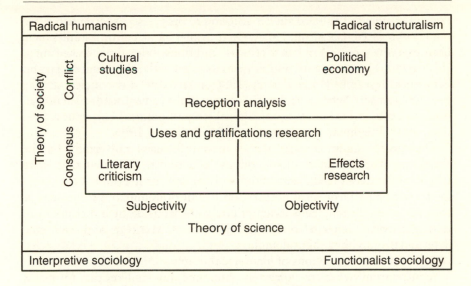

Figure 1.1 Typology of communication studies (from Rosengren, 1994 *Media effects and beyond: Culture, socialization and lifestyles*, pp. 26–7). Adapted with permission of Routledge.

theory (Rosengren, 1994, pp. 26–7). In extending the work of Gibson Burrell and Gareth Morgan, Rosengren argues that the differences between political economy, effects research, literary critism, and cultural studies can be understood in terms of differences in the underlying theory of society, and the underlying theory of science (see Figure 1.1). Political economy and effects research tend toward the pole of objectivity in science, while cultural studies and literary critism tend toward the pole of subjectivity. Where political economy and cultural studies differ on epistemology, or the theories of theory or knowledge, they are on similar poles with regard to ontology, or theories of existence. Both have historically tended to emphasize conflict, rather than consensus.

The competitive political realities of the modern academic marketplace, which can only be lamented or ignored, but not escaped, often means that scholars in one discourse rarely encounter the work of their colleagues in other disciplines or 'schools.' As a result, it is possible for there to be a cyclical process of independent 'discovery' which means that attention to particular issues and commitment to particular methodological approaches moves in waves between disciplines and schools, rather than appearing and disappearing at the same time everywhere.

The criticisms of one school made from within the discourse of an academic competitor are often based on extremely limited samples of the variety of studies identified with that school. For example, in the debates between adherents of political economy and cultural studies, doubts about the commitment of cultural studies scholars to progressive social change are readily expressed (Garnham, 1995). On the other hand, cultural studies have been extremely critical of other critical traditions, both those linked most closely with Marxist theory, and those associated with traditional social and behavioral research. James Curran (1990) referred to this criticism as 'the new revisionism.' Yet another limited critism of the radical academy has been occasioned by debates over multiculturalism and political correctness (Devine, 1996; Friedman and Narveson, 1995; Williams, 1995).

The radical tradition of media studies, influenced powerfully by the Frankfurt School and Marxian political economists, assumed that there was a link between media ownership and content, or it assumed that these media served an ideological function on behalf of dominant groups, rather than societal interest. These assumptions were set aside by a disruption in critical theory associated with the rejection of Marxism and economic determination within cultural studies.

At the same time, notions of ideological domination were being recast as a 'contestation' with an uncertain outcome not unlike the forms of competition in the marketplace of ideas that has been central in liberal pluralist models. Curran (1990) describes the revisionist history of leading figures like Stuart Hall as indicating a 'forced retreat.' Political economists were seen as being among the first to bend as was reflected in a shift in focus away from media ownership to consideration of journalistic practice. The emphasis on 'structural complexity' and contestation within the dominant power bloc is also framed by Curran (1990) as a retreat from the traditional instrumentalist models of ruling-class hegemony which had characterized earlier writing within the political economy of media.

The central point of Curran's review is that these apparent shifts in critical media theory have tended to be discussed as examples of *intellectual progress*, wherein theorists have been shown (by means of powerful critique) the error of their ways. What this representation ignores, however, is the fact that none of these 'schools' or perspectives are ever completely eliminated by a direct frontal assault. To the extent that critics include them at all, reviews of the literature tend to be exceedingly narrow, and as a result streams of research that continue on in the 'defeated' traditions are, for all intents and purposes, invisible to the combatants in any particular debate. Curran demonstrates this point by revealing the parallels between contemporary revisionist work in British cultural studies and earlier work published in the United States. Ironically, some of the revisionists actually appear to be endorsing theoretical positions that have largely been abandoned for the moment by the mainstream of liberal pluralist media scholars. That is, while the revisionists within cultural studies are now gleefully arguing and demonstrating that the effects of media are minimal at best, mainstream effects researchers have turned aggressively towards the demonstration of substantial cognitive effects under the rubric of framing.

Additionally Curran suggests that some researchers, especially historians and social psychologists, have been relatively unaffected by the intellectual and theoretical 'ferment' going on around them. They have, in large part, merely continued to do what they have been doing for quite some time (Swanson, 1996). The fact that the ferment has been contained primarily within the radical tradition has served to obscure the extent to which the movement of the radical core toward the pluralist center has progressed. Dan Schiller asks 'Is such a pluralism, finally, all that can – and should – be salvaged from the oppositional hopes in which cultural studies originated?' (1996, p. 161).

Cultural studies and political action

Cultural studies in Britain and the United States owe much of their focus on textual analysis to their historical roots in literary analysis. With rare exceptions, the primary authors of British cultural studies have come from backgrounds in literary criticism (Garnham, 1988). As a result, their lack of interest in economics and the other social sciences is quite evident, and understandable (Morley, 1992, p. 5). Because of this intellectual history, cultural studies have arrived at an easy accommodation with the humanities and the interpretive approaches more common to the study of literary texts, in ways that remain problematic for more traditional social and behavioral scientists. The preference within cultural studies for models which assume complex and contradictory influences results in an almost hostile avoidance of the linear causal assumptions that are bound into the sophisticated multivariate statistical models commonly used to make sense of complexity within mainstream communications studies (Slack and Allor, 1983).

Where the mainstream empiricist approach of many media scholars produces quantitative content analyses that count the appearance of minorities in specific roles and relationships, the interpretive method of literary analyis emphasizes the style, and occasionally the Freudian symbolism, that reveals the deeper ideological structure of the texts.

These critical readings serve at least two primary purposes within cultural studies: (1) the criticism of representations that distort, ignore, or displace important aspects of the lives of subordinate groups, and (2) the reproduction of critical reading skills, and an informed political sense within the subordinate population. From its earliest moments in Great Britain, cultural studies were concerned with the redistribution of 'cultural capital' through the development of a restricted literary canon that was deemed likely to develop 'the moral sensibility of readers' (During, 1994, p. 2).

Of course, as the movement changed to reflect not only a different understanding of working-class culture, which had also changed in the wake of dramatic shifts in the British economy, the privileged canon was again reconfigured to recognize and valorize more popular, if less commercial, forms. Yet another shift in the focus of British cultural studies emerged in the early 1970s with the adoption of the concept of 'hegemony' as a form of domination that was understood to work through cultural forms previously viewed as authentic. It was during this period that the method of semiotics, and the language of 'signifying practices' and 'discourses' became part of the critical resources of cultural studies. Although analysts would shrink from the language of 'effects' common to American social science, underlying most of these critiques was a tacit, and often explicit, assumption that images *produced* meaning, and established links to social practices that performed the same symbolic role.

Part of the way these messages were seen to 'work' within the ontology of cultural studies is through the process of 'identification' with the characters, relations, and lifestyles presented in the popular media. During (1994, p. 6) suggests that the psychoanalytical structuralism associated with Althusser and Lacan was more influential within film studies than it was within cultural studies. However, the semiotic idea that texts were capable of multiple interpretations, or were *polysemic*, was far more influential on a cultural studies perspective that preferred to emphasize resistance over domination.

While they were likely to seek a comfortable distance from the adherents of a 'uses and gratifications' tradition in American communication research (Swanson, 1996), the emphasis within cultural studies was, in fact, often on the ways in which individuals could create (or construct) new meaning out of the symbolic raw materials that were provided by an increasingly international global media market.

As cultural studies continued to change, the emphasis on resistance gave way a bit to a realization that not all constructive uses of media involved the resistance of oppression. Having a good time, seeking and sharing the pleasurable experiences that consumption provides, also became part of what cultural studies sought to exemplify and encourage.

Thus, when we read many contemporary examples of cultural studies writing, including that explicitly concerned with matters of race, the critical moment is often playful, and is directed toward generating a pleasurable experience for its readers as they enjoy and learn from the creative and expressive *deconstruction* of mainstream media products (Bobo, 1995; Gray, 1995). The production of oppositional texts, accomplished by using bits and pieces from the mainstream, thus becomes part of the 'war of images' that continues to produce a 'split-image' of African Americans and other racial and ethnic minorities in the mass media (Dates and Barlow, 1990). While parody is somewhat rare in the contemporary critical response, it is easy to see much of the playfulness in much of this work as 'signifying.' Dates and Barlow suggest that 'signifying . . . is a rhetorical strategy calculated to reverse dialogue by turning a statement back on itself in order to gain the upper hand in a verbal contest' (p. 13). We should not forget, however, that parody is not itself analysis; it is presumably, and hopefully, the application of an analytical insight to an effort to inform.

While different histories of the development of cultural studies have been written, Stuart Hall is one of the most authoritative sources, and his own reflection on the history of British cultural studies suggests the intellectual movement experienced considerable uncertainty in choosing an appropriate path. Hall suggests that

> it had many trajectories; many people had and have different theoretical positions, all of them in contention. Theoretical work in the Center for Contemporary Cultural studies was more appropriately called theoretical noise. It was accompanied by a great deal of bad feeling, argument, unstable anxieties, and angry silences. (1992, p. 278)

Even though Hall and others associate cultural studies with a form of Marxist critical practice, it has largely been part of the critique of Marxism that was characteristic of the New Left. Like the rest of the New Left academy, scholars working under the banner of cultural studies have paid far more attention to matters of race and gender than those identified with classical Marxist theory. Stuart Hall's engagement with questions of race was made most forcefully in the Center's 1978 publication, *Policing the Crisis* (cited in Schiller, 1996).

Another challenge to the critical mission of cultural studies noted by Stuart Hall is based upon its meteoric rise in popularity beyond the British Isles, with its growth in the United States being the most remarkable, and the most destructive of its original critical mission. In reflecting on American cultural studies, Hall writes

> I don't know what to say about American cultural studies. I am completely dumbfounded by it . . . . I want you to know that my own feeling is that the explosion of cultural studies along with other forms of critical theory in the academy represents a moment of profound danger. (1992, p. 285)

What he feared was that the concerns with power and politics which had supplied the initial motivation behind the critical project might be lost in the move toward formalization and institutionalization. But more than that, Hall felt that the dramatically expanded scope or fields to which the lens of textual criticism was being applied in the American context leaves him with a 'nagging doubt that this overwhelming textualization of cultural studies' own discourses somehow constitutes power and politics as exclusively matters of language and textuality itself' (Hall, 1992, p. 286). This concern is shared by Kahn (1995, p. 154) who laments the absence of any 'credibly political movement explicitly concerned to tackle the rising tide of American racism' among academics so taken with the 'debate on culture and difference' that has become a hallmark of American cultural studies.

This is a concern also expressed by others. David Morley's comments on the dangers of the export of British cultural studies (1992) emphasizes the problematic link of cultural studies with a form of postmodern theorizing which bears little identifiable relationship to its original political project. Bauman (1989) argues that the current debates over postmodernism are reflections of an attempt by intellectuals to 'reestablish their social function on a new ground in a world ill-fit for their traditional role' because they no longer have a 'function' or a responsibility for providing cultural guidance. If culture is now understood as a 'spontaneous process devoid of administrative or managerial centers, free of an overall design, and perpetuated by diffusely deployed powers,' then interpretation, or the search for the meaning of culture, is all that is left for intellectuals to do (1989, pp. 330–1).

Robert McChesney (1996) seems to agree that the professionalization of cultural studies, especially in an American academy that rewards scholars for their success in gaining external funds to support their work, ultimately leads towards the depoliticization of the scholarship. Cultural studies writing seems to actively avoid talking about the politics of culture, and, when it does, it tends to defer to the rule of the market.

Another moment in the history of cultural studies reflects the influence of French critical theorists. Pierre Bourdieu was especially influential in calling attention to the particular 'fields' or 'sites' or 'spaces' in which particular social practices and discursive forms come to reflect their origins in social structure. Again, although cultural studies theorists would reject many forms of ethnography as excessively 'scientific,' it became important for claims about the social practice of media consumption to be derived from direct observation of those practices in their natural and usual settings.

By the time of the emergence of a new conservative political hegemony represented by the Reagan and Thatcher regimes in the United States and Great Britain, the emphasis of cultural studies had shifted toward the celebration of the uniqueness of cultural fields marked by highly particularized social identities. The focus on resistance, which had shifted toward playful creativity, shifted once more toward the celebration of 'difference.' And once again, even though the core of cultural studies had become less political than at any time in its past, most affiliates to this intellectual movement would blanch at the association of their critical social practice with the rush of commerce toward the segmentation and targeting of consumers with the aid of the tools of marketing science (Gandy, 1993). By actively avoiding the methods, assumptions, and claims common to marketing, cultural studies seek to maintain a respectable distance from the disciplinary normalization that Foucault associated with the power of surveillance (Foucault, 1979). One might doubt that they can succeed.

During (1994) has characterized the discipline of cultural studies as being in some disarray, in part because it can no longer rely upon a single analytical approach to reach the different identity publics that its theoretical and political work in the past has helped to create. Its practitioners hope that it is through its emphasis on everyday life, in which media consumption plays such a central role, that 'imaginative intellectual analysis and description may produce liberating effects' (During, 1994, p. 25). Lawrence Grossberg, the American scholar most closely associated with the export of British cultural studies to the United States, has expressed some doubts about the potential of the work in cultural studies that has become linked to the politics of identity (1996). Grossberg suggests that the contemporary theories of identity are 'ultimately unable to contest the formations of modern power at their deepest levels because they remain within the strategic forms of modern logic.' By this Grossberg is suggesting that the politics of identity is incapable of making use of the insights and presumed power of postmodernist theory because, ironically, 'just as we discover that not only particular identities but identity itself is socially constructed, we organize political struggle within the category of identity, around particular socially constructed identities' (1996, p. 93). These issues will be explored in some detail in the next chapter.

As if parallels between a politics of difference and market segmentation were not troubling enough, yet another challenge appears on the horizon. A more recent development within cultural studies appears destined to forge links between the critical academy and the formerly suspect state because of the possibility that cultural theorists might be engaged as advisors to the state in the formation of cultural policy (During, 1994, pp. 19–20). Although his stance seems opposed to this at one level, Toby Miller (1993) suggests that subcultural groups not only have to go on struggling to 'form their identities through the technologies of the self,' but they must then in some way link, or articulate, those identities as material policy interests in the sphere of the state. For Miller, a move toward a new *postmodern citizenship* is necessary because 'to do otherwise would be to utilize identity politics as an end in itself' (Miller, 1993, p. 225). For the social movements which have been linked historically to the politics of difference to make it possible for the state to govern, entirely new forms of identity will have to emerge. From Miller's perspective, it is critical social theory that will bear the burden and the responsibility for helping us to 'lose ourselves' in order to begin again (Miller, 1993, p. 231).

An epistemological divide

Resnick and Wolff (1987) recognize that, at some points of intersection, different theoretical systems will be incompatible with each other. This occurs primarily because different theoretical systems or paradigms have their own means of evaluating truth claims made within. This means that the standards of one theoretical system cannot be used to choose between systems at the same time that there is no external, subordinate set of criteria for truth that is outside and above any contending systems. They also suggest that authors are rarely theoretical purists, and the works they produce are often 'informed by several, often contradictory, theories' (p. 14).

One analytical goal and methodological stance which separates mainstream cultural studies from the traditional social and behavioral sciences is the search for generalizable, rather than universal, claims. Making claims about the general applicability of the conclusions drawn from empirical work generally requires (and assumes) that the observations which are made are representative of a class or category of experiences, relations, or individuals. Cultural studies work tends to deny that it is making claims about generality, and as a result focuses its lens on a single case. This tendency toward 'particularism' is most evident in the comparisons of cultural studies 'readings' of a filmic text, and the kinds of analyses produced by traditional content analysis. A similar tendency is seen in the move by some within cultural studies toward ethnographic observation. Unlike the cultural anthropologists who are credited with developing the ethnographic method, the 'ethnographies' which have become popular within cultural studies rarely make use of multiple 'informants' in order to increase our confidence in the 'typicality' of the case studies they provide.

There are, of course, exceptions, and it is perhaps ironic that Janice Radway, whose germinal work, *Reading the romance*, marked a turn towards ethnography within cultural studies, was careful to note the limitations on the generalizability of her insights into her sample of romance readers (Radway, 1996). The most radical among the proponents of a postmodernist cultural studies suggest that Radway is misguided, because the true audience is always out of reach. In Tony Bennett's critical view:

> The effect of such theories, where they are of literary derivation, is always such as to put the analysis of any and all social relations beyond the reach of any determinate research technique and to constitute them, instead, as a resource for a project of reading that – since the possibility of arriving at a correct reading is denied – is simultaneously the project of a rereading that can never be completed. (1996, p. 155)

After noting that it would be impossible for an ethnography to be 'everywhere' because 'No excursion into the real, no matter how ethnographic, can ever encompass such all-embracing knowing' Ien Ang (1996a, p. 254), suggests that perhaps what ethnographers ought to become is good story tellers about the world. The ethnographic understanding contained in such stories might, from Ang's perspective, be used 'to improve programming for ethnic minorities' (p. 259). This presumes, of course, that which has already been denied – that one could actually capture 'the social and cultural implication' of 'living in the world' as, for example, a non-European migrant in Europe.

I reject the label of cultural studies for this book, not because scholars who identify with cultural studies have not provided arguments, analyses, and claims which have been, and may still prove, useful as a stimulus for empirical investigation and theoretical reflection on matters all too often ignored by political economists. I reject the label of cultural studies because I have come to associate it so closely with the anti-intellectual strain of radical postmodernist thinking that opposes the pursuit of theoretical knowledge, that denies the possibility as well as the utility of generalization, and characterizes political action as meaningless.

If the communication of knowledge or insights derived from theoretical or empirical scholarship results in a reconsideration of dominant views which has as a second-order effect the transformation of racist social practice and the institutions that support it, then this is a goal worth pursuing.

Culture and cognition

The historical development of structural theories in psychology is considerably more complex than any brief review might suggest, so these comments are offered only as a means of indicating the centrality of the concern with structure. Of particular importance to our ultimate concern with determination is the relationship between concrete social experience and cognitive structure.

French sociology, influenced by Emile Durkheim, introduced the notion of the 'collective mind' as well as the belief that this mind was subject to change as a product of social conditions. Durkheim is faulted for his creation of a metaphysical 'collective subject, yet his contribution is fundamental.' Part of his critical contribution marks the moment in which sociology became 'psychologized,' by the acceptance of the view that 'everything social consists of images or is the product of images' (Reigel, 1975, p. 17).

Soviet psychology, especially that associated with followers of Vygotsky, is credited with establishing a dialectical focus on 'psychic activities as the joint outcome of inner biological and outer sociocultural conditions' (Reigel, 1975, p. 19). The influence of Marx on the Soviet psychologists expanded the scope of the dialectic of structural change:

> The interactive process of shifts is not restricted to the activities of the individual, however, but embraces all other individuals in his social world, indeed, all individuals who through their ceaseless efforts over generations have created the cultural-historical conditions under which any present-day descendant grows up and lives. (Reigel, 1975, p. 20)

Differences in emphasis within the behavioral tradition still generate relatively isolated research trajectories, depending upon whether the theorist in pursuit believes that the important determinants of belief structure are based in personality, social experience, or in fundamental biological features.

There are other aspects of cognitive structure that psychologists have developed for us to use in understanding the individual and collective belief systems we still want to refer to as ideology. In his early work on the development of the dogmatism scale, Milton Rokeach (1960) had begun to develop his concept of a belief system that emphasized *openness* as an attribute of an individual's 'belief-disbelief system.' Rokeach's efforts to determine the origins of the structure of this system were not as successful as his development of a method for characterizing existing systems. However, it is clear that Rokeach's approach to decision making provided some of the fundamental insights that guide contemporary work from an information-processing perspective.

While there has been an important and substantial increase in the numbers of scholars who are engaging the problem of meaning from an interpretive stance, it should be clear that the behavioralists have not disappeared, but continue to pursue the nature of meaning through a more explicit shift toward *information processing* and *cognitive science* (Reeves, 1996). At nearly the same time that a shift from behavioral science to cultural studies was occurring in one segment of media studies, this very influential shift was occurring within the behavioral science camp. This shift took place on two levels. First, at the level of the dependent variables, the focus moved from attitudes toward cognitions.

Next, at the level of the independent variables, the emphasis shifted away from purposive communications aimed at persuasion toward more subtle processes that involved cognition and meaning, and involving a rejection of simple outcomes such as attitude change, in favor of more complex transformations of *cognitive structure*. This new perspective opened a way for the study of stability, or resistance to change in cognitions. In this way, empirical results that might have been disregarded by earlier scholarship as a 'minimal effect' became substantially more interesting. A shift away from the goals and intentions of the communicator or source toward the receiver as active processor of information helped to define the contours of this new information-processing paradigm (Beniger and Gusek, 1995).

In the next chapter we examine the nature of beliefs about race as a socially constructed system of beliefs. This system of beliefs is seen as ideological because of the ways in which these beliefs serve to organize and legitimate the distribution of life chances. Racial ideology, like all ideology, is reflected and reproduced in multiple textual, visual, and discursive forms within a social system.

Racial prejudice as a component of racial ideology is rather poorly theorized, and John Duckitt (1992) suggests that the theoretical conversations about race have shifted in response to particular social and historical circumstances. Before the 1920s, prejudice was not conceived of as a social problem, but was rather seen as a natural or commonsense assessment of the backward people who were being encountered as part of colonial or imperialist expansion. After the 1920s, the ways in which prejudice was characterized in different conversations within the social sciences shifted. Prejudice shifted from being merely irrational, and unjustified, until it achieved the status of a more rational response to individual interests.

Constructions of racial and ethnic group prejudice varied from the unconscious defense mechanism to the expression of pathological needs. With the ascendance of culturalist theories in the 1960s, prejudice became an expression of cultural values, such as those of the American South, or an expression of economic self-interest in circumstances where the boundaries of one's identity were extended to include one's racial group. The most recent variants on this theme seem to have almost come full circle in concluding that prejudice is a natural, inevitable outcome of the process of social group formation.

Attitudes and opinions about race

Through their development of the semantic differential technique, Charles Osgood, Percy Tannenbaum and George Suci have also underscored the structural nature of social perceptions (Osgood *et al.*, 1957). Attitude objects, including ideal types, such as 'mother' and 'father,' and 'priest,' can be thought of as occupying a conceptual space defined by the evaluation of that object on three or more dimensions usually labeled evaluative, potency, and activity. Each of these dimensions, but especially the evaluative, can be seen to have an affective, or emotive, dimension. Indeed, as Milton Rokeach argued, 'every affective state also has its representation as a cognitive state in the form of some belief or some structural relation among beliefs within a system' (Rokeach, 1960, p. 399). In understanding the nature of the relations between affective and cognitive dimensions of our belief systems, Bem (1970) also suggests that those things that we believe to be true also tend to be those things that we evaluate positively.

Daryl Bem (1970) provided one way of thinking about beliefs as a vertically and horizontally ordered system. Some of these beliefs are seen as *basic* because they are based on one's own direct experience, or on some credible authority. These beliefs are unquestioned and taken for granted. They are the stuff of *common sense*. Milton Rokeach (1968) suggests that these beliefs enjoy nearly 100 per cent consensus, and the validity of any one of them could be checked 'by asking virtually any stranger who happens along.' Bem refers to these as *primitive* (zero-order) beliefs, and he includes among beliefs of this sort the religious, moral and philosophical beliefs that are central to the foundation of our identity as a rational being.

To the extent that we are able to articulate our reasons for holding some of these beliefs, even if only to make reference to the evidence of our senses, we might call these beliefs *first-order*. Bem (1970) identifies a class of beliefs that we recognize as generalizations or *stereotypes* which have their origins in a cognitive process that generates abstractions from a host of experiences over time.

The *second-order* beliefs that become part of an elaborated value system are dependent upon a process that involves inductive reasoning that is guided by rules of logic. Of course, errors in logic are common, and in combination with the incomplete samples that our positions within the social structure allow us to gather, belief systems are likely to differ from one person to the next. *Higher-order* beliefs within a highly elaborated system are thought to be connected by means of a long chain of syllogistic reasoning (Bem, 1970, p. 11). Horizontal links established through generalization are not especially strong, and the strength of the links is thought to become weaker the further one moves from the fundamental, zero-order primitive beliefs on which they are based. Bem (1970, p. 12) suggests that beliefs differ from one another in the degree to which they are differentiated (vertical structure), in the extent to which they are broadly based (horizontal structure), and in their underlying importance to other beliefs (centrality). An individual's horizontally and vertically structured system of beliefs about race can be understood as a *racial ideology*.

A racial ideology can be thought of as a constellation of beliefs that are held together around a common core. The attributes of the common core may be thought of as making up part of the deep structure of both individual and collective belief systems, that may involve basic assumptions about human nature, as well as links to a system of moral and ethical values. Racial beliefs may be close to this structural core because they involve assessments of the natural and ethical features of different racial groups. As such, they may be stable or enduring beliefs.

We are interested in understanding the role that the mass media play in assigning racial and ethnic groups to their locations in semantic or discursive space, in the same way that we are concerned about the ways in which the media convey the opinions of elites and authorities, or suggest the nature of the rewards that might come from paying attention to irrelevant attributes such as skin color.

Cognition and constraint

The structure of attitudes and opinions developed by individuals and shared among members of social groups and classes is considered to be the product of social experience. Pierre Bourdieu (1977) has developed the concept of the *habitus* to describe the set of objective conditions that are incorporated into a logically structured set of principles and ideals. Bourdieu's elaboration of the process that generates a logic of practice that governs the set of interactions and relationships that are likely to occur within a particular individual's life is one which emphasizes the class basis and class outcome of such a structuring experience (Calhoun *et al.*, 1993). Part of the difficulty we face in understanding the social experiences common to a particular habitus lies in specifying the underlying process through which the cognitive connections are established, reinforced, and changed through experience.

Among the most important linkages are those which we understand as rules, values, and rationales. A system of rules that are accepted as legitimate may be understood as a cultural resource which enables particular forms of interaction to proceed smoothly. We might understand a set of rules as forming a 'structure' that enables the operation of a transportation system composed of intersecting paths or roads. But, of course, the rules that govern the behavior of automobile drivers are not *in* the roads, nor in the cars, *per se*, but are 'in' whatever mental systems people use to organize all the other rules that govern their behavior.

Anthony Giddens (1984, p. 22) suggests that there are particular characteristics of systems of rules which are relevant to our understanding of social reproduction. There are distinctions which are drawn among structured beliefs which are 'merely' cultural, and those which have been elevated for theoretical purposes to the level of *ideology*. Among the things we might recognize as being a part of the ideological structure of a society is a hierarchical ordering of the rules which are treated as being more or less inviolate, and those which are widely ignored.

We will examine what we have learned from social theorists, including Giddens, about the ways in which communication, especially mass media communication, is involved in determining which rules come to lose their force within a given society. We will also examine the ways in which location in the social structure, as defined by race, gender, and social class, also affects the nature of one's commitment to particular rules. But, for the moment, let us examine the distinction between ideology and culture a bit more closely.

There are several concerns which are of theoretical importance to our understanding of ideology. First, there is a need to understand its origins. How is ideology produced and reproduced? Whereas we might recognize a kind of specialization of labor in times of war in which propaganda serves the ideological function of creating a sense of collective purpose in opposing an enemy (Jowett and O'Donnell, 1992), there is no readily identifiable 'central marketing establishment' with responsibility for producing ideological material, while others go about their business producing news and entertainment. The way many critical theorists responded to this problem was to assume that the same ideological function would be performed by all media, and all content, all of the time.

Antonio Gramsci is credited with elaborating the concept of the 'organic intellectual.' This is a social actor closely identified with the interests of a particular class, who 'elaborated the values needed to be promoted . . . and who legitimated the historical role of a given class, its claim to power' (Bauman, 1989). The idea of culture as something that could be consciously regulated and shaped with a corrective intent is understood to be a defining attribute of modern society and its emerging state. The goals of The Enlightenment could be attained through the 'diffusion of right ideas' by an educated elite (Bauman, pp. 318–19). Over time the state's reliance on intellectuals to manage culture has been greatly reduced. The remaining role for intellectuals in the contemporary era is seen to have been shrunk still further as the market has emerged as the primary determinant of culture.

We want to maintain a distinction between the creation or development of a ideology, or system of ideas and values, and their reproduction and distribution through communication. The mass media and the media professionals that work in the industry have not generally been thought of as the originators of ideology. The media were traditionally believed to transmit the ideas of a ruling elite. While the emphasis within cultural studies and critical communications research has been on the nature of a 'dominant ideology,' it should also be clear that there are oppositional ideologies, such as we might identify as an ideology of *resistance*. In the chapters on the media systems and on reflection and representation, we will explore the perspectives which characterize mass media as relatively autonomous actors that on occasion, for reasons of self-interest or social purpose, introduce their own ideological framing into the discourse on social issues and concerns regarding race.

To the extent that a racial ideology represents an ordered system of beliefs, its development and reproduction is not random, but is the product of considered effort. It is perhaps an elitist position that locates the origin of ideology or systems of belief with a select few – the intellectuals. But this is a view expressed by Philip Converse (1964) among others:

> Ideologies are not worked out by people on their own; rather, ideologies are learned. Although many individuals may add their own personal touches to the ideologies they learn, only a handful of the most sophisticated elites make basic changes in ideological frameworks. For the rest of the population, ideologies are institutionalized sets of beliefs that are out there to be learned. Some people learn them quite well . . . others learn only bits and pieces of them, and still others learn nothing at all about them. (Smith, 1989, p. 108)

This is a view which makes an understanding of the ways in which the mass media reproduce and distribute elite opinion important for understanding the nature of the struggle to achieve ideological hegemony in matters of race.

It is not only knowledge of and conformity with social rules that determine individual behavior in day-to-day interactions. Our interaction with others is governed in part by the expectations we have regarding how the other party in an interaction will behave. These expectations are derived in part from our own experience in similar interactions in the past, but they are also derived indirectly from the observation of others. While it is true that information derived from our personal experience is likely to be a more powerful influence on our understanding of the world, by providing the occasion to observe relations which take place outside our day-to-day routines, the mass media become an important source of our expectations about the ways in which others will act toward us, and in response to actions on our part. While we have good reason to trust what we have 'seen with our own eyes,' increasingly what we see has been selected, organized, and perhaps even modified strategically for our consumption by others.

The media are an influential source of the information we use in assessing the nature of opportunity and risk in our daily lives. Media scholars have examined the relationship between what we believe about the hazards or risks we face every day, what the objective facts are, and what the media presents to us. They conclude that there is a closer match between what the media present and what we believe than there is with audience estimates and the facts as they are understood by experts on the basis of statistical evidence (Combs and Slovic, 1979). Some of the most striking disparities reflect the media's excessive interest in crime, as reflected in news media coverage of crime far in excess of its objective links to outcomes like death. For example, Combs and Slovic note that 'Although all diseases claim almost 1,000 times as many lives as do homicides, there were about three times as many articles about homicides than there were about all diseases' (p. 843). The tendency of the media to focus on African American males in reports on violent crime has produced a widely held belief that Black males are dangerous. Indeed, the judicial standard of reasonableness has on numerous occasions incorporated this distorted impression as a justification for a White person shooting a Black male in 'self-defense' (Armour, 1994).

There are a number of explanations for our continued use of and reliance upon the media system, even when we are aware that it provides a distorted picture of our world. Three explanations are particularly important for us to consider: (1) we have few alternatives that are as readily available; (2) we do not make a connection between our continuous exposure to media distortions and the errors we make in subsequent decisions; and (3) we do not suffer the consequences that flow from our ill-informed decisions. An example should make this clear. An employer who chooses not to hire a Black youngster who has responded to his advertisement because he believes that Black people cannot be trusted is not likely to be aware that his assessment of Black youngsters is based largely on media representations of African American youth. This employer is also not likely to suffer any economic loss from his failure to hire this youth because there are many youngsters in need of work, and the White youngster that is eventually hired will do the job just as well as the Black youngster who was denied the job. In this particular case, as in the countless others it represents, it is the Black youngster who remains unemployed who suffers the consequences of a negative media representation.

Thus, it seems that in the absence of equally convenient alternatives, and in the absence of a greater share in the negative consequences that flow from reliance on these media, people will continue to use media that provide distorted impressions. This includes those of us who may be victimized or disadvantaged by such use.

From a critical perspective, our interest in media systems is focused in large part on their role as socializing agents, or as instruments of *cultivation*. The mass media, especially television, are believed to be among the most important social influences shaping the contemporary era, perhaps replacing previously dominant institutions such as the church, state, and school.

Rosengren (1994) identifies several factors that explain the power of the media in this regard. Among the most striking is the reminder that the mass media are active for several hours each day in virtually every home in industrialized nations (p. 16). Of course, this use of power assumes some direct relationship between time with television in comparison to time spent with other socializing agents. Assumptions about the amount of time spent in the consumption of television images are central to the cultivation hypothesis (Gerbner *et al.*, 1994).

Rosengren and Gerbner assume that the effect of constant exposure to the mass media, especially television, may serve to 'temper' the oppositional or transformative influences of other forces of change. This 'conservatizing' influence of the mass media may operate by neglecting, ignoring, resisting, or overwhelming the kinds of cultural innovations that are continually being developed by subcultural, or minority ethnic, groups. This constant struggle will be a central focus of our examination of communications media.

Social structure and determination

The different ways in which social theorists talk and think about social structures are often contradictory and conceptually incompatible, as well as paradoxical and ironic. Bourdieu states quite explicitly that:

> there exist, within the social world itself and not only within symbolic systems (language, myths, etc.), objective structures independent of the consciousness and will of agents, which are capable of guiding

and constraining their practices and their representations. (1989, p. 14)

Outside the extremely limiting discussions of many postmodern theorists (Best and Kellner, 1991), social theorists tend to believe that social structure has a material force, even though social structure is, in itself, *immaterial*, and can be revealed only in the patterns we observe in the behavior of agents. Even though social structure is not directly observable, it is generally considered to be a force which produces, explains, or is implicated in determining observable patterns in a variety of social phenomena.

The existence and character of social structures is inferred on the basis of observable regularities that have meaning within particular theoretical systems. Structure is most often seen as determining or constraining human action while, at the same time, structure is believed to be constituted in and through the activity of autonomous agents whose alternatives for action have not been fully determined or controlled by the structures they inhabit.

Our ability to use structure as an organizing principle is dependent upon the success that different structural models have in describing as well as predicting the interactions, both real and symbolic, that are both the outcomes and origins of these structures. Successful models are those which best describe the relationships between structure and agency. We are uncertain about the nature of social structures because the critical relationships that make up or *constitute* those structures are dependent upon individual mental processes, conceptions, feelings and other highly variable and unstable sources of differentiation and change.

Theoretical analyses of social structures are organized in terms of critical features that we believe have unusual potential to assist us in understanding a given society at several levels of analysis, as well as backward in historical time. We would want such theory to apply to other societies or social systems as well. The selection of one aspect of a social system's structure does not mean that we believe this aspect is more *important* than other structural features; rather, we are suggesting that, within this particular theoretical system, this particular structural element works especially well as an organizing principle.

Class as an aspect of structure

Social class, and the relations between antagonistic classes, has been a primary focus within social theory. This emphasis on class has not been limited solely, or even primarily, to that group of scholars committed to a Marxian perspective. One handbook of research design and social measurement claimed that nearly '30 per cent of all research articles in major sociological journals are devoted to social stratification' (Miller, 1991,

p. 327). Social class is, of course, more than the familiar hierarchical ordering from upper to lower, or working class, or the similarly ordered, but theoretically distinct, Marxist variant which is based on the ownership and control of capital (Wright and Perrone, 1977).

The importance of social class to social theory may be seen in its ready association with measures of the distribution of power and social resources:

> Class is a structure that translates inequality and power into different life-chances for categories of individuals. It is therefore a structural determination of life-chances, a structure which distributes chances to act, and de-limits action spaces, which are often highly resistant to attempts of social actors to change them. (Eder, 1993, p. 12)

This notion of *life chances*, associated most prominently with the social theory of Ralf Dahrendorf (1979), underscores the probabilistic, or uncertain, relationship between any particular location with a social structure, and particular outcomes. Recall that the purpose of social theory is to help us to predict and explain why persons occupying particular structural positions are more or less likely to enjoy a particular quality of life. As a theoretical construct, social class has made an extremely important contribution to our understanding of these outcomes. Contemporary theories about the influence of social location have a basis in theories of social structure that seek to explain the 'accumulations of advantage and disadvantage' that accrue to people who occupy different positions within the social structure (Merton, 1975).

What is important for us to consider in our assessment of those social theories that privilege social class as an aspect of social structure, is the extent to which that theory helps us to understand the nature of *relationships between* elements of the structures defined by class, as well as in structures based on other organizing principles such as race and gender.

A critical aspect of social class is class *identity* or class *consciousness*. We are interested in understanding the role of the communications media in helping to shape the process through which these shared perspectives are formed. Earlier readings of Marx assumed that class consciousness was developed primarily in the context of relations defined by one's experiences as a wage laborer, specifically within circumstances defined by capitalist class relations. Class *position* was primarily determined by one's occupation and one's relationship to representatives or agents of a capitalist class. Contemporary social theorists have come to realize, however, that class identity is complex and contradictory, and that such complexity may reflect the multiple class positions that individuals can occupy at different moments in their daily lives (Wright, 1982; 1989). An employee can also be a supervisor, and may participate in capitalist relations through ownership of stock as part of a retirement plan. Numerous other conflicting positions can be identified, and their salience can vary in relation to many influences, including the coverage of the economy in the news.

Sophisticated theoretical work has also helped us to understand the role of interactions among people of different social classes in the development of class consciousness. Arthur Stinchcombe (1990) has examined the development of class consciousness within the service sector. Relationships within the service or information sectors might also be expected to influence racial group consciousness. In comparing the circumstances of Black entertainers in Harlem to their contemporaries working in Yiddish theatre, Kahn (1995) comes to a conclusion similiar to Stinchcombe's about the consequences of routine efforts to survive economically by satisfying the demands of clients:

> Inevitably this meant that the entertainers of Harlem were more likely to see themselves through white eyes, and to mold their (public) personae according to the tastes of their predominately white audiences, while Jewish entertainers were much more likely to mold their personae to the tastes of their fellow Jews. (1995, p. 119)

The problems of theoretical indeterminancy associated with conflicts between class consciousness and racial identity will be explored more fully in the next chapter.

Recently, a group of social psychologists has offered us a theory of social dominance that uses *caste* rather than class as a structural feature. This perspective emphasizes the social and behavioral, rather than the economic, relationships common to class-based models. The description of this social system includes the specification of two fundamental groups or castes: a hegemonic group on top and a negative reference group on the bottom (Sidanius *et al.*, 1992). Three processes are involved in maintaining the stability of this system:

(a) the differential allocation of social value by social institutions;

(b) the accumulated effect of discrimination by members of the hegemonic group against members of the negative reference group;

(c) behavioral assymetry, or average differences in behavior that both reflects and reproduces the dynamics of this group-based hierarchy system. This assymetry may be induced through socialization patterns, stereotypes, legitimizing myths, and even systematic terror. (pp. 379–80)

An additional set of influences is specified that includes: (a) social comparison and social identity processes, (b) self-esteem maintenance activities, and (c) a social dominance orientation. Within this theoretical system, 'Legitimizing myths are any coherent set of socially acceptable attitudes, beliefs, values, and opinions that provide moral and intellectual legitimacy to the unequal distribution of social value' (Sidanius *et al.*, 1992, pp. 380–1).

Status

Another important aspect of social structure is the status associated with particular class and social positions. Critical differences between Marxian and Weberian perspectives on class and status surround the extent to which status is determined primarily by occupation and the particular relations between the worker and capitalist owners of productive resources, or whether status is more readily understood in terms of *consumption*. The contributions of Thorsten Veblen to our understanding of the link between consumption and status is substantial (Veblen, 1953).

It should be clear that status is conceptual, and that status and its links to self-esteem are relational. Of particular importance to the notion of self-esteem is its link to identity. Individuals form their self-concepts in relation to the reference groups and subcultures they identify with. This identification with referent groups tends to be based on the shared features that we use to characterize people according to race, ethnicity, class and gender. Social status and group identification are also reflected in terms of the characteristics of one's lifestyle. There is a considerable amount of empirical work to be done in order for us to determine whether work or other social relations are the primary determinants of the lifestyle choices made by different racial and ethnic groups, or whether *ethnicity* itself will turn out to be most useful in explaining differences in this regard.

The notion of social status is important to our understanding of the place of individuals within social structures. From a psychological perspective, self-esteem is also critically important because of its relationship to social status and group identity. Self-esteem is not determined entirely by the attributes of an individual, as might be indicated by their demonstrated capacity and accomplishments. People care what others think of them. Of course, not everyone's opinion matters or is valued to the same extent. The esteem of people close to you, either in physical or relational terms, or in terms of shared characteristics or identities, is valued more highly than that of those who are more distant.

Because social status is also linked to the social groups with which one identifies and is identified, and because social status is a central aspect of one's self-esteem, the status of one's reference group becomes important to the individual sense of self-worth. The well-being of the individual is 'inextricably linked to the status of the group to which he or she belongs' and the links are stronger in those societies in which social dominance is defined by group membership (Roe, 1994, p. 185). In most societies, racial group membership is linked directly with social status, and the influence of group status on an individual varies with their identification with their group. A fairly successful index of *racial group identification* involves an estimation of the extent to which one believes that the link between one's own fate and the fate of one's racial group is strong and that group fate predicts individual fate (Dawson, 1994). For an individual with a strong group identification, aspirations regarding one's own status become linked to one's aspirations for one's reference group.

The esteem which is enjoyed by one's reference group, or by one's role models, is not fixed, but can be affected by others who have an interest in maximizing their own esteem, sometimes at the expense of the esteem of others (McAdams, 1995). It important, therefore, to recognize that status and self-esteem, while immaterial, are still socially produced, and have material effects.

Charles Wright credits Paul Lazarsfeld and Robert Merton with specifying a status-conferral function for the mass media. 'Status conferral means that news reports about a member of any society enhance his prestige' (Wright, 1959, p. 19). Of course, some news reports may reduce this person's status if the news is about his arrest for some crime. Status conferral is a media-centric model that emphasizes media power. Alternative models to be examined more fully in Chapter 5 emphasize the uses to which people put the media they rely on. It is possible to consider status enhancement to be the product of informed media use.

The creation of a consumer culture, and the associated *ideology of consumption*, has to be recognized as a critical moment in the transformation of capitalism. Within this contemporary moment, consumption becomes the basis of individual and group identity. The cultural infrastructure, especially commercial mass media, become instruments of social control because of the ways in which they help to construct the indicators of social status. Economic models of household production assume that the consumer as producer of well-being is well informed about how these inputs might best be used (Becker, 1976). These models also tend to assume that the resources that one might need to produce and maintain self-esteem are readily available in the marketplace. As we will see in the chapters on media, these assumptions are not well founded.

Market structure

The analysis of social structure within media systems is a line which divides most pluralists from the more radical scholars of mass communications. Both groups consider structural influence to be an aspect of the social environment that may limit or constrain the ability of the 'corporate controllers' to always have things as they wish. In Graham Murdock's view:

> Structural analysis . . . is concerned with the ways the options open to the allocative controllers are constrained and limited by the general economic and political environment in which the corporation operates . . . . Structural analysis looks beyond intentional action to

examine the limits to choice and the pressures on decision making. (1982, p. 124)

From the perspective of political economy, understood in Murdock's terms as a critique of capitalism, the relations of production, including the relations of symbolic production, are assumed to be of critical importance. As a result, the structure and organization of the media industry become an entry point for analysis. After defining capitalism as 'a social formation determined by the domination of social interaction by a process of material production,' Nicholas Garnham (1990) suggests that truly useful analysis of the structural influence in markets would 'take account of the specific problems of attempting to produce and distribute symbolic forms as commodities, as well as include the determinants of consumer behavior under market conditions' (pp. 10–11).

The structure of markets has been described in a variety of ways by social theorists. Some of the more traditional concerns have been with regard to the *competitive status* of the market (McNamara, 1991; Owen and Wildman, 1992). Mainstream, or neoclassical, economists have developed a number of approaches to describe the competitive status of markets, once they are able to agree on what the boundaries of the market actually are.

The assumed value of describing markets in terms of their competitive structure is based on a set of assumptions about the nature of the relations between the organizations within the market. The level of competition indicates the presence or absence of *power* within those markets. Although the neoclassical discussion tends to avoid direct consideration of power in markets (Bartlett, 1989), the study of industrial organization explicitly recognizes the extent to which real markets depart from a fully competitive ideal (Scherer, 1970; Shy, 1995). Organizations with market power can influence the price and availability of goods and services. The ownership of media enterprises by racial and ethnic minorities has never moved beyond minuscule proportions. Thus, measures of concentration are relatively useless as an indicator of the relatively stable condition of powerlessness of minority interests. However, the ways in which minority ownership, control, and participation in the mass media have changed over time will be examined more closely in Chapter 3.

It is also possible to talk about power within media systems in terms of the structure of *consumer demand*. Economic inequality, like other structural features, can be examined in relation to specific attributes of the communications market, including the rates at which individuals in different classes will acquire communications technology, and spend their income on media products. The same is true for status inequality. While they are highly correlated, racial group membership and these measures of structural inequality represent different structural features that are predictive of media orientation and use.

As will be discussed in the chapter on media systems, the pursuit of greater precision in the characterization of audience segments soon came to add racial identification to the traditional demographic categories of age and gender (Ang, 1991). Thus, the *racial composition* of markets becomes an important structural feature that is now used by market researchers as well as critical theorists as a way to understand the relations between supply and demand (Gandy, 1996b). Changes in the structure of demand reflects, and is reflected in, changes in the quality and character of the media products that become available in different markets.

Race and gender as structural features

If we understand social structures as theoretically elaborated features of social relationships that have a consistent or patterned connection to other features of a society, such as the links between social class and life chances, then it is obvious that race and gender are critically important features of a great many social relationships.

Scholars and political activists have sought to demonstrate that race and gender are aspects of social organization that cannot be fully subsumed within theoretical models organized on the basis of other structural features such as class. The evidence for such claims is often based on the observation that relations of power that affect the life chances of individuals follow social vectors defined in terms of race and gender that seem unaffected by considerations of class.

Racial discrimination is a process that in a great many locales or structural sites does not vary along class lines. We would suggest, for example, that the likelihood that African Americans will be discriminated against in employment, in the market for housing, or mortgages, or home insurance, in the delivery of government services, within the criminal justice system, or in the delivery of medical services does not vary significantly as a function of social class (Dawson, 1994; Sigelman and Welch, 1991).

This is not to suggest that the life chances of African Americans do not vary with their social position, because they do in a great many areas. Instead, the position to be elaborated in this book is that racial status is an indicator of a position within the social structure which is different in theoretically important ways from the positions defined by social class (Omi and Winant, 1994; Winant, 1994).

While there are undoubtedly overlaps, or areas of shared variance, there are substantial areas in which differences in the quality of life are predicted more reliably by means of racial identification than by means of age, gender, or social class. The relationships suggested in Figure 1.2 are not meant to indicate the relative importance of these structural features. First of all, the notion of life chances does not describe a definable set which could be represented as points on a surface. Second, and more importantly,

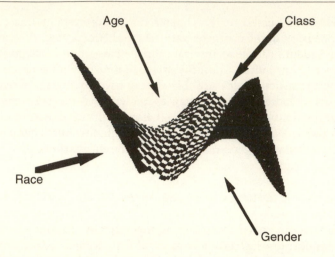

Figure 1.2 Structural influences on the distribution of life chances

some life chances are influenced by race more than others, and the influence of race and the other structural factors is constantly changing.

It will also be important to take due note of the historical contribution that relationships based on race make to the determination of class position in the present and future circumstances of individuals and members of racial groups. Racial discrimination, and the expectation of racial discrimination, may lead African Americans or Latinos to underinvest in education, thereby helping to ensure that their class position and social status will remain subordinate. Such determinations are not well represented by the relationships implied in Figure 1.2.

Agency and structure

Another point of contention which divides those social theorists who engage the notion of social structure is whether structure should be seen as an external force which imposes itself on individuals and limits or constrains their ability to choose, or whether structure is an outcome, or a product, of human activity. Structuration theory responds that both are true. Anthony Giddens (1984) and others have emphasized the duality of structure in models in which structure is conceived of as both product and determinant.

Giddens is an important source of contemporary thinking about the nature of social structure and the ways in which stuctural forces are involved in the reproduction and transformation of social relations in society (Crab, 1992). Although Giddens emerged into prominence in the mid-1970s, many of the concepts at the core of his theory of structuration can also be found in the work of other social theorists, including a less well-known French sociologist, Georges Gurvitch, who was writing about structure in 1962 (Bottomore, 1975). Among the core concepts offered by Gurvitch, and extended by Giddens, is the view that structure is both the product and the source of social or cultural activity.

Changes in social structure are the product of the amplification of the negative, disruptive, contradictory consequences that flow from repeated actions taken by individuals as they make choices in the context of different social relations. Both social change and social reproduction are the products of regularized interactions between individuals and individuals and representatives of organizations.

Understanding the nature of change within complex social systems is one of the more challenging problems engaged by the theory of structuration. Recall the familiar adage: 'the more things change, the more they stay the same.' This paradoxical truism links the potential for dramatic change with a fundamental stability in social systems. At one level of analysis, the impossibility of both stability and change is overcome by a claim that change is taking place only at the surface level, at the level of immediate appearance.

However, without evoking another discussion of false consciousness, we can still be reminded by Marx's warning that 'all science would be superfluous if the appearance, the form, and the nature of things were wholly identitical,' or, as Bourdieu puts it, 'the truth of any interaction is never entirely to be found within the interaction as it avails itself for observation' (1989, p. 16). Thus, it may be that change is taking place only in a subset of a large complex system, and thus real change, important for the subsystem, may not be reflected in any substantial modification of the larger system of which it is a part. This is not to suggest, however, that the impact of this change will not eventually be multpled throughout the system in ways that are massively transformative. Notions of punctuated equilibrium which have been elaborated in the study of complex social systems often trace dramatic changes to events which appeared to be insignificant at the time of their occurrence (Gould, 1992; Somit and Peterson, 1992). Other conceptual approaches incorporate change or instability by defining it as a temporary stage which is bound to be overcome as the system returns to its normal equilibrium state.

Routine interactions expose people to the influence of others. This is what we mean by social influence (Turner, 1991). The importance of routine interactions to a theory of structuration cannot be overestimated. It is routine interactions that provide the 'cumulative instantiation' which produces the powerful assault of 'everyday racism' (Essed, 1991). However, it is important to recognize that not all interactions are equally important in terms of their likely contribution to the reinforcement or change of an individual's cognitive structure, nor to the structure of social relations in which the interaction takes place. We must consider that not all routine interactions that we have are with others who are of equal status. Differences in status means that we are likely to pay more attention to, or be influenced more substantially by, those with whom we share a common status, or otherwise hold in higher regard. From what we have learned from the literature on credibility, *regard* seems to be situational. While status cues may generalize, there are limits to the range of concerns about which we will defer to the authority of others.

Central to Giddens' theory of structuration is his representation of the individual as a knowledgeable actor who engages in goal-directed activities that involve a continuous assessment and adjustment of those activities on the basis of available information. Giddens' knowlegeable actor is engaged in a subjectively rational pursuit of a set of long- and short-term goals, but this rationality is limited by two critical factors. Giddens recognizes that not all the goals that are pursued by individuals are expressed cognitively as an explicit goal. Status enhancement and the maintenance of a person's requisite level of self-esteem are among those goals.

This book is about the role of communications in the process of racial structuration. This process of structuration is akin to the process of racial formation described by Omi and Winant (1994) except there is no single group or agent who can be said to have designed this overall racial project. The mass media of communication will be seen to play a central role in the process, but the advertisers, the regulators, and the audience also have a part and a situated role to play within this structural set. In the next chapter the emphasis will focus more directly on matters of race, racial identity, and racism, and the complex of social practices that ensure the continued existence of race as a critical determinant of the distribution of life chances.

2

The social construction of race

Race is a theoretical construct. It is a product of the realm of ideas, thought, reflection, and perhaps even imagination. Its meaning is negotiated or, as many prefer, contested because of the ways in which that meaning has been linked historically to the distribution of life chances. Dahrendorf (1979, p. 30) defines life chances as 'opportunities for individual growth, for the realization of talents, wishes and hopes' and he suggests that these opportunities are provided by social conditions. Social conditions are to be understood as determining the 'opportunities to choose' that are available within different social structures. Individuals occupy positions in social structures that are established and maintained by allegiances, options, bonds, and ligatures that provide the subjective and collective meaning of those positions. Membership in a racial group is one of the determinants of the influence that social location has over the distribution of life chances. By studying the meaning of race, we can begin to understand its place in the complex of determinations of social structure that we call racism.

The concept of race serves as an entry point for many communications scholars in the same way that social class provides an organizing principle for understanding the functioning of media systems from the perspective of political economy (Garnham, 1990; Mosco, 1996). Debates about whether race, gender, sexuality, or other non-class aspects of personhood, can be more important or fundamental than class relations are unlikely to be solved and, from the perspective of some, represent a wasteful distraction (Resnick and Wolff, 1987). Rather than attempting to argue that race is as important, or more important, than class or any other aspect of social relations that we might believe to be a fundamental determinant of the distribution of life chances, this chapter will illuminate the place of race as an aspect of social structure. It will do so by examining the ways in which communicative acts are involved in the creation and maintenance of the allegiances, bonds, options and ligatures that define social location.

In demonstrating the utility of race as a theoretical construct, a resource that is valuable because of the way it helps us to 'make sense' of the world, we also need to understand the other ways in which the concept has been used in the past. We recognize the irony in the fact that in some nations elite opinion has been directed toward denying the usefulness of racial categories at the same time that culturally engrained systems of assessments and valuations making use of what we understand as racial features continue to operate as a process of racialization (Ratcliffe, 1994). Similarly, at the same time that a postmodernist 'project' seems determined to eliminate further consideration of race, the study of race and racism seems firmly established as an important field of study within a number of social science and humanities disciplines (Solomos and Back, 1996).

At particular moments in history, a complex of forces seems to converge and result in a shift in the direction of scholarly attention to particular social concerns. These shifts have often been accompanied by the temporary abandonment of theories, concepts, and analytical methods, only to see the same concepts and methods re-emerge in slightly different forms. Scholars who have noted these shifts help us to understand the similarities and differences, as well as some of the social forces that may have occasioned the change. Such shifts have been noted in the ways we have come to understand the concept of race (Balibar and Wallerstein, 1991).

These differences in theoretical perspective have also varied between nations and regions at different historical moments. There is some degree of similarity, however, to be found in the ways in which the scholars of different nations have responded to shifts in the racial and ethnic composition of the nation. Earlier relations established through conquest enabled or encouraged periodic migrations that over time produced conflict and contention over rights and resources, and ultimately engendered debates about identity, belonging and otherness (Ratcliffe, 1994, pp. 22–4).

These shifts have occurred for a variety of reasons, including, but not limited to, colonization and other forms of subjugation linked to economic exploitation. Different periodizations of scholarly attention will vary from nation to nation as the relations between Whites and subordinate racialized groups will also have varied. A ready comparison can be seen in the ways in which scholars have engaged questions of race and ethnicity in Australia (Inglis, 1994), those studying race in England (Ratcliffe, 1994), and those in the United States (Allen, 1994).

Numerous scholars have offered a periodization of moments in the development of social theory about race. The shifting of the scholarly focus on race over time can be seen as an example of *theoretical displacement* (Wilcox and Williams, 1990, pp. 386–7). Natural scientists, politicians, religious leaders, and social activists have each, from time to time, taken turns in defining the central characteristics of these stages. Michael Omi and Harold Winant (1994) would suggest that the process of *racial formation* which moves through these and other uniquely identifiable stages should also be seen as reflecting the influence of *racial projects*, or strategic 'efforts to reorganize and redistribute resources along particular racial lines' (p. 56). Racial projects are both discursive and symbolic, in that they are oriented toward the creation of meaning, as well as influencing the allocation of economic and political resources. This perspective suggests that a discursive strategy is often designed to normalize and justify a racial imbalance in the distribution of capital and other social value.

Michael Banton's work is among the most frequently cited periodizations of racial theory (1977; 1987). Banton (1977) has suggested that the social construction of race as a meaningful analytical category evolved through four stages that reflect, in part, the influence of the political and economic concerns of the day: racial typology, Social Darwinism, proto-sociology, and Black Power. In Banton's scheme, racial typology defined an approach that sought to characterize races on the basis of clusters of physical attributes that supported the view that the Black, White and Yellow races were actually different biological species that were fundamentally and permanently distinct. The attractiveness of a racial typology could be understood in part as a reflection of an elite engagement with the excitement and promise of science. It was out of fashion to question *any* application of the 'science' of the moment. 'To be anti-racist in the late nineteenth and early twentieth centuries was to risk being regarded as anti-scientific, unpatriotic, and opposed to progress. The scientific racism of the Progressive period was drawn largely from the real progress made in genetics' (Powell, 1992, p. 112). Assumptions regarding the permanence of racial types was based in part on a naive understanding of genetics and hybridity, in that it was believed that hybrid stocks were sterile (Banton, 1977, p. 89).

Although many students of race these days write as though the biological basis for racial distinctions has been banished by the intervention of social theory, we should note that belief in a biological basis for racial difference has not *yet* been swept away. Surveys of university biologists between 1984 and 1986 revealed that 67 per cent still accept a concept of biological races in the species *Homo sapiens*. A smaller proportion (50 per cent) of physical anthropologists were also so inclined (Lieberman *et al.*, 1992). It should also be noted that, while the scientific or scholarly community may shift to a position where the overwhelming majority rejects the biological model, the residue of the scientific discourse will last for an indeterminable length of time.

Social Darwinism introduced an evolutionary hypothesis as a way to explain the apparent variation in racial characteristics and their relationship in clusters was understood as an adaptation to environmental conditions. The emphasis on heredity and natural selection raised disturbing issues with regard to beliefs about a divine plan, as well as notions about the nature of merit. Banton suggests that the involvement of the British with colonial and imperialist relations with what were conceived of as 'backward peoples' contributed to the attractiveness of Social Darwinism (Banton, 1977, p.96).

Referring to specific groups sharing attributions as *populations*, rather than races, did little to overcome the preference for typologies, as Social Darwinism privileged biology over society. It was not until the 1920s that sociologists, with Robert E. Park as a leading figure among them, engaged the problem of classification from a social systems perspective. American sociologists sought with limited success to replace the concept of race with that of *caste* because of the ways in which caste emphasized the relational aspects of the problem. The focus of the 'Chicago school' of sociology was on the nature of race *relations*, rather than race itself. Park's theoretical model described an evolutionary pattern based on a functionalist assumption about a process of assimilation that would eventually eliminate the problem of race (Omi and Winant, 1994).

Into this expanding discourse on social structure theories about the nature of culture and collective representation helped to elaborate our understanding of racism, as well as our understanding of the role of racial characteristics in race relations. The idea that collective representations were strategic inventions was explored in the context of the economic tensions in the rural South. Race was seen to have been constructed in ways that would provide ready justification for the maintenance of Southern White privilege (Banton, 1977, pp. 115–25).

The construction of race as a problem of social, economic, and cultural relations was also influenced dramatically by the publication of Gunnar Myrdal's monumental work, *An American dilemma: the Negro problem and modern democracy* (1944). Despite the title, Myrdal suggested that the 'Negro problem' was actually a White problem, and would be overcome only when racial barriers were broken down. Myrdal and the small army of scholars who joined him in this massive sociological study would be disappointed to see that no official programmatic response was forthcoming until the United States Supreme Court spoke in *Brown v Board of Education*, and Dr Martin Luther King spoke of his 'Dream.' It was only then that President Kennedy echoed the sentiments and warnings of the Myrdal project, and began the national engagement of the issue of civil rights (Graubard, 1996).

This period was also marked by the introduction of a Marxist perspective on American race relations by Oliver Cox in his book, *Caste, class and race*, which was published in 1948. Cox's approach to the study of racism called for distinction to be made between earlier social formations and those characteristic of capitalist development. Of great importance in this distinction was the fact that the growth of this economic system depended upon a market for labor in which people, rather than merely their labor power, could be purchased. The market for African slaves enabled the creation of a distinction between these two classes of workers. Cox's view reflected the Marxian privileging of 'class as the key to history;

racial division affects the class struggle, but, since class is more important in the long run, racial alignments have to be seen as influences upon class formation rather than the other way around' (Banton, 1987, p. 150). John Rex has continued the Marxian tradition begun by Cox. Rex's approach to understanding racism is critically structural. From his perspective, 'the study of race relations is concerned with situations in which such structured conditions interacted with actors' definitions in such a way as to produce a racially structured social reality' (Solomos and Back, 1996, p. 6).

The fourth stage, which Banton identifies as the 'Black Power' phase, was marked by an emergent nationalism. Black leaders underscored Myrdal's claim that the problem of race was a White problem and that Black people would now become actively engaged in a struggle for self-definition. The intellectual leaders of the civil rights movement began the process of politicizing Black identity. The process understood as 'rearticulation' involved dramatically reorganizing the structural linkages between traditional concepts and symbols. Martin Luther King's incorporation of ideas and images from liberation struggles from around the Third World, including the images of Gandhi's non-violent protest in India, helped to establish a new collective framework through which to understand what it meant to be Black (Omi and Winant, 1994, pp. 99–100).

Black political activists, such as the Black Panthers and the more radical wing of the civil rights movement that included Stokely Carmichael and the Student Nonviolent Coordinating Committee (SNCC), were successful in attracting the attention of the mass media and an emerging cohort of youthful 'revolutionaries.' Banton suggests that, in general, sociologists had been ill-equipped to understand the emergence of racial group identity because they had generally ignored the political aspects of group formation (1977, p. 142). Black nationalists actively used race as a strategic resource in the same way that European and American Whites had used race during an earlier period. The critical difference was that race was not used as the explanation for inferiority, but as evidence that social practice had generated and reproduced inferior socioeconomic status. It was with this political engagement with the construction of race that *racism* came to take on much of its contemporary meaning. An earlier specification of the term emerged with the rise of Nazism in Germany, as the Nazi racial project utilized theories of racial superiority and inferiority (Solomos and Back, 1996).

Around the turn of the century, racism was understood as a belief that race determines culture; in the 1960s, racism and the label of racist was transformed into a pejorative designation. This particular 'ism' was no longer seen as doctrinal, like nationalism or socialism, but indicative of a set of discriminatory practices that could permeate bureaucratic structures and eventually be recognized as 'institutionalized racism' at the same time that individuals could be labeled racist.

Banton suggested that the political dimensions of this movement were truly generative in that racial group identity expanded to include the notion of community. 'The Black community' was expected to have a perspective, a vision, a way of seeing that informed a collective politics. Neo-Marxist scholars like Robert Miles (1988) argue that the concept of race and, necessarily, identity based on race, is a troublesome form of reification, not only in the context of social theory, but also in the context of political action.

Manning Marable (1994) also suggests that Black nationalists tend to reject the emergent contemporary view that 'race' is a dynamic and fluid category. Instead, they argue that race is historically fixed. They also tend to argue as though Black culture was also fixed, rather than continually being transformed through its interaction with other cultures. Marable suggests that the emergence of this nationalist (and separatist) perspective tends to emerge at different historical periods, but especially during times of economic expansion in the capitalist economy that tends to set Blacks further behind other racial and ethnic groups. In such times the status of Blacks is either ignored or justified within the limits of the dominant ideological discourse. These conditions obtained in the 1920s, and the Garvey Movement was the result; they occurred in the 1960s, and Black Power was the response; and they are occurring once again in the 1990s in the form of Afrocentrism.

However, were he editing his book (1977) today, Banton would undoubtedly expand his list to include *Multiculturalism* as the fifth stage in this evolutionary process. Multiculturalism is a political movement that extends the aspect of *choice* involved in constructing what it means to be Black, or Asian, or even White in cultural terms that entail far more than biology and, indeed, emphasizes social origins. A critical definition of multiculturalism would also have to include those aspects of identity and structuration associated with gender. Important challenges to traditional conceptions of racism emerged with the development of a radical feminist social theory. Many of the relationships between race, class, and gender, experienced with special force by immigrant women, has been explored by Anthias and Yuval-Davis (1992).

Multiculturalism as a political project is emerging during a period in which the social leadership of social scientists is being challenged by postmodern theory. The process of identity formation has been made far more uncertain by the celebration of difference, fragmentation, and the kind of chaotic pluralism which is encouraged by a triumphant capitalist market (McRobbie, 1994; Turow, 1997). The contemporary struggles over the right and authority to determine the nature of the boundaries of race help to demonstrate the status of race as a contested domain that was suggested in the early 1980s by scholars at the Center for Contemporary Cultural Studies in Birmingham. The influence of Stuart Hall on the positions on race later elaborated by Paul Gilroy and others of this school is hard to overestimate.

Racial classification

For race to play as important a role as it does within the social structure, as well as in social theory, there must of necessity be a way of determining who is and who is not a member of the privileged and subordinate groups defined in part by race. The guidelines for making such determinations have varied across time and space, and they continue to change as the discourse about race is transformed by politics, commerce, and culture.

Systems of racial classification have generally been based on externally observable characteristics believed to be common to three major racial groups: caucasoid, mongoloid, and negroid. Physical anthropologists helped to develop racial classifications on the basis of what they saw as distinguishing features: forms of the hair (round, flat, oval) which determined whether it would be straight, curly, or wavy; the shape of the nose, ranging from narrow to wide; and head shapes (measured by a cephalic index). The shape of the lips and the eyes and the color of the skin were determined to be less reliable indicators of race because these traits are not in fact transmitted in clusters, but vary independently within and among the three groups that have been identified. Despite our tendency to talk and think most often about race in terms of *skin color* (Lincoln, 1967), this feature is among the least reliable in that there is wide variation in color among the three major groups.

Theories of racial divergence within the species *Homo sapiens* include four causes: (1) natural selection, (2) genetic drift, (3) mutation, and (4) interbreeding (Howells, 1960). Biblical myths, of course, provide an alternative model, but the strategic uses of the myth as part of a racial project are well known.

Migration, conquest, and commerce has throughout time provided the opportunity for sexual relations between people from different races or populations. The children who were the product of these relations not only demonstrated that in fact all people are of the same species, but they also contributed to increasing the variability in attributes within populations, and thereby reducing the reliability of the physical markers that were being used to make racial determinations.

Davis (1991) reports some estimates that place the proportion of African Americans with *some* White ancestry in excess of 90 per cent. As many as 25 per cent of American Blacks also have some American Indian ancestry (pp. 22–3). Many American Indian tribal groups make use of a 'blood quantum' as an initial indicator of 'Indian-ness,' and this quantum varies from one-half to one-sixteenth or, in rare circumstances, any tangible evidence of Indian heritage (Pratt, 1996, p. 241). Because of the way in which legal status depends upon racial identification, some states have developed highly specialized rules to determine when an African American becomes an American Indian. The rule in Virginia specified that persons who were more than one-fourth Indian, and less than one-sixteenth Black, would be defined as an Indian on the reservation, but Black otherwise (Davis, p. 9).

While there are some similarities in the rules which developed in different nations, no other nation ever shared the approach that eventually developed in the United States. The rule of law has been applied in a unique and nearly uniform way to define racial boundaries in the United States. Although it was not always that way, membership of the Black race was eventually determined in the United States by the fact of African ancestry, expressed in biological terms. This rule became widely known as the 'one-drop rule' because it meant that even a single drop of 'Black blood' would make a person Black under the eyes of the law in many Southern states (Davis, 1991). Acceptance of the rule spread from the South to become an understanding that was generally accepted throughout the States by the 1920s.

Racial classification has varied historically in response to changing pressures readily identified in terms of competing economic and political interests. The process of classification involves the assignment of people into groups, or the negotiation of group membership, with the rights and responsibilities that group membership might entail. Because of these entailments, the determination of group membership is an exercise of power that is not often tempered by concerns about justice. As Michael Walzer reminds us, 'the denial of membership is always the first of a long train of abuses . . . . For it is only as members somewhere that men and women can hope to share in all other social goods – security, wealth, honor, office, and power' (Walzer, 1983, p. 63). As we shall see with regard to race, however, the assignment of persons into some groups was designed to justify and guarantee the denial of their access to a host of social goods.

In the United States by 1790 race and gender had been established as critical categories by the grant of voting privileges to White males. The institution of slavery required that a distinction be made between Blacks who were free and those who were slaves (Omi, 1997).

Racial classification remains an important component of government policy determination as the identification of racial group membership is a prerequisite for the determination of whether illegal racial discrimination has or has not occurred. As more examples of racial discrimination are identified, as in debates over environmental racism (Zimmerman, 1994), it is necessary to characterize entire communities in terms of their primary racial composition.

The system of classification that uses both racial and ethnic classifications appears to many to be a hopeless task because the category schemes are inconsistent, reflecting the application of different rules for the identi-fication of different racial and ethnic groups. Hispanics are among the most problematic, in that biology, geography, language, and culture are com-bined in ways that seem to defy uniform articulation and application by government workers. This problem is complicated further by the absence of universal rules indicating which persons in which roles have the responsibility for making a racial or ethnic classification. Rules, once made, are subject to change in response to a complex of political and economic pressures. Prior to 1989, persons of mixed race were assigned to the same racial category as the father; after 1989, assignments have been made on the basis of the mother's race. Because neither mothers nor fathers may be available at the time of death, coroners and funeral directors are left to their own devices in determining the race of the deceased. As you might imagine, such a process generates considerable uncertainty with regard to the usefulness of epidemiological and actuarial estimates of risks by racial group.

Antonio McDaniel reminds us that, while the United States may have many ethnic groups, it is really a matter of race, based in large part on skin color, that forms the basis of structural divisions within the society. He notes that 'Africans did not come to America as Africans, they came as Akan, Yoruba, Ibo, and Wolof.' These African slaves were denied the opportunity to maintain their national and tribal identities as the demands of the political economy of slavery required a more simple classification based on race. The same process applied to immigrant groups who would become classified as Europeans, Asians and Hispanics, and the American aboriginals who would be identified as Indians or Native Americans (McDaniel, 1996).

The negotiation of power over racial classification is reflected in the names which have been attached to different racial and ethnic groups over time. The struggle over naming reflects shifts in the political goals and strategies of the groups over time. These shifts have been 'symbolized by the shifting, and sometimes contentious, history of the way in which the Black-Negro-Colored-African American community has defined and identi-fied itself' (Spencer, 1994, p. 556).

Racial classification becomes increasingly problematic for governments as the simplicity of the Black/White distinction has been destroyed by waves of migration from without and by eddies of miscegenation and transracial reproduction within. McDaniel notes that the tendency for interracial births to be classified as White, except by African Americans, is further complicated by the patterns of intermarriage that vary by racial group. While the number of interracial marriages involving African Americans has increased markedly in the past decade, the rate is far below the rates experienced by Asians (McDaniel, 1996, p. 282). The problem of classifying the products of interracial marriage is especially controversial because the creation of a 'mixed-race' or multiracial category could conceivably result in the disappearance of most of the population that is currently identified as African American.

Ian Haney López's recent book (1996) is focused on the role that American courts have played in defining individuals as entitled to the privilege that designation as White has meant historically. Haney López's analysis concentrates on those cases which ruled on the process of naturalization of immigrants as citizens of the United States. The action of the court was necessitated because naturalization was initially restricted to 'white persons.' Examination of court documents revealed considerable confusion about which criteria were to be used in determining a person's race: 'by skin color, facial features, national origin, language, culture, ancestry, the speculation of scientists, popular opinion, or some combination of these factors' (Haney López, 1996, p. 2). Curiously, a rule of thumb reduced the choices to two – common knowledge and scientific evidence – and, over time, common knowledge won out.

Other influences, including sexism, were also involved in the development of the tortured logic of racial classification in the United States. Haney López notes that, while male citizens could marry alien females and thereby transfer to them the privilege of Whiteness, female citizens who married alien males would lose their former privileged identity (1996, pp. 46–7).

This fact should have ended once and for all any uncertainty about whether or not race was a social construct but, as we shall see, it has not. Indeed, as we will consider below, recognition by critical scholars and progressive activists that race is a social construct has done little to suppress a common belief that it is still necessary and important for the courts to recognize this construction and use it as a basis for legislative and judicial action.

For Asians in the United States, the special character of American racism has produced an almost irresistible pressure toward becoming White to avoid the consequences of being treated as Black (Wu, 1996). By accepting the benefits of 'Whiteness,' Asian Americans can be charged with complicity with the cause of White supremacy. At least for a time many Asians in England avoided this result by accepting the cloak of Blackness, despite the fact that dominant scientific opinion defined them as members of the Caucasian race. In the United States, the courts made use of 'common knowledge' to reject the advice of science in the case of an Asian Indian, Bhagat Singh Thind. The sense which held sway in the court was that everybody knew these 'dark-eyed, swarthy people' were not *really* White.' As a result of the Supreme Court decision in this case in 1923, some 65 Asian Indians who had been granted citizenship 'had their citizenship revoked as their imposed racial identity shifted from White to non-White, and thus from American to non-American' (Powell, 1997, p. 108).

There can be little question that the development of racial classification systems that come to have the rule of law reflects the impact of a complex of economic, social, national, and regional influences. These include sexual relations, and the laws which govern them, migration patterns, and the struggle for economic and legal rights which either bring together, or further divide, members of subordinate racial groups. The rules for racial classification reflect rules for social relations, which ultimately reflect the distribution of power.

During the eighteenth century, when Spain ruled over the Mexican territories, sixteen different categories of persons could be rank-ordered on the basis of ancestry. The uppermost group were offspring of Spaniards and Indians (Mestizos), who inherited the reins of power in Mexico after the Spanish were overthrown (Davis, 1991, p. 89). The overthrow of the French in Haiti produced a similar elevation in status and power for the mulattos who were the product of French and African unions.

Brazil's governments have treated race as a continuum reflected in color, and have avoided the establishment of a legal basis for the determination of racial identity. In Brazil, unlike the United States, ancestry need not determine one's race. Categorization in Brazil is based on a variety of features, including color, and class status seems to shift the relative weight of features such as skin color (Davis, 1991, p. 101). It is only more recently that the links between color and class in Brazil have been explicity labeled racist (Winant, 1994). The contemporary emphasis on race and the color line reflects the emergence of a race-conscious political movement, the Movimento Negro Unificado (MNU), in the democratic opening that the end of military rule provided.

The color line

The importance of color as a hierarchical system in many cultures has long been recognized. The aesthetic dimension of color preference has not always been linked as closely as it might with the hierarchies of status and class. Interbreeding, or miscegenation, in combination with the decision to 'pass,' has over nearly 400 years produced millions of White Americans with some unacknowledged African ancestry. At a moment in American history when racial segregation was strictly enforced in hotels, night clubs, and restaurants, club owners hired African Americans with Caucausian features to serve as 'spotters' – to identify other Blacks who were trying to enter the establishments under false pretenses (Lincoln, 1967, p. 528). The sense of voluntarism about racial identity which is common in the discourse about *hybridity* and *ethnicity* (Anthias and Yuval-Davis, 1992: Omi and Winant, 1994) seems to have lost sight of the traditional circumstance in the United States in which only Blacks of mixed racial heritage who chose to be identified as White were said to 'pass' for White. The phenomenon of 'passing' is not commonly used to describe the assimilation of Latinos, Indians, or Asians. The fact that the 'one-drop rule' is not applied in the determination of membership in these other groups speaks to the very special historically determined meaning of Blackness in the United States.

The acceptance by light-skinned Blacks of the social and economic necessity of a unitary racial identity that ignored the differences that color once brought helped to make the one-drop rule uniformly applied in the United States by 1925. The fact that the renaissance in Black culture, known as the Harlem Renaissance in the 1920s, was led by mixed-race artists and intellectuals underscores the structural importance of the movement through which a common African heritage was being invented and valorized. The celebration of Black artistic creativity was no doubt only a small part of a much more complex process of identity formation, but it is likely that the elevation in status that the Harlem Renaissance produced helped to convince a great many mulattos who might have passed for White that it was no longer a trade worth making (Davis, 1991, p. 60).

In the United States, because of its links to privilege, color became more important to Blacks than to Whites. Lincoln (1967) reports that there was no color consciousness among pre-colonial African tribes, and therefore he attributes the importance of color among American Blacks to the influence of the system of slavery. In the absence of a class system based on ownership of the means of production, a caste system based on skin color reflected the distribution of status markers and whatever other limited economic resources that a closer connection to slave masters might provide. The light-skinned Blacks had more of the privileges, resources, and marks of status than their darker brethren. The expectation, if not the reality, that social and economic benefits could be derived from whitening, remained an issue in the United States through the 1980s. Spike Lee's controversial film, *School Daze*, took a calculated risk in examining the continuing intraracial struggles over the value of benefits one might derive from looking White rather than looking Black.

Among the many things that the former colonies of the British Empire share, one of the more striking is the 'yearning for Whiteness' that the association of color with power during the colonial period helped to produce. Color consciousness is not precisely the same among the former colonies. Teasing out the influence of Europeans on this process has been complicated by the more recent influence of American imperialisms, both economic and cultural. Although there is some controversy regarding the 'true' meanings of the associations of color with the status hierarchies in the Hindu caste system, it is hard to avoid seeing a linkage of color with status in comparisons of the dominant hues of Brahmins at the top, and those of the Sudras at the bottom (Béteille, 1967; Issacs, 1967, p. 372).

Color and power under the apartheid regime in South Africa may have reflected an even stronger linkage than they did in the United States. The extreme numerical disadvantage that Whites faced as a minority group in power in South Africa made the maintenance of a formal mechanism for linking privilege to group membership a vital necessity. For the power of governance to remain in White hands, only persons officially recognized as White could be allowed to participate in the governance of the nation. Adopted in 1947, apartheid was defined as 'a policy which sets itself the task of preserving and safeguarding the racial identity of the white population of the country' along with the separate identities of other racial and ethnic groups in the nation (Legum, 1967, p. 487). The apartheid system established two racial 'buffer' categories between Whites and Blacks: Indians and Coloreds. Coloreds were less than 10 per cent and Indians were around 3 per cent of the population in comparison with approximately 70 per cent who were native Blacks (Davis, 1991, p. 92).

Japan, which was never colonized, has still experienced an evolution in its perspective on skin color that has become linked with a loss of self-esteem, and a representation of the Japanese as racist. Wagatsuma claims that the assessment of 'white' skin as beautiful and 'black' skin as ugly was a fact in Japan long before there was any sustained contact between Europe or Africa (Wagatsuma, 1967). However, more contemporary assessments of Japanese views on skin color reveal a sense of inferiority when Japanese skin color is compared with that of Europeans, and a sense of superiority when Japanese are compared with a great variety of darker-skinned peoples.

It is clear that skin color has a symbolic dimension. Colors have meanings which are primarily connotative because color is interpreted as a characteristic of an object, perhaps indicating an underlying or inherent quality. The connotative meaning of colors is often described in terms of the emotions evoked. Colors reflect, signal, and evoke different moods. The nature of color perception involves many aspects of the social that constructivists have been so vigilant in calling to our attention (Moriarty, 1996). We recognize color not only as a function of the wavelength and intensity of stimuli received by the eye. Recognition and distinction among colors is influenced in part by the extent to which colors are associated with identifiable objects like oranges, or if there are other colors available for comparison (Gregory, 1966).

What is needed is a way to understand the cross-cultural similarity in evaluative responses to different hues in people. There has been much comment about the commonality among Western cultures in their association of black with evil, sadness, and death, and the opposite complex of associations with white: purity, joy, truth, femininity (Gergen, 1967, p. 397). However, it is also fairly easy to find examples of an equivalent symbolic divide among non-White, non-Western cultures. Obvious linkages to evolutionary biology, and a complex of associations between danger and the darkness of night, can be made to explain the apparent universality of the evaluative opposition of white to black. To the extent that these associations have been 'hard wired' into our perceptual facilities, the elaboration and strengthening of this structural framework with additional links and richly detailed examples makes their strategic denial difficult. Trying to shift the location of black in semantic space is a difficult challenge. The results are likely to be unstable and, it would seem, they would also have to be reproduced anew in every generation.

Racial identity and consciousness

Classification is not the same as identity. Classification is a form of knowledge creation that has been associated by Foucault and others with the development and maintenance of systems of power (Rabinow, 1984). The acceptance of one's assignment to a racial group or category is a response to that power that can be understood as a form of domination. In an important sense the acceptance of administrative labels is a form of submission to an external authority. While the acceptance of a classification as a marker or index of one's identity may be enabling, often it is not.

Not everyone who accepts classification as a member of a racial group shares the same level of comfort or ease with that assignment. Individuals will differ in the extent of their attachment or identification with the group. Estimates of group cohesiveness reflect attempts to assess the extent to which members of the group share interests, feelings, and commitment to group goals. An individual level index of attachment to the group has been defined in terms of group consciousness or identity.

Because antagonism is clearly an aspect of race relations, several definitions of racial identity and consciousness include an oppositional dimension (Cross, 1995; Jenkins, 1995). The extent to which persons are identified with, or possessed of, group consciousness may be assessed in terms of (1) the extent to which they perceive differences in life chances in group rather than in individual terms; (2) the extent to which they see their own position as being structurally rather than personally determined; and (3) the extent to which they see their group as hostile toward and dominated by members of another group (Hurst, 1972). Studies of Black identity, race consciousness, and self-esteem have included system blame as a critical component of the overall concept of racial group esteem (Hughes and Demo, 1989). The absence of a significant correlation between system blame and self-esteem suggests that the Black consciousness need not include strong links to feelings about discrimination (Smith, 1995).

The identification of others as different from oneself, and from members of one's group, would also imply that one would not ordinarily agree with them, or see the world in the same way. Because members of antagonistic groups see the world differently, members of the one's own or *primary* group would not ordinarily expect to be influenced by members of an antagonistic group. The only ways in which members of such a group could influence members of another is through the exercise of *power* that might be seen as illegitimate (Turner, 1991, p. 172).

Michael Hecht and his colleagues have offered what they call a 'communication theory of identity' that has 17 assumptions about the nature of identity (Hecht *et al.*, 1993). Although this work has been organized and presented for the purpose of understanding African American communication from an Afrocentric perspective, the assumptions have a universal character, in part because of the openness of the descriptive system.

First, they suggest that identities are dialectically determined. In part, this means that identities are emergent, and continually being elaborated through social practice (of which communications practices are central). Identities within this system are multidimensional, but can be understood in part through reference to ordered structures or meanings, assumptions, and expectations. The relational aspect of identity within this theoretical system makes it easy to see how each individual can develop and maintain a number of potentially different identities in which race may vary in its importance or centrality.

Because identities emerge in relationships, and each relationship is different – indeed, they will be different at different stages of any relationship (stranger, friend, lover, spouse, etc.) – the self that an identity refers to means something different, depending upon which relationship is engaged by an inquiry, or in reflection.

Racial identity is not limited to an individual or personal frame of reference. Individuals can be seen to be, whether they intend to or not, as acting as a member of a racial group, rather than as a unique individual. In this sense, identity is enacted through behavior, especially through *communicative behaviors* (Hecht *et al.*, 1993). Recognition of the ability of some individuals to engage in 'code-switching' or adopting the speech patterns and linguistic styles of the dominant group as well as that of one's own group has long been a part of the study of intercultural communication (Asante and Gudykunst, 1989).

Because every social interaction is a relationship between two or more individuals, and those individuals are likely to differ in terms of power or status, some of which may be associated with their social role or position, the contribution of any interaction to the development of the identities of participants is most uncertain. However, most interactions that make up our lives are routine, and therefore do not vary substantially from day to day. It is the routine nature of interactions that provides the possibility for analysis and subsequent characterization of the process of identity formation.

Racial identity is also constructed or defined at the level of the social group. Aspects of identity, especially those which afford the group a basis for pride, are jealously protected and reproduced through a variety of myths, rituals, and symbolic activities. Groups can therefore be said to 'possess' their identity, even though, strictly speaking, racial and ethnic groups are themselves theoretical constructs, rather than operational entities. Racial identity, as possessed and defended by groups, is thus understood as a kind of social instrument, a resource that can be used in the struggle over other resources. It is a strategic resource that might be built according to a theoretically informed design, if it were not for the actions of others with competing goals in mind.

Identity and reference groups

Membership in, and identification with, a racial or ethnic group is a matter of fundamental theoretical concern because of the role that reference groups play in the organization of social influence (Turner, 1991). Identities are extremely complex and multidimensional, but are also a central feature of our interactions and relationships. Although we have no basis for making a direct comparison, it seems clear that racial markers are among the more important aspects of our identity, and the importance of race varies with the extent to which racial identification is associated with negative outcomes.

Turner argues that

> similar people in the same situation not only tend to act in the same way but expect to act in the same way. In so far as we categorize ourselves as similar to others in the same situation (in relevant respects), it is natural and logical to think that we should tend to respond in the same way. In so far as we do, we should experience subjective validity. (Turner, 1991, p. 161)

This sense of subjective validity, which Anthony Giddens (1984, p. 375) discusses in terms of *ontological security*, leads us to believe that we understand the world, including our identity and our place in that world, as it *really is*, rather than as a product of our own 'biases, prejudices and idiosyncrasies' (Turner, 1991, p. 161).

The literature on the nature of social influence generally agrees that the influence of the ingroup is greater than that of the outgroup, although this influence reflects the strength and the appropriateness of group identity for the behavior in question. Where social identity is seen to be relevant, and the social cues that are available within a particular context make a *particular* identity salient, the research suggests that people are more likely to conform to standards that this reference group treats as normal and appropriate.

It seems likely that dominant groups are likely to serve as the reference groups for subordinate groups in a great many aspects of routine existence. Under these conditions, the orientation of members of subordinate groups is likely to be upwards, rather than downwards, in the status hierarchy. This orientation toward the dominant group means that attributes that characterize a dominant group are often more likely to be evaluated more positively than attributes of a subordinate group. This suggests that members of subordinate groups tend to suffer in comparisons made with dominant groups. Of course this assumption does not hold in circumstances in which the dominant group is not perceived to have any legitimate claim on its dominant position. Groups that construct the dominant group as oppressors are less likely to grant very many of the features that distinguish members of the dominant group from their own a higher value. Indeed, William Cross (1995) identifies two different forms of oppositional identity that may be developed by African American youth: one he terms defensive, and another alienated. The defensive oppositional identity may be misinterpreted as a form of acceptance of domination (Kitano, 1991) because it is a form of identity developed primarily by Blacks who are, or seek to become, 'functional within the larger society' (Cross, 1995, p. 185).

It is important to recognize, however, that groups which are dominant on one dimension need not be dominant on others. It also means that individuals who are members of groups which are lower in social status in some dimensions may be higher in others. African American males have achieved dominance in several fields of athletic competition, such as basketball, boxing, and track and field sports. Whites, who are dominant in a great many other spheres that determine economic and social status, seem willing to grant the legitimacy of African American status in these areas. While there may be a tendency to explain these apparent exceptions to a racial status hierarchy as an evidence of genetic predisposition, rather than the product of individual effort, the evaluation of the achieved status is generally positive.

The influence of reference groups is readily transmitted to its members through a recognized leader or expert. Leaders may take advantage of their knowledge regarding differences of opinion when they urge members of their group to consider issues as members of the group rather than as individuals (Turner, 1991, p. 170). The role of leadership, and struggles over the character of a group's identity, will be examined later in the discussion of identity politics.

Cognitive structures or schemas

Understanding the social construction of race requires us, at some point, to understand the role of perception in the formation of identity, and in the comprehension and evaluation of the relationships that make up our day-to-day existence. A structural orientation toward perception is one that pays particular attention to the relationships between the attitudes, images, and impressions of self and others that have been shaped through direct and mediated experience. Cognitive schemas represent a useful way of thinking about perception in a way that is informed by structural thinking. These schemas are not unlike the notion of habitus developed by Bourdieu (Bourdieu, 1989; Bourdieu and Wacquant, 1992; Calhoun *et al.*, 1993). Bourdieu's critical stance associates the forms that habitus takes with the system of domination that structures it: 'the mental structures through which they apprehend the social world, are essentially the product of the internalization of the structures of that world . . . cognitive structures are themselves socially structured because they have a social genesis' (Bourdieu, 1989, p. 18). Past experience in the social world generates memories which affect our experience of the present.

Psychologists have suggested that our memories are organized thematically. These thematic structures are called schemas. These thematic maps are elaborated, and the links between images and impressions are developed and reinforced over time through a process of social learning. Schemas are the mental theories that we use to make sense of the world. Already existing schemas facilitate the processing of new information, in part by selecting, sorting, encoding, and storing new information within the structures already in place. New or conflicting information may be treated in a number of ways, including the further elaboration of existing schematic structures. The same structures facilitate the retrieval of previously stored information.

Four different kinds of schemas have been identified (Taylor, 1984, p. 149):

(1) A *person* schema organizes an understanding of a typical person, or a specific individual, and it may include traits and goals.
(2) A *self*-schema includes knowledge of one's own psychology, and provides a complex, but accessible, verbal self-concept.
(3) *Role* schemas engage intergroup perception and stereotyping because they describe appropriate norms and behavior for broad social categories, such as those defined by age, race, sex, and occupation.
(4) *Event* schemas include prior knowledge of the typical sequence of events in standard social occasions.

The system of schemas may also include a 'procedural social schema' which has no specific content but may provide guidance in navigating the cognitive structure and processing information.

Graber (1984, pp. 154–73) identified six such schemas in her study of the ways in which people processed the massive flood of information presented to them by the news. In addition to strategies for the judgement of persons and institutions, her schematic frameworks included cause-and-effect models, empathy perspectives, and guidelines for the application of cultural norms.

The kinds of self-schema that may be developed over one's lifetime may include assessments of personal efficacy and situational competence. The experience of success is undoubtedly the source of self-schemas that organize impressions of one's competence. Institutionalized racism and widespread discrimination operate in ways that ensure that Blacks and other subordinate racial or ethnic groups have very few opportunities to experience success as a contribution to self-esteem, and as a central component of their self-concept. This fact explains the importance of social location as a predictor of personal, but not group, assessments (Allen *et al.*, 1989; Hughes and Demo, 1989).

The kinds of cues that are provided by communications are of central importance to the extent that they activate particular schema. The theory of *priming*, which has become so important to specialists in political communication, suggests that comments and symbols presented in the early parts of a story, or even in an entire news program, can activate a particular schema, which influences the ways in which much of the information that follows is processed and stored (Iyengar, 1991, pp. 132–3). A number of factors combine to determine which schema will be activated. These include how recently, and how often, they have been activated in the past (Fiske, 1984, pp. 175–6).

The structure of cognitive schemas is also believed to involve links to emotional responses. *Activation* of a person schema dominated by racial identification, and linked with an unpleasant experience that occurred in the past, may produce an unpleasant reaction to an individual defined primarily in racial terms.

Person schemas are believed to influence the ways in which our perceptions of others are organized. Stereotypes are the short-hand rules we use for categorizing others. Self-schemas might also be thought of as stereotypes of the self (Turner, 1991, p. 159). As parts of our identities, self-schemas provide models of what we can do, and what we should do, or how we ought to respond in different circmstances (Hecht *et al.*, 1993, p. 162).

We categorize those who we believe are different from us into category systems that have less variety than the systems we use for people we think are more like us. In addition, after we have categorized a person as a member of a particular group, that classification affects how we characterize their behavior. The same behavior performed by a member of another group will be characterized in different ways on the basis of the structure of beliefs we have already developed about those groups. Thus, some observers of a White child who takes an eraser from another child is likely to be seen as *assertive*, while a Black child doing the same thing is likely to be seen as *aggressive* because of the ways in which their person schemas for Whites and Blacks have developed over time (Fiske, 1984, p. 161).

The priming of racial stereotypes has also been shown to influence the assignment of responsibility for outcomes which are otherwise ambiguous. The presentation of negative stereotypes of African Americans led Anglo respondents to blame both Rodney King and Magic Johnson for their misfortunes (Power *et al.*, 1996). Those who were primed with counter-stereotypical cues were far more likely to make external or situational attributions for Rodney King than they were for Magic Johnson. The differences are explained in part by the complications that sexual behavior introduced into these comparisons.

In another priming experiment, Sniderman and Piazza (1996) asked two groups about affirmative action, and about their opinion of Blacks. The experimental and control groups differed in terms of which question was asked first. Given the contemporary opposition to the expression of comments that could be read as racist, it was quite striking to find that 43 per cent of Whites who had just been asked about affirmative action perceived Blacks as irresponsible and lazy. A much smaller proportion (26 per cent) offered the view that one would expect, had respondents been asked their views on Blacks first (Sniderman and Piazza, 1996, p. 59).

The nature of cognitive structures is believed to be such that a change in any component will of necessity produce a change in those components that are most closely related to it. Some aspects of cognitive structures are believed to be more central or more highly linked than other aspects. This means that changes in more central or more highly linked components will have wider repercussions for the overall cognitive structure.

Because of their centrality, racial stereotypes are rather easily activated or primed. In a series of experiments, all that was necessary to evoke the readily available stereotypes of American or Arab workers was the use of 'typical' names (Bodenhausen and Wyer, 1985). The activation of stereo-types by such methods has also been shown to interact with other elements of complex stereotypes, such as whether particular crimes were more or less typical of the primed group. When the crime 'fit' the stereotype, the punishments were more severe, and when the crime was inconsistent with the traditional stereotype the punishments were more lenient (Bodenhausen and Wyer, 1985, p. 278). The activation of stereotypes seems also to help override the effects of other relevant information that is available to guide decision makers.

There is evidence, however, that in some cases information which is inconsistent with established schemas is actually more likely to be remem-bered than information which is consistent. There are a number of explana-tions that might be considered, including an assumption that such inconsistencies are remembered because of the extra work that is done in order to 'handle' the inconsistency. It seems likely, however, that far more often inconsistencies are ignored, or soon forgotten, because they are not seen as being important or worth the effort to bring them into agreement with existing opinions. Indeed, it is often only when someone else (like a cognitive theorist) brings the contradiction to light, that a process of realignment aimed at reducing cognitive dissonance begins.

These schemas are very resistant to change, in part because they facilitate the reinterpretation of different, even contradictory, information so that it can fit within well-established schemas. Overcoming schemas, such as those incorporating racial stereotypes, often requires active monitoring of one's cognitive processes as well as practice in counter-arguing with the components of one's own schemas (Fiske, 1984, p. 405).

While we can identify a number of studies that demonstrate that priming can influence social perception by activating particular schemas, and that the use of oppositional, or counter-stereotypical, primes can shift attributions of responsibility (Power *et al.*, 1996), we have little reason to believe that the effects of such interventions will have a sustained or long-term influence on an individual's cognitive structure. The number of stereotype-consistent exposures an individual is likely to experience seems likely to overwhelm the impact of most atypical exposures in a relatively short period of time.

Devine (1989, p. 15) suggests that 'inhibiting stereotype-congruent or prejudice-like responses and intentionally replacing them with nonprejudiced responses can be likened to the breaking of a bad habit.' It involves a substantial commitment and resolve on the part of the individual, and it may require the rebuilding of a large part of the individual's cognitive structure because of the multiple links that a particular racial stereotypes may have within that structure.

Cognitive theorists continue to develop their understanding of the ways in which cognitive structures, including stereotypes of racial and ethnic groups, are created, reinforced and, with some difficulty, transformed. Theories of cognitive development have much in common with concepts at the center of Giddens' structuration theory (1984). Once developed, a cognitive structure affects the processing of new information, generally in ways that strengthen or reproduce the existing structure. It is the very nature of the cognitive structure that makes it likely that information which is contrary to, or inconsistent with, existing stereotypes is rejected, forgotten, or even transformed in order to make it consistent with well-established views (Graber, 1984).

Giddens recognizes that social structures do change, or are transformed. Cognitive structures change as well but, like social structure, stability rather than change is the rule rather than the exception here too. One explanation for stability in cognitive structure is in the mutuality or multiplication of force that may be generated through multiple linkages. Well-elaborated cognitive structures are difficult to change because there are so many linkages between concepts. Changing a single idea, understanding, or schema involving matters of race may require change in a host of related constructs (see Figure 2.1). This process of readjustment involves work, and perhaps even substantial cognitive discomfort, such as might be involved with admitting that you were wrong about something that you had stated so authoritatively just moments ago. It is far easier to reject the

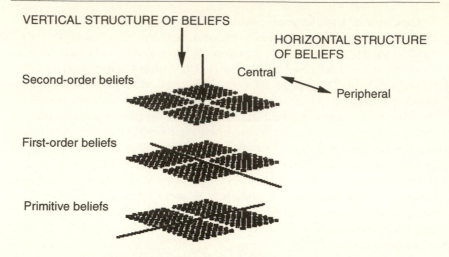

Figure 2.1 Multidimensional structure of beliefs

validity of the competing information than to change an entire system of belief (Graber, 1984, 141–3).

Although it seems necessary for there to be some form of cognitive structure that organizes thinking in general, and thinking about race in particular, there remains considerable uncertainty about what we actually know about cognitive organization (Kuklinski *et al.*, 1991; Wilcox and Williams, 1990).

Some of the difficulties that cognitive scientists have had with understanding the nature of cognitive structures are related to the impossibility of observing these structures directly. Claims made about the character of individual and group structures are based on patterns observed in responses to stimuli or to survey questions. The underlying assumption being made is that associations at the level of measurement indicate associations in those structures that are beyond observation. Differences in reaction time (latency) are believed to reflect the amount of effort required to solve a problem or respond appropriately to incoming information. Differences in effort are assumed to reflect structural differences in the kinds of associations between images and other components of a schema. Quicker reaction times imply the presence of a readily accessible, well-ordered schema.

Non-experimental studies that make use of the concept of schemas rely on correlation and correlation-based analytical designs. Factor analysis is a statistical technique that is frequently used as a means to 'reveal' or 'uncover' the underlying structure of the unmeasured factors believed to operate as sources of constraint or influence on attitudes and behavior. Correlational studies have inferred the existence of cognitive structures. On the basis of such studies, researchers have claimed, for example, that positive and negative stereotypes about Blacks represent two separate and distinct schemas, rather than the ends of a single distribution (Allen *et al.*, 1989, p. 433).

By means of a sophisticated structural equation model, Allen and his colleagues were able to assess the contribution that measures of social location and involvement with Black community-based activities made to the formation of racial schemas. The schema, or theoretical model, that they characterized as a 'racial belief system' was reflected in a set of beliefs about the nature of group interests, and the relation between those interests and the interests of other groups. The relation of these competing interests to social class was also assessed. Their analysis provided some empirical support for the traditional claim that, as Blacks move up in the social hierarchy, the strength and the character of their racial group identification is likely to be reduced.

Unfortunately, individuals are not aware of, and are generally incapable of describing, the characteristics of their cognitive structures. Giddens has referred indirectly to this problem in his discussion of three levels of consciousness as they relate to an agent's awareness of the motivations that guide her actions (Giddens, 1984, pp. 6–8). There are *unconscious* motives which are not available to the individual, even though their influence is presumed to be substantial; there are motivations at the level of *practical* consciousness, which is believed to serve as the primary guidance system for the knowledgeable actor, but this cognitive realm is thought to exist below the level of active awareness; and there is *discursive* consciousness. The kinds of reasons and justifications that individuals are able to provide quite readily are thought of as part of this realm.

We are not at all sure that the reasons that people do provide in response to survey questions are in fact the *actual* motivations that govern their actions. This uncertainty is not entirely a concern about misdirection or intentional lying by respondents, but a recognition that some of the motivational pressures and drives are simply not recognized, or are not available for articulation at the discursive level. While greater self-awareness is possible, it is thought to require intervention and practice before it becomes reliable (Ball-Rokeach *et al.*, 1984, p. 32). It does seem likely, however, that the kinds of reasons that lead to an aversive racial response are not going to be immediately available to individuals. The negative affect that leads people to want to avoid contact with 'others' who are far down on their social contact hierarchy is less likely to be held consciously, especially in the context of dominant social values in opposition to racism (Hilton and von Hippel, 1996, p. 257).

As noted in the earlier discussion of epistemological difficulties, there is also no *sure* way of determining whether the inferences that cognitive theorists draw from differences in response rates, or other behavioral responses, are anything more than artifacts of the theories behind the measures. That is, because we cannot observe mental processes directly, we need to develop theoretical models which help us to conceptualize that process, that help to make the 'black box' a bit more transparent. Sometimes the approaches to measurement that these theories seem to invite actually limit the insights that an empirical investigation might provide. As we have noted several times, the ways in which questions are asked, or problems are posed, may activate, prime, or trigger particular schemas, and thus what we conclude about the presence, absence, or character of schemas may actually be the products of inquiry, rather than social experience (Zaller, 1992).

Self-esteem

Self-esteem is believed to be an important part of our identity or self-concept. Like other schemas, self-esteem is a multidimensional construction. What we think about ourself includes, to a greater or lesser degree, depending upon aspects of personality having to do with 'other-directedness,' what we believe others think about us. Concern with what others think of us may lead us to adjust the ways in which we might otherwise 'present' ourselves to the world. The *presentation* of self requires decisions about language, style of dress, and even the subjects about which we willingly express some interest and expertise in conversation. Aspects of presentation may include the selection of other attributes of personal style that emphasize or de-emphasize racial group identity.

One theoretical model, informed by notions of economic rationality, or the pursuit of self-interest, interprets actions taken to support group interests as being, in the final instance, an investment in one's own well-being. That is, to the extent that the well-being of one's group influences the well-being of the group's members, it makes sense for group members to act in the interest of the group. Among those things which are understood as being in both group and individual interest is the *social status* of the group. Group status is a core component in individual self-esteem. Because people care what other people think of them, they have an interest in what is thought about the groups they are associated with. For the same reason, they also have a rational interest in contributing to the esteem or reputation of their reference groups. Indeed, it is suggested that members of groups will actually cooperate in order to enhance the status of their group, even if it means acting in ways that damage the esteem of other groups (McAdams, 1995).

To the extent that status or esteem is like other economic goods, its distribution is limited by its relative scarcity. Interactions involving esteem might be thought of as a 'zero-sum game' in which increases in status for one group necessarily mean a decrease in status for another. Thus, it seems rational for members of one group to attempt to raise the status of their own group by lowering the status of others. Manipulation of status is achieved primarily through communication, although it can be readily argued that an entire system of laws and social practices can be, and has been, developed to institutionalize the production of group status.

Such practices include the ways in which members of ingroups may be punished for acting in ways which might increase the status of the disfavored group. Laws against miscegenation, or intermarriage, could be seen as efforts to maintain the utility of the boundaries that defined group membership. Shunning of group members who associate with, or communicate excessive 'respect' for or interest in, members of the subordinate group is one of the ways in which preferred behavior might be reinforced.

Dawson (1994, p. 57) argues that the salience of group interests is determined in part by the connections that an individual makes between the status of her group and her own personal well-being. The degree to which she believes that her own life chances are dependent upon the treatment and well-being of her racial group as a whole is the extent to which she identifies with that group. This model, which Dawson refers to as the 'black utility heuristic,' implies that the use of group interests as a proxy for personal interests is both rational and efficient. A similar concept called 'linked fate' was included in the National Black Election Panel Study (NBES) conducted between 1984 and 1988. Participants were asked if they thought that 'what happens to black people in this country will have something to do with what happens in your life.' Responses could vary from 'not at all' to 'a lot' (Dawson, 1994, pp. 77–9). As we will discuss in Chapter 5, group identity measured in this way was a powerful influence on individuals' perceptions of social reality.

The maintenance or enhancement of self-esteem is posited as a powerful drive that explains a great many aspects of race relations. There is, however, a distinction between maintenance and enhancement that may explain some of the differences we observe in the ways in which individuals as members of social groups engage in communication and seek out, and on occasion avoid, exposure to information (Ball-Rokeach *et al.*, 1984).

It has generally been assumed that Blacks use Whites as a standard when they make many of the social comparisons that are part of the process through which self-esteem is managed. The presentational aspect of self-esteem management for Blacks is also presumed to be dominated by White standards and opinions. That is, Blacks are assumed to be aware of and influenced by the opinions that Whites hold about Blacks. An alternative model, and considerable supportive evidence, however, suggests that the opinion of Whites is far less important to Blacks than the opinion of parents, friends, and teachers in certain aspects of life that are linked to racial identity (Hughes and Demo, 1989).

Kitano (1991) provides an elaborated model of a process through which a 'negative ethnic identity' is developed. The process begins with early childhood socialization, and is reinforced through the interactions that the

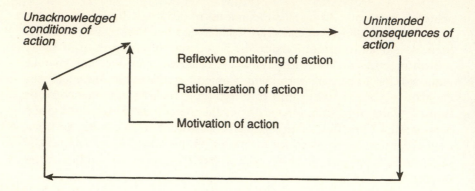

Figure 2.2 Reflexive monitoring of action (from Giddens, 1984: *The Constitution of Society: outline of the theory of structuration*, p. 5). Reproduced with permission of Blackwell Publishers and University of California Press.

minority child has with members of the dominant group. The mass media, the schools, and other institutionalized sources of cultural images reinforce the images of inferiority that the child identifies with. Kitano suggests that it is the nature of the different relationships which minority group members enter into during their socialization as young adults that leads them to develop a variety of identities, while Whites need only develop one (p. 93). Of considerable importance to Kitano's model is the way in which minorities are rewarded for conforming to stereotypes, and punished for departures from the ascribed norm. Thus, 'the final stage of ethnic identity is achieved when ethnic individuals internalize the stereotyped roles preferred by the majority' (p. 95).

If the maintenance and enhancement of self-esteem plays such a central role in the lives of individuals, it is also important to think about and understand the ways in which *reflection* or self-assessment occurs. Giddens refers to such assessments as part of the process of 'reflexive monitoring' (1984, pp. 41–5). It may be that every decision we take is assessed in terms of its effect on self-esteem (Figure 2.2). This would necessarily include an assessment of the presentational aspects of the choice, in that our appearance to others is an important component of self-esteem. Understanding how an individual would manage the complex system of accounts in order to maintain and extend self-esteem is at least as difficult as understanding how individuals choose between different goods and services that are supposed to 'maximize their subjective utility.'

Part of the difficulty in understanding how decisions are made with regard to self-esteem has to do with limitations in what we know about how low self-esteem, or the loss of self-esteem, is experienced. Psychic pain is real. Embarrassment is felt strongly, and therefore actively avoided. But how should it be measured so that we can compare different states and different people? Reliable measurement will be needed for us to understand how our choices are controlled by our efforts to avoid this psychic pain, and to realize the pleasures that 'feeling good about myself' implies? Presumably, individuals will seek information that promises to make themselves feel good, or better, about themselves, and avoid that which would do the opposite. Presumably they have guidance about what they can expect from particular information sources from experience, and from other reliable sources (most likely from members of their social network).

Individuals are also likely to engage in active information seeking when events, circumstances, or encounters have recently contributed to a loss in self-esteem. Of course, this becomes extremely complicated and difficult to predict. The availability of information about the impact of action, policies, circumstances, threats, etc. will vary with the circumstances, network of relationships, communicative interactions, and media use that affect an individual's access to information. Thus, interaction with members of one's racial or ethnic group, membership in formal and informal organizations that are concerned with group interests, reliance and use of group-specific media, and receptivity to the influence of group elite opinion, all contribute to the salience of group status on personal identity. We will examine some of these issues in the context of discussions of the 'uses and gratifications' tradition in Chapter 5.

Ethnicity and ethnogenesis

So far, our discussion has focused primarily on race and racial identity. On occasion a convenient phrase 'racial and ethnic group' has been used, in a way that suggests comparability or easy substitution. Race is not the same as ethnicity. For some, race is thought of as a component of ethnicity, and is thus subordinate to or less important than ethnicity. This is not the view that I take in this book. You will recall our initial discussion of race as an unstable, and thereby unreliable, basis for classification. Because most definitions of ethnicity include a host of components or variables, each of them subject to massive variation in specificity, ethnic classification is even less reliable than classification by race. Further, because ethnic identity depends on, indeed invites, a greater degree of active choice than racial classification allows, instability and unreliability abound. Ratcliffe (1994) suggests that an interesting and troubling empirical project might involve the attempt to measure ethnicity: 'Ignoring the thorny problem of "situational ethnicity" the most realistic measure may well be a composite variable combining geographic origin, birthplace and religion . . . . Consciousness of group membership could then be assessed by questions on "self-image" which may stress a number of differing dimensions such as colour/class/religion/nationality and country of origin' (Ratcliffe, 1994, p. 115).

Nevertheless, despite the difficulties involved, for a number of reasons that will be explored, ethnicity has emerged as a dominant construction in the discourse on race, bypassing earlier class- and nation-based theories of similarity and difference (Anthias and Yuval-Davis, 1992; Omi and Winant, 1994). Many authors make use of all three concepts because of the ways they allow them to make claims based on strategically useful constructions of the past (Wallerstein, 1991, p. 78). The past is useful in this way because its reality, at least its *social reality*, is so malleable. Wallerstein sees the emergence of these three concepts as reflecting the dominant conflict of the historical moment when the terms emerged. Race expressed the relations between capitalist core and its periphery; national categories expressed the competition between sovereign states. He associates labor specialization within nations with the 'ethnicization' of the labor force that helps to manage the socialization, the reproduction, and the rationalization of inequality within those states. The observed high correlation between ethnicity and occupation around the world is offered in partial support of his claims.

The turn toward ethnicity by social scientists and policy actors helped to accelerate the shift in the definition of race toward the social and away from its biological basis. The identity complex which is ethnicity includes biology as well as culture and, perhaps, also political ideology. However, because the development of the concept of ethnicity in the United States was influenced so powerfully by a concern with immigration, and the integration of White Europeans into the American mainstream, theorists were ill prepared to understand the specific barriers to assimilation that were associated with color and race. At the same time that scholars studying White ethnics examined the variety that national origin, religion, language, and other cultural differences produce, other students of ethnicity tended to treat Blacks as though there was no variation in ethnicity in this population worth studying (Omi and Winant, 1994, p. 22).

Just as we recognize that the concept of ethnicity is relatively new, it must also be recognized that the relationships and commonalities that ethnicity and ethnic culture refer to are also continually changing and may be understood as being 'historically and socially emergent' (Hecht *et al.*, 1993, p. 18). The character and shape which such an emergent phenomenon takes on is believed to be linked in critical ways to a process of *identification*. According to Hecht and his colleagues, 'the creation and maintenance of ethnic culture interacts with the establishment and expression of ethnocultural identity' (p. 19). Neither the ethnic cultural form, nor the group or individual identities can be thought of as unitary or homogeneous. Just as we are coming to accept the view that there are multiple, competing, and even contradictory class identities for individuals (Hecht *et al.*, 1993; Wright, 1989), there are also identities in which gender, race, and sexuality are being developed as resources in a continuing struggle for dominance. Shohat and Stam (1994, p. 344), have commented on the level of complexity that contemporary identity politics has achieved. They describe an absurd identity ritual that hybridity might produce in which a speaker identifies herself before an audience as a 'Chicano-identified, feminist, heterosexist, anarchist Anglo artist.'

The process through which these new ethnicities emerge, or are produced as resources, has been discussed as *ethnogenesis*. Ethnogenesis includes a transformation in the social valuation of ethnic identity as in those cases in which ethnicity 'has been transformed from a social liability to a desirable identity to be achieved' (Fitzgerald, 1992, p. 115). The creation of ethnic identities can be seen as a way in which subordinate groups are able to escape some of the negative consequences that occur when they are classified and labeled by dominant groups. According to Fitzgerald, 'it would appear that the upsurge of ethnicity (ethnogenesis) is only related to the perceived socioeconomic gains it allows individuals whose identities have been submerged or whose status has been denigrated in the past' (p. 123). There is evidence to suggest that this holds true in the case of Native American Indians, in that there has been a 225 per cent increase in the population of American Indians in the United States between 1960 and 1990. Michael Omi suggests that 'These changes are driven by shifts in attitudes toward American Indians, a romanticization of the past and tangible benefits tied to American Indian identification' (Omi, 1997, p. 15).

Important differences can be seen in the critical tensions in the evolving naming practices for Native Americans that include preferences for the use of tribal names, as well as acceptance of a general classification as Indians. Similar struggles have emerged over the labels that identify people as Hispanic or Latino rather than Mexican, Salvadoran, Cuban or Puerto-Rican. Martin Spencer suggests that the multiplicity of origins for recent Asian immigrants to the United States makes them the least likely to develop a common or collective identity (Spencer, 1994, p. 558). However, it is not clear that there is any empirical standard against which we might compare the variety of 'origins' that Africans actually had.

Stuart Hall's (1996) discussion of the 'new ethnicities' reflects both the important differences in the construction of racial identity in the United States and Britain, and the tensions between biology, place, and social practice in the construction of identity. At one moment in the UK, 'Black' emerged as a term that some scholars and political activists applied to immigrants both from the Indian subcontinent and the Caribbean, as well as to native-born citizens of African descent. The British bureaucracy tended to ignore the biologically based racial classifications that would assign many Indians to the Caucasian group. The British government defined marriages between Indians and Europeans as interracial (Davis, 1991, p. 159). From Hall's perspective, it seems clear that Black identity is not guaranteed by nature, and not entirely by national origin, and thus must be constructed 'historically, culturally, politically' (1996, p. 446). It also seems clear that 'the term "black", however inclusively it is defined, cannot accommodate the diversity of ethnicities of potential importance in the field of "race"' (Gabriel, 1994, p. 4). We should not, however, overstate the extent that agreement over the application and use of terms indicating racial identity is universal. Ratcliffe (1994, p. 120) suggests, without directly challenging Hall's claims, that the term Black was not generally accepted among the South Asian population, and especially not among those who were middle class.

Conventional definitions of ethnicity assume some degree of commonality, and a limited degree of choice or arbitrariness about such classification. Individuals become members of such groups by birth. They are born into them. At the same time, it is the sense that one 'belongs to' an ethnic culture that helps to define one's ethnic identity (Hecht *et al.*, 1993, p. 30). Competing definitions introduce a substantial element of choice which reflects a greater emphasis on the cultural aspects of emerging definitions of ethnicity, as well as the more strategic goals which are believed to flow from the creation of a ethnic identity, such as the pan-ethnic identities we accept as Asian American or Hispanic.

Ethnogenesis may also be applied to the process of ethnic identification that is developed in the service of commercial interests with the support of government action. We have the case of Singapore, in which a desire to create a viable market for tourism involves the creation of a national identity and the transformation of ethnic culture into 'cultural capital' (Leong, 1989). The requirements of marketing operate to 'erase' distinctions between ethnic groups within the nation. For the purposes of tourism, only four ethnic cultures are officially recognized in Singapore: Chinese, Malay, Indian and 'Others.' The reality is that 'there are boundaries within a given "Chinese" group, where at least sixteen categories can be distinguished on the basis of language/dialect and province of origin in China' (Leong, 1989, p. 82). Curiously, the 'resurgence of ethnicity all over Southeast Asia can be partly attributed to the revival or re-creation of diverse traditions of the past for the purposes of a tourist industry and a new nationalist spirit consequent upon political independence' (Leong, 1989, p. 91).

The interest of a state in producing uniformity by smoothing over the differences in the features that would otherwise serve as markers of ethnicity and race can also be seen in the problems of creating a national ethnic identity for Jews in Israel. The historic migrations of Jews around the world has produced a great variety of racial types among the peoples who would come together as Israelis (Issacs, 1967).

Where threatened by intermarriage, specification of matrilineal or patrilineal determinancy helped to define membership within an ethnic group. Thus, the question of 'who is a Jew' could be answered with some confidence in some circles by a determination whether or not the person's mother was defined as a Jew. Of course, the need to answer this question became particularly urgent when the creation of a Jewish state made the determination of group membership a political necessity (Issacs, 1967, pp. 360–1).

Other commonalities that help to define ethnic cultures include rituals and practices, including the preparation and presentation of food, as well as physical features thought to be characteristic of the group. Historically, ethnic groups also shared a common geographic origin, such that Asians, Africans, and Europeans can be defined in continental terms.

Of course, common political heritage equates ethnic identification with the *nation state*, producing French, Germans, Italians, Nigerians, and the like. Of much more recent origin is the creation of hyphenated ethnic identities reflecting an immigrant past. Hence the peculiar tradition of naming in the United States that recognizes Irish-Americans as ethnic immigrants, must, ironically, accommodate a contradictory construction in the case of Native Americans, because they are a people for whom their place of origin was renamed following conquest. Ironically, the label 'Native American' originally applied to a political party in the United States that sought to exclude 'foreigners' from holding public office, and seeking to extend the number of years before the route to citizenship could be reached through naturalization (Myers, 1960, p. 110).

It is also important to take note of the existence of thousands of 'nations' that are not officially recognized because their sovereignty has never been formally acknowledged (Shohat and Stam, 1994, pp. 32–6). Many of these 'captive nations' are composed of indigenous or tribal groups that would meet the traditional definitions of a 'people' but they have been 'incorporated' into political units formed through colonization. Their language and culture is distinct from that of the nation state of which they are a part. Their status remains subordinate even after the wars of liberation swelled the ranks of the United Nations. Dozens of 'forbidden nations' whose traditional lands have been divided by historical forces have organized and petitioned for recognition under the banner of the Unrepresented Nations and People's Organization (Frederick, 1993, pp. 49–53).

Although we have witnessed the rise and fall of a widespread concern about cultural imperialism, we continue to find numerous examples of peoples which have opposed homogenization. Despite the intimate relationship between Puerto Rico and the United States, the people of this small island have apparently struggled mightily and successfully to maintain a sense of Puerto Rican identity. Pressures to 'Americanize' have failed; indeed:

> this pressure and the visibility of the United States in Puerto Rico have heightened awareness of the differences between the island's Hispanic-Caribbean culture and the culture of the mainland . . . . The vigor of their defense of Puerto Ricanness has responded to the aggressiveness of the United States' efforts to subdue it . . . . It has

prevailed, in part, through the intrinsic dynamism as well as the deliberate cultivation of symbols of identity. (Morris, 1995, p. 169)

Ethnics as foreigners

The links between ethnic identity and nation state have become especially salient at the turn of the century. The changing character of the industrial order has affected the demand for labor, which has had a significant impact on the extent to which nations are able and willing to absorb large numbers of foreigners who are distinguished by their cultural practices, if not by their physical appearance. These foreigners make up the ethnic division of labor that fits within a structure of racialized differentiation and stratification that is strikingly similar from nation to nation within Europe despite obvious differences in the fine details. Variations in the ways in which immigrants are integrated into the society of the industrializing host are reflected in the ways in which xenophobia becomes either manageable or an extremely dangerous response to difference.

The political tensions are underscored in a period of dramatic global change because of the ways in which ethnicity has been linked to national identity. This identity is, as Marie Gillespie suggests, contradictory: 'Modern nations typically try to constitute themselves as an ethnos, or ethnic unit, in order to exclude others; but at the same time, the dominant ethnic group often adopts the strategy of concealing its own ethnic status and attributing ethnicity only to "others"' (Gillespie, 1995, p. 10). This process differs from country to country.

France has been a 'country of immigrants' for much of its modern history (Ubbiali, 1995, p. 118). Immigration to France has served to overcome the labor shortages generated by the country's negative population growth, and immigration has played this role for a longer period than the most recent immigration of laborers from India and the Caribbean that eventually heightened the concern with foreigners in England. Like Britain, France was one of the most important colonial powers that maintained close links with former colonies, and the process of decolonialization was accompanied by substantial migration to the mainland. These immigrants tended to settle in a small number of urban centers which tends to increase their salience to French nationals. The fact that the greatest number of these immigrants are from North Africa also contributes to their apparent 'otherness'. As with other European nations, France sought to close its doors to immigrants following the economic crises of the early 1970s.

Ubbiali (1995) suggests that, because the number of foreigners in France has remained relatively stable since 1974, the upsurge in ethnic hostility has to be associated with exploitation by politicians of the anxieties generated by economic crises. In France, the extremist position was expressed by the National Front and its leader Jean-Marie Le Pen, perhaps taking a feather from the cap of an earlier nationalist leader in the UK, Enoch Powell (Favell and Tambini, 1995; Miles, 1988). Public opinion surveys in France in 1990 indicated that Arabs and Muslims were the least welcome, with Blacks and Asians not far behind, despite the fact that marriages between French and North Africans have continued to increase (Ubbiali, 1995, p. 125). Reports of conflict over expressions of ethnic identity, such as the wearing of Islamic veils and headdresses in French schools, have multiplied, suggesting that resistance to multiculturalism is strong and is being cultivated in the press. As in the United States, the New Right in France has 'managed to displace the debate about racial discrimination into a debate about culture' (Ubbiali, 1995, p. 128), effectively crippling the relatively weak anti-racist movement on the left.

Favell and Tambini (1995) suggest that the response to the problem of foreigners in Great Britain is less like the rest of Europe and more like the United States because the government's response to racial discrimination in 1976 was modeled very much on civil rights legislation passed in the US in the 1960s. Robert Miles (1988) also suggests that the influence of migration in Britain was similar to that in the United States, except that the migration was from India and the Caribbean. Both sets of migration gave rise to a sociology of race relations and, as a result, the anti-discrimination infrastructure in England made use of the racial and ethnic distinctions common to the American condition (White/Black/Asian/Other) and ignored discrimination based on nationality, culture, or ethnicity. Indeed, in the British case, 'discrimination based on any other kind, particularly the rejection of certain cultures or ethnic behavior as "not British" cannot be pursued in legislation unless it can be reduced to racial prejudicial terms' (Favell and Tambini, 1995, pp. 151–2). Thus, even though Margaret Thatcher and other political actors might speak to the threats represented by 'immigrant culture', traditional concerns about race were never far below the surface. While racially motivated crimes are described as a familiar, almost daily, occurrence in the the British inner-city, these crimes are defined statistically as racial, rather than a concern with foreigners.

Like England and France, the Netherlands has experienced periods of foreign immigration resulting from a shift in relations between them and their former colonies, as well as from periods of active recruitment of foreign 'guest workers' from the 1950s to the 1970s. The racial aspect of Dutch xenophobia is evident in the fact that it has been primarily the Turks, Moroccans, Surinamese, Antillese and other dark-skinned immigrants who have been the targets of more recent violent assaults (Ter Wal *et al.*, 1995). Despite a liberal tradition, and the existence of several anti-racist organizations and programs of intercultural education in schools, there is considerable evidence that prejudice and concern about 'the loss of Dutch culture and tradition' is well established and growing in the Netherlands.

At the same time, Eastern Europe has also experienced the dramatic collapse of communist and state socialist governments. To the extent that the label 'totalitarian' and an ideology of socialism implies a suppression of the ethnic hostilities that existed prior to the integration of these states into the Soviet bloc, the collapse of this infrastructure of social control created a political vacuum that invited appeals to ethnic solidarity (Gellner, 1995). At one extreme, such appeals devolve into a call for 'ethnic cleansing' and genocide (Petrovic, 1995). This was clearly the case in the former Yugoslavia when political leaders convinced enough of their people that the only solution to the economic difficulties they were experiencing lay in the creation of independent and ethnically homogeneous nation states. Persons of the 'wrong' ethnic group, who had co-existed under the umbrella of an integrated Yugoslavia, now found themselves defined as foreigners, and the subject of vicious propaganda blaming them for all the problems of the nation. Eisenstein notes that 'the use of violent nationalism and ethnic cleansing have created thousands of refugees. These refugees have become the new "others" in western Europe. England and Germany have tightened their borders against them. Once again, one hears that Germany is for the Germans' (1996, p. 57).

This problem was especially acute in Bosnia-Herzegovina because there was no overwhelming national ethnicity; rather there was a division among ethnically distinct Muslims, Serbs, and Croats. The constraints on an individual's free choice of ethnicity were sharpened here because the outbreak of war 'created a situation in which even the most nationally disoriented individuals have developed a heightened consciousness of their national affiliation, due to the fact that when they are attacked they have already been classified as such by their enemies' (Petrovic, 1995, p. 49).

Even in Denmark, a small nation with a very homogeneous population, problems of ethnic hostility can emerge. The flow of migrant laborers from Turkey and Pakistan in the late 1960s, who stayed on after the global recession of 1973 marked the end of an open-door policy, increased the potential for ethnic tension because these immigrants and others from Vietnam were readily identified as 'different' (Mouritsen, 1995). Public opinion surveys in Denmark reveal a dramatic increase from 22 per cent in 1984 to 42 per cent in 1988 in respondents who think that 'immigration is a serious threat to our national identity' (Mouritsen, 1995, p. 98). By 1990, as many as 44 per cent of Danes agreed that 'immigrants and refugees were an important cause of Denmark's economic problems' (p. 99). Mouritsen leaves little doubt that the mass media bear responsibility for the shaping of Danish opinion regarding foreigners through their emphasis on social problems that are linked to foreigners.

Australia represents a relatively unique racial and ethnic formation. The subordinated group is traditionally identified as an indigenous Aboriginal population whose autonomy was reduced dramatically by the massive immigration of Europeans beginning in 1788, and by subsequent immigrations from Asian nations after 1970 (Inglis, 1994). The 'settler colonialism' that characterized the relations between Whites and Aboriginal people in Australia has much in common with the relations that developed between Whites and the Native American Indians, including a period of active dispossession of native lands.

Inglis (1994) notes that official policy toward Aborigines shifted from assimilation to segregation and back to assimilation again as the relative size of the Aboriginal population shifted. When the Aboriginal population was granted full citizenship rights in 1967, attention shifted to the problem of determining Aboriginal identity as it was linked to government programs designed to reduce the disadvantage that a history of racial discrimination had produced. Earlier, the determination of Aboriginal status was based in part upon measures of association, such that a child who habitually associated with or lived with Aborigines would be deemed an Aboriginal (Markus, 1988, pp. 48–9). Markus (1988) suggests that racial consciousness in Australia actually went through four phases, which includes a period between 1890 and 1940 that he associates with the 'flowering of racial consciousness.' It was during this period that Australia implemented legislation designed to bar the immigration of persons of color from Asia, Africa, or surrounding islands. This period also marked an increase in government efforts to control the Aboriginal population through forceable collection in reserves and, where possible, through disenfranchisement.

To the extent that official classification entails self-identification, a process of ethnogenesis has been initiated in Australia as well as in other nations. The outcome of the process is a kind of pan-Aboriginal identity which smoothes over the distinctions between groups in order to facilitate the distribution of benefits linked to ethnic identity.

The impact of globalization

Research into ethnic cultures within industrial economies has been quite limited, focusing primarily on expressive aspects of youth cultures, and ignoring for the most part the other aspects of family, work, and political activity which are critical components of cultural identity. Cultures change. They change through absortion, incorporation, translation, invention, indigenization, synthesis and a host of other variously theorized processes. Because of the centrality of culture in most definitions of ethnicity, we must assume that ethnicity also changes. It is historically and socially emergent (Belay, 1996; Hecht *et al.*, 1993, p. 18). Those forces that can be identified as influences on culture must, of necessity, be seen as influencing ethnicity. Thus, a host of historical forces linked with trade and conquest, as well as direct and mediated interaction, are recognizable as factors that are transforming the nature of ethnicity.

Critical scholarship has traditionally tended to privilege aspects of culture and ethnicity that might be characterized as 'traditional,' especially when it might be argued that external forces are responsible for the threats and challenges that traditional culture faces from external forces. Cultural imperialism is a charge made in defense of traditional cultures faced with an almost certain transformation that would be brought about by a complex 'informational infrastructure' serving the interests of multi-national corporations (Boyd-Barrett, 1982).

The spread of mass media, supported by commercialization and the increased acceptance of advertising as a means of finance as well as a cultural force is credited with the most substantial transformation of culture. 'The planet is not turning into a single global village but into a collection of highly segmented clusters of consumers sharing a common lifestyle despite being separated by great distances' (Barnet and Cavanagh, 1994, p. 178). Belay (1996, p. 342) prefers to describe the current status as a 'single interactional space.' The critical problem he suggests we need to engage theoretically is the difficulties people will face in managing the multidimensionality of their own 'cultural self,' rather than a problem of dealing with cultural 'others.' This multidimensionality that Belay refers to is reflected in the five types of identity which he sees as particularly salient in global environment: (1) sociological identities (religion, social class, gender, etc.), (2) occupational identities, (2) geobasic (rather than racial) identities (Asian, African, Latin American, etc.), (4) national identities, including American co-cultures), and (5) ethnic identities (pp. 324–6).

Recent scholarship provides arguments based on economic theory that underscores the importance of language and market size to the competitive advantage that nations like the United States realize in the global cultural markets (Wildman and Siwek, 1988). While evidence of comparative advantage may have gained ground as a challenge to the cultural imperialism hypothesis, it does not deny the impact of imported cultural materials. Demonstrating this impact invites the same charge of essentialism that has been raised in the debates about race because of the fact that the boundaries of culture are not real, but are socially constructed (Kahn, 1995).

Global communications media, especially satellite television, are just part of the mix of influences producing new cultural forms and identities. Tourism, as well as migration in search of economic and political alternatives, must be recognized as factors which increase individual awareness of similarities and differences in culture.

Among the more interesting examples of the influence of globalization on the social construction of race and ethnicity is the way in which the flow of cultural materials helped to make the civil rights movement, and then the more radical Black Power movements, the source of an emergent racial political identity in many nations of the world. The military dictatorship in Brazil was forced to respond to a 'black soul' movement which developed among Black urban youth. Because the ways the youth identified with the

North American movement was so superficial, limited to the Afro hairstyle, Motown records, and the Americanized dashikis, the military was able to attack the movement as 'un-Brazilian' (Winant, 1994, p. 144). A more recent cultural movement seeks to re-establish links more directly to the African roots of Black Brazilian heritage. The Afrocentric musical group, Olodum, has reached a level of popularity far greater than that of the black soul movement of the 1960s. What the effect of this contemporary movement will be on Brazil's 'racial ambivalence' is most uncertain.

Paul Gilroy's writing on the ways in which cultural materials flow back and forth between the regions of the Black Atlantic (1993) underscores the complexity that is produced within markets as the international media industries respond to shifts in the character of demand produced by migration. This new global marketplace has also been influenced by the rise of a new consuming class which has become cosmopolitan on a global scale. The character of this new market will be explored more fully in the next chapter.

Identity politics

The elaboration of ethnic similarity and difference that we have discussed as ethnogenesis, and have recognized as having been complicated by the global marketing of cultural materials, is not a process that has proceeded smoothly. Instead, ethnic and racial identity has become a site of often rancorous debate in the context of what some have referred to as 'the culture wars.' The debates over multiculturalism are a critical component of that debate.

The ways in which the Black Power and civil rights movements transformed the economic value of racial identity for African Americans and other Black people around the world, also helped to stimulate other nascent identity movements among other ethnic minorities. At the same time, other social movements that shared a common opposition to oppression and discrimination based on gender, sexual orientation, physical attributes and differences in capacity have come to be associated with a radical egalitarian project that has been successfully demonized by the conservative right as political correctness. 'These movements joined, in an informal way, to generate a common political mood of victimization, moral indignation, and a self-righteous hostility against a common enemy – the White male. All of these groups felt oppressed by the ruling White male elite of American society or, in some cases, Western civilization in general' (Spencer, 1994, p. 559). One relatively thoughtful observer associates political correctness with a sense of defeat among leftists:

> PC has its roots in more respectable intellectual and political positions. It is the refuge of Marxists who have lost faith in an order in history, or at least in the ability of human beings to understand that

order . . . the crucial ingredient in the formation of the PC outlook is despair of the progressive aspirations entertained by one's forebears (or one's earlier self), and the resulting adoption of a fortress mentality by groups who used to try to change the world. (Devine, 1996, p. 28)

The struggles across the ideological divide between right and left have also been reproduced in part as occasionally acrimonious debates among critical scholars on the left.

Much of the public attention to the issue of political correctness in the United States has been focused on college and university campuses, where administrators and faculty have struggled over speech codes and actions taken against charges of racial and sexual harassment (Scanlon, 1995). Related battles on campuses focused on attempts to revise the canon of key disciplines in the social sciences and humanities to reflect the contributions of those cultures excluded by an emphasis on European sources.

It may be as some claim that the effort to reduce the availability or prominence of negative images may actually operate to restrict the range of subjects that can be discussed and materials that can be read and criticized (Fox-Genevese, 1995). As we will consider in examining social reproduction and change a growing unwillingness to express overtly racist beliefs created a need for social scientists to develop alternative measures of racism and prejudice that might be more sensitive to modern, sanitized forms of racism. It is certainly clear that it is no longer socially acceptable for people to be explicitly racist in public conversation. It also seems that this form of racial awareness leads many to believe that it is inappropriate for Whites to comment, especially to comment critically, on the behavior of Blacks or members of other subordinate groups.

This demand for 'civility' is also understood to place legitimate demands on elite members of racial and ethnic groups to 'police' those members of their own group who have not successfully incorporated the new sense of public manners. Actions or statements by Louis Farrakhan, the outspoken leader of the Nation of Islam, are regularly held up by Whites as requiring comment by 'responsible' African Americans.

Part of the struggle within universities over the canons of scholarly enterprise can be understood in terms of a struggle over culture as more broadly understood. The location of this struggle within the university reflects an evolving conception of 'cultural capital' as a newly valuable form of 'human capital.' Cultural capital has a basis in the mastery of the kinds of skills that help to ensure success in the academy. Aspects of cultural capital may also include forms of symbolic mastery that win approval elsewhere in the capitalist economy (Merelman, 1994). The evidence on many fronts, at least in the United States, is that Whites, as the dominant cultural group, have given way in several areas to the cultural challenge from African Americans. The recent publication of *The Norton anthology of African American literature* (1996) might be seen as the penultimate mark of canonical legitimacy, even if that legitimacy is defined by the approval of a wing of the White academic establishment.

The debate over multiculturalism in the United States is seen as having established a link between race and culture, and reinforces the conceptualization of race as an affirmative and affirming choice (Merelman, 1994, p. 13). Multiculturalism as a rationale for cultural differentiation along racial lines represents a symbolic vacuum which has no obvious contender for primacy. Zillah Eisenstein (1996) notes that multiculturalism 'as a politics, can be used for very different purposes by those who seek to use diversity opportunistically for corporate interests, or by those who wish to destroy the euro-american hegemony of corporatist transnationalism. Both of these usages often employ multiculturalism as a code word for race, sometimes creating a racist backlash' (pp. 63–4).

The liberal tradition that served as the mythic basis for talk about equality between the races assumed similarity between people and claimed that differences were only skin deep. It was thought that, by eliminating restrictions and limits that operated at the surface level, true equality could be achieved. Multiculturalism denies that this kind of equality has any lasting value. Adherents argue instead that Whites, Blacks, Asians, and Native Americans are different at a deeper, cultural level, and that the preservation of these cultural differences is a legitimate choice.

The debate over multiculturalism has at times been quite heated, and has produced some 'strange bedfellows' in terms of traditional ideological guideposts. In part the difficulty reflected in this often confusing debate has to do with the contradictory nature of the struggle over resources, and the claims that might be made from the position of racial identity. Post-structuralists find themselves in the contradictory position of wishing to avoid the loss of control that essentialist labelling represents, at the same time as they are active supporters of the affirmative action, redistributive, and group rights policies that depend upon those very same restrictive classifications (Shohat and Stam, 1994, pp. 342–6). Grossberg (1996) agrees, suggesting that 'it may seem somewhat ironic that just as we discover that not only particular identities but identity itself is socially constructed, we organize political struggle within the category of identity, around particular socially constructed identities' (p. 93).

The marketplace has not been confused by the debate. It has responded actively to the possibility of a multicultural future. There has been a literal explosion in commercial media seeking to exploit the benefits of a self-segmenting taste culture. This 'riot of difference' challenges our traditional understanding of politics and the public sphere. The movement toward more racially homogenous media, and a growing number of research reports that demonstrate the influence of racial identity on responsiveness to advertisements using own or other race actors (Qualls and Moore, 1990; Whittler and DiMeo, 1991) may result in more rapid movement toward a period of even greater salience of racial identity, despite its increasing hybridity. This is a conclusion that one must also draw from Turow's recent study of the pursuit of racial and ethnic segmentation of markets (Turow, 1997). In the next chapter we will turn our attention more fully on the role that these segmented media may eventually come to play.

The development of an active politics which depends upon control over the framing of ethnicity and racial identity has meant that some acts of identification become the focus of attack by combatants in the 'culture wars.' The sense of an extreme multiculturalism that is understood as a radical relativism represents to some a denial of the possibility of progressive politics:

> At a deeper level, though, any possibility of a moral perspective gets erased by a position fashionable among some of our post-modernist academics, that there can be no absolutes, no truths, and hence, no grounds for moral judgements. There can't be a left if there's no basis for moral judgement, including judgements that will cut across group or gender or ethnic lines. There can be no left where the only politics is the narrow politics of identity. (Ehrenreich, 1992, p. 337)

Ehrenreich is joined by Devine (1996, p. 33) in suggesting that:

> the effect of postmodern rhetoric is thus to unsettle all institutions and practices without distinction, including those that protect deviants from the wrath of the majority; and at the same time to cut the heart out of any possibility that the resulting confusions could be resolved in a progresssive, or even a coherent way.

In the same way that mainstream media are criticized for failing to reflect the diversity within minority populations, the cultural activists have also engaged in hostile criticism of minority authors whose publicly constructed identity falls outside the approved range. Even autobiographical works in which the author is unquestionably the most *authentic* source of knowledge about his or her identity are likely to be appropriated for use in struggles that the authors may not have decided to enter, or may have entered on the wrong side.

Fernando Delgado (1993) tells of the debates which emerged in response to the publication of Richard Rodriguez's autobiography, *Hunger of memory* (1982). Published at a time when both nationalism and conservatism were on the rise in the United States, Rodriguez's book became one 'hill' in the battles between the groups who identified themselves variously as Latinos, Hispanics, Mexicans, Mexican-Americans and Chicanos. Mainstream White or 'Anglo' critics tended to praise the book, while Chicano critics were more generally opposed to the book and the ways they felt it was being misused within larger political debates.

Rodriguez was himself attacked for 'his complicity with the dominant, mainstream, Anglo-American world,' a complicity which was made worse in the eyes of the critics because he had been 'appropriated' by the right wing (Delgado, 1993, p. 12). From within the emerging, but contested, cultural canon, Rodriguez was seen 'not to fall within the bounds of a Chicano ideology, even as he is labeled Chicano by those who misuse the term as a synonym for the ethnic and cultural terms *Mexican-American* and *Hispanic*.'

Delgado's analysis of this particular case underscores the contradictory aspects of the struggle for cultural hegemony. Cultural critics felt compelled to respond because the dominant Anglo culture had put Rodriguez forward as an example of the correct path toward integration into the American culture. Yet, the only way the Chicano critics seemed able to respond was within the context that had been defined by this claim. Thus, ironically, the critics can be seen to actually be functioning hegemonically because they have accepted the terms of the debate set down by the dominant cultural group. For Delgado, 'Chicano authors and critics have failed to subvert because even in resistance they have allowed and accepted the hegemonic terms of engagement' (1993, p. 14).

The criticism by Dana Cloud (1996) of Oprah Winfrey's biography notes the distinction between autobiography and this special form. While both are constructs, a biography 'reveals more about cultural ideologies than about its purported objects, the personalities of popular heroes' (p. 119). It is not at all clear, from Cloud's analysis, that Oprah could have actually written her own history and avoided the charge of tokenism and complicity with what it conveys. For Cloud, 'Oprah's' identity and her politics are securely located by framing narratives within liberal individualism and an oppressively gendered meaning system' (p. 132). Neither Winfrey nor General Colin Powell can escape the fact of their tokenism, and the hegemonic consequences that would flow from their being held up as 'representatives of the black élite as "proof" that the system is just and that racism is a thing of the past' (p. 133).

Some of the battles being waged in print among African American cultural critics have centered on questions about the kinds of solutions that ought to be considered for the seriously degraded circumstances of Blacks in the nation's cities. These have been debates about the place of culture, and the importance of finding or in some way constituting a culture of liberation. Molefi Asante, as the primary source of intellectual leadership for a contemporary cultural nationalist movement charges Cornel West with misrepresenting the theory of Afrocentricity (Asante, 1987; 1990). Asante explains West's failures as a reflection of his desire to speak to (and perhaps for) a predominantly White audience.

Charged by both West and bel hooks (hooks and West, 1991) with *essentialism* because of the claims that he makes for the existence of a distinct African American culture, Asante counters that being essentialist is precisely what liberation requires (1993, p. 43). Asante seems quite comfortable with 'employing essentialism strategically' rather than 'falling into essentialism' as one would fall into logical traps.

West's approach to what he calls the 'dilemma of the Black intellectual,' emphasizes the need to move forward by sifting, selecting, combining whatever insights, guides, resources, and competencies one encounters, without any special preference or privilege granted on the basis of their origins (hooks and West, 1991, p. 146).

Afrocentricity, Asante's own contribution to critical theory, argues for placing 'African ideals' at the center of any analysis that involves the culture and behavior of African people (Asante, 1987, p. 6). It actively denies the centrality of Eurocentric perspectives. It does not declare them false, only incomplete in some regards, and overreaching in many others. Asante describes his work as metatheoretical, engaged in explaining a cluster of theories. He suggests that it would be nonsense to claim uniformity in black communicative behavior, but he insists that the 'variance among blacks is less than between blacks and non-blacks' (p. 37). The origin of the similarities among Black people's communicative style is African, pure and simple: 'Communication styles are reflective of the internal mythic clock, the epic memory, the psychic stain of Africa in our spirits' (p. 48).

Asante's Afrocentrism privileges those elements of African American culture that his analysis can link to an African past. Whereas most White, and some Black, critics see 'Ebonics' as little more than a non-standard and inferior approximation of English, Asante celebrates it as 'a creative enterprise, out of the materials of the interrelationships and the energies of the African ancestral past' (1987, p. 57). Manning Marable (1995, p. 194) suggests that:

> populist Afrocentrism was the perfect social theory for the upwardly mobile black petty bourgeoisie. It gave them a vague sense of ethnic superiority and cultural originality, without requiring the hard, critical study of historical realities . . . . It was, in short, only the latest theoretical construct of a politics of racial identity, a world-view designed to discuss the world but never really to change it.

Asante rejects the biological basis for concepts of race, noting the European origins of that particular concept that affected W. E. DuBois' thinking on the subject. Instead, Asante argues that the concept of 'blackness' might be understood more usefully as a philosophical rather than a biological question (p. 125).

These philosophical differences have occurred at other moments in which the status of African Americans has taken a sharp turn. John Spencer directs a similar charge at other Black scholars he identifies as postmodernists opposed to multiculturalism (1993). He suggests that Shelby Steele and others who wish to deny the usefulness of racial identity are suffering from the malady that Steele has named 'racial fatigue.' This fatigue is most troublesome for those African Americans who thought that they had escaped the burden of race (Cose, 1993). No sooner had they begun to enjoy some of the privileges that cultural capital provides than they find themselves still saddled with the burdens of Blackness. They apparently tire of being represented by, and representatives of, their race. The fact is, there is no escape from the influence of racism, even though the way one experiences it may vary with social position.

The reproduction of racism

Just as we are able to identify differences between scholars, activists, and critics in the ways in which they understand race and ethnicity, there are also critical differences in the ways that these observers understand racism and its longevity. The orientation of psychologists to the problem of racism is understandably at variance from the primary perspectives of sociologists or political economists. But psychological theory is not stable, and it has evolved in theoretically important ways that occasionally intersect with other streams in social theory.

John Duckitt (1992) argues that much of what we know about stereotypes and *racial prejudice* reflects the influence of the particular social and political concerns that dominated the social agendas during the eras in which attention to other theoretical concerns went into decline. He notes, for example, the prominence of theories of individual-level personality, such as the *authoritarian personality*, that were of central importance in the 1950s, and the emphasis on sociocultural explanations that were prominent in the 1960s and 1970s. In his view, it is not that these earlier theories had been rejected, or replaced, but that there had been a shift in attention toward particular issues or questions that earlier theories simply did not address.

Duckitt (1992) suggests that, prior to the 1920s, there was little scientific uncertainty about the racial superiority of Whites, and the inferiority of Blacks, and, as a result, 'the concept of White prejudice or White racial attitudes was not a scientific issue of any significance' (1992, p. 1183). The 'race theories' of the day were focused on describing and explaining the inferiority or backwardness of Blacks. A number of convergent influences, including the emergence of a Black civil rights movement in the United States in the 1920s, emerging movements that challenged the legitimacy of colonialism, the need for national mobilization against a common enemy, and the movement of Jews into the profession of psychology, all raised challenges to the validity of theories of racial superiority. Social psychologists, led by the work of Floyd Allport, began to shift their attention toward the problem of explaining White prejudice, rather than Black inferiority.

World War II and the atrocities linked to the racial ideology of the Nazis served as a kind of a critical event that stimulated, or at least marked, an important shift in the orientation of scholars concerned with prejudice. To the extent that the Holocaust was a kind of 'collective madness,' it seemed appropriate that a pathological personality type was the most likely explanation. Prejudice was pathological, and prejudiced individuals were sick. The research task became one of identifying the 'personality structures and characteristics making individuals prone to prejudice and ethno-centrism' (Duckitt, 1992, p. 1186). Scales identifying an 'authoritarian personality' or assessing the extent of 'dogmatism' or 'tolerance' were developed during this era.

Once more, near the end of the 1950s, the field shifted from individual differences to concerns about the nature of broad social and cultural influences. Prejudice in the American South had to be explained in terms of cultural norms, as it no longer seemed reasonable to rely upon theories of individual psychopathology as an explanation for such widespread atti-tudes and social behavior. Efforts to understand continuing racism in terms of socialization were relatively unconvincing and attention shifted to the problem of 'identifying and explaining those intergroup conflicts of interest and social structural conditions that underlie racist and discriminatory social systems' (Duckitt, 1992, p. 1188). It seemed that it would be necessary for psychologists to move into theoretical domains that had previously been the province of sociologists and political economists. But psychologists showed only limited interest in attempting to explain preju-dice as a function of group interest. The shift in emphasis had to await the challenge from experimental evidence that demonstrated the power of group identification (Dovidio and Gaertner, 1986).

Racism defined

In the same way, and for many of the same reasons, the definition of racism has changed along with the shifts in the meaning of race, and the framing of race as a social problem. According to Omi and Winant (1994, p. 70), 'the absence of a clear "common sense" understanding of what racism means has become a significant obstacle to efforts aimed at challenging it.'

Racism needs to be distinguished from bigotry, which includes all forms of intolerance, but has been used most frequently in the examination of religious persecution (Myers, 1960).

Racism also needs to be distinguished from ethnocentrism. It is reason-able to expect that people will see the world from a perspective that reflects their social position and, as we have suggested, race is a critical feature that defines social position. However, the fact that one sees others in ways that reflect the racial origins of one's point of view is not automatically racist. It is not racist to recognize patterns in appearance and behavior that are part of the defining characteristics of other groups. It is not even racist to dislike some of those habits, and to prefer the company of persons who think and act as you do. 'What is racist is the stigmatizing of difference in order to justify advantage or the abuse of power, whether that advantage or abuse be economic, political, cultural, or psychological' (Shohat and Stam, 1994, p. 22).

Of course, this definition leaves open the possibility that non-Whites can be racist, and it even allows that Whites can be victims of racism. Racism is an evil that varies in degree. Not all racisms are the same, and even adherents of the traditional definitions of racism favored by many Blacks that links racism with the exercise of power must recognize that Blacks, Latinos, and other non-Whites who have been oppressed still have power that can be, and has been, used racially (Winant, 1994).

Racism is more than disdain and fear of persons of another group defined by biology and culture. Racism (and sexism) are linked in important ways to the economic systems which reinforce and depend upon it (Balibar and Wallerstein, 1991). Understanding racism fully requires that we understand how racism operates to distribute material resources. Racial discrimination is the primary form through which the exercise of power transforms prejudice or ethnocentrism into the experience of racism. Myrdal (1944) identified a 'rank-order' of discriminations that reflected an underlying structure of attitudes, opinions, and preferences of Southern Whites toward Blacks. Southern Whites might be distributed along a racism scale in accordance with the extent to which they wished to deny African Americans the free exercise of choice in actions that varied in intimacy (Davis, 1991, p. 61):

(1) marriage or sexual contact with White women
(2) less intimate personal relations
(3) use of public facilities
(4) political participation
(5) rights under the law
(6) economic activity.

A variety of legal, and extra-legally enforced restrictions on the rights of African Americans in these areas came to be implemented far outside the Jim Crow South. They became part of the definition of American racism.

Philomena Essed provides a more comprehensive definition of racism (Essed, 1991). For her, racism must be understood as a 'system of structural inequalities and a historical process, both created and recreated through routine practices' (p. 39). More formally, she notes that racism is 'defined in terms of cognitions, actions, and procedures that contribute to the development and perpetuation of a system in which Whites dominate

Blacks.' Domination implies the exercise of power. This power may be exercised by individuals, but it depends upon its origins in the structural position of a dominant group. Essed argues that racism is both structure and process, in that forms of domination exist and are reproduced 'through the formulation and application of rules, laws, and regulations and through access to and the allocation of resources' (p. 44). Reflecting the influence of Giddens, Essed suggests that racism is also a *process* in that structures exist only through the 'everyday practices through which they are created and confirmed.'

Her special contribution to our understanding of racism rests with her explication of the notion of *everyday racism*. For Essed, 'everyday racism is the integration of racism into everyday situations through practices (cognitive and behavioral . . .) that activate underlying power relations' (Essed, 1991, p. 50). Her emphasis on the routine nature of racism reduces the importance of individual events, acts, or instances. Each 'instantiation of everyday racism has meaning only in relation to the whole complex of relations and practices' (p. 52).

To the extent that everyday racism is normalized and widespread, it may be thought of as institutional. For some scholars, racism is distinguished from prejudice, but such a distinction introduces problems with regard to intent:

> Conceptually, separating the constructs of racism and prejudice clarifies the fact that attitudes do not always lead to particular behaviors and that certain behaviors can have the same devasting effects, with or without an attitudinal component. This separation made it easier for people to focus on the concept of *institutional racism*, where consequences are negative even though the intent might not be malevolent. (Katz and Taylor, 1988)

Omi and Winant's (1994) definition of racial projects would seem to require some level of awareness or purpose, although they would not deny the reality of the racial disparity that 'innocent' decisions may produce.

We understand racism, then, as involving fundamental aspects of human nature. While the social and biological tendencies toward ethnocentrism and prejudice seem to be universal, it is also clear that there are important individual and group differences in the extent to which racism influences social practice. The influence of the social factors, at least, can be seen to vary in relation to aspects of culture, including the nature of economic and social inequality. Cultural influences operate through their determination of interaction between members of different racial and ethnic groups and the character of socialization. Stereotypes and other classificatory schemes are not predetermined by some identifiable social logic, but are the result of a complex social process. For the moment, we will focus on those aspects of racism that depend in part on cognitive constructions.

Racial ideology

Racial ideology is a system of beliefs that is incorporated into a range of discourses in ways that reinforce and reproduce beliefs and assumptions about individuals because of their identification with a particular racial group (van Dijk, 1994, p. 112). This system of beliefs is ordered in a way that we can understand usefully in terms of its structure, or the relationships between its component beliefs, attitudes, and values.

Although he was not writing specifically about the particular racisms we understand and encounter today, Stuart Hall (1986) suggested that there are some insights that we can take from Gramsci's work that make the influence of the social structure in the area of race meaningful. In this piece Hall extends Gramsci's work first by suggesting that racism and racist practices are likely to reach most sectors of the society, although its influence is bound to be quite uneven. But it is Gramsci's contribution to our understanding of the nature of racist ideology that Hall reserves for his closing remarks. Among the issues, uncertainties, and questions that Gramsci's insights make ripe for study are the nature of working-class racism, the contradictory and unstable character of the 'self' which is at the base of any ideological formulation, and the importance and possibility of ideological struggle that might be produced as we engage the processes through which the victims of racism are also victims of the 'very racist ideologies which imprison and define them' (p. 27).

It can be argued that the cognitive structure which each individual develops and maintains is that which best meets his or her requirements with regard to the maintenance and enhancement of self-esteem. The extent to which an individual's personal belief system matches the dominant structure of beliefs is a reflection of the extent to which they have internalized the dominant ideology. Those who benefit from the distributions of life chances that such an ideology supports are most likely to agree with, or otherwise share, the dominant ideology.

The following are claims about the roles that media play in reproducing and distributing the dominant ideology. The ideological role of a media system may be understood in part through an examination of the relationships between the social representations in media and in dominant ideological structures:

(1) The ideological framework reflects the interests of the group providing the social representation.
(2) The representations have similar content and structure.
(3) The structures of cognitive schemas are similar to those in the social representations.
(4) The schemas are consistent with other knowledge and belief, that is they are plausible, and therefore acceptable.

(5) The authors of the representations are thought to be credible and reliable. (van Dijk, 1994, pp. 114–15).

A racial ideology may be seen to provide an operational constraint on behavior in the same way that a political ideology provides constraint. The stronger the influence of an ideology, the stronger the correlation between attitudes and policy preferences consistent with that ideology (Converse, 1964; Smith, 1989, pp. 105–58). Although political ideologies and racial ideologies may share many features in common, some political scientists argue that they are conceptually and empirically distinct (Sniderman *et al.*, 1991).

Racial ideology is implicitly evaluative. It may also involve a *comparative* ranking, which is reflected in the establishment of a *racial hierarchy* which arrays racial and ethnic groups or 'types' in terms of their value, their attractiveness, the legitimacy of their claims, etc. Within the dominant racial ideology of those social systems dominated by Whites, Whites are always situated at the top of the racial hierarchy. Stereotypes tend to minimize the differences between the 'others' at the lower end of the scale. It is still possible, of course, for scholars to determine which aspects of racial identity are operationally more or less important as guides when dominant groups are pressured to distinguish between groups near the bottom of the hierarchy (Shah and Thornton, 1994).

In his examination of the nature of the ethnic hierarchy in place among Dutch youth in the Netherlands, Hagendoorn (1993) found a scale-like structure that placed northern Europeans at the top, and Moroccans and Turks, who come to the Netherlands as guest workers, at the bottom of the preference order. Hagendorn took special note of the fact that this preference ordering did not vary according to the respondent's attitudes about race and ethnicity. Even 'non-racists' tended to have a similar structure of evaluative preferences.

Preferences for groups thought to be close to one's own group, and the desire to avoid members of groups thought of as distant from one's own group, are also based on a characterization of the behavior of distant group members as 'deviant.' Groups may be characterized in terms of the extent to which they differ from one's own group in terms of the values assumed to guide their behavior. The characterizations and the assumptions that are a part of them are part of what we recognize as racial stereotypes.

Of course, awareness or *knowledge* of racial stereotypes does not necessarily mean that an individual is a racist, or even holds racist beliefs. Devine (1989, p. 12) observes that 'even for subjects who honestly report having no negative prejudices against Blacks, activation of stereotypes can have automatic effects that if not consciously monitored produce effects that resemble prejudiced responses.' The fact that such stereotypes can be activated or brought to mind through a process of priming in both high and low prejudice individuals underscores the difficulty involved in eliminating the place of racial beliefs in our cognitive structures. The nature of priming effects, where very subtle cues evoke or activate a structured set of stereotypic images or impressions, increases the potential influence that mass media or other communicators may have on the reproduction of racism.

Racial stereotypes

Social learning is not limited to direct personal experience, but is mediated by means of communication, including mass communication media (van Dijk, 1994). 'The combined result of these processes . . . is that by the time we are adults (and undoubtedly well before then) we all have well-established stereotypic conceptions of numerous social groups' (Hamilton and Trolier, 1986, p. 137).

Racial group stereotypes are part of the symbolic environment in which we live. Stereotypes are recognized as both a limitation and a resource. Some scholars suggest that stereotypes are the result of a motivational process, and that stereotypes are developed and used because of the ways in which they serve the 'intrapsychic needs of the perceiver' (Hamilton and Trolier, 1986, p. 127). While it seems clear that stereotypes are used by everyone as an aid to social perception, we are just beginning to understand how stereotypes come to be as the product of social interaction, and how they become incorporated as a resource within our cognitive structures, and how their subsequent use contributes to the reproduction of racism.

While the evidence is slim, the general conclusion about the role of motivation for the use of stereotypes is one of 'context-dependent functionality' (Hilton and Von Hippel, 1996). Stated simply, we use stereotypes when they help us to achieve the goals or interests that vary from context to context. Thus, while the use of stereotypes can be motivated by the need to defend one's ego, or self-concept, stereotypes are also useful in routine information-processing tasks that have no readily identifiable competitive or conflictual aspects. The fact that the activation of stereotypes is automatic, akin to an unconscious reflex (Devine, 1989), suggests that their utility is well established, perhaps even the product of the long-term evolutionary adaptation of the species.

It seems likely that stereotypes become part of our understanding of our surroundings from the first moments of our efforts to make sense of the world around us. Indeed, evidence suggests that 'stereotypes are well established in children's memories before children develop the cognitive ability and flexibility to question or critically evaluate the stereotype's validity or acceptability' (Devine, 1989, p. 6).

Our concern with the use of stereotypes is not based primarily on their usefulness as a resource for managing the complexity in our social environment. The convenience which such classifications provide does not come without some cost. That cost is the biasing of our perceptions. Cognitive theorists argue that these social categories 'can bias the way we process, organize and store it in memory, and make judgements about members of those social categories' (Hamilton and Trolier, 1986, p. 133).

If the dominant feature of the stereotype of a young African American male involves his violent aggressive manner, then the description of a young man that emphasizes *this feature* is likely to evoke the image of a Black male, and in the absence of other information he is likely to be identified and evaluated as such.

Racial stereotypes include belief systems as attributes or traits that are assumed to characterize most of the members of identifiable groups. We evaluate other groups in terms of the extent to which we believe they share important beliefs, especially those beliefs that engage moral and ethical principles.

Stereotypes are not limited to personal attributes or traits; they are also used in the communication of normative boundaries around what we believe to be appropriate social roles for members of particular racial and ethnic groups. Stereotypes are akin to role dimensions of person schemas. While occupational roles are among the most important roles we organize in our person schemas (given the part that work plays in the construction of our own social identity), there are also important social roles within the family and the community which are likely to be defined in stereotypical ways.

One of the factors in cognitive processing that makes understanding of the role of stereotypes so difficult is the influence of the *distinctiveness* of particular features or cues associated with individuals or situations. While race is a readily identifiable cue, its distinctiveness may vary with the context in which it is one among many potentially relevant cues. Cognitive theorists suggest that distinctiveness affects perception through its influence over the attention we pay to things in our environment. The salience of race is structurally determined in large part. Because the White majority is just that – a majority – it is possible for other aspects of personhood to be more important than their race. However, minority status raises the salience of race, and increases the likelihood that race will be activated as a relevant feature. It is minority status that makes every minority person a representative of his race, and the more extreme the minority status the greater the salience of race.

Individual differences in the perceived distinctiveness of racial and ethnic cues are readily explainable in terms of the background and experiences of each person. Persons, behaviors, clothes, or other features that one has little direct, personal experience of by definition makes these features unfamiliar and distinctive and, as a result, they are likely to be the focus of attention within a complex perceptual field.

The victim-blaming tendency that has been identified in studies of *attribution* patterns leads people to identify internal motivations, drives or tendencies as being responsible for the problems that 'others' experience. The use of internal explanations for positive outcomes may be used when the behavior of members of 'those' racial groups is contrary to the dominant stereotype of that group. The 'exceptional' Black person is exceptional because this particular individual is different from other members of the group.

Racial thinking

The development of cognitive maps and elaboration of cognitive structures is dependent upon the amount and quality of information one processes on a day-to-day, routine basis. The information that an individual is likely to receive about members of outgroups is more likely to be mediated either by other individuals or by the mass media. This information is likely, therefore, to have been structured in some way by the interests which motivate or govern those sources. To the extent that information about members of an outgroup is available from these sources, dependence on those information sources is likely to produce and reproduce a distorted or biased image of the outgroup (Ball-Rokeach *et al.*, 1984).

The theory of *media dependency* underscores the variety of ways in which the influence of a media system may be felt by individuals (Ball-Rokeach *et al.*, 1984, p. 7). Individuals will differ in the extent to which they depend upon the mass media as the source of the information they need for:

(1) understanding themselves and the world around them
(2) guidance in making decisions about activities and relationships, as well as for
(3) solitary and social recreation.

Media choices are rationally informed, but like most choices they are limited by the characteristics of what the market, or other socially structured institutions, provides for their use. Members of minority racial or ethnic groups will also select from those media on the basis of their availability as well as their perceived utility. Racial group identity will be seen to influence, and be influenced by, the character of the specialized media available to them. Decisions about which media to use may be influenced by advertising and promotion as well as by the recommendations of members of a person's friendship network. Persons who are more closely identified with their own racial or ethnic group are more likely to have more of their friends from the same group, and are thus likely to receive recommendations regarding the value of targeted media from members of their own racial group.

Media dependency is believed to play a critical role in the process of media effects and, by extension, in the social construction of race:

the greater the media dependency, the greater the level of attention during exposure, the greater the level of affect toward the message and its senders, and the greater the likelihood of postexposure communication about the message – and thus, the greater the probability of message effects, intended or unintended. (Ball-Rokeach *et al.*, 1984, p. 13)

What we understand about the nature of identity formation leads us to believe that the mass media perform a critical symbolic function in providing role models that we use in self-evaluation. We make adjustments on the basis of comparisons between who we think we are at present and who we think we would like to be in the future. That projection, or *ideal self*, is often informed by reference to *role models*, and those role models are, more often than not, accessible to us primarily through the mass media.

Strategic construction and unintended consequences

Jannette Dates and William Barlow (1993) describe a critical tension within mass media as a 'war of images.' The battles in this war continue to be fought to determine who will determine the representation of African Americans and their cultural heritage in the mass media. The principal combatants in this war are identified as Whites and Blacks, with Blacks largely responding 'to the omissions and distortions of the former' (p. 3). This battle is framed as an ideological struggle, with Black creative energies being focused on a resistance movement of the sort common to the struggle of subordinate classes throughout history. The metaphoric construction of war is unmistakable:

By the 1850s, the slavery controversy had engulfed the nation in a war of political rhetoric and racial imagery. For the first time, key stereotypes in the arsenal of the proslavery forces, like the contented slave and the benevolent master, were being seriously challenged by antislavery activists at public forums and in the media. (Dates and Barlow, 1993, p. 8)

Of course, the idea of battling images competing for hegemony over consciousness is a useful way of understanding the ways in which stereotypes emerge and become transformed or displaced by more powerful images over time. It is not clear, however, that this notion of struggle is broad enough to include the other relationships which are a part of the process of cultural reproduction.

If we examine the metaphor of war more closely, we can see that the conflict frame is ill equipped to explain the strategic and expressive, as well as exploitative or profit-seeking motives that have guided image makers over time. It will be important to consider how the relative importance of these different goals may have shifted with the increasing commercialization of media, and with changes in the racial and ethnic composition of media markets. This will be an important part of the discussion in Chapter 3.

The idea of war, or the 'battle for men's minds' is a familiar theme in the analysis of propaganda. Propaganda is understood as a strategic resource that involves a 'careful and predetermined plan of prefabricated symbol manipulation to communicate to an audience in order to fulfill an objective. The objective that is sought requires the audience to reinforce or modify attitudes and/or behavior' (Jowett and O'Donnell, 1986, p. 15). Propaganda is the antithesis of the kinds of communication that Jürgen Habermas (1987) has elevated to the status of an ideal, in that propaganda is not directed toward the goal of understanding, but toward the manipulation of consciousness and the subsequent control of behavior.

While much of the criticism directed against the images of racial and ethnic minorities is focused on the false, biased, or distorted character of the images, propaganda is not always, or even primarily, false. What is critical to underscore in the definition of propaganda is the extent of design and intentionality. We may wish to distinguish between the consequences that flow from intentional acts and those which are neither intended nor anticipated. As Giddens makes clear, the unintended consequences of action must still be connected with the actor, and be included within any conception of her agency (1984, pp. 9–14). For Giddens, understanding the ways in which the unintended consequences of action may interact with institutionalized practices is critical to understanding the reproduction of racism.

> Repetitive activities, located in one context of time and space, have regularized consequences, unintended by those who engage in those activities . . . . What happens in this second series of contexts then, directly, or indirectly, influences the further conditions of action in the original context . . . . The unintended consequences are regularly 'distributed' as a by-product of regularized behavior reflexively sustained as such by its participants. (Giddens, 1984, p. 14)

Should the definition of propagandist apply to an individual artist, driven only by the desire to express herself? It seems most would fall short of the definition of propagandist in that artists at least claim to have little interest in affecting behaviors beyond the continued consumption of their works. Yet, at the same time, we can bring to mind numerous examples of communicators who were, in fact, actively engaged in an effort to influence attention, awareness, and opinion. Certainly the cadre of Black film-makers like Spike Lee, or Haile Gerima, have commented on the educational, motivational, and persuasive goals of their works.

Uncertainty about the nature, extent, and significance of intention in the production of cultural materials is heightened in the case of those media for which authorship must be shared. Books, articles, speeches and the like are generally identified with a single author. While a play may have a single author, at the point of its reception by an audience, actors, directors, and the designers of sets and costumes each come to share in the authorship. It is unlikely that all are ever of one mind in terms of their understanding of the story, or the understanding that the author hoped to generate in the audience. It seems especially likely that actors, directors, and authors will differ considerably in the messages they *intended* to convey even in the case of skits, programs, or films in which Black actors reluctantly perform in stereotyped roles.

A racially disparate outcome may be produced by an objectively neutral action because the outcome is a 'byproduct' rather than the target of reasoned action. Giddens emphasizes the importance of the 'unintended consequences of action' (1984, p. 5) because of the implications that they have for our understanding of the agency of those knowledgeable actors, who are actually quite ignorant in this regard. Unintended consequences, especially those which occur outside the range of vision of this actor, have a potential to influence and limit this actor's subsequent actions because these consequences become part of the 'unacknowledged conditions' of future actions (Figure 2.2). The cognitive response to an unintended affront may be anger and hostility, and the response may have negative consequences for the knowledgeable, but ignorant, agent. Examples in the realm of mass media abound.

J. Fred MacDonald reflects this view in his assessment of the strategies used by television producers who responded to the demands for increased visibility by African Americans. Because the primary audience for prime-time television programs, including situation comedies, had been middle-class White viewers, the Black characters tended to be 'culturally and socially assimilated and at least middle-class . . . [and] usually exhibit the bourgeois values, habits, and attitudes that are so familiar in white characterization' (MacDonald, 1992, pp. 278–9). The attempt to attract the mainstream White audience guaranteed that the 'authentic' qualities that would make African Americans distinct from other racial and ethnic groups would be largely absent from view. But it is hard to imagine that producers 'intended' to 'shortchange' African Americans, either by ignoring them initially, or by presenting an unrepresentative view in response to a complaint. However, because we think that representation matters, both in terms of absence and in terms of abstraction, the role of intention is secondary, but not irrelevant.

While television programmers may be aware of the unintended consequences that flow from these choices, cultural critics also recognize the inherent contradictions in attempting to reflect the diversity of African American personality and culture when only a very narrow window of opportunity is presented by the marketplace. How does a producer present the Black poor and working class without providing material that might reinforce the stereotypes held by Whites? MacDonald argues that 'given the historic intolerance of the dominant culture in the United States, it seems myopic and even dangerous for blacks to tolerate portrayals of themselves that are not complimentary' (p. 281).

MacDonald suggests, however, that some efforts to overcome the problem of narrow, sanitized representations of Blacks risks generating more serious harm to racial solidarity. The popular television series *In Living Color* is a program which generated considerable debate and tension among African Americans, in part because of the ways in which it seemed to glorify life in the ghetto and to ridicule the achievements of the Black middle class (Gray, 1995; MacDonald, 1992). Similar skirmishes in the 'culture wars' around the value of 'gangster rap' and other forms of 'Black street culture' reveal the tension between the search for success in the marketplace and success in the public sphere (Dawson, 1993).

Indeed, as will be explored more fully in Chapter 3, the 'triumph of the market' and substitution of efficiency as a normative basis superior to fairness or social justice increases the likelihood that these contradictions will be lamented, but interpreted as outside the reach of legitimate political action (Herman, 1995).

Ethnic humor

Ethnic humor is understood to 'work' because it relies upon readily available stereotypes for the 'resolution of the problem' at the core of the joke. It is argued that ethnic or racial humor also usually works in a *conservative* fashion in that 'it works in a given society, within and between sub-groups, to reinforce accepted values, goals, and ideals. And these accepted values are, more often than not, the values of dominant groups' (Lewis, 1987, p. 67).

The use of ethnic humor represents another critical site at which we might observe, or at least theorize on, the nature of structuration and the reproduction of racism. Studies of what we think of as ethnic humor are of fairly recent vintage, and have been generally linked to an interest in understanding the nature of racial prejudice (Goldstein, 1976). Michael Pickering (1994) has argued for the re-examination of a British television show, *The Black and White Minstrel Show*, which enjoyed a success run on the BBC between 1957 and 1973, despite its reliance on the traditions, if not the openly racist humor, that characterized earlier forms of minstrelcy. In pointing out the talent of these Black artists, Pickering still warns that 'the discourse of sexist and racist humor can seep through into other discourses, and its clichés and stereotypes may contribute to a symbolic lexicon from which fear and prejudice are able to derive their self-sustaining expression' (p. 330).

Ethnic humor is defined as 'a type of humor in which fun is made of the perceived behavior, customs, personality, or any other traits of a group or its members by virtue of their specific sociocultural identity' (Apte, 1987). Telling a joke that depends upon such stereotypes reinforces the symbolic structures in which stereotypes exist and do their cultural work. The joke works because it is understood, and we understand or 'get' the joke because we possess knowledge of the stereotype. And, unless our response to the joke is hostile and resistive, getting the joke is likely to increase the structural importance of the stereotype by establishing yet another link for it to the somewhat unique circumstance in the joke. If we repeat the joke, seeking the rewards we get from bringing pleasure to others, we reinforce the stereotype still further.

Part of the analytical problem that ethnic humor represents is contextual. It is argued that humor in general is an essentially social act, where the quality of the joke, and its success in evoking laughter, depends very much upon context – who tells the joke to whom (Zijderveld, 1983). Because the social context of joking is frequently one of social exchange, where we are expected to laugh in response to the 'gift' of a joke, and further to reciprocate with another equally productive joke, responding with either outrage or analysis would be seen as inappropriate. Criticism is therefore usually inhibited by the usual social context in which jokes are told. This is a structural constraint, and its usual product is the reinforcement of racial and ethnic stereotypes.

As with other occasions of exchange within and outside markets, not all participants trade as equals. People are said to possess a 'sense of humor' if they are able to laugh, that is, to be amused, but for targets of racial or ethnic humor to achieve or maintain their status they often have to be amused 'at their own expense' (La Fave and Mannell, 1976). For persons in subordinate positions, the psychic costs are likely to exceed the level of injury that is part of the self-deprecation common to other forms of humor. Not unlike other forms of victim blaming, a target who does not find such jokes amusing is seen as deficient, being unable to 'take a joke.'

We have no solid basis for independently evaluating the *quality* of a joke, or the quality of a television program or film. A joke's power to amuse depends so much on the context and the way it is delivered. Perhaps it may depend even more on what the audience brings to it. Where racial features in stereotypes influence perception because of their salience or distinctiveness, humor often produces its effects because of the perceived incongruity of the behaviors represented in the joke (Fry, 1987). Like distinctiveness, incongruity is subjective assessment, both individually and culturally. Whether one 'gets the joke' or not depends on the nature of one's experiences cumulated over time.

For some observers, the history of ethnic humor reveals parallels with the history of ethnic identity. Initially, ethnic humor was used as an expression of superiority of natives over immigrants, and over the children of Black slaves. Some of the emergent derogatory stereotypes of the time were later adapted for use by these subordinate groups as a marker of a past that they had moved beyond, or as a means for expressing hostility toward still other ethnic groups (Boskin and Dorinson, 1985). Used in this way, these stories may have served to strengthen group identity and cohesiveness. On the other hand, because of the voluntary and dynamic nature of racial and ethnic identity, it is also possible that a member of the target group may be amused by jokes about his group because he no longer has a positive personal identification with the group (La Fave and Mannell, 1976, pp. 120–1).

Telling or sharing jokes about one's own racial or ethnic group is not always a sign of self-hatred, however. It may

> on the contrary, signal a strong sense of group identity, for the laughter . . . [these jokes] elicit is not a laughter with whites at the expense of blacks, but rather an in-group laughter which stands proof of ethnic pride and self-consciousness. It is the same kind of gallows humor – suggesting invincibility and a sense of superiority noted in studies of Jewish humor. (Zijderveld, 1983, p. 51)

Telling jokes may also be used as an index of racial or ethnic identity, perhaps as a 'test' of ethnic competence. Among American Indians, 'razzing,' a form of joking akin to 'playing the dozens' among African Americans, is used as vehicle for confirmation of 'Indian-ness' (Pratt, 1996). It is also a resource for socialization, used to inform an individual of the ways in which they have been judged to have deviated from the group norm, and to indicate what kinds of behavior are more appropriate. Pratt (1996) suggests that:

> Indian humor, as is true of other forms of humor, is based upon stereotypes that only members of the community are privy to. It is assumed that you are truly one of us when you can understand and will not have to ask about meanings, or what was seen to be humorous about a story or joke. (p. 251)

Here, as in other places, the influence of group identity is substantial, and the salience of identity is socially determined. Changes in the *politics* of identity have also helped to produce changes in the symbolic function of humor, and perhaps to an even greater extent small talk among strangers. The emergence of a movement among Whites to oppose the forms of privilege that Whiteness brings produces suggestions for ways in which responses to jokes can be subversive (Winant, 1997). Whites who are told a racist joke by another White are advised to respond to the joke teller by saying 'I know you told me that story because you thought I was White. It is a mistake that is frequently made, but I am not White and I am offended by your joke.'

Whether such radical subversion of racial identity and the privilege associated with it have any potential for success is something that we might begin to assess in the context of a media system which continues to shape the dominant construction of race. This is the focus of the next chapter.

|3|

The media system

The role of the mass media in the construction and reproduction of race and racism is to be understood in the context of mass media systems and institutions. Widely distributed or mass media content can be understood as the product or output of a production and distribution system. Mass-produced cultural materials are industrial products. Indeed, within the critical perspective associated with the Frankfurt School, the media are part of a 'culture industry.' This critical formulation sees the media as an essential component in the control of society through control over the formation of individuals and their relationships to institutions within society (Adorno and Horkheimer, 1979; Hardt, 1993). Unfortunately, the Frankfurt School critique has not historically been much concerned with race. Indeed, some of the attempts by Adorno to position African American jazz as an example of bourgeois false consciousness reproduced the racist constructions of an African savage that were in common usage at the time (Bayles, 1994). Understanding the place of race in the culture industry thus remains an unrealized goal of critical social theory, and that goal is the focus of this chapter.

At one level, communications media are to be understood as technical systems which are governed by tradition as well as by contractual relations. To a certain extent, which varies from country to country, the operation of media organizations is constrained by formal systems of laws and regulations. These communications policies govern access to media outlets through a variety of administrative means which vary from the reservation of frequencies and time slots, and tax policies designed to increase minority ownership, to employment policies designed to stimulate active recruitment, retention, and advancement of minorities. In some cases, government policy includes strict limits on racially inflammatory speech, as well as requirements that broadcasters ascertain the 'interests and needs' of minority groups within their coverage areas. Organizations of media professionals have also, from time to time, established race-sensitive policies related toward ownership, employment, and consideration of minority group interests as they relate to the accuracy of group representations. Their policies may, in fact, be more important than any of the policies established by government agencies.

In addition, the operation of these industrial organizations reflects the influence of distinct and interacting social forces that include the vagaries of consumer tastes and preferences, as well as the differential economic values that the marketplace assigns to different classes of audiences or consumers. In the neoclassical economic paradigm, prices are used as surrogates of value, and thus govern the allocation of resources within a society. It is this underlying mechanism that constrains 'the desires of participants and coordinates their actions. In the economic approach these market instruments perform most, if not all, of the functions assigned to "structure" in sociological theories' (Becker, 1979, p. 9). It is the interaction of all these influences that determines the racialized character of the information and symbolic materials that are produced and distributed within markets and through a variety of non-commercial media systems.

Our examination of media systems in this chapter will emphasize the relations between the supply of content, the distribution of news and entertainment material, the assessment and valuation of audiences, and the continually changing mechanics of direct and indirect financing. A variety of Marxist and neo-Marxist perspectives have sought to explain systematic patterns in media content as deriving from and being determined by those who owned and controlled media systems (Murdock and Golding, 1979). This early work has been elaborated and extended in response to challenges to assumptions about the extent to which owners actually controlled industrial production in an era in which management had become a technical speciality (Murdock, 1982). We will explore some of the problems these critical theorists encountered in their efforts to represent media content as performing an instrumental function in support of the interests of a ruling class.

Because the pursuit of profit within the commercial segment of the media system depends upon advertising revenue for a large share of its income, production decisions have had to accommodate the desires of advertisers as well as the desires of individuals and groups within the audience. We will examine the ways in which different forms of financing help to determine the influence that different actors bring to bear on media decision making. In an era that is characterized by 'globalization,' the influence of actors in foreign markets is also quite substantial, and it will be seen to complicate the ability of media scholars to specify precisely which sets of actors dominate the media systems in any market (Litman and Sochay, 1994).

Because not all media are explicitly profit oriented, and therefore not governed entirely by a capitalist logic, we must also examine the ways in which these organizations make production decisions, and the ways in which the content they produce is similar to or different from that produced by commercial media. The primary media of this type are the state-run, or state-supported, 'public service' broadcast media operated by the British Broadcasting Corporation (BBC) in Britain, the Public Broadcasting System (PBS) in the United States, the Canadian Broadcasting Corporation (CBC) in Canada, and numerous other examples from around the globe. There are very important insights to be gained from the changes that have taken place in these systems as the spread of commercial media has accelerated in the past decade. These changes demonstrate that economic structures and a marketplace logic have a determinant influence even on systems which are not themselves part of a fundamental, or even a subsumed, capitalist relation (Mosco, 1996; Resnick and Wolff, 1987).

We will also examine the relatively underdeveloped body of scholarship which examines the nature of audiences, especially their tastes and preferences for particular media content. We have come to recognize that even though mainstream assumptions about 'consumer sovereignty' are easily challenged from a variety of positions that go beyond recognizing the influence of advertisers, consumer demand still plays a role within the media system that cannot be ignored. Even if the assessment of audience tastes and preferences is based on incomplete information and inadequate theory, media producers do attempt to provide consumers with some approximation of what they are willing to 'purchase' or invest their time with. This imprecise technology of audience assessment, which can be thought of as 'ready, shoot, aim,' results not only in a characteristic structure of supply, but also in measurable shifts in what audiences *actually* do when they adopt the audience role.

The production system

When we talk about the mass media system, we generally refer to the numerous interconnecting networks of individuals and organizations that are involved in the production and distribution of symbolic materials at any point in time (Figure 3.1). Media scholars frequently emphasize different subsystems, such as production and distribution, while others emphasize the ancillary services, such as marketing and audience research, while still others focus on the regulatory bodies that are involved in setting limits, or bringing about a transformation in the traditional orientation of decision makers within the system (Turow, 1992).

While at some analytical levels these differences may not actually matter, there are often good reasons for differentiating between media systems in terms of what we think of as the primary characteristics of the medium. For example, differences in the costs of production may be the basis for distinguishing between broadcast and print media. Differences in the costs of distribution may be the primary reason for distinguishing between broadcast and theatrical film. However, alternative video distribution

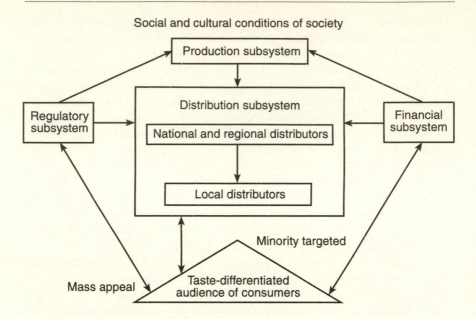

Figure 3.1 Mass media system (adapted from deFleur and Rokeach, 1982: *Theories of mass communication*, p. 177). Reprinted by permission of Addison-Wesley Educational Publishers Inc.

systems, such as video cassette rentals, and direct broadcast satellites have transformed the economics of the film industry (Wasko, 1994).

There is much talk and considerable hype surrounding the potential for convergence between media. For strategic reasons, competitors within the electronics industry are rushing to develop a single 'information utility' that will make the output from a host of different media systems accessible through an integrated system in the home. Yet there are still bound to be important differences in the nature of the work that goes into producing the 'first copy' or the original (Baldwin *et al.*, 1996) that we need to explore.

In order to understand the structure of these media systems and the ways in which they appear to be changing, we begin with a list of some of the primary actors and the relationships between them. Joseph Turow, following earlier work by George Gerbner, has identified 13 different actors that are likely to have some influential role within a mass media industry (Turow, 1992, p. 22). Because of the industrial character of the mass media today, only the 'creator' and the 'public' generally perform their media system roles outside a formal organization, and even the creative work is being commoditized at an increasing rate.

Characterizing these different positions within the media industry as *power roles* is a useful way to reveal the underlying structure of the industry. Turow's perspective on this aspect of media industry structure underscores the importance of control over *resources* as a defining aspect of the relations between participants in the industry. By examining the changing coalitions between institutional actors that develop over time, one can begin to understand how this power structure has evolved in response to critical events, technological change, and shifts in organizational form and style, as well as shifts in the philosophy of government as it applies to the media system.

Examining changes over time underscores the importance of history to the process of structural change. Thomas Cripps suggests that Black cinema in the United States has emerged out of African American history, but that this particular story has its own history of struggle: 'first, of struggles of a weak minority for a protective censorship, then a century-long campaign to affect Hollywood movies at their source, and finally a parallel line of race movies' (Cripps, 1990, p. 131).

Although we will examine in more detail the claims that have been made about the variety of ways in which a particular program, message, or unit of symbolic material can be interpreted, we want to emphasize the moment of production in this chapter because it is at this stage that the media text is thought to be inscribed with what Stuart Hall defines as the dominant or preferred meaning through a process of encoding. Encoding takes place within the moment of production (Pillai, 1993). While the nature of any links between media texts and ideological or hegemonic interests remains to be established, there is also a generalized and well-placed concern with the *accuracy* of these representations. These will be examined in more detail in the next chapter but, for the moment, our concern is to understand how media products come to have particular characteristics, some of which may be readily seen to serve ideological functions.

Media scholars and activists have been convinced that the quality of representation is determined in part by the level of participation by minority group members in important creative and decision making capacities within the media industry. This reflects a view that a communicator is more likely to be able to faithfully reproduce or represent experiences and perspectives that she has had direct and substantial experience with. There is a long history of activist pressure to increase minority participation in different media industries at all levels, including ownership of media organizations and facilities.

There are also likely to be important interactions between the structure of media organizations and the structure of the markets in which they operate. For example, Liebler (1988) found that the greater the prominence of Hispanics in a news organization's primary market, the greater was the role of ethnicity in the organization's newsgathering efforts. On the other hand, the more integrated or pluralistic the community, the less influence ethnicity seemed to have on the journalist's work. Similar differences were noted between journalists who worked for Spanish-language and those who worked for English-language media. It should be noted that Mexican Americans were more likely to be employed with English-language media than other Latino journalists. This is a point which underscores the analytical problems that are created when scholars and marketers ignore the cultural differences and social experiences that identify Latin Americans.

It has been argued that without participation representation can never reach the level of accuracy, at least within the news media, that is required by a democratic system of governance (Bates, 1995; Udick, 1993). There have also been voices raised in opposition to these claims, not primarily because they deny the assumptions of special capacity, or oppose affirmative action (Splichal, 1992), but because they find the *burden* of ethnic representation too heavy for minority communicators to bear (Schement and Singleton, 1981).

A more highly developed stream of media scholarship has sought to understand how a process of *socialization* would operate so as to ensure that media professionals would produce content that was well integrated into and consistent with the dominant ideology. This is a central concern for a Marxian critical theory that makes claims about a hegemonic process in which workers from the lower and middle classes still manage to produce content which is supportive of, or at least not directly challenging to, the interests of the ruling elite (Cantor, 1980).

Race and the commercial imperative

Nicholas Garnham (1990) has argued for the necessity of understanding the mass media as economic entities concerned directly with profit, and indirectly, through advertising, with the realization of profit by other economic organizations within the economy. While not denying the importance of an ideological role for these organizations, Garnham, as a political economist, privileges the economic within a complex of determinations. In the same way, while the reproduction of racism unquestionably has an ideological dimension, and media do play an ideological role, the economic logic of capitalist markets can be seen to complicate that role. A critical understanding of communication and race must engage this logic and its conflicts and contradictions directly.

In contrast with much of the contemporary work on media which *assumes* a market orientation, we want to emphasize the fact that the introduction of a capitalist logic into the production of culture is a relatively recent and largely incomplete process. As Nicholas Garnham reminds us, capitalist relations are continually being established anew in areas of social life which had previously existed outside the direct influence of the market. The form of a particular media industry in a particular nation at particular moment in time should be understood as 'a specific form which grew within a pre-existing social formation and is involved in a process of expansion and conquest of non-capitalist sectors, a process which is incomplete and contradictory' (1990, p. 36). In the view of Dan Schiller (1994), there are no 'transhistorical reasons' for the expansion of capitalist relations in a particular way in a specific place:

> It is, rather, the host of specific conditions and pressures exerted by a capitalist political economy, forever requiring new markets, new materials and production processes, and new and cheaper sources of appropriately skilled or deskilled labor, that must be connected with the capitalization of any particular form or practice of information production. (p. 99)

At the same time, Herbert Schiller suggests that there has been an acceleration in the decline over the last 50 years in the amount of creative and symbolic output which remains outside the control of market forces (Schiller, 1989, p. 32). The speed with which the commercial imperative has come to dominate the process of cultural reproduction has consequences for the ways in which the media can be relied upon to serve an ideological role within the context of racial projects.

A great many of the policy debates about privatization and deregulation in media systems are emanations that flow from the disruptions of traditional relationships threatened by the expansion of capitalist relations (Schement and Curtis, 1995). Media scholars have not emphasized the processes through which the arts and popular cultural materials have been incorporated into the commercial market. The work has been distressingly ahistorical. Market structures have been taken as given, and far too often assumed to be at or near the competitive ideal imagined within the mainstream economic literature. Scholarship directed at understanding how markets really are, and how they got that way, is only now being published to any great degree (Baker, 1994a; McChesney, 1993; Mosco, 1996). There are barely more than a handful of studies which focus on the ways in which markets oriented toward racial and ethnic minority populations have developed.

Production for the market

Production for the market is a defining aspect of capitalist relations in the production of culture. Dan Schiller defines a commodity as 'a resource that is produced for the market by wage labor' (Schiller, 1994, p. 98). Understanding the nature of the process of commoditization is central to our perspective on the changing importance of race and race relations to the supply of media materials with racial content. Commodification represents a shift in the locus of power over production decisions. Prior to commodification, goods were produced on the basis of their potential for meeting individual and social needs. As commodities, the decisions about whether or not to produce a particular good is based upon whether or not it can produce a profit in the marketplace (Mosco, 1996, pp. 143–5). Within the neoclassical model, the value of commodities is established in the market. However, that value, indicated by its price, is not solely, or perhaps not even primarily, determined by the range of uses enabled by the structural or material characteristics of any particular good. Advertising and promotion play an increasingly important role in determining both price, value, and utility of commodities in the market.

Estimation of the demand for media requires some knowledge of who the actual or potential consumers of content might be. The estimation of demand requires some knowledge of consumer tastes and preferences. It also requires some knowledge of the distribution of wealth, and the propensity to consume media products that is likely to vary with income or wealth. It is for this reason that much of our attention in this chapter will be focused on the ways in which *audiences* are understood and pursued within commercial and non-commercial media systems.

There are also critical differences within and between media systems in terms of the relations between producers, audiences, and others with financial interests in those relations. Because of the nature of broadcast technology, there is no simple reliable way to enable a direct exchange of capital against value received. Advertising may be understood as one of the ways in which this problem was addressed. Because advertisers pay the costs of production, *they*, rather than the members of the audience, exercise a determining influence over what is produced and distributed by broadcasters. Because advertisers are relatively uninterested in the consequences that flow from media consumption that are not directly related to the purchase of their products, the ways in which programs designed to attract the 'desired audience' may affect the ignored or 'accidental audience,' is rarely a matter of concern. That is, advertisers seeking to introduce upscale Anglo audiences to their new brand of salsa are unconcerned about the impact their ads have on the reproduction of stereotypical impressions of the Latinos who traditionally included such condiments in their cuisine. These consequences, which economists refer to as 'externalities' will be examined more closely in the next chapter.

Our focus on audiences as a critical component of the media system is not an attempt to shift attention away from the production system. It should be clear that the audience is a social construction that reflects the interests of actors in various positions of power and authority in the media system. Individual consumers of media ought to be understood as having only negligible amounts of power with which to influence the system as a whole, or any of its formal organizations. It is the audiences as conceptualized by the more powerful actors, especially those in the production and distribution system, that are the primary concerns of this chapter.

James Anderson has developed a well-elaborated and quite useful way of distinguishing among these constructed audiences (1996). Anderson distinguishes between what he calls 'formal' and 'empirical' audiences. Among the formal audiences, Anderson distinguishes between 'encoded' and 'analytic' audiences. The analytic audiences are created in theory, but they may also be creatures of empirical assessments such as surveys and experiments. What matters in their creation is that their characteristics are determined by the assumptions of the knowledgeable agent who may write or produce content with this audience in mind. The encoded audience is the audience for whom a particular line is written, or a troublesome scene is reshot because 'our audience' prefers such representations.

The empirical audiences are a more highly elaborated set including: 'transcendent' audiences, 'aggregate' audiences, 'surrogate' audiences, and the audiences produced by ethnographic research, the 'situated' audience. Still other empirical audiences include the 'strategic' audiences, which would include media activists and critics, whose audience experiences are focused on producing readings 'on behalf' of their constituents, and the 'engaged' audiences that we might recognize as 'superfans.' A special but undertheorized audience described by Anderson is the 'emergent' audience member who has knowledge that is shared with persons who have actually 'consumed' some media product, but they have gathered this knowledge indirectly through conversation and other social interactions.

For our purposes, the three different kinds of audience which have been constructed from the perspective of commerce and governmental actors deserve our attention (Ang, 1991). Ang makes a distinction between 'audience-as-public' and 'audience-as-market' primarily in order to develop a temporary distinction between government public service and commercial interests. Audience-as-market should be further divided to include the construction of the audience as commodity. It is the nature of financing through advertising that is the basis for thinking about different audience segments as commodities produced efficiently by means of a sophisticated industrial technology (Gandy and Signorielli, 1981).

A somewhat more radical perspective sees the audience as *labor* in order to incorporate media use into a traditional Marxian model of exploitation (Jhally and Livant, 1986; Smythe, 1977). According to this view, what audiences are doing when they watch commercials on television is working – producing surplus value for capitalists. Smythe defined these media consumers as 'the commodity audience' (Meehan, 1993). While the compensation derived in terms of pleasure, relaxation, or other satisfactions derived from viewing the content that surrounds the commercials may be thought of as socially necessary, media capitalists derive additional, or surplus, value from their viewing and processing of commercial messages.

Some have argued against this interpretation of the nature of the 'work' that audiences perform, suggesting that this work involves 'making sense' of the media content we consume. Part of this *sense making* involves understanding how the consumption of media (and advertised products) contributes to our always present concerns about increasing status and maintaining self-esteem (Streeter, 1996, pp. 289–308). This involves considerable work in observing and processing the ways in which others, including others who are in one's reference group, work, relate, and consume. These observations are not limited to people we encounter and observe on the street, at work, or during our social lives. The people we encounter in mass media content are part of the raw materials we have to process in order to succeed, and to appear culturally competent.

It is also fairly common for media critics and scholars within and outside the academy to think of media audiences as *victims*. This is the view that will be examined in Chapter 5 where the use of media will be associated with particular harms. This view has been challenged somewhat in recent years by a view offered by other media scholars who prefer to think of audiences as *competent agents* who use the media for their own often creative and playful purposes. Although the academic media scholars are generally thought of as peripheral to the primary media systems, there are times when their criticism has affected the behavior of other powerful actors within the media system such that the overall character of images and representations has been changed in important ways.

Music and commercialization

There are differences between media and cultural forms whose origins have been commercial, and in which the influence of commerce has increased and has been transformed by technology. The music industry has been transformed by the commercial imperative. It has been shaped powerfully by race, racism, and racial politics. And it has been shaped by the cultural origins of its sources.

Musicians are no different from other creative actors in that they are forced from time to time to make compromises. Musicians compose and play music that on occasion departs from what they personally enjoy, or from what they believe to represent their interests, or their individuality as artists. Among those sources of pressure on individual musicians is the commercial market and the consumers that it organizes into audiences and markets. When a group of international musicians was asked about the circumstances surrounding their own musical compromises they said overwhelmingly that 'they modify their own musical preferences to suit what they perceive to be the tastes of their target audiences' (Robinson *et al.*, 1991, p. 240). The blending of different national styles which is described by one group of observers as 'bricolage' will continue to serve as a constraint on the freedom of musicians to play what they wish. Even though we may be witnessing a decline in the influence of the United States and other traditional centers of the global culture industry, 'the process of bricolage is not one of absolute "free" choice but one of constraint compromised between what might be desired creatively and what will be accepted commercially' (p. 249).

When commercial acceptance is not an empirical but a theoretical criterion, the influence of commerce on musical culture can be quite perverse. Richard Peterson (1994) underscores the influence of market researchers on the ways in which marketing ultimately shapes not only the structure of musical markets but also helps to shape the audience's expectations and appreciation of different musical forms. Peterson suggests that there are important cultural implications that result from the tension between different spheres of influence that reflect differences in social constructions of the audience. The markets sought by radio stations and their advertisers are not the same as the markets conceived by the record companies, and *none* of these are an exact match for the interests of the actual audiences for this music (Peterson, 1994, p. 173).

What he identifies as the 'categorization constraint' is a structural pressure within the music industry to categorize every artist and record into a particular slot – preferably one which is well established, and perhaps one in which the particular company has a dominant position. This kind of opportunistic classification often results in an artificial separation of musical types, such as that which developed over time between blues and country music. The creation of segmented markets oriented to different racial and ethnic communities emerged as the dominant strategy, and the development of 'race records' targeted to African Americans was a familiar result.

As Peterson and others note, producers actively shaped, or 'shoe-horned', performers into these predetermined categories, which from the producer's perspective seemed to be the most appropriate way to reach racially targeted segments. The result was that a *market* emerged that was racially divided, even though the *audience* for these forms of music was not originally divided in this way (Peterson, 1994, p. 177).

William Benzon (1993) suggests that the substantial interest shown by Whites in African American cultural forms reflects a dissatisfaction with the inability of traditional European forms to satisfy the emotional needs at a level set by contemporary American culture. Benzon's analysis includes references to Erik Erikson's (1968) claims regarding the incompleteness of cultural adaptation, which he offers as an explanation of racist stereotyping. 'Each culture cultivates some characteristics at the expense of others. The neglected characteristics may then coalesce into a negative identity which members of a given society will often project onto members of some other society or culture.' Benzon suggests that Europeans 'were disposed to see blacks in the image of the emotionality and sensuality they were rejecting in themselves' (p. 410).

At the same time, Benzon reminds us, Whites were the almost exclusive audiences for the 'uptown' clubs in which Black performers pursued

expressive limits unavailable to Whites within their own culture's repertoire. Finally, Benzon suggests, because the rebellious artist has been
provided a special place on the margins of White culture, it also became
permissible for these artists to *imitate* the cultural forms of African
Americans, and to present these synthetic forms to the broader mass of
Whites. Simon Jones (1993) among others agrees with the historical
character of this relationship arguing that:

> black music has been perceived by whites as a sign of 'authenticity'
> and 'sexuality' and as a 'pure' 'uncommercial' folk form to be
> protected and preserved. From the long tradition of white bohemian
> romanticization of jazz through the various subcultural appropri-
> ations of blues, r&b, and reggae, successive generations of whites
> have lived in their own particular 'imaginary' relation to black music.
> (p. 103)

Jones also calls our attention to the differences between the consumption
of Black music in the United States and in Britain. It seems likely that, in
the same way that commodities in general tend to be stripped of the history
of their production, exported cultural commodities are even further alienated from the conflicts and tensions that marked their production and
consumption in the United States. This relationship in the United States
was seen to be markedly different from the relations that developed
between White Britons and the producers of Afro-Caribbean music (Gilroy,
1987; Hebdige, 1979).

Citing a theory of creation, imitation, and abandonment that he credits
to LeRoi Jones (Amiri Baraka), Benzon describes a pattern of interaction
between African American and European American culture in which Blacks
abandon a musical form after Whites adopt the form for themselves. The
prime example is the blues, but Benzon suggests that it 'happened succes-
sively with ragtime, traditional and swing jazz, rock and roll, and most
recently with rap' (Benzon, 1993, p. 415). Jones (1993) adds that phono-
graphs made it possible for White musicians to learn from and imitate
Black performance styles in ways that sheet music did not permit. The
videos on 'Yo MTV Raps' and other such shows provide young Whites
today with the opportunity to cross the cultural distance between their
suburban communities and the 'hood' as 'visual tourists.' This experience
produces the sentiments they repeat among themselves.

Benzon's description of the relationship between Black and White cultural forms does not tell us what the future will bring, however. Although
he seems to suggest that the incorporation of African American musical
forms into White culture influenced the 'loosening up' of that culture, it is
not clear whether he means to suggest that the next level of Black cultural
expression would have to move to an even more liberated and demonstra-
tive form. In his view, it was the movement of Black performers like
Michael Jackson and Lionel Richie into the mainstream that created the

'vacuum' in popular music, rather than some dissatisfaction with what was being produced by these Black artists (Benzon, 1993, p. 421). Yet, we might accept that the combative elements, the visceral level of anger in the lyrics of rap, may indeed suggest the kind of escalation in the stimulation that long-term desensitization tends to produce a taste for.

The fact that the audience for rap is primarily White and male, and the fact that only a few White artists have succeeded in producing successful imitations of the form, leaves us uncertain about the future of the cycle (Vaughn, 1992). The fact that *Ebony* magazine did not publish any feature articles on rap until it was already commercially successful, and then all but ignored its cultural significance (Fenster, 1995), reflects an unwillingness by some cultural agents of the Black middle class to accept this particular music as its own (Bayles, 1994).

Jones (1993) also offers us a way of thinking about the relationship between the center and periphery that evokes an earlier moment in history when material resources, rather than cultural identities, were being mined, expatriated, processed, and then exported back to the Third World. In his view, Black and Third World musical cultures have more recently served as the artistic 'colonies' that are being raided periodically by Western artists and music companies. For Jones and others the 'world music' explosion of the 1970s is an example of the ways in which the capitalist market 'plunders' the cultural assets of societies that are at the same time seeking status as partners in the service of a 'universal consumerism' (Middleton, 1990, p. 293). Others suggest that the world music market has been made much more complicated because of the different realities of migration. Making distinctions between an exploitative market where the music of the periphery feeds the needs of a market in the core, and one in which music from the periphery re-establishes and reproduces the cultural links between the expatriate and his former home, is a problem noted by Hebdige (1979, p. 432) in his comments on the history of Island Records and its market among 'homesick rudies' in the UK.

Increasing concentration in the music industry, not unlike that which has taken place in the other sectors of the communications industry, has generated a greater determination within the industry to find a market that extends beyond any single nation's boundary. In the 1980s, the US record industry made more money in the international market than it did at home (Robinson *et al.*, 1991, p. 49). The need to identify and promote musical stars internationally is reflective of a similar drive that attempts to create, and then exploit, the visibility of international stars in the cinema (Barnet and Cavanagh, 1994). Where film and television programs are assessed in terms of how well they 'travel,' concern about 'geographical agility' permeates the international music industry as well (Cohen, 1994, p. 130). As a result, the dominant firms in the industry have incentives to 'obscure and overcome subnational and national boundaries in order to market their products as widely as possible.' This has meant that musical and cultural styles will increasingly be stripped of their local identity so that they can circulate more easily. While the emergence of different kinds of 'placeless' musics, like 'House' and 'Hip-Hop', are increasing, music identified with regions, cities, and even neighborhoods seems likely to continue to emerge on the edges of this market in search of the possibility of worldwide commercial success (Cohen, 1994, p. 132).

From the perspective of some observers, however, the sense of placelessness is not seen as problematic. Instead, it is seen as enabling, and the process which produces it is therefore referred to as *deterritorialization*. For example, the emergence of a Chinese ethnic music subculture in the United States is seen as an advance over the days in which 'Chinese musicians were on exhibit by Phineas Barnum and when the sounds of exotic instruments escaping from dark basements could only be caught by a few adventurers venturing into mysterious Chinatown' (Zheng, 1994, p. 284).

The commercialization of the music and culture of indigenous people raises a set of unique problems not generally considered when we talk about cultural exchange. Because music and dance have such an important role in the rituals that are used for healing, spiritual engagement, and social reproduction, providing access to cultural performance may mean providing access to knowledge that ought not to be shared. Access to certain rituals is forbidden not only to 'outsiders,' but, because the knowledge in many rituals is a part of the traditional structure of power, status, and authority, access is even limited within the indigenous community. Fiona Magowan (1994) discusses the kinds of solutions that some of the Yolngu of North East Australia have developed as a way for them to manage their entrance into the commercial music industry.

Aboriginal popular music groups attracted the interest of the Australian music industry in the 1970s. One of the more successful of these groups, Yothu-Yindi, became known internationally on the basis of their first album, *Tribal Voice*. Euro-Australian access to the ritual texts is limited by the use of a Yolngu dialect, but other performance techniques, as well as the images selected for the album cover, have been designed both to convey and engage this external audience's appreciation of Yolngu culture. This effort at outreach is especially strong when songs mix English and Yolngu language. The English text in these recorded performances tends to be explicitly political.

Magowan reports that this form of strategic communication is not entirely new, as previously restricted and sacred objects had been revealed in 1957 in an effort to achieve mediation between Christianity and Aboriginal religion (1994, p. 152). In her view, the participation by the Yolngu in an international market that has expanded so dramatically in the wake of interest in 'world music' has been guided by political as well as financial interests. Some of these groups have been especially successful, therefore, in using an indigenous *relational* aesthetic to serve both political and cultural ends.

The audience-as-public

Governments have played a central role in the nurturance, reproduction, and preservation of culture throughout their history. Before the emergence of formal states and cultural ministries, kings and traditional rulers supported the arts and cultural forms. Governments participate actively in the reproduction and transformation of ethnic identities through their involvement with mass media systems. Governments may operate, finance, and regulate media systems in ways that encourage assimilation, cultural preservation, or some variant of both (Husband, 1994; Riggins, 1992). Even government decisions about what will be the national language, and whether the use of other languages will be encouraged or discouraged, will influence the ways in which ethnic cultures survive in the face of globalization and other forces of change.

Governments have recognized the importance of the arts and entertainment for the development and maintenance of a national identity. Stokes (1994), for example, suggests that control of music has been especially important to the leaders of the newly emerging states who hoped to forge a national identity out of the pieces left from a colonial past. In many cases, music, and the broadcasting systems that controlled much of its distribution, was a vital arm of government cultural policy. Stokes suggests that 'musical styles can be made emblematic of national identities in complex and often contradictory ways' (p. 13). It is not that this music *produces* a national (and ethnic) identity, but it puts a sense of identity 'into play' in a way that few other symbolic forms can: it can be performed, danced to, listened to, and thought about. Depending upon the ways in which other social facts interact with this music, a very special identity can be formed (p. 24).

Governments have believed, as many still do, that music helps to 'produce orientations toward reality,' and, because of this potential, encouraging some and suppressing other forms seemed to make good political sense. Music is understood to have 'positional values' with which one could rank and rate, and compare musics to each other (Middleton, 1990, p. 253), and then determine which types were worthy of support:

(1) It can have *communicative value*, in terms of whether it does, or does not have something of interest to 'say.'
(2) It can have *ritual value*, as in its role in creating solidarity.
(3) It can have *technical value*, in terms of its accord with norms and standards.
(4) It can have *erotic value*, in terms of its ability to involve and energize the body, and, of course,
(5) It can have *political value*, in terms of explicit political content and orientation.

Reily (1994, pp. 92–4) describes the ways in which the *Estado Novo* in 1930s' Brazil sought to consolidate its power through strategic control over the nation's music. The state-owned National Radio established contracts with the most popular of Brazil's singers to ensure that they would sing the emerging nation's praises. Carmen Miranda and others 'became agents in the propaganda machine.' The carnival in Rio was made official in 1934, and the state provided funds for those samba schools that were 'willing to use their parades to glorify patriotic symbols and national heroes.' Dependence on government funds meant that most sources of 'high art' would be influenced by the cultural project emerging out of Brazil's new Department of Culture. Opposition to this form of cultural nationalism was extremely limited. It was not until the redemocratization of the nation in the 1970s that certain aspects of Brazil's cultural history were opened up. Central among these aspects is the celebration of Brazil's African musical heritage (Winant, 1994, pp. 144–5).

While the allocation of state resources for purposes related to ethnic communities may be expressed in terms of a desire to preserve valuable cultural resources, the underlying motivations and pressures that influence government decisions are far more complex than any public pronouncement would suggest. Reflection on the justifications given in support of local content requirements, or an earlier articulation of the *media imperialism* hypothesis (Schiller, 1969; 1976), will reveal some of the tensions that exist between actors within and between nations. Communication scholars have, unfortunately, not progressed very far in this direction (Nordenstreng, 1993).

Riggins (1992, pp. 8–11) identifies five different models that characterize the dominant approaches to the management and control of ethnic media that have been pursued by different countries at different points in their history. The interests of the ethnic communities are clearly subordinate in each:

(1) By choosing an *integrationist* model, states would be able to monitor, and thereby constrain, any minority movement toward separation or independence.
(2) The *economic* model is both multiculturalist and integrationist but it focuses on targeted communication because of its promise of educating an ethnic workforce more efficiently.
(3) A *divisive* model provides a strategic distraction by pitting rival ethnic groups against each other in a classic divide and conquer move.
(4) A *preemptive* model is seen in cases where the state establishes its own minority media so that the oppositional potential of privately operated ethnic media will be limited by the economic realities of production.
(5) The *proselytism* model applies most readily to ethnic media funded by churches, with the consent of the state.

In Australia, the government has established a Special Broadcast Service (SBS) as an ethnic broadcasting network akin to the BBC, but programmed with local and imported programs for ethnic communities (Molnar, 1990). Ironically, during its early years, it defined Aborigines as the indigenous race, and therefore not a target for 'ethnic' programming investments. Molnar suggests that Aborigines are either invisible or presented in limiting stereotypical ways on the primary network, the Australian Broadcasting Corporation (ABC).

A unique alternative form of Aboriginal broadcasting has emerged through the successful efforts of the Central Australian Aboriginal Media Association (CAAMA). After a period in which it produced programming for a community radio station, CAAMA acquired its own public radio station from which it broadcasts in Aboriginal languages. CAAMA acquired a commercial television license in 1987. The fact that few Aborigines have had the kind of technical training needed to operate a television facility has meant that they are a minority within their own broadcast organization. A novel program, the Broadcasting to Remote Area Communities Scheme (BRACS) has been designed to enable Aborigines in remote areas to use radio and television as a way to promote and preserve aspects of traditional culture. However, its low level of government funding, in an era when governments around the globe are reducing their support for social programs aimed at minorities, would suggest that the long-term impact of this program will be minimal (Maharey, 1990).

The existence of ethnic media does not guarantee the availability of a reliable stream of alternative and oppositional information and cultural forms. It is difficult, if not impossible, for those who produce and distribute ethnic media to operate independently of the media system which surrounds them. Their day-to-day existence is organized from within the majority culture. No cultural barrier could keep its influences from seeping in and becoming integrated with the structures of a subcultural understanding of the world. The ways in which ethnic media depend upon resources, including content and expertise, often in the form of employees or consultants, guarantee that external influences will be felt.

Outside the United States, public service broadcasting has been the primary means through which the modern state has been most directly involved in the shaping of mass culture. However, state involvement in cultural production may also include direct assistance through the provision of a funding subsidy for the production of motion pictures, support for the arts and humanities through grants and special education, and institutionalizing access through museums and national companies. Governments also provide indirect support by establishing and enforcing regulatory limits on foreign competition. All these forms of government support have come under increasing attack all around the globe in recent years.

The United States has been unique historically in its preference for a commercial rather than a government-run system. Public service broadcasting was marginalized in the United States in the 1930s when a proposal to reserve 25 per cent of the spectrum for education and other non-profit broadcasting services was defeated. A small educational service that struggled to survive in the space created by an underfunded and highly politicized 'public broadcasting service' never grew to have a fraction of the influence of public broadcasting services in other nations (Herman, 1995).

In the UK, the public service monopoly was broken by the introduction in 1955 of direct competition from commercial broadcasting in the form of Independent Television (ITV). In 1964, competition from within the government system was initiated with the launch of BBC2. The year 1981 saw the introduction of Channel 4, initially funded by a required subvention of the commercial system. With the introduction of Channel 5, and the move toward direct commercial financing for Channel 4, broadcasting in the UK has become a model for the future commercialization of public service media.

The original public broadcasting services in the UK and in other European states were bound to be challenged by the commercial competitors that they helped to nurture and develop. It is in the nature of the commercial system to expand through capturing and integrating other systems into its logic and structure. Garnham sees the global challenge to public service broadcasting as a specific example of the general process of the 'industrialization of culture' (1990, p. 120). But the original rationale for the development of a state monopoly seems also to have been assured of instability on other grounds. The original rationale for the kind of public service broadcasting exemplified by the BBC was 'one in which an enlightened political and cultural elite imposed its tastes and views of the world by means of the "brute force of monopoly" upon a public whose views and tastes were not to be trusted' (Garnham, 1990, p. 129). This rationale could not expand to accommodate the changes in the nature of the civil society that accompanied the expansion of its active membership.

The introduction of competition into the British broadcasting system also introduced a critical rupture in the ability of the state to define popular culture and, through this control, to successfully define aspects of 'Britishness' that also included ideas about citizenship (Ang, 1991, p. 115). The BBC had abandoned the theory of public service that had been established by its first managing director, John Reith. Where the state, through the earlier model of the BBC, would take the public by the hand, as it were, and 'lead it in a previously determined direction,' the new BBC would be an 'honest broker.' Where a former goal was one of a universal sense of national identity and common interests, reflecting an identifiable moral order, the hallmark of the modern BBC became that of *diversity*: 'diversity of interests represented and of tastes catered for, even if it concerns minority interests and tastes' (Ang, 1991, p. 116). James Snead (1994, p. 121) suggests that 'the existence of "establishment" channels for funding and exhibition, such as the BFI and Channel 4, as well as the output of various filmmaking collectives' created an environment that was more supportive of British Black film-makers than that which was found in the United States.

The introduction of Channel 4, with its special commitment to 'minority audiences' and the community of independent producers who were expected to serve those interests, provided a very special opening for productions by racial and ethnic minorities in the UK (Curran, 1992). Funding for public broadcasting in the United States also increased the participation of independent minority producers, but a substantial part of this funding was derived from private foundations, rather than solely from government tax revenue.

The BBC has also made overtures to the rest of the European Community as part of a program developed by its Equal Opportunities Department. 'Public Broadcasting for a Multi-Cultural Europe' sought to define a role for public broadcasting in a multicultural project by increasing the participation of Black and other ethnic minorities in broadcasting, as well as to outline guidelines and standards of good practice. Specifically, the goal was 'to strive toward high quality multicultural mainstream programming which promotes harmonious relations between different ethnic, religious, cultural and linguistic groups; to develop joint strategies for using educational and social action broadcasting as a means of countering racism and xenophobia within Europe' (Benjamin, 1995, pp. 109–10). As with most such initiatives, minority group members remain sceptical about the level of commitment that administrations and media professionals actually share with regard to these lofty goals.

Ross Eaman (1994) suggests that public broadcasting was justified in the Canadian case because of concerns about the threats to Canadian culture represented by the powerful commercial industry in the United States. Cultural nationalists in Canada argued that to 'the extent that Canadians consume foreign cultural products, they are in effect re-creating other cultures' (p. 13). While this might not be bad in itself, Eaman suggests that it may also mean that Canada would not be actively re-creating its own national culture.

Not even Canada's private industry was thought to be powerful enough to survive on its own against the force of the much larger American market. But more importantly, according to Eaman, there are social needs that are unlikely to be met by any commercial system, no matter how well financed. The only question was whether it made sense to leave it up to a

cultural elite: to decide what those needs were, and how they ought best be met. Canada's eventual move toward greater reliance on an audience measurement system developed by A. C. Nielsen, for the purposes of guiding a market-driven, audience maximization system, would suggest that Canada's public broadcasting service will become a weaker, rather than a stronger defender of its national and minority ethnic cultures. (Eaman, 1994, pp. 198–226)

The same tensions that marked the transformation of public service broadcasting in Canada and the UK were reproduced throughout Europe, and ultimately around the globe, as state-controlled communication systems gave ground in response to the demands and pressures of the commercial market (Herman, 1995; Smith, 1991; Straubhaar, 1995). Smith (1991, pp. 46–50) describes a number of approaches that have been followed as states bowed to what seemed an unavoidable outcome: the elimination of state monopoly and the replacement of a public service rationale by a commercial logic. Each of these strategies modifies the structure of the media system, and therefore has a slightly different potential for shaping the character and quality of media content each system will make available to its audience.

(1) *Denationalization* refers to the process through which the government no longer owns or even indirectly controls media.
(2) *Liberalization* refers to the process through which the state monopoly receives direct competition from commercial entrants.
(3) *Commercialization* refers to the process where a state subsidy, perhaps financed by license fees, or from general funds, is supplemented, or eventually financed entirely from the sale of commercial time.
(4) *Re-regulation* is a term to describe a shift in the purpose of government regulation from that of public service to the facilitation of corporate competition.

Each strategy increases the influence of the marketplace. Some increase the influence of transnational corporations and global market considerations more rapidly than others, but all move in the same direction. To the extent that liberalization increases the openness of national markets to foreign sources, including those introduced by means of high-capacity delivery systems, such as satellite, cable, and VCRs, the challenges to the survival of unique cultural identities linked to geopolitical boundaries will only multiply (Raboy, 1990, pp. 335–9).

Audience-as-market

We distinguish between audience-as-market and audience-as-commodity primarily to accommodate the distinctions between media which are produced for consumption by audiences and are financed by direct payments from members of audiences and those media which are financed by advertisers or other third parties. The reason for this distinction is based on the belief that the one who pays the piper calls the tune. While it remains to be determined empirically, it seems reasonable to assume that direct payment by consumers produces a media supply that is more reflective of, and responsive to, popular taste and sentiment. As the composition of the audience for any media channel changes, we can expect the content which best characterizes that channel to change as well. As changes in population demographics reflecting migration and economic well-being increase the collective power of minority audiences, we should expect an increase in the production of material specifically targeted to that audience. This seems to describe recent shifts in the motion picture industry. Less dramatic shifts in the character of television content may reflect the fact that it is the audience, rather than the content, which defines the primary commodity produced within that particular industry.

Understanding the demand for media

Understanding the audience-as-market requires understanding what different kinds of audiences seek from media, including what they are willing to pay for this content or experience. Understanding the audience is important because producer conceptions of the audience is a primary determinant of what content is produced and how it is promoted. The response of consumers to available media is not governed entirely by the nature of what is supplied by the media industry. We will see that the nature of consumer demand also changes in response to important shifts in culture, in response to critical events, and in response to shifts in the economy, including changes in the nature of media technology.

Bruce Austin (1989) suggests that three broad motivations help to shape our interests in and preferences for different leisure activities. First, media consumption may fill a *social need*. This is a need to interact with others. Sharing media is like sharing meals in that it can help to establish and maintain social relationships. Talking about the media experiences that people share in common, even though experienced at different times and in different places, serves to strengthen the social bonds between people. Talking about movies, television shows, books, and records provides a way to assess the extent to which you and an acquaintance share interests.

Commonly experienced media can facilitate communication within and across social boundaries. The mass media provide raw materials, phrases, images, jokes, vignettes, etc., any of which can serve as a metaphorical resource that can be used to make a point with some confidence that its meaning will be clear. Gamson (1992) provides some examples of the ways in which people use mass media as a conversational resource. The fact that people introduce references from news, recent films, advertising slogans, or even phrases from popular songs into conversations in support of points they are trying to make underscores the value of the contribution that commonly experienced media make to social relations.

Second, there is a host of *psychological* needs that media are believed to serve. Media help individuals to manage their different emotional states. To the extent that media can 'take you away from it all,' they represent a means of escape from the pressures of daily life. The audiovisual media are especially useful as an engaging distraction because of their ability to transport consumers to a different time and place. People not only have a need to relax, but they also have a need for *stimulation*. Stimulation can be provided by a variety of different genres or types of content: action adventure, horror, suspense, and erotic themes can all be arousing. The amount of stimulation that media provide may explain why audiovisual media like movies or television are considered by some to be addictive (Smith, 1986).

Third, mass media also help to meet *intellectual* requirements. Historical dramas are appreciated not only because they are entertaining stories, but because they serve an educational function. This *educational* function is served by media that provide a 'window' into circumstances, cultures, and relationships outside one's personal experience. Of course, the satisfaction of a person's intellectual curiosity may also be serving a psychological need.

Consumer demand also has a structure. While economists tend to talk about aggregate demand, producers respond to *segments* of the market and, as we will see, an orientation to audience segments has become even more important in an era in which producers have enhanced knowledge of consumers' tastes, preferences, and resources.

Often producers and financial backers assume that Whites will not want to see films that are about Blacks or other racial or ethnic minorities. Jesse Rhines (1996) suggests that 'Black films must be presented to white distributors in particular ways that are consistent with white audience stereotyping of Blacks in order to predict crossover success' (p. 70). Rhines gives the example of Eddie Murphy films in which success with White audiences appears to be likely only when Murphy's film has a great majority of White characters. Films with a predominance of Black or minority characters are believed to have to conform to stereotypes of Blacks as violent, and this is felt to explain the economic success of films like *Boyz in the Hood* and *Menace II Society* that have Black actors and Black cultural settings. Otherwise, a very fine line has to be drawn in order to include enough material of interest to Black audiences, in that Blacks are such regular movie goers that they account for 25 per cent of theatrical revenues.

The same assumption that Whites will respond more readily to familiar stereotypes is offered as an explanation for photo editors in newspapers using images of African Americans to illustrate stories about poverty. Gilens (1996, p. 535) suggests that 'photo editors may be aware that popular perceptions of the poor as largely black are misguided, but may choose to "indulge" these misperceptions in order to present to readers a more readily recognizable image of poverty.'

We should recognize that rationalist models of consumer behavior assume that consumers make informed choices. These choices include mass media products. The preferences that consumers reveal over time may reflect the ways in which they believe media might be useful in helping to produce one or more of the underlying values that all rational consumers are said to pursue (Becker, 1979). It should be clear, however, that mass media, and information goods in general, are different from other goods in terms of the amount of information that is available to consumers to guide their choices.

We recognize that the relation between use value and market or exchange value (price) is not fixed or given. Advertising plays a special role in shaping consumers' expectations regarding media products (Jhally, 1990). Advertising and marketing play a central role in shaping consumers' expectations regarding the pleasure, or other kinds of utility, that they can expect to derive from the acquisition and consumption of media. The character of that advertising may include a racialized construction of the audience that will, as a result, influence the racial composition of the eventual market. Reviewers, who presumably have no stake or interest in how many people attend a movie or watch a television series, may conceivably serve as agents or representatives of the public. What they have to say about a book, film, record, or play can affect the value that an audience, or segments of an audience, will place on that media product.

As we will discuss in Chapter 5, the consumption of *symbolic material* may also have positive or negative consequences for individuals. We will want to consider what is the nature of the *informational environment* in which consumers can expect to find the information they need in order to inform themselves about the benefits and the risks of consuming popular media goods. Debates about whether Whites are competent to review Black films or African American literature are not only about whether the authors will receive a fair assessment of the quality of their work. This concern is also about whether or not the self-interest of Black consumers is likely to be served if they rely upon reviewers who may not have their particular interests in mind when recommending media products. It seems quite unlikely that White reviewers will have considered the consequences for self-esteem that might result from minority children viewing *Pocahontas*, or some other extremely popular film that involves racial constructions.

Racial and ethnic differences in media preferences

In several studies of differences between racial and ethnic groups in terms of decisions to consume media, Neuman (1991) and Frank and Greenberg

(1980) found that the differences between groups were actually quite small. It was clear that Hispanics had an interest in Spanish-language programming, and it was also clear that Blacks had a preference for programs that featured Black actors and explored aspects of African American culture. But it was not at all clear that there were any significant differences in media preferences at the level of more basic program attributes, genres, formats, or even motivations for using media. However, in a subsequent analysis of this data performed for the Corporation for Public Broadcasting (CPB), somewhat different conclusions about the nature of Black and Hispanic viewing were drawn (National Analysts, 1981).

The Black and Hispanic respondents were examined as independent audience segments. They were described in terms of their distribution across 14 *interest segments*. These segments had been defined empirically through the use of correlation-based statistical techniques that revealed the underlying structure in these viewers' orientation toward 139 different interest items. Both Blacks and Hispanics viewed more television than the average viewer. Because their reasons for viewing were not different from the mainstream, the report concluded that their high levels of viewing 'may result from financial or other situational constraints which may restrict access to alternative leisure activities' (National Analysts, 1981, p. 12). There was no explanation for the greater than average preference that African Americans showed for situation comedy and musical programs. Even with the removal of those programs that were identified as 'black oriented' there was *still* a greater preference for these genres among Blacks.

The study by the Corporation for Public Broadcasting (National Analysts, 1981) suggested that it was the influence of racial and ethnic identification in combination with familiarity with the cultural contexts that explained the revealed preference of African Americans for programs with Black characters. The choice of television programs (and other media products as well) may be a reflection of racial or ethnic identity. As complex and involved as ethnic identity has been revealed to be, for this fact to be useful as guidance to media producers, additional information about audience expectations is required.

If content providers were interested in producing an African American audience, it seems that a sure-fire solution would be to include Black actors and situations that had a readily identified link to African American culture. The uneven, but continually expanding, number of such programs available in media today would seem to suggest that programmers and advertisers made exactly that decision. The dramatic increase in the presence of African American males in leading roles in Hollywood films reflects the importance of the African American audience to the industry. Because Blacks tend to go to the movies more often than other segments of the population, their share of the box office is almost twice their presence in the population. In addition, according to one analysis, the concentration of African Americans in those urban markets where films can open with an impressive set of early returns increases the importance of Blacks to those who invest in films. The fact that the leading roles that African American males are capturing are primarily in the extremely popular action-adventure genre also demonstrates the extent to which Black actors are also acceptable to the young White movie goers who are also heavier than average contributors to the Hollywood bottom line (Austin, 1989; Kinnon, 1997).

Racial identity and media use

Understanding the influence of racial and ethnic identity on the choice of media is an important but extremely challenging problem. Because identities are not fixed we are likely to be in error if we rely upon simple or surface attributes to assume what a individual's identity is, or to understand how that identity will be used in a particular choice situation.

The identities which are defined by race, gender, and class, or social position, are likely to be a powerful influence on our media choices. However, our 'present' identities, defined externally on the basis of objective features, may not actually be the identities that guide our media use. Who we are may not be who we intend to be. Thus, it is important to recognize the influence of *anticipatory socialization* as a factor that explains the tastes and preferences of media audiences. This is especially relevant with regard to young people who are in the process of developing both preferences and expectations. Keith Roe reports several studies of youth in Sweden which indicated that 'although the relationships between social background and most music preferences were very weak, some music tastes were related to anticipated future status' (1994, p. 190). Consistent with claims made by Pierre Bourdieu and others who link schooling with the formation of class trajectories (Bourdieu and Passeron, 1990), Roe also notes that youth who preferred socially disfavored music actually 'anticipated getting lower status jobs after leaving school' (p. 190). More extensive analysis led to the conclusion that 'over time, music preferences are seen to be related to differential educational achievement and to anticipations of future status' (p. 195).

It has been suggested that one of the motivations for media use could be the maintenance of one's ethnic identity, and the links to one's racial or ethnic heritage (Ríos and Gaines, 1997). One study that explored the media usage patterns over time of individuals from 13 different ethnic groups in the United States found that ethnic identification and the desire to maintain or strengthen that identification was a significant predictor of ethnic media use (Jeffres, 1983). But we should be cautious in our acceptance of the conclusions we draw from these studies because of the different ways in which they have measured or assessed ethnic or racial identity.

For example, one study of the influence of cultural identity on media use among Hispanics presented respondents with nine options for self-identification. Among those clearly associated with Latino ethnicity, they included Chicano, Mexican, Spanish American and Mexican American (Korzenny *et al.*, 1983). One of the major conclusions reached in this study was that Hispanics were not homogeneous in their media orientations and behaviors.

There are also differences in the ways in which the goal of maintaining one's ethnic identity is defined in these studies. The desire to maintain one's connection with one's 'mother country' is of particular interest for recent immigrants, but it is relatively meaningless for African Americans who may know little about which country or region of the African continent is their ancestral home. For many Blacks, an interest in knowing about the experiences of others like themselves in the African diaspora is reflected in an interest in news and entertainment involving people of African heritage around the world.

In his comments on the Jamaican Rasta in England, Dick Hebdige (1979) develops a caricature of a lost soul who is exiled from Africa, Jamaica, Britain and Brixton, and ultimately the 'real world', and must 'occupy an exalted position in some imaginative inner dimension where action dissolves into being' (p. 427). From Hebdige's perspective, the character of the music as an expression of Rasta culture was a highly cultivated form of withdrawal that met rejection with rejection (p. 438). How can we understand the identity that governs the use of this music by these folks?

At the time of its introduction, *Ebony* magazine was targeted to an upwardly mobile, primarily Northern Black audience. Integration was the cornerstone of *Ebony's* editorial policy, and the success of light-skinned Blacks was a prominent feature. Perhaps if one considered an interracial marriage the penultimate form of integration, surpassed only by 'passing' as White as the ultimate form, then *Ebony's* dependence on advertisers that proffered skin-lightening creams and stories that featured interracial marriage makes perfect sense. News stand sales certainly appeared to demonstrate a preference for such stories. Among the most popular issues that *Ebony* published during its early years was one focusing on romances between Black GIs and German fräuleins. The other was a feature on 'Five million US White Negroes' (Burns, 1996, pp. 114–15). What kind of racial identity shall we assume these readers were motivated toward preserving?

Audience-as-commodity

Framing the audience as a commodity is an unusual, if not a radical, view that has emerged from the study of media financed through advertising. From this perspective, audiences are akin to industrial products, and the attributes of programs, generally thought of as production values, including special effects, popular stars, exotic locations, and scripts from well-known authors, are the inputs or resources that are used to produce audiences of different quality. Statistical techniques such as linear regression can be used to estimate the contribution to audience size of particular program attributes (Gandy, 1981a; Gandy and Signorielli, 1981). Adjustments in programming reflect an assessment of how well particular attributes of programs appear to attract the interest of particular audience segments.

For much of its history as a business, the dominant view within the television industry in the United States was that the primary audience was White, and that it would be difficult to find 'properties about blacks that can also be appreciated by whites' (Gitlin, 1985, p. 181). The number of programs with Black characters was generally small, and the small number of programs that featured dramatic actors and themes of racial conflict appeared irregularly. The impact of successes like *Roots* was extremely short-lived. The periodic success of Blacks in situation comedies allowed the networks to be inclusive while deriving the benefits of using Blacks as 'comic relief.'

Success in producing and marketing audiences as commodities requires a reliable means of assessing the quantity and quality of the commodity. Within the past 20 years one group of auxiliaries within the media system, the audience measurement industry, has increased the importance of audience demographics for both producers and advertisers. Hugh Beville (1985) describes the origins of the broadcast ratings services in the United States. The first surveys conducted for advertisers by Archibald Crossley in 1929 established general principles which have changed only in the extent to which they have increased the precision with which they specify demographic groups. Methodological problems involved in measuring poor and minority audiences became increasingly troublesome as the fortunes of media organizations that targeted those audiences suffered from undercounting or biased estimates (pp. 226–8).

The commercialization of broadcasting and the influence of advertisers evolved much more slowly in other nations. In Britain, a consortium of manufacturers which had been organized in 1922 to exploit the commercial potential of radio was replaced by the British Broadcasting Corporation (BBC) in 1926 with a public service mission. In Canada, the Canadian Radio Broadcasting Commission (later to become the Canadian Broadcasting Corporation, or CBC) was created in 1932 with the responsibility to develop a broadcast monopoly that would operate in the national interest, with public service rather than profit as its goal (Raboy, 1990). The Canadian experience with broadcasting was unique in that it encouraged the development of a French-language service which not only contributed to a sense of difference within the emerging national identity, but it left the English-language service especially vulnerable to the influence of the more solidly financed commercial media broadcasting from Canada's neighbors to the south.

Print media like newspapers are generally financed by advertising as well as by circulation revenue. Although the relationship is not perfect, we can assume that the greater the proportion of revenue derived from circulation, rather than from advertising, the more the editorial decisions can be seen as responding to evidence of audience interest (Baker, 1994a).

The influence of advertisers or commercial sponsors on the nature of media content is not as straightforward as one might imagine. Advertisers are not only concerned with gaining access to the audience so that they might deliver their persuasive appeal; they are also concerned that their appeal be placed within a symbolic environment that increases the likelihood that their message will be favorably received. Thus, they are concerned that the surrounding material should not insult, threaten, or even change the mood of the audience in a way that would weaken the impact of their advertisement.

Ideally, advertisers in print media would prefer to have their ads appear adjacent to stories or features which emphasize the benefits that can be expected from consuming a product like theirs. The worst possible placement would be adjacent to a story that described the health risks associated with using the product. Communication scholars have examined the correlation between the amount of advertising revenue received from alcohol and tobacco accounts and the amount of editorial content exploring the health risk associated with the use of these drugs, and the evidence suggests that the influence of advertisers is strong (Smith, 1978; Tankard and Pierce, 1982). As we will examine further in the context of minority and ethnic media, commercial media with small and unsteady budgets will be even more susceptible to the influence of these advertisers.

Segmentation and targeting

The production of audiences for sale to advertisers is the dominant practice within the commercial media industry, even though the primary discourse relies on metaphors akin to war. The segmentation and targeting of consumers along racial and ethnic lines has become more of an active strategy since the early 1980s. Although presented in what we might characterize these days as the laughably overdrawn claims of Frankfurt School critics, Adorno and Horkheimar (1979) presented an early view of segmentation and targeting that still seems to express the hopes of marketers working today:

> The public is catered for with a hierarchical range of mass-produced products of varying quality, thus advancing the rule of complete quantification. Everybody must behave (as if spontaneously) in accordance with his previously determined and indexed level, and

choose the category of mass product turned out for his type.
(p. 351)

While sensitivity to the charge of discrimination may have tended to temper the discourse of race within the marketing community, few doubt that race and ethnicity has been utilized in the development of commercial appeals. The social facts produced and reproduced by aversive racism – the racially homogeneous neighborhoods that are so characteristic of the United States – helped to elevate the usefulness of a technique called *geodemographics*.

Without using race as a variable in the clustering models, Jonathan Robbin's PRIZM (Potential Rating Index for Zip Markets) system sorted the 36,000 zip-coded communities into 40 different 'lifestyle' clusters that still had a very high degree of racial and ethnic uniformity (Weiss, 1988). Weiss notes that 'segregation in housing has hung on more tenaciously than any other aspect of racially divided American life' (p. 34). African Americans were concentrated in just a fraction of the PRIZM clusters, and none of them, including the group labeled 'Black Enterprise', was among the top fourth of the socioeconomic ladder (p. 48).

The decision to pursue ethnic targets has, over time, increased the value of defining those markets with greater precision. While we are far from approaching the infinite regress implied in Ang's criticism of audience research (1991), distinctions within ethnic market segments based on class and culture are being identified and pursued. These distinctions will be especially important within the Asian and Latin markets where country of origin is associated with substantial differences in culture that are linked to tastes and preferences for media and consumer goods.

In order to succeed in targeting a market, marketers believe they have to learn as much as possible about them. This involves using the computer to develop lists, and then to manipulate

> vast files of information about individuals or households: their past purchase records, their membership in organizations, their subscription to particular kinds of publications, and their demographic characteristics, or at least their residence in neighborhoods that could be described by distinctive attributes. (Bogart, 1991, p. 204)

While most of the talk about segmentation and targeting emphasizes getting to know the desired audience, it should not be forgotten that targeting one audience segment means excluding or ignoring another. Newspaper publishers question the value of expanding circulation if the new readers are not seen as desirable: 'many advertisers, retail and national, were doubtful about the value of low-income readers who accounted for only a minor part of total consumption for their products or services' (Bogart, 1991, p. 157). Bogart also notes that publishers were being advised by securities analysts to adopt the magazine model and target the upper half of the market, ignoring the less desirable customers. In one sense, the newspapers found themselves 'between a rock and a hard place' because they feared that media activists and critics would soon charge publishers with 'discrimination and insensitivity to minority needs' (p. 158).

Critical reflection on the impact of the increased support of ethnic media provided by mainstream advertisers raises the possibility that the social control of difference that might have been achieved through integration and assimilation might be achieved even more effectively through segmentation, a form of economic segregation. We assume that advertising and other forms of persuasive communication are more effective when they have been designed with a particular audience in mind. Targeted advertisements are designed to reach racially and ethnically identified audiences, and they are more likely to do so when they reach individuals who have already invested in ethnically specialized media (Turow, 1997). Targeted communications should, therefore, have a greater potential influence. To the extent that these messages explicitly or indirectly replicate dominant cultural themes, but present them in subcultural forms, they are likely to be even more effective than messages designed for mass consumption. This is the logic that supports the placement of special 'public service announcements' and health warnings that are targeted to minority audiences in the commercial breaks adjacent to the programs that these audiences tend to view. The evidence that segmentation and targeting of ethnic media are also being used in explicitly political ways is quite substantial (Gandy, 1996b; Subervi-Velez, 1992).

It does not matter whether commercial products or political candidates are the theme of targeted messages. For them to work well, they must resonate with aspects of an individual's identity. Ethnic identity is likely to be salient within the context of ethnic media; thus the design of these appeals tend, at the very least, to emphasize positive links between mainstream and ethnic cultural beliefs, while ignoring or downplaying the points of departure.

The 'preferred audience'

The audience production approach (Gandy, 1995) suggests that the audiences produced by different media techniques are not only of different 'quality,' but that the demand for those qualities varies dramatically within the marketplace. One might think that within a capitalist market, at the end of the day, the only thing that matters is whether a consumer has the money to acquire the commodity being offered. Race should not matter. Indeed, it might be argued that race itself does not matter, it is only that race is being used as a *proxy*, an indicator of the likelihood that a particular individual will become a customer. Further, it might be argued that a form of *racial triage* has been brought into play, where some groups are already loyal consumers, and really do not need to be attracted by specialized ads, and another group is most unlikely to consume, and therefore should also be ignored. The triage would recommend focusing on a particular target group. The use of a triage in this way, however, risks the possibility that those who already consume will note that they are being ignored and seek to punish the manufacturer by withholding their support in the future.

Herman Gray suggests that the opening up of the television industry to a greater variety of representations of Black life was not guided by any sudden interest in Black culture. Instead, it was a recognition within the industry that 'to the extent that black-oriented programs were cost-efficient and advertisers could be attracted, such programs were well worth the risk' (1995, p. 68). The remarkable economic and popular success of *The Cosby Show*, along with the increased popularity of other Black media personalities, including sports superstars like Michael Jordan, 'helped to focus, organize, and translate blackness into commodifiable representations and desires that could be packaged and marketed across the landscape of American popular culture' (p. 68).

There are also status-linked complications. It may be that those who are not consumers, but might be enticed to try the product on the basis of an appeal which includes references to the gains in status or self-esteem that come from use of the product, might doubt the claims in the advertisement if they see persons they think of as low status also consuming the product.

Because these marketing strategies are considered proprietary, in addition to being potentially explosive if their widespread use was revealed to the public, one rarely finds explicit discussion of these contradictory influences on the marketing decision. However, in the absence of such strategies, one would expect that the composition of people in advertisements would reflect the composition of the intended audience. This is the assumption which governed a study of the relationship between magazine ads and the racial profiles of their readership (Snyder *et al.*, 1995). African Americans were substantially underrepresented in advertisements in particular magazines, in that Blacks appeared in 5.2 per cent of the ads, but actually represented 14.8 per cent of the total readership. However, if these same data are examined from the perspective of who the preferred readers of the ads might be, it is easier to understand why Whites were more likely to be in major roles in the ads in the general interest magazines, while Blacks were more likely to be portrayed in major roles in the ads in the magazines targeted to Blacks.

One cannot, however, rely fully on the characteristics of advertisements as an indication of advertiser 'interest' in a consumer segment. Dwight Brooks (1995) identifies the World War II era as the point at which the marketing community in the United States began to develop an orientation toward an African American market as a distinct advertising target. His analysis of the trade literature leads him to date the commercial interest in an African American market far earlier than might be assumed if one focused primarily on the appearance of Blacks in mainstream advertisements.

Brooks suggests that the marketing community made use of Black consultants as a solution to the contradictory tensions between an underlying economic interest in expanding into new markets and the set of assumptions, based in a history of racism, about the ways in which a Black consumer *should* be approached. It was ironic and paradoxical that Blacks were being identified as a group to be approached on the basis of racial characteristics, but at the same time advertisers were being warned against using traditional stereotypes of Blacks because they would be viewed as offensive. It seems that advertisers initially chose silence because, without the expertise that Black advertising firms would later provide, they did not know how to proceed.

Then, as now, the industry turned to research in order to learn about the nature of the Black consumer and then, later, how best to present a product. Early discussions in the trade press noted the potential that the Black press represented, even though it was not generally thought of as an advertising vehicle for mainstream commodities. The industry was helped in understanding both the nature of the market and the potential of the Black press by a study which the publishers of *Ebony* magazine commissioned (Brooks, 1995, p. 41; Burns, 1996).

In his benchmark study of the African American market, Gibson (1969) identified four reasons why an unrecognized and undervalued consumer market defined by race existed in the United States. Among them was his claim that the people who comprised this market suffered 'forced identification' in addition to having definable purchase patterns. The forced identification was due in part to the 'highly visible and different outward appearance' that identified Gibson as 'a member of a minority group having an imposed subordinate status in American society.' Improving this status was, therefore, at the center of this consumer's concerns (pp. 8–9). The fact that African Americans tended to be concentrated in urban centers where they often made up 25 per cent of the population also spoke to their reality as a *market*.

Brooks notes that some of the evidence from early research which compared this Black consumer market with the mainstream, undifferentiated White market evaluated some of the differences in ideological terms. Black consumers were believed to prefer expensive, higher quality items than their incomes would seem to indicate (if White expenditures were taken as the standard). The conclusion was that Blacks were attempting to overcome a 'legacy of inferior social status' through consumption at levels above their means (Burns, 1996, p. 42).

The 1990s have been marked by the emergence of a substantial Black middle class. With more than one million Black families reporting household incomes in excess of $50,000, as well as a taste for literature reflecting their educational attainment, it was only a matter of time before the industry would respond. Publishers have now identified this market as one of the fastest growing segments among folks who buy books (Brown, 1995). There have been several earlier periods in which African American authors achieved visibility and some financial success. The Harlem Renaissance was followed by a period in which angry Black writers used the shock of harsh criticism as an entry to a market that did not sustain its interest. The most recent period began in 1989 with the success of Terry McMillan, who rekindles some of the reader interest that Black women writers like Toni Morrison and Alice Walker had discovered in the 1980s. McMillan's *Waiting to exhale* made the *New York Times* bestseller list in 1992 and held that position for 38 weeks. This dramatic success all but assured its further success as a motion picture starring Whitney Houston.

Roberta Astroff (1988) identifies 1966 as the beginning of the period during which the advertising trade press appeared to have begun actively pursuing a Latino market. Despite the fact that there are more than 20 million people of Hispanic origin living in the United States, a fact that would make the US the fifth-largest Spanish-speaking country in the world, this linguistic market remains largely underdeveloped. While there are now networks which are competing to provide Spanish-language programming to this large market, the primary source of the program materials is from beyond the borders in Mexico or elsewhere in Latin America.

When the US advertising industry made its early attempts at organizing an approach to this market, it was confused about the nature of Latino ethnic identity. The industry appeared to be genuinely confused about how to characterize this population. Clearly, the Hispanic market was defined by more than language and national origin, but confusions about the place of race, culture, and class often led the industry to fall back upon traditional stereotypes. Considerations of economic efficiency led the industry to construct the Latino market as a single, homogeneous entity. It is not clear whether the smoothing over of the distinctions between Hispanics that race, class, and culture produce for the purposes of marketing efficiency actually results in a homogenization of Latino culture, but the influence of the industry on the symbolic environment cannot be ignored.

If the differences in media preferences between racial and ethnic groups are influenced primarily by stylistic differences, rather than thematic differences, then the interest of advertisers in reaching these audiences within an editorial context in which these features are more salient would be a primary consideration in the decision to produce and/or distribute targeted, rather than general, audience programming.

The segmentation of audiences into narrower and narrower slices, reflecting differences in tastes, preferences, or interests, might be thought of as having no limit. Certainly much of the marketing hype about the new media gives the impression that the digital age will be the age of highly targeted, perhaps even individualized, personal media (Baldwin *et al.*,

1996; Willis, 1994). Narrower and narrower segments would have content matched with more and more specialized commercial and other appeals. Neuman (1991) describes this process as one of fragmentation, but suggests that several important constraints will continue to operate in ways that will at least slow down this movement, if not make it impossible to achieve. Turow (1997) suggests that segmentation is improved, or made more precise, through the use of 'signals of distinctiveness' which suggest to the 'visitor' whether he or she belongs in this audience. With magazines, the covers are the primary signalling devices, and different techniques are used by different radio formats. However, 'in radio, as in the restaurant, people who don't know immediately whether the place is for them will find out after a few minutes inside' (p. 101).

Changes in media technology, especially the convergence in form that will be enabled by the move toward digitalization, will mean that the full range of media content will eventually be delivered to the home electronically (Baldwin *et al.*, 1996). Different content providers will have to compete more directly with each other for the attention and the loyalty of this audience. The elimination of meaningful differences in the character of the delivery systems only means that the extent of duplication that exists across media may decline. It does not mean that the actual variety will expand.

There is evidence, however, that audiences *have* responded to the increased options that changes in media supply have produced. As the number of television channels has expanded, and as this expanded market has enabled competitors to survive by dividing the audience for particular genres between them, members of the audience have realized a net gain in the amount of program material that they prefer. This has meant that more people are now being exposed to fewer different kinds of media products (Webster, 1989).

Early efforts at capturing the African American market involved the rebroadcast of off-network series in Monday through Friday strips. Rupert Murdoch's Fox network also introduced a new Black talent as a successful competitor into the late night talk show arena – *The Arsenio Hall Show*. Fox also introduced a controversial, but highly successful, variety program, *In Living Color*, as well as an even more controversial but less successful series about an integrated family, *True Colors* (Gray, 1995). By 1996, the existence of a substantial African American consumer market, in combination with the tendency for racial segregation to to keep Blacks clustered in the cores of the nation's larger cities, had led newly emerging networks of UHF stations to target this Black audience directly (Storm, 1996).

At one point in 1996, 17 currently produced television programs featured African Americans as central characters. Twelve of these shows were being produced for two new 'networks' that had been cobbled together in cities with large Black populations. In combination with Fox, the two newest networks were moving in to capture the market that the three larger networks appeared to have abandoned. Only two situation comedies on the older networks featured Blacks, while more than half of the comedies on the newer networks began the 1996 season with Black characters featured. These networks were not 'putting all their eggs into one basket,' however. The nod they made toward the African American audience segment was concentrated strategically into two *different* week-day evenings, scheduled so as not to be in direct competition with each other. Other nights of the week, action adventure programs, including fantasy and science fiction, was designed to capture other 'fringe' audiences seeking an alternative to the prime-time network offerings being targeted at upscale White youth.

Market structure and performance

Within mainstream economic theory, the performance of industrial markets is assumed to vary with their competitive structure. The traditional view was that the greater the level of competition the greater the performance of the market (Scherer, 1970). A few media scholars have adopted this particular structural approach to evaluate the performance of media indus-tries in their markets (Busterna, 1989; Gomery, 1989). While media scholars from a Marxist tradition have focused on the nature of media concentration, they have rarely sought to make use of the empirical estimates of either market structure or media performance that have been developed and used by mainstream economists.

We have to ask: why does concentration of ownership matter? Concen-tration of ownership implies concentration of control. The more media entities that individual capitalists or, more realistically, large media organ-izations control, the more likely they will be able to govern decision making about the content which those entities will produce and distribute. If, as the Marxian view suggests, the interests of these controllers is in any way ideological, that is concerned with the social rather than solely with economic matters, then greater control of the production system means greater ideological control.

There is inherent in this model, however, a fundamental assumption that ought to be noted. If all commercial media share a common status as capitalist organizations, then we should assume that at some level their owners share common interests in the reproduction of an ideology that is supportive of capitalist interests. This fundamental interest in the survival and prosperity of the underlying system should not change because one capitalist organization owns and controls more entities than another. Nor should it change because one owner or one organization extends its control to different forms of media in a process known as *conglomeration*.

Graham Murdock and Peter Golding specify the kinds of theoretical and empirical work that they believe would be necessary for us to pursue

critical inquiry into the nature and consequences that accompany changes
in the character and extent of media concentration (1979, p. 35). They
suggest that first we would have to specify what the leading or dominant
ideology actually is. This would involve specifying its assumptions as well
as its central propositions. Second, we would have to identify the existence,
and perhaps the priority or relative dominance, of this ideology within the
content of different media. The third and perhaps most difficult requirement they set before us is that we would have to specify the standards and
practices within the media industries that operate to ensure that this
particular ideology is favored.

I would add, at this point, that we would also have to articulate the
reasons why we would expect these standards and practices to change as
the structure of ownership changes. As we will see, in discussions to come,
if the primary distinction between media organizations is no longer defined
primarily in terms of class, then we should be able to specify a great many
reasons for changes in structure to be accompanied by changes in content.
That is, if the relevant structural charateristics are enlarged to include race,
ethnicity, or some other sociocultural basis upon which the identification of
common interests may be formed, then shifts in structure, *including*
changes in the concentration of ownership, may indeed produce substantial
changes in media content.

Unfortunately, consequences that flow from changes in the concentration
of ownership among capitalists is woefully undertheorized. If concentration
of ownership does have consequences for ideology, it may not be a direct
reflection of the ways in which capitalist owners differ on matters of ideology. Differences in content may reflect the differential *salience* of ideological concerns in the matrix of influences on day-to-day decisions. Two
content providers may share the same ideological goals, but may differ
substantially on the ways in which they believe those goals can and should
be reached. Differences in strategy may produce differences in content, even
though the underlying beliefs and motivations are the same. Differences in
the ideological content in media may also reflect the influence of decisions
they have made about how to reach a particular audience. Production
decisions may reflect the use of different assumptions about the tastes and
preferences of different kinds of audiences.

Most of the theoretical and empirical work in this area points to
consequences that flow from private or institutional, rather than social,
concerns. The content provided by capitalist firms is likely to vary as a
function of the extent to which its programming is believed to affect the
orientation of consumers or government to the company and any of its
products. This is a concern that is especially salient for media organizations
that have direct financial interests in other industrial sectors of the
economy. For example, media owners that are also involved in the production of chemicals, or military technology, or consumer products, can be
expected to develop editorial policies designed to protect their firms and,

secondarily, their industries from bad publicity (Baker, 1994a). The effect of concentration and conglomeration within media industries would most likely be a decline in what one analyst has described as 'editorial vigor' (Thrift, 1977). The investigational journalism produced by such conglomerates is thought to be less likely to focus on the misbehavior of corporations, except to identify and punish 'bad apples.'

Industrial organization

Within the mainstream of media economics, the usefulness of what is generally referred to as the *industrial organization model* is severely limited by the traditional specification of performance in narrow economic terms (Figure 3.2). The traditional approach (Scherer, 1970) suggests that the performance of industrial markets ought to be evaluated in terms of

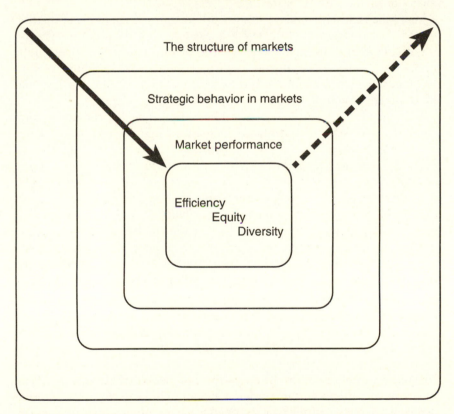

Figure 3.2 Media industry analysis

(1) productive and allocative efficiency, (2) progress, (3) full employment, and (4) equity. None of these criteria are traditionally interpreted as applying to concerns about diversity, representational accuracy, ideological cohesiveness, or even support for democratic principles, through increased public participation in governance. However, communications scholars have begun to suggest that almost any performance measures could be used to assess the influence of changes in market structure.

For example, Joseph Dominick examined the influence of several economic factors, including competitive structure, on the changing character of motion picture content (Dominick, 1987). Dominick developed a 13-category system with which to classify the films released each year by the Hollywood motion picture industry. By placing each film released by the major studios into one of these 13 categories, Dominick was able to develop three statistical measures that we might see as indicating media system performance. The difficulty for Dominick's analysis, and for other studies that have used this approach (Baker, 1994b), is that the film industry is already a tight *oligopoly* and its structure has not varied very much during the past 50 years.

John MacManus has taken a slightly different approach to the evaluation of media performance (1994). He has argued that it is the profit orientation of media organizations that makes it difficult for them to meet their public service obligations. He compares quality of commercial station news with the standards that a social responsibility orientation would produce, and the commercial stations are described as performing badly.

As the tendency toward concentration and cross-media conglomeration continues, and is being reproduced in markets that were formerly dominated by government monopoly, mainstream economists are beginning to reconsider whether the ideal of a fully competitive market even makes sense as a standard in communication markets. Many argue for the development of a new standard of 'workable competition,' or an even lower standard of 'contestability,' in which it is the mere *possibility* of competitive entry that would condition the behavior of firms in the market. Observers of the rapidly changing telecommunications market suggest that oligopoly will become the norm in these markets, in part because the high costs required for the development of these systems means that smaller firms are unable to participate (McNamara, 1991).

Economies of scale

Competitive structure is not the only aspect of media markets that has been the focus of attention for media scholars. Other features have been identified as critical determinants of the extent of diversity in content. Interactions between the size of firms, the size of their markets, and the kinds of investments that are made in technology help to determine the extent of content diversity we might observe.

Neuman (1991, p. 129) suggests that the underlying economics of mass communications do not actually promote diversity. The economies of scale in both production and distribution favor the reproduction of *sameness*, rather than variety. It is a special characteristic of information goods that makes the economies of scale more important in the communications market than in the markets for other industrial commodities. Economies of scale refer to the tendency of the costs for producing or distributing some products to decline as the number of units increases (Litman, 1988). These scale economies may be realized through greater efficiency at larger scales of organization that include financial advantages that accrue to organizations which purchase inputs in large quantities and are therefore granted discounts that smaller organizations do not enjoy. Some of the most important sources of scale economies in communications industries have to do with the cost structure of production, reproduction, and distribution of the industry's products (Picard, 1989, pp. 62–7). These economies are also affected by the use of computers and network information systems (Mulgan, 1991).

The costs of gathering the news, or producing a film, or even mounting a dramatic production, can be thought of as 'first copy costs.' Different media have different cost structures that reflect the costs of the materials that are used up in producing the first copy. There are also differences in the salaries paid to the people who write, produce, direct, print, and perform in the different media. The first copy costs may be thought of as 'fixed costs' because, on the average, they are quite similar from day to day for similar media products and, thus, costs can be allocated well in advance. The variable costs are those which reflect the number of 'copies' that have to be delivered to consumers. Here the differences between media become considerably more important. The unit costs of reproduction for print media decline more slowly because each copy uses the same amount of paper and ink and machine time. The unit costs of reproduction for broadcast media, however, drop very rapidly because, once the program is broadcast, the *consumer* actually pays for the reproduction of the information by their radio or television set. More importantly, there is no additional production cost incurred as the second, fifth, or even fifty-thousandth member of the audience tunes in. The variable costs for those media that distribute 'copies' of their program materials over wires are not zero, but costs of serving each additional user through electronic distribution systems are relatively insignificant. Clearly, the incentive within communication markets is to produce a commodity that the largest possible audience would like to consume, and then deliver it to them at the lowest possible cost. This economic reality generates the tendency toward sameness rather than diversity within network-based media systems.

Economists have identified the existence of massive economies of scale, as well as the influence of advertiser financing, as the primary explanation for the decline of direct competition among newspapers in American markets (Baker, 1994a; Litman, 1988). The absence of advertiser support has been identified as the most important reason historically for the failure of African American and other ethnic minority newspapers.

What we need to pursue, however, is a way to understand the special case of magazines. Here we have seen a dramatic expansion and considerable success among vehicles targeted to racial and ethnic markets. Although it was not always the case, magazines being published these days are more specialized than other mass media. As a result, they may act as if they are in a market all of their own. They are oligopolists, and may enjoy some of the advantages that monopolists enjoy. This *product differentiation* strategy so common to magazines reduces the threat of direct competition. Of course, this status is likely to be threatened when the size of the market reaches a point at which the economies of scale would support another entrant. Wolseley (1990) claims that there is at least one magazine available for every human special interest. He argues that Blacks need their own magazines whenever they 'have cultural differences from the nonblacks, cannot obtain white services, have been forced into their own groups, or have special problems of little interest to nonblacks and so not worth much space in the white journal' (p. 167). As Blacks and other members of minority groups have been perceived as being able to respond financially to these particular needs, specialized magazines have appeared.

Magazines depend upon circulation revenue to a greater extent than do newspapers. When the readers of a magazine value it highly, it is easier for publishers to pass the increased costs of production and distribution on to the customer. However, it should be clear that the economics of magazine publishing logically supports a greater focus on upscale, wealthier consumers who are less price sensitive than is possible for newspapers which, in general, have become more dependent on retail or mass market advertising as the costs of production and distribution have increased.

Peterson (1964) identified an aspect of magazine publishing that explains their somewhat greater vulnerability to those periodic shifts in an economy that tends to push minority and other publishers into bankruptcy. The attractiveness of advertising revenue sets into motion a very dangerous pattern. Publishers expand circulation in order to attract advertisers, but most of the advertising revenue has to be used to pay the additional production and distribution costs that circulation revenue does not cover. Presumably, the publisher has already trimmed these costs to an absolute minimum, so that if advertising revenue declines, either due to competition or to a downturn in the economy, the publication will fail. To the extent that subscriptions have been paid in advance, the possibilities for adjusting the prices of magazines are relatively limited. Thus, for magazines, increasing circulation without also increasing advertising means a loss rather than a gain in net revenue.

Not only is there a tendency toward concentration and away from direct competition in media industries, but there also tends to be an absence of stable or expanding diversity in styles, genres, or formats. This claim is, understandably, open to the criticism that the categories used in these comparisons are inventions, and therefore it is impossible to say whether diversity has really expanded, narrowed, or stayed the same (Neuman, 1991, p. 141). However, the logic underlying the claims that Neuman and others make suggests that much of what we perceive as variety in the media is the coming and going of 'fads' that have a very short history. Thus, despite the increase in the number of different types of material, over time, the market tends to provide a common, stable, and familiar core. While there may be a great many new 'fringe' products introduced into the market, their lives are usually short. If some in fact do stay in the market, they tend to remain on the fringe.

The influence of scale economies also limits the numbers of participants that can enter the market and remain competitive. The requirements for control of one's own production and/or distribution equipment represent a barrier to the competitive entry of minority group members into many media markets. In those industry sectors where there is substantial ethnic diversity, we are seeing the results of scale economies. The greater number of special interest magazines reflects the relatively limited scale of investment required to enter that market. During the years in which they were making their entry into the market, the *Negro Digest* and others like it could be pasted up on a kitchen table and still appear competitive (Burns, 1996). However, the costs of entry into broadcasting and the newer electronic media markets are much more prohibitive. Successful entry into these markets by persons of color nearly always requires cooperation and partnership with Whites.

The influence of scale economies is also a factor in determining the structure and character of global media markets. An analysis of the global market that challenges the assumptions of the cultural imperialism model (Read, 1976; Schiller, 1969) is one that underscores the competitive advantage that the scale of a linguistic market provides. This view, expressed well by Steve Wildman (Wildman, 1994; Wildman and Siwek, 1988), and extended by David Waterman (Waterman and Rogers, 1994), suggests that, because the quality of production bears a positive, if not a perfect, relationship to the amount of money or resources used up in its production, those markets which have more money available as a function of the size of the market are likely to produce the more attractive and commercially successful products. This competitive advantage is demonstrated clearly in the video market, and is suggested to operate in other media markets as well.

Indirect support of this model can be seen in the results of surveys made of musicians around the world as part of a study of popular music and cultural diversity (Robinson *et al.*, 1991). Musicians were asked to name musicians who had been influential in their own development, but who were not directly known by them. They report that in 'every location but the United States, more of the musicians named foreign musicians; even 20 per cent of our US musicians cited British musicians as particularly influential' (Robinson *et al.*, 1991, p. 234). At first glance, this would suggest that we have an international music culture, and musicians are likely to have been influenced by outsiders. But, while this was generally true, the tendency seems to vary with country size. Canadians, who also lived in a large country, were second to those in the US who named their own 'compatriots' as being influential and overall a general rule was observed: the larger the country the more likely musicians were to name own-country influences. The influence of market size and economies of scale in production is seen in the fact that while Anglo-American music dominated the influence process, in part because English is the dominant global language, and the American market is the dominant source, US musicians identified British influences only 20 per cent of the time, while US references were made 60 per cent of the time (p. 235). Scale, rather than language, seems to explain the direction of cultural influence.

The audience and aggregate demand

Turow (1992) suggests that the role of the public or the audience is quite limited as a actor with power within the media system. This is a view which is also consistent with the mainstream economic perspective on the role of individual consumers. As individuals, they are essentially powerless to influence either the price or the quality of the goods and services which are offered.

Consumers are *price takers* rather than price makers. They have only the ability to exit the market – to withhold their attention or their fees. The power of their voice is extremely limited, and it depends upon the willingness of regulatory agencies or courts to pursue complaints that they might make against some entity within the marketplace. The same is also supposed to be true for media providers in the idealized world of economic theory. The reality, however, is that few media markets are fully competitive, and as a result providers have considerable power to determine both price and the standards of quality for symbolic goods and services. Turow (1991) suggests that, when members of the public organize in order to increase their power relative to other actors within the media system, they 'take on' another kind of power role: they become public advocates.

Despite the powerlessness of individuals in their role as consumers or members of media audiences, we cannot doubt that audiences as 'markets' or market *segments* do have a collective influence on the media system. The sum of individual decisions to invest time or money in acquiring or attending to a particular media offering can be understood as an expression of consumer demand. The managers of commercial and non-commercial media organizations do respond in important ways to this aggregate demand.

The literature on audience behavior identifies a variety of other structural factors which influence individual decisions about the use of media which are reflected in aggregate patterns of demand. Age, employment status, income, number and age of children in the household, and measures of community, church, or political involvement are all useful predictors of the decision to watch television, to read books, to go to the movies, theatre, concerts, etc. When examined at the aggregate level, this information helps to explain shifts in the patterns of media consumption.

Jorge Schement (1994) identifies important demographic shifts in the population that are certain to affect the nature of demand for new telecommunications services. Among the more important of these shifts is the change in the characteristics of the household. A dramatic increase in the number of single-person households has taken place over the past 50 years. As we will discuss in more detail in Chapter 5, the ways we understand and respond to mass media varies in response to the influence of the context of media consumption. The increase in single-person households means an increase in the amount of solitary media consumption.

Bruce Austin (1989) notes that there was a dramatic increase in the population in the United States between 1900 and 1930, and this expansion in population was also accompanied by a similarly dramatic shift of the labor force out of the fields into the factories, which also meant a migration of that population out of rural areas into the nation's cities. This is a period in which the motion picture industry emerged and moved rapidly into maturity as a recreational form. Austin also notes an additional factor that explains the relationship between commercial recreation and urbanization. The concentration of populations within smaller geographic space made it possible for recreational activities such as movies to take advantage of scale economies. Because at the turn of the century most commercial recreation required people to leave their households, the development of neighborhood theatres reflected the power of these scale economies in interaction with shifts in population centers, such as the dramatic migration of African Americans out of the rural South into the cities of the industrial North.

The class structure of public entertainment also changed with the motion picture. Austin suggests that before movies achieved their overwhelming popularity in urban centers, commercial amusements were segregated by race, class, and gender. Movies, in his view, were considerably more democratic, although in some regions segregation by race continued to be the rule.

Other shifts in the character of the population within a geographic market have been associated with changes in the fortunes of the industry. These shifts have also marked changes in the nature of supply. The increase in the size of ethnic populations, through immigration and birth rate, will increase the ethnic market as long as the members of these population groups identify ethnically or racially and, as a result, exhibit a willingness to consume targeted media.

An important change in the character of immigration has affected the structure of racial and ethnic markets in the United States. Between 1820 and 1970, Europe supplied the majority of immigrants to the United States. By 1980, an even larger majority of immigrants were coming from Asia and Latin America. As peoples of color, these new immigrants, along with the African Americans already occupying positions on the fringe of the American cultural mainstream, are expected to face more difficulty in assimilating into the dominant culture and, as a result, will become part of an evolving 'confederation of minorities' (Gutiérrez, 1990). The growth of ethnic populations does not, by itself, guarantee increased advertiser support of media that attract these audiences. Advertisers must believe that there is a market worth reaching, and that it is efficient to reach them through ethnic media, or ethnically identified appeals in mainstream media. Because they tend to be spread among rural reservations, and are more diffused when they live in the larger cities, Native Americans have not emerged as a significant market for American advertisers (Gutiérrez, 1990, p. 12).

The geographic clustering of ethnic populations facilitates the targeting of commercial appeals which enables the successful operation of ethnic media. Because these media provide the content that reinforces ethnic identity, this develops into a system that tends to reproduce itself. The presence of vibrant ethnic communities tends to attract ethnic immigration, which further reinforces the demand for ethnic media that help to smooth acculturation. Larger cities become multicultural, and the correlation between ethnic population rank, ethnic media presence, and targeted advertising expenditure is actually quite strong. Gutiérrez (1990) identifies Los Angeles as a kind of multicultural kaleidoscope because of the number of different kinds of Asian, Latino, and African American media outlets that were operating in the metropolitan area. A curious and contradictory process seems to be unfolding in these postmodern cities as national advertisers are convinced of the value of making targeted buys in ethnic media. These 'media and advertising systems identify and reinforce cultural and linguistic differences while they promote consumption of mass-produced products' (Gutiérrez, 1990, p. 13).

Variation in the patterns of media consumption is not captured entirely by shifts in population parameters. Media consumption is also a reflection of shifts in cultural and subcultural perspectives on leisure. There are quite remarkable differences between nations in terms of the amount of television watching, movie and theatre going, and participation in recreational sports. These are reflections of differences in national culture. Some of these differences may reflect quite different constructions of the meaning of work and its relation to leisure. This may be seen in the average number of days, weeks, and hours that individuals work in different countries.

Austin (1989) defines leisure as pertaining to 'activities that are non-obligatory, consciously and personally selected, and essential to people's physiological and psychological well-being.' Leisure is understood as serving several purposes or functions for individuals: (1) 'a means for balancing, correcting, or compensation for the tensions, strains, and obligations of workaday life,' or (2) 'the means to provide such essentials as self-fulfillment, growth, satisfaction, and self-expression' (p. 26). Karl Marx is said to have favored the pursuit of improvements in the level of technology because the resultant improvements in productivity would increase the amount of time that workers would have available to improve themselves, or realize their individual human potential through the productive use of their leisure time. The development of an industrialized recreational industry also depended upon the development of an orientation toward consumerism in which 'spending replaced thrift as a social value' (Austin, 1989, p. 29).

As suggested earlier, aggregate demand for particular media reflected the availability of the audience to consume. This varied with the nature of the medium, including whether or not it required consumers to leave the home. A second determining influence on the demand for a particular form of media is the availability of competing alternatives or substitutes. We note that the demand for motion pictures reached its peak between 1946 and 1948 in the US at around 90 million tickets per week. In 1949, theatre attendance dropped by 20 per cent, and continued to drop to around 54 million per week by 1951, and to less than 20 million by 1984.

A large part of this drop in movie attendance in 1949 can be explained by the introduction of a competitive alternative – television. Here was a technology that provided a close approximation of the motion picture experience that did not require leaving the home. Accessing television did not require purchasing a ticket each time one wanted to view it, and cost of viewing television did not rise with the number of people viewing. Movie going as an activity changed so much that the industry changed the definition of frequent movie goers to include those who went to the movies at least once a month, whereas before the introduction of television people tended to go to the movies at least once a week (Austin, 1989, p. 39).

Technological innovations continue to provide alternatives to previously dominant forms of recreation. The VCR increased the shift in the focus of recreation toward the household. Cable television increased the number of channels which were available in the household. Shifts in national policy toward greater competition increased the numbers of commercial alternatives in those countries where there were only a few government-managed television stations available. The household penetration of VCRs in those markets proceeded at a much faster rate than in the US and in other markets which had more than one station available. The development and subsequent popularity of video games only extended that trend.

Because the media industry was not especially interested in the non-White household in the 1970s, little effort was expended to explain the sizeable and increasing gap between Whites and non-Whites in terms of the amount of time spent watching television. Although Nielsen's estimates were household data, and could not tell us much about individual viewers, the increase in the differential between White and non-White households from 7 hours in 1974 to 20 hours in 1979 was substantial. It seems unlikely that any change in the average size of non-White households would explain the difference. A more likely explanation was the fairly sharp increase in unemployment for Blacks that was not matched in the experience of Whites (US Bureau of the Census, 1979). This conclusion is supported by the higher than average levels of daytime television viewing in Black households in 1979–80. It has also been suggested that Black/White differences in television use exist because the 'recreational alternatives that vary with social class for the majority population have been limited historically by racist practices in the US, and as a result, many blacks have turned instead to vicarious participation in the wider society through television' (Gandy, 1981a, p. 113).

Differences in preferences for programs with African American characters would explain most, but not all, of the disparity between Whites and Blacks in terms of what they revealed were their favorite programs. A comparison of the top 20 White programs in January 1980 with the 20 favorites in Black households found only 7 programs in common. Seven of the programs in the Black top 20 had predominantly non-White casts. Only one of those programs, *The Jeffersons*, made it to both lists (Myrick and Keegan, 1981).

Media access, regulation and reform

The structure of the media industry is not determined entirely within the market, nor is its performance with regard to race determined entirely by market values, or the interplay of supply and demand. The government, through legislation, regulation, and court decisions, is an important actor that may be thought of as an unpredictable if not an autonomous force with considerable power. Government regulations vary dramatically between countries in ways that reflect different historical traditions, not the least of which are based in traditions of the state control of broadcasting media. In the United States, where the broadcast media have historically been operated through private control, policy with regard to matters of race has moved through various forms of content and structural regulation.

Because of the interpretation of the First Amendment as barring government restrictions on private speech, a preference for structural regulation has been seen in a somewhat half-hearted pursuit of diversity in content through efforts to achieve diversity in employment and ownership of media entities.

The shape of mass media policies in the United States, Australia, and Britain has responded to expressions of public sentiment that have at different times had the character of social movements. Montgomery (1989) describes the efforts by several groups to influence the ways in which their communities were represented in the media. Direct pressure by advocates from representatives of a variety of social movements influenced both portrayal and hiring of group members. Kellner (1990) suggests that, while several social movements were able to influence television portrayals, Blacks were more successful. That success is explained in part by the much broader mobilization that the civil rights movement represented. A more important influence was the recognition that African Americans represented a substantial, but as yet unexploited, economic market. Although there was some early resistance from Southern broadcasters, by the late 1960s an increasing number of prime-time series included African Americans.

Administrative units concerned with limiting discrimination, improving diversity, and ensuring minority access to communications and information resources have been established. In Britain, the 'specific laws, statutory and voluntary organizations which have been established with the specific project of fighting racism' are studied under the label of a 'Race Relations Industry' (Anthias and Yuval-Davis, 1992, p. 156), and the communications media have been a central focus of its work.

The extent to which these entities actually pursued their goals as aggressively as they might is difficult to determine, although it is clear that changes in the ideological core of government policy, such as that associated with the Reagan and Thatcher administrations, produced a retrenchment in government activism.

Fife (1987b) reminds us that the US Federal Communications Commission (FCC) was not only subject to 'capture' by the industries it regulated, but it was also influenced by other interests if they were sufficiently motivated, and were able to mobilize enough resources to bring pressure on the agency. The civil rights movement in the United States represented just such a political force, and its influence on the FCC and the media it regulated ought not to be underestimated. Part of that influence included a 'demonstration effect.'

Other social movements reflecting the interests of women, gays, and environmentalists followed the lead established by the civil rights movement, and helped to maintain a level of sensitivity to group interests that had not been achieved at any earlier moment in American history. Classen (1994), on the other hand, argues that the efforts to realize civil rights in media systems would not have succeeded if there was not also a sizeable consumer movement emerging within American society. He notes that the FCC had already begun to respond to emerging consumer concerns in 1960 by modifying broadcasters' reporting requirements to include evidence that might be derived from survey- and interview-based 'assessments' of community needs and interests.

Fife (1987b) underscores the importance of the network of resources that the civil rights movement helped to develop. The multidimensional character and institutional reach of this movement enabled it to realize so many of its goals in a fairly short period of time. The activists were organized, and they were relatively well funded from a variety of sources that included foundation and government grants. The movement had powerful advocates within the government bureaucracy in the form of a radical FCC commissioner, Nicholas Johnson, and an activist Black commissioner, Benjamin Hooks.

As Fife suggests, the citizens' broadcasting reform movement in the United States had its beginning with the involvement of the United Church of Christ (UCC) with a coalition of civil rights activists in Jackson, Mississippi. The movement not only succeeded in having the license of television station WLBT-TV revoked in 1969, but it also established a judicial landmark determining that members of the audience had 'standing', or a legal right on the basis of their genuine interests as consumers, to participate in regulatory deliberations (Classen, 1994; Rowland, 1982). The legal arguments put forward by the UCC team focused on the economic interests of the public. It framed those interests in terms of 'investments' that consumers made in receiving equipment. 'This argument provided the awkward equation through which the court defined local African-American concerns as synonymous with those of the American consumer' (Classen, 1994, p. 84).

Still, the citizens' reform movement has to be recognized as having produced a significant shift in the structure of American broadcasting. It increased the salience of minority group interests, increased the involvement of local community organizations in programming decisions, and helped to elevate the value placed on the employment of racial and ethnic minorities within the media industry. If we think about the civil rights movement as a critical event – a shock to the system – we ought not to be surprised that a correction, or a response to a demand from other interests that had been displaced temporarily at the helm of government, would operate to undo much but not all of the 'damage' to the system that occurred during this very special moment. While the movement has all but faded from view, the effects of its 'shock' to the structure of traditional relations can still be seen in the expanded and improved representation of minorities, especially African Americans, in American television programs.

As Maxwell (1988) notes, however, the benefits that the Chicano wing of the media reform movement enjoyed are much harder to identify. Part of the explanation for some of the differences between the African American and the Chicano wings of the reform movement was the ways in which the movements were funded. A federally funded agency, the Community Relations Service (CRS), was formed under Title X of the 1964 Civil Rights Act. It funded several Chicano civil rights efforts, but Maxwell identifies a national media conference which gave birth to the National Chicano Media Council (NCMC) as the most important product of CRS funding (p. 96). Rather than continuing to support NCMC, the federal government funded the development of more centralized coordinating arms, like the National Telecommunications and Information Administration (NTIA) and its umbrella program for minorities, the Minority Telecommunications Development Program. As a result, Maxwell (1988) argues: 'While nominally expanding the scope of minority media, these state-run organizations have limited the agenda of media reform by promoting the entrepreneurial ethos to which, according to Rowland [1982], the media reform movement generally has fallen prey' (p. 97). Maxwell sees this case as yet another example of an 'internal colonization' process. The involvement of the government, foundation, and industry funding ensured that the 'consciousness of Chicano activism' would not be legitimated within the reform movement.

The experience of Chicano media activists reflects the more general response of a dominant system to demands from smaller oppositional movements. The pattern for Latinos in communications was the same as the response of American capitalism to Black demands for civil rights:

> leaders and leadership organizations were legitimized; demands recast as acceptable reforms; symbolic activities were carried out as acknowledgement of demands; issues were de-politicized as much as possible; and there was no fundamental change in the existing social order. (Fife, 1987b, p. 493)

Ironically, the transformation of a claim by an aggrieved group or class into an expression of concern for the rights of individual consumers may have set in motion the redefinition of the public interest standard from its previous basis in a higher moral standard involving collective notions of the public good to a market-determined summation of what consumers, on the average, were willing to purchase (Polic and Gandy, 1991). The emergence of the 'marketplace standard' as a replacement for a traditional moral/rational 'public trusteeship' standard marked an important shift in the orientation of the Federal Communications Commission (FCC) away from its accommodation of minority interests in the United States (Polic and Gandy, 1991).

Wimmer (1988) argued that the future for minority involvement in the mass media in the United States would depend upon the ability of media activists to transform the language of rights and fairness into the language of efficient markets, and then to find convincing evidence of market failure. Wimmer's efforts to define marketplace failure in terms of unsatisfied demand and continued use of stereotyped representations of minority group members had little chance of reversing, or even slowing down, a move toward the elimination of existing programs to increase minority participation through affirmative action.

The claim that minorities were members of identifiable subcultures, with unique interests and viewpoints that not only ought to be respected but ought to be served by an efficient marketplace, was a view that met with ready opposition within the government. The FCC resisted the idea that a preference should be given to minority applicants because it doubted that minority ownership would guarantee minority oriented, and therefore more diverse, programming. It took action by the DC Court of Appeals in 1975 to instruct the FCC that, in the absence of evidence to the contrary, its policy should be guided by the 'reasonable expectation' that minority ownership would enhance diversity (Kleiman, 1991). The FCC responded with two policies, distress sales and tax certificates, that most observers identify as having produced a measurable increase in minority ownership.

However, almost as though they had been informed by the discourse of indeterminacy which had become dominant within cultural studies, a vocal and increasingly powerful conservative minority within the Supreme Court in 1990 (Metro Broadcasting) suggested that government ought not to assume, nor act upon the assumption, that race or ethnicity would determine how people think or act (Kleiman, 1991). In oral arguments, Justice Scalia aggressively challenged the assumption that there were distinct racial and ethnic ideologies. And, even if there were such things, Scalia argued that they ought not to be sustained, but dissolved in the 'melting pot' of the American cultural mainstream.

What evidence there was available to the Court at the time was hopelessly contradictory (Fife, 1987a; Singleton, 1981). Marilyn Fife's study of minority ownership and minority images in news was funded in part by a competitively awarded grant from the National Association of Broadcasters (Fife, 1987a). Several important findings were reported in this study. First, there was evidence of 'narrowcasting' or targeting, in which minority owners programmed for their own racial or ethnic community. It also seemed that minority owners who chose a 'mainstreaming' approach, perhaps out of competitive necessity, still evidenced a 'commitment to cultural pluralism rarely seen in majority-controlled TV outlets' (Fife, 1987a, p. 110). Fife suggested that the only positive function that could be served by a station in which the racial or ethnic group represented by the ownership was virtually non-existent in the marketplace, and therefore unlikely to be the subject of local news, is that which might be seen as accompanying an expansion of the economic base of minority entrepreneurs. This is, of course, not a content-based assessment of structural influence, although it might be seen as contributing to change in the structure of the industry. It is argued that increasing the number of minority broadcasters will increase their 'clout' or influence within the industry, just as others have argued that increasing the numbers of minorities on media staffs, perhaps beyond a 'critical mass,' will increase their influence on the editorial policies of the organization.

Minority ownership

At the mid point of the citizens' reform movement, support for the development of 'Black capitalism' was understood as a non-threatening structural response because the underlying capitalist logic would actually work to support and reinforce the existing relations within the market, rather than providing a substantial challenge (Fife, 1987b). The change in the presence of Black capitalists was dramatic, but not significant in relative terms. Minority ownership of commercial broadcast stations barely reached one-half of 1 per cent in 1978, but it had increased to 3 per cent by 1994 as a result of a complex of policies instituted in response to activism (Bush and Martin, 1996; Wilson and Gutiérrez, 1995, p. 222). Minority ownership in newer media that were likely to be affected by the 'convergence' of computer and telecommunications systems did not attract the same kind of movement attention and, as a result, has not grown in the same way.

Whereas the evidence was unclear with respect to the relationship between minority ownership and programming, there is solid evidence of a positive relationship between minority ownership and minority employment. By comparing Black-owned with White-owned Black formatted radio stations in 1980, David Honig found a highly significant difference, with Black owners hiring more Black employees. This disparity was the greatest in the officials and managers and sales positions – the areas in which minority employment in broadcasting was the lowest (Honig, 1983).

In 1981, the US Congress had granted the FCC the authority to use a lottery method rather than comparative hearing as a way of accelerating the granting of licenses for new communications services. The FCC adjusted its minority ownership policies with regard to broadcasting to accommodate the lottery method, but determined that concerns with diversity would not be affected by using such methods to allocate common carrier licenses. As a result, a dramatically successful cellular telephone service developed without significant minority participation. It was not until the election of Bill Clinton in 1992 that diversity of ownership in small business, without regard to an impact on diversity of content, was again specified as a goal of the FCC's licensing activities. Before the Commission's plans for minority preferences in the new digital telephone service (PCS) were implemented, however, a series of Supreme Court cases established the requirement of 'strict scrutiny' before racial preferences could be justified. When the courts rule that affirmative action requires 'strict scrutiny' they are saying that, unless compelling evidence can be provided that racial disparities are the result of illegal discrimination ('pervasive, systematic, and obstinate discriminatory conduct'), then policies that show preferences for minorities are likely to be ruled an unconstitutional denial of due process – unfairness to non-minorities. This implies an evidentiary standard that will be almost impossible to achieve (Bush and Martin, 1996).

By early 1997 impact of this policy shift was already in evidence (Adelson, 1997). Minority ownership of broadcast facilities had slipped by 10 per cent in just one year. AM radio ownership had slipped to 3.6 per cent, FM radio to 2.2 per cent, and television stations to 3.0 per cent. This decline is in part the result of the release of massive amounts of capital in search of consolidation in broadcast properties after the Telecommunications Act of 1996 all but eliminated barriers to multiple station ownership, allowing up to eight radio stations in a single market to be owned jointly. One minority entrepreneur, US Radio's Ragan Henry, gave up his status as the owner of the largest Black-owned radio group in exchange for a $140 million windfall he realized by selling his group to another able to play in a market in which prices had risen to 15 times cash flow. Media activist David Honig concluded that this was 'the worst environment for minorities in this industry since the 1950s' (Adelson, 1997, p. D9).

In England, the shift in policy toward privatization had positive benefits in terms of Black ownership of broadcasting entities. Benjamin (1995) reports that prior to 1989 most of the Black music on the airwaves had been provided by 'pirate' or illegal stations. Although Wicked Neutral and Kicking Radio (WNK) eventually failed, its owners did gain a license in 1990.

Minority employment

Benjamin (1995) describes a rather dismal picture of minority employment within journalism in England. She notes that of some 63 editors of the mainstream quality press none are Black. There are no Blacks among the 75 editors of the national tabloids, and there are only around 20 Black journalists out of 4,000 working for the mainstream press (p. 58). The picture is considerably better in the United States.

A 1994 report by the Federal Communications Commission (FCC) interpreted the growth in minority employment within the broadcast and

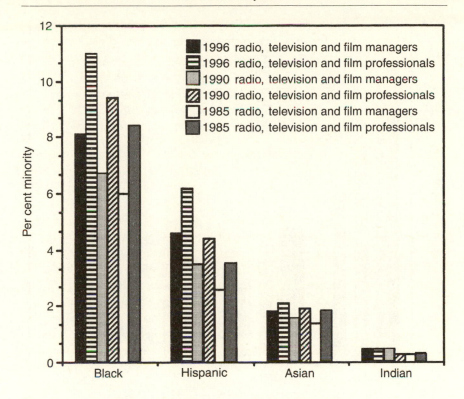

Figure 3.3 Minority presence in broadcasting

cable industries as an indication of the success of their efforts to guarantee Equal Employment Opportunity (EEO). The increase in minority presence within the cable industry was three times greater than that within the industry as a whole, bringing the proportion to approximately 25 per cent, with the share of minorities in 'upper-level' positions estimated at 20 per cent (Federal Communications Commission, 1994). The FCC reported that despite the gains the proportion of minorities employed in broadcasting remains below comparable figures for the overall national workforce. This fact reflects the failure of media organizations to engage in active recruitment of minorities.

Data gathered from the US Equal Employment Opportunity Commission (EEOC) suggests the impact of two institutionalized forces on the employment of minorities in media industries. Formal EEOC guidelines within the FCC, and a commitment within the American Newspaper Publishers Association (ANPA), appear to have resulted in market increases in the employment of minorities in both managerial and professional positions in broadcasting (Figure 3.3) and in the newspaper business (Figure 3.4) between 1985 and 1996. We might ascribe the slight and rather uneven

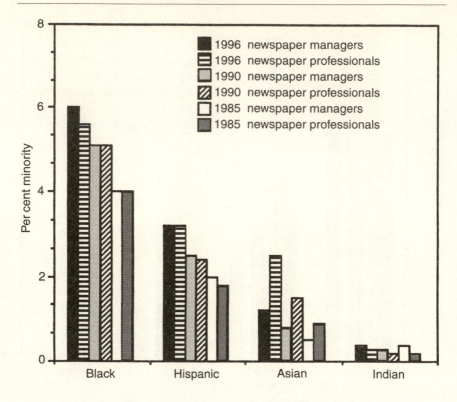

Figure 3.4 Minority presence in newspapers

increases in minority employment in the motion picture industry over the same period to the absence of any initiatives within the industry prior to 1995 (Figure 3.5).

The absence of African American film-makers from the slate of 1996 Academy Awards nominees (one film-maker out of 166 nominated) was described as a 'national disgrace' by *People* magazine, reflecting an impression shared by many who noted that fact that Blacks make up 12 per cent of the population, 25 per cent of movie goers, but only 3.9 per cent of the Academy's membership (Waxman, 1996).

The increase in minority employment that media advocacy helped to stimulate also helped to generate a critical mass of minority professionals within media organizations who have assumed some of the responsibility for monitoring media practice that community groups had established. These minority professionals have organized into professional organizations defined by racial and ethnic group background. The Asian American Journalists Association, the National Association of Black Journalists, the National Association of Hispanic Journalists and the Native American Journalists' Association came together in a joint conference in 1994 to

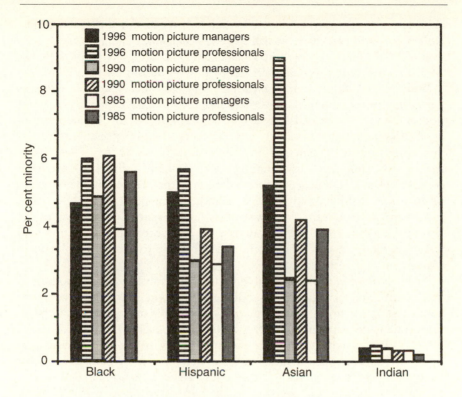

Figure 3.5 Minority presence in motion pictures

develop their strategies to influence media performance through both criticism and praise.

If minority journalists find themselves having repeatedly to confront issues of ethnic and racial insensitivity on the job, they are bound to put their jobs and their careers in jeopardy. Even if the courts and the Commissions have turned away from these concerns, then a vigilant public may be the only insurance against a return to an earlier period of ethnic insensitivity. There are examples that demonstrate that media owners will still respond if the protest is dramatic enough (Lieb, 1988).

Access

Generally, the focus on media access has been limited to a consideration of the extent to which minority voices are heard as a function of the access that minority communicators have to the means of communication. This is reflected in the discourse among activists and researchers on ownership and employment. There is also a reason for us to be concerned about access to the means of reception. The number of African Americans with access to cable television helps to define the kind of market that an entrepreneur like Robert Johnson can reach with his cable-based Black Entertainment Television (BET). Data reported in 1993 claimed that 90 per cent of Blacks with cable television were subscribers to BET (Tait and Barber, 1996).

With regard to telecommunications services, this kind of access is considered in relation to the assumption of 'universal access' that the grant of a monopoly to the Bell system was to guarantee. With the break-up of the Bell system, concern about universal access, and especially access by minorities and poor, emerged in policy discussions about 'safety nets.' Access to communications technology was framed in terms of an overall concern about a confluence of forces that were threatening public access to information (Schiller and Schiller, 1988). Discussion of the electronic superhighway emphasized the ways in which disparities in access to the new media would further disenfranchise the poor, especially minorities who were less likely to own computers and subscribe to information services (Anderson *et al.*, 1995).

An analysis of current trends in computer use found that, in addition to the contribution of income or social class to a widening gap in access to computers in the home, racial and ethnic characteristics appeared to be an independent determinant of access to these resources (Bikson and Panis, 1995). While Asians are among the most likely to have a computer at home, Hispanics, Blacks, and Native Americans are among those least likely to have such access. These data suggest, however, that unlike measures of income and social class, the gap based on race and ethnicity has remained constant between 1989 and 1993, rather than widening (p. 30).

The passage of the Telecommunications Act of 1996, driven largely by the desire to realize the economic gains that unbridled competition is thought to bring, represents a serious threat to the logic of universal access, in part because of the technical difficulties in assigning shares of access costs to competitors with vastly different levels of involvement and power in the emerging markets.

Minority media

Ethnic media in the United States are not alternative media in the sense that they are treated as substitutes for mainstream media. They are not. These media are generally not in direct competition with mainstream media for anything other than advertising support. They provide information that the other media do not provide, and thus they are the primary, rather than an alternative, source providing access to what, for all intents and purposes, is 'another world' which is invisible in the mainstream media.

John Downing has examined ethnic minority radio broadcasting in the United States. His emphasis on media owned and operated by minority group members reflects his recognition that the involvement of the White minority in ethnic media has been guided by a variety of motivations. For the most part, ethnic minority media have been operated as a medium of resistance and solidarity for populations that have been the victims of racism (Downing, 1990).

Data gathered by the National Association of Broadcasters (NAB) in 1986 indicated that, of some 10,000 radio stations in operation, slightly more than 2 per cent were owned by minority group members. Downing's analysis of the NAB data indicated that these minority-owned stations were not in those markets one might expect if minority group presence was used as a predictor. While there were stations in those markets which programmed materials of interest to those communities, the stations were not likely to be owned by minorities. The distribution of minority-owned stations more closely reflected the lack of minority access to the kinds of financial resources that would be needed to acquire a station in a major market.

In their study of Spanish-language media Gutiérrez and Schement (1981) described an industry that more than doubled in size in five years, from 250 radio stations offering all or part of their programming in Spanish in 1973 to 600 stations in 1978. There were also 21 television stations listed in 1978, where there were none listed in 1973. Focusing on those 64 radio stations which were primarily Spanish-language in 1978, Gutiérrez and Schement note that *75 per cent* were owned by non-Latinos. When they looked at the top ten Latino markets where the bulk of the radio listeners would be found, nearly 90 per cent of the stations were owned by non-Latinos (p. 186). They also determined that Latinos were poorly represented among the management of these stations although, not surprisingly, Latino owners were more likely to hire Latino personnel. Similar findings had been reported in an earlier study of Black format radio. Among the 310 radio stations that were self-identified as programming a Black format, only 16 were owned by African Americans in 1969 (Ferretti, 1970).

The Black press in the United States

The foremost authority on the Black press in the United States, Roland Wolseley (1990), argues that a distinction ought be made between media which appeal to the interests of African Americans and those which are owned and managed by Black people. But, for Wolseley, ownership is not enough. The Oakland *Tribune* was owned and edited by Robert Maynard, a noted Black journalist, but its orientation was toward the mainstream, and it could just as well have been owned by non-Blacks. Thus, Wolseley adds the requirement that the publication has to be intended for Black consumers for it to be included in the category of Black press. For a variety of reasons, many having to do with the unsteady economic condition of much of the Black press, as well as its arms-length distance from the mainstream associations of publishers, there is no reliable estimate of the number and combined circulation of this institution (Wolseley, 1990, p. 16).

The working definition being used to identify the Black press in Britain is undoubtedly more expansive than Wolseley's. Because of the definition of 'Black' as a racial and ethnic category, newspapers owned and operated by Africans, Asians, and West Indians are included in a category that supports the claim that 'London is fast becoming the Black newspaper capital of the world' (Benjamin, 1995, p. 1). Wolseley adds a touch of realism to his working definition of the Black press by suggesting that all of the social, cultural, and political purposes behind the institution of a Black press 'are superseded by that of earning a profit from advertising and circulation or reaching the listeners and viewers essential to independent survival' (p. 6). Black newspapers in the South were also limited by their dependence on the good will and forbearance of White printers who would, from time to time, refuse to reproduce Black newspapers if they disapproved of the content (Pride, 1951, p. 182). White printers exercised their substantial power in the North as well. Until *Ebony* magazine became large enough to threaten the loss of its business, its printer acted as a censor and refused to publish pictures of interracial marriages (Burns, 1996, p. 102).

The emphasis on profit, more often than not, operates to limit the political potential of the Black press, as well as the press of other subordinate groups. Steiner (1992), on the other hand, identifies a group of alternative women's publications that explicitly 'repudiate the language of business in order to embrace the language of sisterhood' (p. 123). Feminist media in Steiner's view are clearly motivated or constrained by the pursuit of profit. Differences between the generally conservative Southern Black press and the more dissident version emerging in Northern cities reflects the conservatizing impact of the structural constraints that economic dependency represents (Pride, 1951).

The Black press need not always be a dissident press. The oppositional role of the press undoubtedly reflects an assessment that publishers make of the circumstances and concerns that are recognizable themes in the thinking of their readership. The first newspaper published by and for African Americans, *Freedom's Journal*, was created in 1827 in part in response to the refusal by a New York paper to publish a letter responding to racist attacks being published in the press (Kessler, 1984). This adversarial response would come to characterize other Black newspapers that promoted the Abolitionist cause, and still others that would help to catalyze the struggle for civil rights. Although Frederick Douglass had ready access to a number of White Abolitionist newspapers, he created his own paper, the *North Star*, in 1847, in part to demonstrate that African Americans could in fact succeed as a dissident voice in the marketplace of ideas.

While there are always variations around any core, it can be said that the Black press in the United States does have an identifiable point of view (Pride, 1951). This point of view is derived from its historical role as a medium of protest, even though protest has been toned down considerably as the Black press evolved into a commercial venture. In Wolseley's view, the Black press still 'crusades' more than the White press because it has more to crusade for (Wolseley, 1990, p. 202).

Yet, the Black press finds itself in an unusual circumstance as it approaches the new millennium. The poor African Americans who most need this press as their advocate have never really been a part of its audience. The Black middle class has increasingly turned away from the Black press to make use of mainstream sources of information more closely linked to a mainstream lifestyle. The Black press that serves this upscale readership seems committed to both reflect and reproduce the idea that one achieves status through consumption. Many of these upscale publications are periodicals in which the editorial tone suggests that 'the primary goals of young black men should be to become nationally famous sports stars paid millions and owning posh homes. Such is not the atmosphere in which a fight for civil rights or social justice thrives' (Wolseley, 1990, p. 401). Because of its inherently conservative orientation, based in part in its pursuit of capitalist goals, this press also finds itself unwilling to embrace, or be embraced by, the more militant Blacks out of fear of losing the advertising support they have come to depend on.

Reginald Owens suggests that most studies of African American newspapers fail to appreciate the extent to which these papers have served historically as 'weapons of the African American elite in the war of cultural symbols and politics' (Owens, 1996, p. 97). This initial role for the Black press was to be recreated at different times in the history of American racial politics. The importance of this press waxed and waned in response to changes in the economic, social, and political fortunes of African Americans. Using a variety of indicators of oppression that included lynchings, executions for rape, executions for murder, and maternal mortality, Owens demonstrates a link between trends in the circulation of Black-owned papers and peaks of oppression. While the correlation between oppression and *circulation* is negative, the opposite is true for newspaper formation. As the number of acts defined as racial oppression increased, the number of newspapers published by African Americans (standardized as the number of papers per thousand Blacks in the population) also increased (Owens, 1996, p. 107).

The divergence between the formation and circulation figures can be explained as a function of the emergence of conflicting ideologies at times of crisis for African Americans. During these periods competition among Black newspapers offering alternative ideological views results in declining circulation for the individual papers, which is measured, therefore, as a declining average. However, Owen's figures suggest that as circulation among mainstream newspapers has continued to fall, total circulation among African American papers has remained steady when measured against population. The fact that publication activity increases during periods of oppression can be taken as evidence that the Black press still plays a vital role within this minority community.

The publisher of *Ebony* magazine, however, decided quite early to distance his publication from the rest of the Black press. Ben Burns, editor of both *Negro Digest* and *Ebony* magazine for Johnson publications, claims that *Ebony* was always committed to focusing on the 'happier side of Negro life.' He reports that 'for the first time, a national Black periodical openly rejected negativism and advocacy of a cause: the persistent theme of the Negro press from the start' (Burns, 1996, p. 88). John Johnson wanted to appeal to the growing Black middle class, and did not want to offend them or, perhaps more importantly, the advertisers who were just beginning to recognize their market potential. An article in *Tide*, one of the primary journals of the advertising business, seemed to validate Johnson's position by 'praising *Ebony* for "taste and restraint to avoid the taint that afflicts so much of the Negro press"' (Burns, 1996, p. 94).

Teresa Mastin's study (1996) of advertising in *Essence* magazine underscores the continuing perceived vulnerability of minority publishers to the pressures of the market. Her analysis reveals some of the ways in which dependency on the market serves as a constraint on editorial policy. It is fairly well established that magazines in general, and women's magazines in particular, are dependent upon tobacco advertising and that their editorial treatment of the health threats associated with smoking is less than it would be if they did not rely upon revenue from the tobacco industry.

Essence magazine had a greater reliance on cigarette advertisers than did most other magazines which targeted women as readers (9 per cent of advertising revenue, for *Essence*, versus 5 per cent for other women's magazines). Mastin found a significant negative correlation between editorial content and the amount of cigarette advertising. Surprisingly, and perhaps more importantly, this relationship remained even while *Essence* was increasing its focus on the health concerns of Black women (Mastin, 1996, p. 226). The fact that its senior health editor explicitly acknowledged the risk publishers take in alienating tobacco companies underscores the status of this binding constraint.

Another study of cigarette advertising (Pollay *et al.*, 1992) underscored the tendency of this industry in particular to target segments defined by race, culture, and class. Because of the relatively homogeneous character of the readership of particular magazines, they are prime vehicles for targeted tobacco ads. Tobacco advertising in magazines increased sixfold after the industry shrank from the assault of counter-advertising that the FCC seemed to be encouraging in the 1970s. In a comparison of *Ebony* and *Life* magazines in the period between the 'discovery' of the Black consumer and the industry's withdrawal from television, Pollay and his colleagues find 'clear and obvious targeting of a black audience from at least 1950' (p. 56).

It is not only dependence on advertisers that has softened the political sting of Black media. In Wolseley's view, all media are responding to an underlying hedonism in media. Altruism and good will seems to have evaporated in the pursuit of pleasure (1990, p. 401).

Foreign-language media

Félix Gutiérrez and Jorge Schement have been pioneers in the study of Spanish-language broadcasting in the United States (1981). Their primary concern was an assessment of the extent to which the informational and cultural needs of Latinos in the US would be met by an industry dominated by foreign owners. In an important way, their framing of these concerns as a question of international communications policy established an important linkage to the theoretical debates about the New World Information Order, and the concept of cultural imperialism (Nordenstreng and Varis, 1974).

A finding that raises questions about the autonomy that minority owners are able to exercise within the context of a competitive capitalist media market is that Latino owners did not appear to program more public service programming than did non-Latino owners (Gutiérrez and Schement, 1981, p. 188). They recognized, however, that their estimation of the influence of minority ownership was extremely limited because of their reliance on the kinds of data that were reported to the FCC. This is one of the primary concerns about positivist analyses of media performance that have been raised by Edwin Baker (1994b). Baker argues that the assumption of a need to use statistical indicators, as well as a reliance upon data gathered to meet industry or government needs, introduces a distortion, a blind-spot in the analysis of media (pp. 17–19).

Other important comparisons were made by Gutiérrez and Schement. They cited studies that compared English-language and Spanish-language stations in the same market that indicated that the English-language stations provided more local news and information than the Spanish-language station. Of course, such differences in performance, if the categories were actually comparative, might be explained in terms of the relative wealth of the two stations. The wealthier station could afford to put more reporters in the field.

A more complicated argument about the value of localism in non-news programming would have to be made in order for similar comparisons to be made between Spanish-language and English-language television. However, Gutiérrez and Schement did provide evidence to suggest that viewers of Spanish-language television received a schedule which contained programming that came primarily from Mexico, with additional material from

Venezuela, Spain, Argentina, and Brazil. While this material was popular and profitable, it displaced coverage of news to the fringe hours of programming. Whatever the explanation for the differences they observed between Spanish and other broadcast stations, their analysis suggested that the structure of the media market resulted in an ethnic minority population that was likely to be underserved by its media.

In the next chapter we will examine the performance of media – those directed toward the mainstream, and those targeted to national minorities. The change in the performance of those media should be understood in the context of a variety of contending influences that have shaped production decisions.

4

Reflection and representation

How should we assess the role of the world's media as it relates to the problem of race? Denis McQuail's approach to the assessment of media performance is one that privileges the contribution that media make to realizing the public interest (McQuail, 1992). McQuail recognizes that the concept of public interest is actively contested, in part because of the seeming impossibility of specifying the boundaries of 'the public.' He also notes the ways in which the concept has changed as the influence of the marketplace has transformed that which we understand as the public sphere. His overall framing of the concern with media performance reflects a mainstream functionalist emphasis on the contribution that media systems make to the operation of society as a whole. Our focus in this book is on the role that the mass media play in the reproduction of racism. This is a concern with the well-being of individuals as well as with the social systems in which they make their lives. Within the context of a functionalist model, we might want to assess the extent to which the media have shaped the ways we understand the differences we associate with race and ethnicity. We would want to know whether the media contributed to an understanding and an appreciation of difference. Such an assessment would of necessity require an examination of the extent to which the media reflected and represented the great variety among people and their circumstances. That assessment would also evaluate the ways in which the media helped to shape participation in the public sphere by informing individuals of their interests, including interests that are determined in part by their membership in racial and ethnic groups.

So far we have taken the position that the reproduction of racism takes place through a multidimensional structure of routinized relationships that are governed by well-structured systems of beliefs and opinions. Those beliefs and opinions are generated, integrated into cognitive structures, and reinforced by direct and indirect experiences. The mass media are the primary source of those indirect or mediated experiences; thus we cannot doubt that the media play an active role in the reproduction of racism.

While the media's role in this process of structuration is continuous, scholars and political actors in general tend to ignore its performance in the area of race until some crisis or critical event increases public awareness of the failure of media to perform its pacification function. That is, media have come to be seen to fail in their responsibility to provide an accurate representation of the lives, interests, and concerns of racial minorities most often when racial violence erupts onto the front pages of the nation's papers, and becomes the lead story on the evening news. In the United States, evidence of such a failure began to mount after a series of riots took place in the summer of 1967 (Kerner, 1968).

The Kerner Commission Report, named after its chairman, Otto Kerner, then governor of Illinois, included only a brief chapter on the role of the news media in the wake of the riots. Most of that chapter focused on the ways in which the media covered the disturbances, but the last two pages emphasized the more general failure of the press to cover the problems of the Black ghetto. In charging the press with a failure to communicate, the report suggested that:

> they have not communicated to the majority of their audience – which is white – a sense of the degradation, misery, and hopelessnes of living in the ghetto. They have not communicated to whites a feeling for the difficulties and frustrations of being a Negro in the United States. They have not shown understanding or appreciation of – and thus have not communicated – a sense of Negro culture, thought, or history. (Kerner, 1968, p. 210)

The Commission also saw as problematic the fact that the newspapers seemed not to be aware that a sizeable part of their audience also happened to be Black. As a result of this blind spot, the biased and incomplete image of African Americans that was being presented to Whites was likely to be perceived by Blacks as insensitive and indicative of an institution that was unworthy of its special position of trust. It seems that the American press had not taken to heart the recommendations offered by an earlier scholarly and professional assessment of the press that reflected a remarkably similar concern. The Commission on Freedom of the Press, known more popularly as the Hutchins Commission, identified five areas in which the press had *a social responsibility* to perform:

(1) providing a truthful, comprehensive, and intelligent account of the day's events in a context that gives them meaning;
(2) providing a forum for the exchange of comment and criticism;
(3) projecting a representative picture of the constituent groups in society;
(4) presenting and clarifying the goals and values of the society; and

(5) providing a full access to the day's intelligence (Commission of Freedom of the Press, 1947, pp. 20–1).

Some have argued that the Commission set goals which were impossible for it to meet if the press was also going to maintain its contemporary claims to journalistic objectivity (Udick, 1993). Perhaps the failure of the press to meet these social responsibilities should not have been a surprise, as the press was increasingly concerned with realizing a consistent profit. However, after finding that the press had failed to exercise the social responsibilities it had identified as its own, the Kerner Commission insisted that the nation's press, and the rest of the mass media, needed to move immediately toward integrating Blacks into its content, in part by integrating Blacks into its editorial staff (Kerner, 1968).

The other mass media – motion pictures, fictional television, and even popular music – have from time to time been the target of political and scholarly attention because of the belief that deviant or socially disfunctional behavior was being stimulated by its content. But, here, the causal models that predict and explain these impacts are far more complex, and the number of major initiatives has been small. As a result, at least in the United States, no broad-based, comprehensive media research project has had the study of race relations as its primary focus (Lowery and DeFleur, 1983).

Of course, there is some basis for treating representations in the news as different from representations in fictional entertainment media. As we will discuss in the next chapter, audiences bring different expectations and orientations to different media experiences. These expectations are believed to temper or modify the impact of such exposure. Representations in the news, documentary film, and historical drama, might at one level be expected to be more accurate than representations in media that have entertainment rather than information as their purpose. Bias or distortion in the news might therefore be seen as a more troublesome shortcoming than similiar forms of bias in recreational media.

Arguments in support of assigning a special performance requirement to the news media may also take note of the fact that there are far fewer outlets for news than there are outlets for entertaining fare. This suggests that the potential impact of representations in the news would be greater because not many people would be exposed on a regular basis to alternative representations of any particular event, or the complex of perspectives that shape its meaning. If biased representations within the news are relatively consistent across relatively long periods of time, far more people will have been exposed to common representations that are assumed to be fact rather than fiction.

We also recognize that consumers do not select media primarily for the advertising messages they contain. Indeed, consumers are turning increasingly to alternative media, or are making use of remote control devices to avoid commercial messages. Nevertheless, advertisements are media content and arguably have consequences for the structure of racialized beliefs that flow from repeated exposure to them.

This chapter will focus on two aspects of media content that media scholars have identified as especially important to its performance in the reproduction of racism: the accuracy of representation as it might relate to the reproduction of cultural values, and the accuracy of media's reflection of social reality as it might inform social policy. Whereas problems in the accuracy or completeness of representations of racial and ethnic groups and their relations with other members of society are assumed to have important consequences for the development of self-image and personal identity, communications scholars have also focused on the ways in which media bias threatens the ability of individuals, or society as a whole, to make informed choices within the marketplace, or within the public sphere. Both concerns should be addressed.

A fundamental assumption of the rational models underlying neo-classical economics and other contemporary theories of the competent goal-seeking agent is that individuals are guided in their decision making by models of social reality. These models provide a kind of confidence or 'ontological security' which is necessary for the performance of even routine tasks. The validity of these models is continually evaluated, in part through a process of stock taking or 'reflexive monitoring' (Giddens, 1984). As Giddens suggests, however, individual agency is limited, in part because this knowledge is always incomplete, and reflects biases in the information environment which mass media help to construct.

Individuals make use of and rely on the mass media for much of their reflexive monitoring of this environment, and in their assessment of the validity of personal and culturally privileged theories about the nature of the world. While the primary emphasis within the communication literature is on the use of the news media as the sources for surveillance and for interpretive assessment, Gerbner and others (1986) have argued that fictional media serve similar functions. Thus, fictional and non-fictional forms bear some responsibility for the social construction of the realities in which we pursue our day-to-day existence. Because of this, the performance of the mass media has to be evaluated in terms of the quality of its representation of the lives of people of color. Thus, a concern with media representation is a concern with its impact on, or consequences for, individuals, groups, and entire societies. This is a concern which is focused in large part on the ways in which communications affect the distribution of power. We believe that 'symbols (words and images) affect power as they affect expectations of power' (Lasswell *et al.*, 1949, p. 19), and as they affect assumptions about the legitimacy of power.

Blindspots, stigmas, and stereotypes

Media scholars have approached the study of media reflection and representation from a variety of perspectives, reflecting differences in ideology, purpose, and training. For some, the analysis of media content is guided by a theoretical interest in the relationship between characteristics of communicators, and the attributes of the content they produce. For others, the focus is on the potential impact that exposure or consumption to such representations are believed to produce. Whether the focus is on the production or the reception side of the media equation, a description of the content is required.

The criticism usually directed against the media is that the representations of racial and ethnic groups, as well as the relations between the races, are inaccurate, reflecting individual, institutional, and cultural biases toward subordinate groups. Although misrepresentation can take many forms, the primary outcome of these analyses informs a criticism of media bias – bias that results in a production system that oversupplies negative images of minority group members.

Within studies of news media performance in particular, scholars consistently find an institutional bias toward the production of 'bad news.' Such a slant all but guarantees that stories about racial minorities will emphasize the negative outcomes, the failures, and the misbehavior of members of minority ethnic and racial groups. Critical examination of journalistic traditions also reveals an emphasis on conflict, rather than cooperation, between racial and ethnic groups. Some of the more recent critiques extend this primary determination of bias by focusing on the *limited range* of character types and roles that tend to be assigned to minority characters portrayed in mainstream entertainment media (Shohat and Stam, 1994).

In general we see that the media are charged with continuing to rely upon racist stereotypes, emphasizing negative aspects of behavior, and suggesting deficiencies in morality and intelligence that stigmatize an entire population. At the same time the media are seen to ignore available evidence and examples of the highest levels of discipline, achievement, and commitment that have sustained these communities through centuries of oppression.

A substantial number of studies which examine media content out of concern for the representation of race make use of formal, quantitative content analysis. This technique, which is claimed to have originated within the field of communication, is defined formally as a 'research technique for making reliable and valid inferences from data to their context' (Krippendorff, 1989, p. 403). For our purposes, the operative word is *context*. In this definition context refers either to the circumstances surrounding production, or to those surrounding reception.

The standard empirical assumption that frequency, or placement, or emphasis reflects the *importance* assigned to some particular element or feature of content allows content analysts to use comparative statistics to support claims about relative importance. Krippendorff suggests that this emphasis on scientific objectivity and statistical significance, however, makes it less likely that formal, quantitative content analysis will help us understand the kinds of issues that are more likely to arise in the approach of literary, historical, or psychoanalytic studies (1989, p. 407). At the same time, the unique or idiosyncratic nature of such interpretive analyses raises concerns about the extent to which such 'readings' are likely to be shared by all, or even most, members of the audience.

Because content analysts generally focus their empirical lens on media texts, and not on the complex varieties of ways in which content is received and understood, claims made about the nature of these effects are always open to challenge. For example, the critical perspective of the Cultural Indicators Project (Gerbner, 1973; Gerbner *et al.*, 1979) associates the portrayal of patterns of victimization with a demonstration of White male power in society. Conservatives interpret those representations as an expression of sympathy for victims, and add that the perpetrators of such violence are nearly always punished. Further, they ask what the liberal interpretation would be if the reverse were the case. They ask:

> what if most prime-time violence were perpetrated by blacks and women on helpless white males? Would feminist and civil rights leaders welcome the change as politically progressive because it portrays their constituents as socially dominant? Or would they decry the negative portrayals of criminal blacks and aggressive women as a racist and sexist reinforcement of establishment thinking? (Lichter *et al.*, 1994, p. 421).

They suggest further that: 'In real life violent crimes are committed disproportionately by blacks, youths, and low-income groups. In prime time violent criminals are mainly wealthy white, mature adults, especially businessmen' (Lichter *et al.*, 1994, p. 418). Although their critical interpretation emphasizes different consequences, the analyses produced by the more progressive Cultural Indicators team actually point in the same direction. Utilizing a 'risk ratio' which compares demographic groups in terms of the imbalance between characters that are killed and characters that kill or are violent, the Cultural Indicators team concluded that women and young people, including young men, as well as non-Whites and the poor, were victimized relatively more often than they committed violent acts in the world of television (Gerbner *et al.*, 1979).

It is important to recognize that the racial characteristics of criminals in fictional television programs are the product of a complicated negotiation between artists and network officials who have been sensitized by periodic charges of racism. This has certainly been the case with regard to the presentation of African American males as criminals. As a result, producers have had to negotiate the introduction of Black criminals into scripts. They persisted because, from their perspective, it was highly unrealistic to make all the criminals White. Todd Gitlin tells the story of *Hill Street Blues*, an extremely popular television series which was located in a 'real' precinct in which the criminal element was 'almost 100 per cent black or Chicano.' The producers negotiated an accommodation with the 'standards and practices' folks in New York: 'they put a mixture of various ethnic types in the station, so that you had a counterbalance for the problems that we might be confronted with as broadcasters . . . saying that all of the bad guys are Chicanos or blacks'. The result was that the 'junkies encountered by Hill and Renko [detectives in the series] eventually were cast as one black, one white, one apparently Hispanic, and the fourth wholly unrecognizable; the one who pulls the trigger – seen only for a split second – is white' (Gitlin, 1985, pp. 286–7).

However the distribution of characters by race comes to be, it is difficult to sustain a claim that, at the manifest level, there is much uncertainty about what is available to be read, observed, or heard. The polysemic openness would have to come into play at the level of individual interpretation. Such interpretation must, of necessity, involve the complex of experiences and orientations that each member of the audience brings to each engagement with a communicative text. Our problem in assessing media performance is not so much that the televisual text is polysemic, but that the social theory that we need in order for us to link representation and consumption to social consciousness is so woefully underdeveloped. We will discuss some of these difficulties in greater detail in the next chapter.

Some studies make explicit comparisons between racial groups. When the representations of one group differ substantially from the representations of another, especially when the status and circumstances of the others is similar, a conclusion of racial bias seems justified. This analytical approach represents an advance over studies which merely identify and enumerate the use of different racial stereotypes. One study compared the representations of African American and White representatives to the United States Congress (Barber and Gandy, 1990). Nine major metropolitan newspapers were examined between 1979 and 1983 to determine how the White and Black politicians tended to be presented to the readers.

Informed by the literature on assessments of political competence, 12 different characteristics of political actors were used as the primary basis of comparison. In addition, an analysis of quotations attributed to the politicians was used to identify the subject areas in which the press treated the politician as being competent to speak. It was expected, and confirmed, that the press was more likely to quote African American politicians on local and racial matters, and less likely to quote them on congressional affairs. In addition to reporting the frequencies for each of their measures and noting the differences in the treatment of Blacks and Whites, Barber and Gandy (1990) also made use of a statistical technique called discriminant analysis to determine how well one might predict the race of a politician on the basis of the way he or she was treated in the press. More than 70 per cent of the politicians were correctly identified by race on the basis of the different ways that the press framed their stories. Among the more powerful predictors was the appearance of the politician's name in the headline, and in the inclusion of comments about the politician's leadership ability. On the basis of this analysis, Barber and Gandy (1990) concluded that the press engaged in discrimination in its coverage of Black elected officials.

On occasion, content analyses that examine structural relations make direct comparisons with other more 'objective' assessments of the social reality of minority group members. Such analyses might compare employment and other government statistics with the proportional representation of minority group members in news or television fiction. In one example of this kind of analysis, David Atkin and Marilyn Fife (1993–4) examined the influence of race and gender on the ways in which particular groups would be presented in local television news. They hypothesized that the recently improved status of White women would result in their being represented more accurately than African American men or women. On the basis of a content analysis of 27 hours of local news broadcast in the Detroit market, they concluded that race, by itself, did not determine the representation of particular groups. Contrary to their expectations, White females were the only group that was significantly *under*represented. Being male led to overrepresentation, without regard to race, although White males were the most overrepresented. An assessment of positive or negative framings of these subjects may have helped to explain why their findings did not support their initial hypotheses.

Other studies have examined the relationships between minority representations or *framing* in the media and particular structural features of the markets in which particular representations are most common. While Gandy (1996a) looked for and found significant differences between newspapers in their use of a discrimination frame that was associated with the proportion of African Americans in the newspaper market, Campbell (1995) was struck by the '*sameness* of the racial mythology' in local television news programs broadcast in 29 different American cities. The fact that Campbell's analysis relied upon an interpretive, rather than quantitative, content analysis may explain the apparent difference between the conclusions of these two studies.

Although, as we will discuss in the next chapter, the media are an important influence on our understanding of public issues, the understandings that the media help to create are quite often at variance with other evidence about the nature of reality. The media influence the salience, or the perceived importance, of particular social problems, but their coverage of those problems comes and goes in waves of emphasis which bear no direct relationship to actual changes in the status of those problems (Cook and Skogan, 1991; Funkhouser, 1973). The reasons for this departure are complex, involving the interests of the media as well as their bureaucratic sources (Gandy, 1982). It seems likely, for example, that the periodic crime waves that emerge in the press are largely a response by the press to public relations efforts by the police or politicians seeking to create an electoral issue (Fishman, 1980). In 1996, the press created a sense that there was a wave of racially motivated arson directed at Black churches. As with other such media-created crises, evidence to support claims of a dramatic increase in this particular racist crime was weak at best.

The press is intimately involved in the reproduction of racism. As van Dijk (1992) suggests, the news media may participate in the survival of racism by denying its existence. According to van Dijk, the voice of the press is especially shrill when the charge of racism is hurled in its direction: 'No newspaper, including (or especially) the more liberal ones, will accept even a moderate charge of being biased, while allegations of racism are rejected violently' (p. 103).

The press plays an active role in the denial of racism by joining in the counter-attack against those who actively oppose racism. In an analysis of what is referred to as 'the Honeyford affair' (a story involving the headmaster of a British school who had published articles in opposition to multiculturalism that many Asian parents found racist), van Dijk provides examples of the press coming to the defense of the headmaster. He was praised for his courage, the anti-racists were labelled 'hysterical', and the defense of multiculturalism was labelled anti-British (van Dijk, 1992, p. 104).

The traditional determination of newsworthiness that has been institutionalized within the modern commercial press is one which privileges the sensational (McManus, 1994). The O. J. Simpson story combined a sensational crime with the additional benefits of visible celebrity, flavored with the special tension of interracial sex (Hutchinson, 1996). Although few crime stories have all these attributes in anything approaching the magnitude of this story, crime is a reliable source of sensational copy. Underlying the attraction of crime stories is the notion of threat or risk. It is presumed that the audience has an interest in knowing about dangers in the environment. Yet, if the public depended upon the press to inform them accurately about the risks they faced, they would be ill served.

Both quantitative and the more qualitative approaches to an assessment of representation often identify a set of common stereotypes or idealizations that are expected to occur repeatedly in other programs or examples of a particular media form. These primary constructions or *exemplars* are often pointed to as evidence of the existence of a constraint on the variety or richness of likely portrayals of minorities. The ease with which coders, or critical observers, can identify or characterize a television or film character as an exemplar of an ideal type might stand as evidence of the commonsense reality of such a stereotype. There is room for us to expand our understanding of the nature of stereotypes so as to be able to explain the similarities and differences in the character types which are prominent in stories about African Americans, but are relatively rare in stories about Asians, Hispanics, or Native Americans.

Along these lines, there is also a need to understand how competing stereotypes change in their relative importance over time, or as the structural relationships between dominant and subordinate populations shift or are transformed by critical events. Studies of the images of the Native American are especially useful in this regard in revealing the tensions between the image of the 'savage' and the image of the 'noble red man,' and the ways these images began to change with the emergence of a community of independent Indian film-makers (Hilger, 1995; Weston, 1996).

Asian scholars argue that, unlike White ethnics, Asian Americans continue to be looked upon as foreign 'strangers' in their native land. Like Hispanics, Asian Americans complain that they have had few opportunities to succeed in television. The one significant exception to this conclusion is also a subject of controversy and concern. Television news directors have not only accepted, but appear almost to demand as a necessity, that their stations hire a female Asian anchorperson. Critics refer to this as the 'Connie Chung syndrome,' after the CBS news personality of the same name (Hamamoto, 1994, p. 245). The revealed preference for minority female anchors is interpreted by some as reflecting a desire by the White male establishment to meet diversity goals by having a minority female paired with a White male anchor, rather than the other way around. There is also the claim that Asian women are seen as exotic, but non-threatening, and therefore appealing to the mainstream White audience. Seen through the interpretive gaze of cultural studies we understand how this examplar is being constructed by the media establishment: 'Once subdued and wrested from her male defenders, the fantasy-ideal of the Asian woman can then take her rightful place at the side of the Euro-American conquerer as war bride, as mail-order wife, as whore, as TV news anchor' (Hamamoto, 1994, p. 246).

Scholars who have examined the comparative representation of minorities underscore the ideological nature of news coverage in particular. Hemant Shah and Michael Thornton (1994) remind us that racial ideology operates at an unconscious, 'taken-for-granted' level, and that these assumptions have been incorporated into journalistic routines. Elements of this racial ideology 'are woven into the news narrative with the tools of linguistic emphasis, which include positioning, placement, treatment, intensity and striking imagery.' Comparisons between minorities enables an important ideological function to be performed. 'Good' minorities can be held up as examples, and the evaluative impressions associated with them can be cognitively linked to other aspects of the ideological system which are also evaluated positively. Not surprisingly, Shah and Thornton's analysis reveals that mainstream magazines' coverage of Blacks and Latinos tended to suggest that:

> Latinos successfully assimilated while blacks stubbornly refuse. Not only does this depiction imply that assimilation into the white mainstream is natural and proper, it insinuates that any ethnic or racial minority can assimilate into the mainstream if they desire, and that a failure to assimilate is an indication of group or individual shortcomings, not systemic problems with society itself. (1994, p. 156)

Stability and change

We have argued that the best way to understand the nature of social structures is to examine the ways in which they change. The theory of structuration leads us to explore this change in terms of the ways change is produced by knowledgeable actors continuing to seek the realization of personal and collective goals. This kind of purposive action almost by necessity includes efforts to overcome the constraints of structure through oppositional efforts that, on occasion, involve acts of open resistance.

Changes in the representation of subordinate racial and ethnic groups reflect the impact of these oppositional moves. At the same time, changes in structure will also reflect the impact of efforts of dominant groups and institutions to regain control over relevant systems and relationships. Responses to resistance may be understood as accommodation, but they may also include strategic attempts at the co-option and incorporation of oppositional forms within the mainstream in ways that are least disruptive of a more central, or more widely linked, set of social relations. As we have suggested in the discussion of media markets, changes in representation may also reflect a response to an assessment of changes in the market, and the profits that might be gained by responding to minority tastes and sensitivities.

Janice Radway's investigation of the mass-market publishing industry reveals the ways in which media industries have become more and more sophisticated in avoiding the risks of the marketplace. These strategic moves have important consequences for the readers of the genres that an industry develops and then promotes (1984). While audience tastes undoubtedly play some role in the increased popularity of particular genres, Radway suggests that we have to consider the ways in which these genres come to be marketed, including the ways they are made to appear through packaging, and the ways in which audience demand is actually created through advertising.

One is able to make claims about structural causality only by examining the relations over time between relevant structural forms: structures in representation and ideology as well as the structures inherent in the shifting relations between supply and demand. These comparisons depend upon the kinds of temporal divisons or periodizations that identify those moments in history when changes are most reflective of underlying social processes.

Wilson and Gutiérrez (1995, pp. 152-8) suggest that five phases can be identified that characterize the ways in which each non-White group is treated by the mass media, as follows.

(1) *An exclusionary* phase, in which people of color are invisible or absent from mainstream media.
(2) A phase in which people of color are identified as a *threat* to the existing social order.
(3) This phase is followed by one in which fear and apprehension escalates into open *confrontation*. After the confrontration subsides, movement of the nation into a post-conflict status is required.
(4) A *stereotypical selection* phase, which is seen to be necessary as a means of neutralizing White anxiety and apprehension about these potential threats still within their midst. These representations reinforce historical stereotypes, but the images selected are more comforting in that they help to define the non-Whites as being 'in their place.'
(5) The final phase is identified as an ideal – multiracial coverage.

Wilson and Gutíerrez's stages reflect an earlier proposal by Cedric Clark which was described by Greenberg and Baptista-Fernandez (1980, p. 5). For Clark, the first stage was one of non-recognition, or invisibility, which is soon followed by a stage in which visibility occasions ridicule. A later stage features minority group members in regulatory roles, where they are shown upholding the virtues and standards of the mainstream society. Here, Clark was referring to roles as police officers or others responsible for maintaining law and order. If minority members also appear as criminals during this phase, the struggle between the 'cops and robbers' tends to be resolved in ways that help build the 'respect' that minority characters require before they finally achieve a more egalitarian and representative portrayal.

Mary Ann Weston (1996) organizes her analysis of the changes in the ways in which journalists framed their coverage of Native Americans into similar historical phases. However, Weston's approach reveals these changes in relation to important policy debates or dramatic events that marked critical junctures in the relations between Indians and White society. This view makes the phases seem less natural or universal because of her specification of the historical influences involved.

Her focus is on modern, twentieth-century representations, and some events and issues she uses as temporal markers include the 1930s debates about the Indian Reorganization Act, World War II and the unique role of

Indian soldiers as 'braves on the warpath,' debates about relocation that re-emerged in the 1950s, and the period of Indian activism in the late 1960s and early 1970s that included the takeover of Alcatraz Island, and the occupation of Wounded Knee, South Dakota. More recent debates over political correctness had emanations reaching into Native American consciousness that Weston saw in Indian criticism of the use of Indians as mascots and symbols for athletic teams. The period of Indian activism was marked by an identifiable shift in the still stereotypical representation of Native Americans in ways that reflected the development of considerable skill in manipulating the press by staging dramatic events. In the most recent period, Native American journalists joined the ranks of other minority journalists who could be counted upon to challenge and criticize mainstream representations.

Ed Guerrero has identified five cultural–political moments or 'junctures' that he uses to make sense of the racial images in Hollywood commercial film (1993). He identifies several forces that intersect in complex ways that ultimately determine the images of Blacks in commercial cinema:

(1) Hollywood's ideology of racial domination,
(2) Hollywood's fiscal strategies and shifting economic fortunes,
(3) the oppositional challenges of Black activists, including their efforts to increase Black participation and control over the production of Black cinematic images and, more complexly,
(4) the influence of particular historical moments that favor some forces and influences over others (p. 5).

Just as representations of African Americans and other minority group members change over time, the ways in which the issues which affect their lives are presented for consideration also change over time. These changes have consequences for the ways in which public policies come to be supported or opposed by political elites.

Gamson and Modigliani (1987) have examined the ways in which the media discourse surrounding affirmative action changed over time. Stephen Steinberg (1995) describes the egalitarian strategy as one which is in full retreat, being led by former liberal supporters. Gamson and Modigliani identify five critical events which provide the occasions for the 'sponsors' of particular frames to attempt to influence press coverage of the underlying issue. They begin with the introduction of 'The Philadelphia Plan' in September 1969, include the Supreme Court decision in the Bakke 'reverse discrimination' case in 1978, and end with the decision by the Supreme Court in the case of the Memphis firefighters in which the Court ruled that seniority should be considered first, even though its use would mean that Blacks would continue to be 'last hired and first fired.'

What the analysis by Gamson and Modigliani reveals is that, over this ten-year period, the fortunes of particular frames that would affect the availability of resources for making sense of the issue of affirmative action changed dramatically. In their analysis of television news, the 'package' of frames they identified as 'delicate balance,' because of the way in which it expressed the necessity of assisting Blacks without harming Whites, all but disappeared by 1984. In its place was an oppositional package they called 'no preferential treatment.'

Their analysis of news magazines and political cartoons did not identify similarly strong shifts in dominant conceptual frames, although their analysis of editorial columns also reflected the shift between delicate balance and no preferential treatment frames. In discussing those forces which help to determine the life of particular issue frames, Gamson and Modigliani suggest that these changes in culture are the 'product of enterprise.' Issues have 'sponsors' who make use of professional specialists whose duty it is to influence media practitioners (Gandy, 1982). The failed life of the 'delicate balance' frame is explained in part by the fact that it needed active sponsors (Gamson and Modigliani, 1987, p. 165). The success of 'no preferential treatment' was attributed to the active promotion by a neoconservative network that included authors, columnists, research institutes, and well-funded organizations.

The success of the 'reverse discrimination' frame was not explained entirely by the existence of powerful and well-financed sponsors. 'It met the needs of working journalists for balance and dramatic form . . . it had strong positive resonances with larger cultural themes of self-reliance and individualism, and used antiracist and equality symbolism to neutralize the favorable resonances of its major competitor' (p. 170).

The patterns of stability and change differ within and between media, reflecting in part the complex of structural relations between producers, audiences, financiers, critics, government regulators, and shifts in the larger cultural environment.

News media

There are important differences between media in terms of the ways in which the content of their news items is ordered. The *discursive* structure of television news differs from that common to newspapers, and both differ from the *narrative* structures that are common to prime-time television fiction or theatrical film. Teun van Dijk (1991) has provided consistent leadership in suggesting how we ought to go about understanding the role of the press in the reproduction of racism. His approach to discourse analysis shares a great deal in common with formal content analyses of media. Informed by his detailed analysis of the press, van Dijk recommends that we pay special attention to the ways in which headlines are used to frame stories about race. Headlines are important for both cognitive and ideological reasons. Not only do headlines 'prime' readers in ways that influence their processing of stories, but they are also influential in determining which stories are even read.

Headlines are seen to play an ideological role when a journalist or, more likely, an editor assigns a headline which does not match the primary focus of the story. The ability of the headline to either 'promote' or to 'downgrade' the central issues of the stories allows an editor to influence the ways in which readers will process and understand stories. In an analysis of the ways in which major American papers covered a wire service story about discrimination in mortgage markets, Goshorn and Gandy (1995) discovered that only one newspaper used a headline that emphasized the fact that Whites were more likely to be granted mortgages than Blacks, despite the fact that nearly a quarter of the lead paragraphs actually featured that aspect of the story. This was a clear example of demoting the lead.

Detailed analysis of headlines can also provide an assessment of an editor's orientation to the problem of race, in that the use of quotation marks around terms like racist or racism indicates 'journalistic distance or scepticism' (van Dijk, 1991, p. 57). Analysis of the use of quotes around particular words may also serve as an indication of the movement of the concept into common practice or acceptance. For example, in the coverage of the debate over affirmative action at the University of California Berkeley campus, the San Francisco *Chronicle* tended to put the term 'bias' in quotes as a reflection of editorial doubt about the charges of discrimination being made by Asian activists. During the continuing life of the controversy, however, the quotes were eventually removed (Takagi, 1992, p. 43).

Structural analysis of units as small as the headline can also reveal something about the ways in which racial perspectives are being shaped. The positioning of actors within the headline is telling. When minorities are mentioned first, they are more often perpetrators or agents of negative action. Although van Dijk suggests that Blacks are rarely represented as victims, Gandy's (1996a) analysis of stories about social risk found that headlines were far more likely to frame stories in terms of Black victimization or loss than about White success whenever racial disparity in outcomes was part of the story.

An important aspect of discourse analysis identified by van Dijk is a characterization of the newspaper's use of particular sources, and the extent to which those sources are granted the right to speak, as when a journalist quotes them directly. He suggests that 'quotations allow the insertion of subjective interpretations, explanations, or opinions about current news events without breaking the ideological rule that requires the separation of facts from opinions' (van Dijk, 1991, p. 152). For the journalist, the quote becomes a *fact* in itself. Of course, analysis of the press reveals that not all sources have access to the readers, and not even all those identified by name are given the opportunity to speak. Minority group members are quoted less often and less extensively. When they do get to speak, their time on the stage is brief, and they are usually 'allowed' only to speak as victims, rather than as critics or accusers.

The analysis of different newspapers often reveals a striking similarity in the ways in which stories are framed, issues are explored, and explanations are put forth. 'This suggests that a very powerful ideology is at work, a unifying framework that is routinely applied when understanding and evaluating ethnic affairs' (van Dijk, 1991, p. 201). At same time, van Dijk's analysis reveals important differences in the ways that conservative and more liberal elite newspapers treat racial concerns. He also found differences between nations, in that the blatant racism he found in some of the right-wing newspapers in the UK would be extremely difficult to find in the United States, the Netherlands, or in Scandinavian papers. However, van Dijk was explicit in stating that the differences he observed were not fundamental, but were differences in degree that tend to show up in the rhetorical styles that different papers seem to prefer (p. 249).

Colleen Roach (1993) has provided an analysis of the success and failure of the movement to establish a New World Information and Communication Order (NWICO) with the assistance of the United Nations (UN) and its activist subunit, the United Nations Educational, Scientific, and Cultural Organization (UNESCO). Guided by a critical theory that linked economic and cultural domination, complaints from the Third World tended to focus on the unidirectional flows of news, television, advertising, and communication technology from the industrialized countries of the West. UNESCO provided financial support and institutional legitimacy for a small but steady stream of content analyses that criticized the ways in which Third World nations were being represented in the Western press.

UNESCO also supported a series of studies of media performance with regard to race and ethnicity that began with the publication of *Race as News* in 1974. *Ethnicity and the Media* was published in 1977, and it examined the ways in which race was covered in the British provincial press and the treatment of Punjabis in the Canadian press, as well as an assessment of the role of the press in covering the conflict in Northern Ireland.

Race as News made use of formal content analysis, but also sought to understand the structural influences that explained the structures of representation. It was argued that the structure of news values, reflecting in part the racial makeup of the primary audience, meant that minority groups would have to rely upon 'negative behavior' in order to attract the attention of the press. The fact that news media were also staffed by White personnel added to the tendency of the press to define news worthiness from the perspectives of Whites. The British press was criticized for its failure to examine the underlying basis for racial conflict, and part of the explanation for this failure was the press's reliance on a 'conflict framework' that resulted in the identification of scapegoats, rather than deeper structural causes (Halloran, 1977). That is, the press tended to ignore the realities of life for Black Britons until those realities came to be understood as a threat to the interests of the White majority. Those stories would be organized within a conflict frame through which Blacks could only be seen as at fault.

'Race in the provincial press' was described by Halloran (1977) as a follow-up to an earlier study of the British news media, but this study had its focus on the provincial rather than the national press. This was justified by the belief that the provincial press had a different commitment to its community and its social responsibility that deserved to be examined. Analysis of this press revealed striking parallels to the kinds of criticisms that had been mounted against the American press. The coverage of race was routinized. It was generally limited to the coverage of crimes involving violence or, on occasion, human interest stories that relied upon familiar but negative stereotypes of racial minorities. The dominant frame in coverage was a *problem* frame. Black immigrants were linked with social problems, at the same time as serious problems between Blacks and the police were all but ignored.

The conclusions arrived at suggest that, even though there were subtle differences between provincial and national media approaches to the question of race, both institutions handle race-related material in ways that 'serves both to perpetuate negative perceptions of blacks and to define the situation as one of inter-group conflict' (Halloran, 1977, p. 15). Structures of meaning were seen to govern the day-to-day routines of news production, and, despite the apparent awareness of the inherent biases in these structures, these journalists still managed to produce a stereotypical and negative representation of Blacks and other immigrants.

In 1986, UNESCO published a supplement to these two reports which focused on the racial unrest and concern linked to a period of increased immigration into the United Kingdom (Jones, 1986). The press was charged with complicity for its role in providing Enoch Powell with the means to amplify his racist sentiments, and to distribute his calls for Black repatriation to all who would hear it. The British press was charged more generally with two shortcomings: (1) treating race and color *difference* as news, which was seen by some as reinforcing stereotypes, and (2) maintaining the 'neutrality' that a gatekeeper role implied. This stance by the press was seen as inexcusable because 'neutrality in a biased situation feeds bias' (Jones, 1986, p. 5). Charles Husband's assessment of the media's performance charged the press with making it difficult for Blacks to feel at home in the UK: 'A continuous assumption implicit in much of the news programming is that in various ways you and your kind are an unwanted burden, a black parasite on a white society' (Jones, 1986, p. 6).

Coverage of conflict

Within news coverage, the coverage of racial conflict deserves special emphasis. This is so in part because conflict is often unexpected, and represents a departure from the routine. In such cases, journalists are more likely to rely upon a readily available framework of stereotypes and ideologically structured interpretations that oversimplify and distort both the circumstance and the participants.

Carolyn Martindale's study of news media coverage of African Americans was pursued in part as an assessment of the extent to which the press had taken the charge by the Kerner Commission to heart (Martindale, 1986). You will recall that the Kerner Commission was brought into being in response to a violent explosion of Black anger, and a concern about the ways in which the press had covered the riots that sprang up around the country. Analysis of the ways in which the press covered such stories after that time might provide a basis for assessing whether any lessons had been learned, or whether the employment of more African Americans had influenced the coverage of urban unrest.

The riots which erupted in Los Angeles in 1992, following the acquittal of the police officers accused of beating a motorist named Rodney King, have received more scholarly attention than any of the previous disturbances in the United States (Ramaprasad, 1996). The riots were covered as a racial story, as evidenced by the consistent reference to the race of the participants. By 1992, Los Angeles, which was the site for this violent response to injustice, was a very different city from the one in which the Black ghetto of Watts erupted in 1965. Los Angeles had become even more of a city of immigrants. By 1990, more than 40 per cent of the residents of the city had been born outside the United States, and nearly half spoke a language other than English at home. Approximately 35 per cent were speaking Spanish.

Reflecting the constraints of a mainstream analytical model that privileges comparisons, Ramaprasad (1996) provides a detailed description of some 473 stories published in four major American papers, and then compares the coverage in the *New York Times* to that in the *Los Angeles Times*, the *Chicago Tribune*, and the *Atlanta Constitution*. Not surprisingly, proximity as a traditional determinant of news value resulted in greater coverage in the Los Angeles paper. Another analysis of the *LA Times* coverage indicated that the local paper published no fewer than 21 and as many as 78 riot stories *each day* during the height of the media's attention cycle (Atwater and Weerakkody, 1994).

Overall, the papers did not devote much space to an analysis of the causes of the riots. 'The individual's behavior is reported as a public safety threat, with a focus in coverage on law enforcement rather than on the behavior as a symptom of a problem' (Ramaprasad, 1996, p. 92). The relative absence of interpretive analysis, and the prevalence of factual episodes that identify individuals and link them to the actions they have taken, tends to privilege the assignment of individual responsibility or blame, and tends to ignore the responsibility of particular institutions, or the society at large (Iyengar, 1991).

Other observers took issue with the accuracy of the frames that journalists relied upon to bring the audience into the story. The media tended to present the disturbance as a *Black* race riot, not unlike the Watts riot in 1965. This framing, and the subsequent coverage, ignored the fact that participants as well as victims were not only African Americans, but Anglos, Asians, and Latinos (Abelmann and Lie, 1995). A multiethnic frame did not, however, perform very much better than the dominant frame in suggesting systemic or institutional causes of the riot:

> The interethnic conflict frame leads to explanations, which, in keeping with the prior reifications of each group, locates the conflict's cause in each group's characteristics. Rather than focusing on the broader political economic context, the presumed interethnic conflict pits one homogenized group against another. (Abelmann and Lie, 1995, p. 160)

A Mexican American paper, *La Prensa* of San Diego, was explicit in charging African Americans with victimizing both Latinos and Asians (Miles, 1992, p. 51). Rather than emphasizing group characteristics, it offered a *sociological* explanation. In *La Prensa*'s opinion, Blacks saw themselves being replaced in the pecking order by Koreans, and they also feared the loss of what little political power they had managed to accumulate over the years to Latinos.

Erna Smith's analysis (1994) suggests that the primary focus of television news was on Black–White relations. A smaller proportion of stories emphasized the relations between Blacks and Koreans but, in general, television coverage tended to downplay the involvement of Latinos. The mismatch between the representation and the reality was quite dramatic in this regard. There was also a tendency for the images selected to represent the violence in the streets of Los Angeles as featuring Blacks most prominently. Smith claims that 'almost all of the most violent rioters on television news, such as those shown assaulting people and burning property were African Americans, and blacks comprised the majority of people shown looting' (p. 7). Arrest records tell a strikingly different story of a riot in which most of the people arrested for rioting were Latinos (Miles, 1992).

Smith's analysis suggests a difference between newspaper and television coverage, as well as some unexpected differences between local and national stories. Whereas Ramaprasad (1996) found only the most minimal attention being paid to the causes of the riots, Smith found causal themes in more than half of the broadcast stories. However, the emphasis on individual blame and responsibility still tended to dominate. Most of the blame was placed on rioters who were characterized as 'lawless, immoral, and greedy people' (Smith, 1994, p. 9). Smith did find that the network news stories differed from local coverage, in that networks tended to focus a bit more on underlying social causes, and less on individual lawlessness. The networks also tended to focus on members of minority groups as victims, while the local stations tended to focus on them as criminals. Perhaps, for some of the structural reasons we have discussed in the previous chapter, the networks were able to come closer to the journalistic ideal of objective, balanced coverage. The local stations, which were in direct competition for ratings and revenue (McManus, 1994), tended toward the more sensational coverage, which was likely to generate troublesome consequences for race relations in Los Angeles.

The riots that erupted in several British cities in 1985 were examined by van Dijk (1991). Here too, the emphasis was on the criminal behavior of Black inner-city youth, and there was avoidance of analyses that would point toward inequality or frustration as a justifiable basis for the rage being displayed by these youngsters.

Not all interracial conflict results in violence. Some analyses of the press have described the ways in which the press has been a willing participant in the political, but non-violent, struggle between racial camps, in what might be seen as a 'purification ritual.' James Ettema (1990) tells the story of a 'ritual cleansing' in Chicago that took place in the spring of 1988. This case exemplifies what functionalists might identify as a necessary and ultimately highly valued role of the press. Steve Cokely, an aide to the acting mayor of the city, had been accused of making anti-Semitic remarks to Black Nationalist audiences. After describing the history of this racially charged 'social drama,' Ettema describes the role of the press as much more than the 'transmission of mythic tales to mass audiences.' In his view, 'the progression of political purification rituals was, at the same time, a progression of story frames' which ultimately resulted in 'the production of political reality' – the removal of an irritant to the well-being of core interests in the Chicago community. The failure of acting mayor Eugene Sawyer to maintain the liberal coalition between Blacks and Jews that had elected Harold Washington resulted in the eventual election of Richard Daley, and the end of a brief 'progressive' era in Chicago politics.

Tense relations between Whites and the Maoris of New Zealand also served to stimulate a move to evaluate the performance of the press in the coverage of racial and ethnic concerns (Spoonley and Hirsh, 1990). While the media organizations in New Zealand have begun to modify the ways in which the Maoris are covered in the news, in part by increasing the number of Maori professionals involved in news production, those professionals are still challenged by 'the way their language is spoken and written, and the continual portrayal of their people as victims, bludgers, no-hopers and perpetrators of violence by their peers' (Webber, 1990, p. 147). The emphasis on crime or violence among the Maoris reflects the influence of news-gathering routines, and ethnocentric standards of newsworthiness. Covering the Maori world is considered a low status assignment unless the story is about a major scandal. The majority of community events (*hui*) which different Maori groups schedule during the year tend to be ignored by the news media.

Mary Ann Weston's study of the portrayal of Native American Indians in the news (1996) provides an example of the ways in which stereotypes continue to function within the news even though the social status of the subject groups, as well as the general sensitivity of the population, has changed. Weston underscores the importance of journalistic practices which produce a pattern of representations which are not objectively false or grossly inaccurate, but nevertheless seem likely to reinforce stereotypical views. Weston's analysis also revealed important differences between coverage in national and local press. Consistent with theories of community pluralism (Donohue *et al.*, 1985), and related theories of the journalistic response to power (Donohue *et al.*, 1972), she found that stories which were published in cities further from the actual incidents involving conflict with Native Americans tended to rely on traditional stereotypes (Weston, 1996, p. 122).

Weston's analysis of coverage of Indian activism in the 1960s and 1970s raises a concern to which we must return. She suggested that the Indians had become relatively skilled in manipulating the press by staging events, such as the takeover of the former prison at Alcatraz. This success in controlling their representation became the basis for a further criticism of the press by Weston, because the journalists apparently failed to exercise their responsibility to question and challenge their sources. In her view the resultant 'positive images of Native Americans seemed a newer version of the noble savage' (Weston, 1996, p. 148).

Poverty and race

The extent to which the public is willing to support public policies designed to eliminate the influence of racism reflects in part the extent to which they believe that the economic disparity within society is both excessive and is the result of unlawful or immoral discrimination. That is, media representations of poverty may help to frame it as a problem only for members of minority groups and, further, news coverage may suggest that most of those in poverty are undeserving of a helping hand.

In their study of press coverage of issues surrounding a massive reduction in public services in England in 1976, Golding and Middleton (1982) suggest that the press responded to a need for an explanation of the economic crises facing the British government. The response of the press involved their return to familiar stereotypical images and constructions of the poor that had functioned ideologically so well in the past. They noted that the press made good use of cartoons as an especially efficient way of recalling and activating dormant but accessible stereotypes. Among the most important uses of these stereotypes was to distinguish between the 'deserving and undeserving poor' (p. 65). Golding's and Middleton's analysis revealed that over the latter half of the 1970s this distinction tended to make use of racialized images of the 'deviant superscrounger' who was taking advantage of the welfare system: 'More commonly, scrounger stories involving ethnic minorities are couched in "adjectival racism" – the gratuitous use of ethnic labels when irrelevant to a story – in the routine of local fraud and abuse stories' (p. 93). They conclude that 'While blaming the victim remains the cornerstone of our conceptions of poverty, the grinding and enduring misery of the poor is unlikely to evoke other than contempt, malign distrust or a corrosive pity' (p. 244).

Recently, an analysis of news media in the United States (Gilens, 1996) examined the media construction of race and poverty between 1988 and 1992, and produced evidence of an assessment of poverty that may have helped to accelerate the call for welfare reform. Gilens noted that public opinion surveys revealed that the American public tends to substantially overestimate the proportion of Blacks among the nation's poor. He argued that 'the public's exaggerated association of race and poverty not only reflects and perpetuates negative racial stereotypes but it also increases white American's opposition to welfare' (p. 517). Gilens' extensive analysis of stories about poverty in three leading news magazines included both text and photographic images. A 10 per cent sample of televised news stories about poverty was also subject to analysis.

The analysis of news magazines found a dramatic overrepresentation of African Americans in stories about poverty. There were twice as many pictures of African Americans than would have been predicted from objective statistics about the racial character of poverty. Arguing that the public is more sympathetic toward the elderly poor, and finding that the elderly poor were 'virtually invisible among the magazine poor' (p. 522) and, further, that Blacks are underrepresented among the elderly poor that do appear, leads Gilens to conclude that the image of African American poverty is doubly biased. The concentration of Blacks among the 'undeserving' poor is also reinforced by an underrepresentation of Blacks among the working poor. Similar patterns were observed in his analysis of the television news stories. Gilens interprets the consistent, multidimensional pattern of misrepresentation of African Americans as evidence of the 'operation of a consistent prejudice' (1996, p. 536).

The cause célèbre

The trial of O. J. Simpson and the beating of Rodney King require special attention because they brought an unusual amount of attention to the issue of racism in the United States. In this way, the 'media event' is akin to a blockbuster film in terms of its reach or its cumulative impact on different members of a media audience. John Fiske (1996) suggests that

> O. J. Simpson, Rodney King, Clarence Thomas, Willie Horton, Mike Tyson [and] Marion Barry are all different people, but they are all resonant media figures of the 1990s because they are all Black men whose mediated racial identity was sexualized, whose masculinity was racialized, and who were all, whether found guilty or not, criminalized . . . they figure as embodiments of the white fascination with and terror of the Black male and his embodiment of a racial-sexual threat to white law and order. (p. xv)

Fiske claims that the 'media coverage of the O. J. Simpson case was rarely overtly racist, but in a society as deeply if covertly racist as this one, it did not need to be for the whole affair to widen the divide between the races' (p. xxvii).

The criminal trial of O. J. Simpson is widely discussed as the 'trial of the century.' However, the meaning of that trial in the context of a continuing discourse on race has to be examined in the light of the racial violence that followed the first verdict in the trial of police officers charged with beating Rodney King. Although the trial was a news event, its impact on the media system spread far beyond those boundaries, generating scores of books claiming to offer an insider's perspective on some aspect of the case and the trial.

Press coverage of Simpson's trial also heightens the contradictions between a massive commercialization of the Black athlete and the risks that advertisers take in choosing a representative whose identity is defined in racial terms (Hunt, 1997). Tiger Woods' popularity reportedly surpassed that of basketball superstar Michael Jordan after his capture of the Masters golf tournament. A five-year contract to make this youngster the spokesman of American Express's financial management services suggests not only a desire to derive the benefits of global visibility, but a blindness to the downside risks that come with being Black in America. Black superstars are 'not exempt from racial stereotypes. One misstep can turn the cheers into jeers' (Hutchinson, 1996, p. 129).

In addition to refocusing public awareness of the substantial ideological divide between Whites and Blacks in the United States that had been suggested by Hacker (1992), the trial of O. J. Simpson underscored the ways in which sponsors of competing racial frames might struggle to dominate editorial representation of the issues at hand. The characterization of Simpson's lawyers' efforts to remind the court, the jurors, and the general public of the role that racism continues to play in the administration of justice as 'playing the race card' suggests that a dominant and preferred reading of the defense's strategic move was the perspective of the White majority. Such a framing evokes a game theoretic assumption that 'any gain by African Americans – real or imagined – is considered to be a loss by whites' (Higginbotham *et al.*, 1997, p. 33).

The coverage of the Simpson trial also occasions an analysis of the Black press and a comparison of the mainstream with the alternative press (Shipp, 1994). Much of the early coverage of the case in the Black press was marked by avoidance of the question of Simpson's guilt or innocence. This absence is seen as consistent with a tradition of emphasis on the positive features of Black celebrity. There is a tendency in this press to avoid the coverage of wrongdoing by Black elected officials that is so common in the mainstream press. Coverage in the Black press may also explain the increasing divergence between White and Black assessments of Simpson's innocence from the time of his arraignment to the announcement of the verdict.

The trial of heavyweight champion boxer Mike Tyson also generated an extensive amount of press coverage and thereby attracted the attention of media scholars. Even though he examined more than 500 news items, Lule (1995) did not produce the kind of numerical or statistical analysis common to traditional content analyses. Instead, Lule sought to 'demonstrate that the reporting on the Tyson trial did invoke a larger drama around the boxer, a drama indeed structured by demeaning and racist cultural archetypes' (p. 178). The archetypical character of this press coverage was most clear in the consistency with which stories relied upon one of two primary stereotypical portraits. Tyson was 'either a crude, sex-obsessed, violent savage who could barely control his animal instincts or he was a victim of terrible social circumstances' (p. 181). Lule suggests that both these portraits were demeaning.

Agreeing with Stuart Hall (1982, p. 88) that 'ideological distortions do not occur "at the level of the conscious intentions and biases of the broadcasters"' (Lule, 1995, p. 190), Lule also suggests that such clearly racist stereotypes may continue to be reproduced by the press because they are 'embedded in the narrative conventions and journalistic canon' which is instilled during academic and on-the-job training. It is not that journalists are necessarily racists, but merely that they are journalists doing the jobs that they have been selected, trained, and socialized to perform.

Film and television fiction

Although the news and theatrical films are consumed for different purposes, and as a result these media are assumed to differ in their social role, the criticism of their social performance is quite similar. One feature of scholarly criticism of minority representation is the observed tendency of film producers to rely on readily available stereotypes of identifiable racial or ethnic groups. As we have suggested, the use of stereotypes is readily understood as an economically rational production decision. Stereotypes are easy to capture on film, as most actors can readily call the more familiar images to mind and then use them to guide their own performance. Stereotypes are also readily processed by audiences. The unusual or even counter-stereotypical representation, on the other hand, is distracting, in part because it may take more mental effort to process than the more familiar and 'contextually appropriate' stereotyped behaviors.

It is the importance of stereotypes to the experience of reception that explains the commercial success of some films and the failure of others. Some observers suggest, following this logic to its conclusion, that the representations of racial and ethnic groups in very popular films can be taken as quite reliable indicators of the beliefs and orientations that the majority of the movie-going public actually holds (Woll and Miller, 1987, p. 5). Considering the fact that members of the minority groups who are portrayed in this way are actually overrepresented among the audience for these films, there is an important contradiction that we ought to address. We will do so in the next chapter.

Because of the functional utility of stereotypes, it is fairly easy to call to mind those stereotypes which are consistently used to represent racially typed characters. Even though it is rarely the focus of critical discussion, there are readily identifiable stereotypes that apply to generic Whites, or 'Anglos', as well as ethnic Whites (Davis, 1996). At the same time, some ethnic groups are not the beneficiaries or victims of stereotypical representations because the cues we use for making ethnic assignments are not so well drawn.

There is, as has been noted, some difficulty with distinguishing the precise ethnicity of the many groups that are referred to as Hispanic or Latin. Perhaps because Mexican Americans are the largest of the Hispanic groups in the United States, theirs is the image which has been most prominent in film and television representations of Latinos. Berg (1990) claims that there are very few non-stereotypical portrayals of Hispanics in the Hollywood film. He offers us six basic Hispanic stereotypes that are assumed to indicate Mexicans, rather than Cubans, or Puerto Ricans, or other Latinos:

(1) *El Bandido*, or the Mexican Bandit, is typically presented as shifty, treacherous and dishonest. He is 'driven to satisfy base cravings . . . and routinely employs vicious and illegal means to obtain them' (p. 294).

(2) The *Halfbreed Harlot* is 'a slave to her passions . . . she is a prostitute because she likes the work, not because social or economic forces have shaped her life' (p. 295).

(3) The *Male Buffoon* is, in one sense, a foil for the bandit . . . Berg suggests that the 'characteristics that are threatening in the Bandit are made targets of ridicule' in the Buffoon (p. 295).

(4) In a similar way, the *Female Clown* is used to temper the threatening sexuality of the Harlot. Berg identifies Carmen Miranda as an exemplar of this stereotype.

(5) He suggests that we owe the stereotype of the *Latin Lover* to Rudolph Valentino, an Italian immigrant to the United States who exuded a kind of suave, sensual, and tender but dangerous sexuality.

(6) The last of the primary stereotypes identified by Berg is the *Dark Lady* – that 'mysterious, virginal, inscrutable, aristocratic – and alluring' personality (p. 296). Being just out of reach is what Berg suggests is the basis of Anglo fascination with this particular stereotyped character. For him, the best example of this type was Dolores Del Rio.

Berg suggests that these primary and some other secondary stereotypes have really not changed over the decades in which Hispanic characters have appeared in Hollywood films. What little change he finds in these representations is associated with an increase in Hispanic film-makers, and perhaps more importantly, a growing recognition by Hollywood that there is a substantial Latino audience that spends considerably more on movie going than the general population (Chávez, 1996).

Donald Bogle (1974) identifies five stereotypes of African Americans that were prominent from the very earliest attempts to demonstrate American film artistry. Although he does not claim that these very same stereotypes remained dominant throughout the history of the industry in the United States, other scholars readily find his Tom, Coon, Tragic Mulatto, Mammy, and Brutal Buck in the filmic portrayals of African Americans in every decade.

The mid 1960s have been identified as a critical moment during which dramatic changes took place in the portrayal of racial and ethnic minorities in television. The situation comedy as the primary vehicle for delivering ethnic humor to the mass audience was not always in great demand within the broadcast industry.

Two programs which emphasized racial or ethnic subjects failed to survive their transition from radio to family television. The first, *Amos and Andy*, featured portrayals of African Americans that the NAACP summarized as being stereotypically 'inferior, lazy, dumb, and dishonest.' The second was *Life with Luigi*. This was a program that Italian Americans opposed for presenting similarly offensive portrayals. Only *I Remember Mama* survived for a time, perhaps because the Norwegian immigrants who were featured did not represent a sufficiently threatening economic or political challenge to the sponsors of the show. For more than a decade, American television turned away from ethnic humor as an audience building resource (Lichter *et al.*, 1994). The one notable exception was Desi Arnaz, who played Ricki Ricardo in the very popular series *I Love Lucy*, that he produced with his wife, Lucille Ball.

By 1965, however, the proportion of Black television stars had increased dramatically, with characters appearing in a host of genres beyond situation comedy. The increase of Black characters in a broad range of roles was accompanied by a number of story lines that engaged social issues linked to race. However, the level of engagement of issues of assimilation and discrimination was largely unsatisfactory.

> The message is that everyone, regardless of race, creed, or color, deserves an equal chance at the good things in America. With a little understanding and tolerance, all groups can get along and even flourish in American society. Bigotry and intolerance still exist but can be overcome when people learn more about each other. (Lichter *et al.*, 1994, p. 356)

In an example from the popular *Sanford and Son* series produced by Normal Lear, the young son, Lamont, flirts with, and then ultimately rejects, identification with his African heritage. The accommodation the show recommends through Lamont's struggle is that 'traditional ways are fine, but they just don't fit into modern America. He agrees with his father that they are more American than African' (Lichter *et al.*, 1994, p. 358). In his analysis of the 1984–85 television season, Gray suggests that the programs that featured Blacks prominently were all 'predominantly assimilationist in tone and texture' (1986, p. 237).

At the same time that they were presenting a message of interracial and intercultural accommodation, American television series dramatically increased the number of episodes in which interracial personal relations were featured. These relationships were nearly always free of conflict, and were only occasionally represented as problematic. The message seemed to be that 'people of every creed and color naturally get along together, aside from the odd burst of mindless bigotry or misplaced nationalism' (Lichter *et al.*, 1994, pp. 362–3).

In 1977, the US Civil Rights Commission published a landmark analysis of the ways in which women and minorities were represented on television. This report, entitled *Window Dressing on the Set* (Franzwa, 1977), was published in part as a challenge to the Federal Communications Commission (FCC) and the ways in which its regulation of broadcasting had failed to ensure accurate representation of minorities. Reflecting an already widespread official preference for structural rather than content regulation, the Civil Rights Commission assumed that representations would improve if and when women and minorities were hired in key decision making positions within the industry. Derived from an analysis of prime-time and Saturday television broadcasts between 1969 and 1974 that had been produced as a component of the Cultural Indicators Project (Gerbner, 1973), this report set the standard for the analysis of the demographics of television. It also included an analysis of a composite week of news programs broadcast by the three national networks, but this analysis was limited to the demographics of 'newsmakers.'

The analysis of prime-time television included occupational roles among the demographic indices that compared White with non-White television characters. Because of the focus of the Cultural Indicators Project on the portrayal of violence as a symbolic resource for demonstrating the cultural rules of the road, the report took due note of the race and gender of those who were violent and those who were victims.

While many critical analyses had focused on the stereotypical representations of minorities in situation comedies, this report emphasized the roles that minorities played in action adventure series. Nearly half of all non-White characters were in this sort of program, thus the *symbolic function* of television violence could be performed with regard to Whites and non-Whites as well. The analysis revealed that non-White males killed more frequently than they were killed, and non-White females were killed far more often than they killed (Franzwa, 1977, p. 37). Apparently the image of the violent Black male was already coming into sharp focus during this time.

Concern about the ways in which Black family life was being presented on television led Greenberg and Neuendorf (1980) to study the ways in which family interactions were portrayed. Of 19 Black families portrayed during the sample period, more than half were headed by single parents, and the traditional nuclear family was exceedingly rare. Only 25 per cent of the White families portrayed were headed by single parents. During this period when Black families were being represented by *Good Times*, *Sanford and Son*, and *That's my Mama*, sons rather than daughters were the most active initiators of relations between family members. In the White families, the husbands and wives were the most active characters.

Overall, during the period of the 1970s, Black males were the most active characters, and they interacted more often with other Black males. Because they saw their scholarly role as being limited to providing descriptions, Greenberg and Neuendorf made no claims about the consequences that might flow from such representations, nor did they assess whether the television representations differed from the reality of Black family life. It is worth noting, however, that African Americans fared much better than Hispanics during the 'stereotypical selection' phase that Wilson and Gutíerrez (1995) identified. An analysis of prime-time television between 1975 and 1978 identified only 53 characters out of some 3,500 characters who could be characterized as Hispanic (Greenberg and Baptista-Fernandez, 1980). The few Hispanic characters that appeared during the early years of American television could be readily identified as one of three major character types: he could be funny, crooked, or a cop. The female character types that were more common in film tended not to be featured in the small number of series that featured Latinos in the 1970s.

An analysis of programs broadcast in the fall of 1977 compared the representation of Blacks with those of Whites (Baptista-Fernandez and Greenberg, 1980). By 1977, nearly half of the African American characters were in situation comedies, with an additional one-fifth in Saturday morning cartoons. Black life on television in 1977 was still segregated. No Whites appeared in shows with more than four Black characters, while nearly half of the Black characters appeared in such shows. Indeed, six shows accounted for 41 per cent of all Black characters appearing during the sample week.

Ten years later, a study of the 1987–88 American television season was designed (Stroman *et al.*, 1989). It used an analysis of the representations of African Americans in prime time to evaluate how broadcasters had responded to the criticisms directed toward television by the Kerner Commission 20 years earlier (Kerner, 1968). During this period, African Americans on television were being portrayed as belonging to either the middle or the upper classes, with their high-status occupations providing a consistent theme. Not only had Black characters become wealthier, competent professionals, but their physical appearance also moved closer to the mainstream ideal. Whereas Black women on television described in previous studies tended to be obese, only 14 per cent of the women in the 1988 season could be classed as obese.

The movement toward the development of television series which included more Black and White characters as regulars, or individual segments which seemed designed as a counter to racialized emphasis on difference, led some observers to challenge the underlying logic (DeMott, 1996). Demott suggested that mass media have been engaged in the presentation of an image of sameness, including the sense that racial equality had been achieved. This message had been communicated most powerfully by the cozy, friendly relationships between Blacks and Whites on some of the most popular, and therefore widely viewed, television programs. In most of the examples of interracial relationships that he cites, initial anxiety and tension is soon overcome, and the White or Black outsider is soon admitted to the fold. Demott finds little difference in his assessment of a spate of television commercials in which Blacks and Whites interact easily as 'buddies.' The same good buddy theme is consistently being reproduced in films, with the *Lethal Weapon* series starring Danny Glover and Mel Gibson combining action and humor into a duet of sameness.

DeMott's catalog of examples from recent motion pictures includes a rather extensive list of economically successful films featuring racial harmony. He places Whoopi Goldberg's *Sister Act* up near the top of his list, because of the way it provides a woman's version of the interracial buddy film. The crowning example for DeMott was an episode on the cable television series *The Larry Sanders' Show*, in which tension between Whites and Blacks over affirmative action is finally resolved strategically by bringing Whites and Blacks together in opposing the one Black character who will not or cannot fit in. For DeMott, this 'sameness-mongering' is part of a cruel hoax, an attempted cover-up of the more serious problems in society that is doomed to failure.

Some of these problems feature prominently in a relatively new form of television, the 'reality' drama, in which dramatizations of allegedly real events are presented. Robin Andersen (1995) provides an extended critique of these 'reality-based' police shows. She interprets the narrative discourse of these shows as producing a 'sense of the barbarism of young black men.' She suggests that the media portrayals of urban crime in a program like *Night Beat* repeatedly provide images that evoke 'waves of revulsion' almost magically in response to the mantric incantation: 'drugs, criminality, young black men.' From her perspective, this media narrative is not intended to inform or explain the association between race, poverty and crime, but to 'evoke fear, fascination, and spectacle' (p. 184). For Andersen, the violence which is *poverty* is too *real* for reality-based programs, and has therefore been excluded.

Her analysis brings the ideological into electromagnetic alignment with the structural when she concludes that 'the media's propensity for telling drug stories that feature young black youths being hunted down is cheap, exciting, and convenient entertainment, and their demonization has become acceptable' (Andersen, 1995, p. 194). She argues further that the cultivation of fear of Black men as an instrument of social control may be strategic as well as convenient. Rather than discussing the real political and economic origins of crime, these reality shows provide little more than a diversionary spectacle.

Exemplars

Some media criticism emphasizes individual cases, rather than making claims about the prevalence or central tendency of filmic representations. Although not often stated explicitly, however, the use of extended examples is strategically designed to make a claim about the social impact of these representations. Such claims have a more reasonable basis when it can also be claimed that the extent of public exposure or reach was substantial. Thus the more popular films or television programs are likely to play an important role in the reproduction of racism to the extent that they are popular, and their popularity increases the probability that these media texts provide the raw material that is used in the production of social talk about race.

Michael Eric Dyson (1993), an African American cultural critic of some stature, identifies his work as part of a much needed contribution to the development of a 'mature and oppositional criticism of black culture' (p. xix). He suggests that this washing of the dirty cultural linen must be done in public rather than 'handled in secrecy away from the omniscient gaze of white society' (p. xxiii). This criticism is thought to be instructive in the ways it 'promotes the preservation of black culture's best features, the amelioration of its weakest parts, and the eradication of its worst traits' (p. xxv).

He, along with other Black scholars writing from their vantage points in elite universities, take regular aim at what they call 'neonationalist racial essentialism' (Dyson, 1993, p. xxix). Dyson finds examples of this particular flaw in the films of Spike Lee. While Dyson is generally supportive of Lee's attempts to make an audience think and talk about racism, he suggests that Lee 'nevertheless slides dangerously close to a vision of "us" and "them," in which race is seen solely through the lens of biological determinism' (p. 25). He goes on to suggest that it is Lee's neonationalist leanings that condemn many of his characters to be archetypes that are not much more subtle than the stereotypical caricatures that a racist film industry has used historically to represent the 'breadth of black humanity.'

Although his criticism is far more tempered, Herman Gray (1995) offers a criticism of a popular, but controversial, comedy/variety program *In Living Color*. This program was one of the early successes of the Fox television network. Fox, and its notorious owner, Rupert Murdoch, had determined that it could succeed in a marketplace dominated by the three mainstream networks by capturing the fringe audiences viewing during late night. To a significant extent, this was an audience of disaffected White youth. The program succeeded with a very heterogeneous slice of the youthful 14–25-year-old target demographic. Its success may have come at the cost of a clear unambiguous cultural statement from its young Black producers. Instead, Gray suggests that the program revealed a troubling ambivalence about race, class, gender, and sexual orientation.

As a comedy program, its use of parody and satire relied upon traditional and derogatory stereotypes of Blacks, especially those who were working class, poor, or gay. At the same time, as Gray notes, Whiteness was also a 'consistent object of ridicule, satire, and commentary.' And, some of the time, 'sketches that parody white liberal guilt or white fear of black criminality actually name and engage the dynamics of white privilege and power in relationship to Blacks' (1995, p. 141). The problem, from Gray's critical position, is that the satirical formula comes dangerously close to trivializing issues which are worthy of far more serious analysis and comment. Ultimately, for Gray, the program fails as a cultural resource because its ambivalence does not provide a base from which to engage serious concerns. As a result, this special opportunity is not only squandered, but it may, in fact, have resulted in the further crystallization of racist cognitions.

Advertising

Wilson and Gutíerrez identify advertising as 'the media's not so silent partner' (1995, p. 109). In their view:

> Advertising, like mining, is an extractive industry. It enters the ghetto and barrio with a smiling face to convince all within its reach that they should purchase the products advertised and purchase them often. It has no goal other than to stimulate consumption of the product; the subsidization of the media is merely a by-product. (p. 137)

However, in the same way that mining affects the communities that surround it by generating clouds of dust, clogging the roads with traffic, and eventually leaving ugly scars where there was once a grassy plain, advertising also has its negative external effects. Theorists believe that advertising not only reflects a society's myths and ritual, but that it is also implicated in its transformation.

Advertisements which have been produced for one segment of the population have historically made liberal use of stereotyped representations of others outside the target market. The rationale for the use of these stereotypes is often based on a perceived need to evoke the 'exotic' and the 'foreign' in an effort to create a sense of cultural authenticity for products which have been sanitized and mainstreamed for the domestic market. Only protest, competitive failure, or an expansion of the target market has led advertisers to change their approach. Cultural sensitivity among advertisers seems as rare as environmentalism among strip miners.

Wilson and Gutíerrez make this point by describing two different advertising campaigns initiated by the Frito-Lay Corporation. Both campaigns were for corn chips, but the first campaign used a negative stereotype embodied in its incredibly offensive cartoon character, 'the Frito Bandito.' The iconic image of the campaign had a bad Spanish accent, the requisite sombrero, a handlebar moustache, a pot belly, and a pair of six-guns. As the campaign unfolded, he was uncontrollably driven to steal corn chips from a series of unsuspecting victims. The first campaign generated a vocal and sustained opposition that included protests organized by the Mexican American Anti-Defamation Committee against Frito-Lay, and the promise of boycotts against the stations that carried the ad. Only time will tell whether the protest against the 'Frito Bandito' will herald a new age in the representation of Latinos in the same way that the protests against *Amos and Andy* affected the representation of African Americans.

The second campaign for a similar product introduced ten years later was barely noticed, except for its success in bringing Tostitos into the American living room. The second campaign used a live actor to evoke the more positive stereotype of the Latin lover. Wilson and Gutíerrez note that national advertisers have tended not to generalize from their experience with African Americans to their treatment of Latins or Asians. Instead, advertisers have developed an increased level of sensitivity to each minority group in turn, perhaps reflecting an awareness of the economic and political power that these groups represent, rather than any universal rejection of negative stereotypes as a marketing resource.

Recently, perhaps in an ironic response to the public discussions about political correctness, or perhaps because the stereotyped image was just too powerful to waste, another manufacturer introduced a brand of flour tortillas and used an image that was almost an exact copy of the 'Frito Bandito,' but in this case the manufacturer named him and the brand 'Gringo Pete's.' Perhaps they hoped that the tag 'gringo' would not disturb or interfere with the more well-entrenched linkage between tortillas and their Mexican origins in the minds of Anglo consumers.

Advertisers, editors, and program producers are all influenced by their impressions of the target audience, and their response to ads (Qualls and Moore, 1990). Advertisers avoid controversy, and they have historically threatened to pull, or actually have pulled their ads from media when the adjacent content of media threatened to tarnish their product with guilt by association. Protest against a particular advertising campaign is a form of controversy in which the product itself becomes controversial. Under those unusual circumstances, other advertisers fear association with offensive and controversial ads. But it is not only protest that has occasioned the change in the representation of racial and ethnic others.

Content analyses of commercial advertisements have varied in their level of sophistication. The approach of mainstream scholars has not been much different from the ways in which they have approached the rest of media content. Many studies of advertising and minorities have focused on the changing image of African Americans over time. Some begin by noting the relative absence of Blacks in the ads. One study of 20,000 ads published in the *New York Times* between 1963 and 1964 found only 11 ads with pictures or representations of African Americans (Boyenton, 1965). The performance of the *Times* had not improved substantially by 1975, while the visibility of Blacks in television commercials had already begun to improve by the early 1970s (Culley and Bennett, 1976). Some of these studies also criticized the relatively limited and stereotypical roles that Black actors are allowed to play in the ads. They also noted that Blacks appeared more often in institutional rather than product ads. Still others examined the relationships between actors in the ads, noting the fact that Blacks rarely appear alone, but stand out as the one dark face in the crowd (Culley and Bennett, 1976).

Some have noted the way a particular image is changed as the advertiser's perception of the market changes. Marilyn Kern-Foxworth (1994) recently published an extensive historical review and criticism of the representation of African Americans from a perspective that assumed that the representations of Blacks affected not only Black self-image, but also affected the relations between Blacks and others in the society (Kern-Foxworth, 1994). Kern-Foxworth provides an extended discussion of the 'mammy' stereotype, exemplified best for her in the continually changing, but always limiting, image of Aunt Jemima. Identified as one of the oldest trademarks in the United States, pictures of this buxom, warm, and comforting woman graced packages of pancake mix and other household products.

While Jannette Dates (1990) associates differences in the representation of African Americans in the mass media with the level of interest advertisers had in reaching the Black consumer, analyses of the ads in Black-oriented media suggest that the determining influences are considerably more complex. Michael Leslie (1995) has examined the changing image of Blacks in the advertisements in *Ebony* magazine. Leslie observed that the skin color of the models used in those advertisements became darker for a brief period, perhaps in response to the heightened emphasis on Blackness in the 1960s, but the ideal had returned to the fair-skinned Eurotype by the end of the 1980s.

Writing in 1976, Michael Chapko's analysis of *Ebony* ads published between 1964 and 1974 actually revealed a steady increase in the number of integrated ads to a peak in 1970, and then decreasing slightly thereafter. Leslie's data, however, show the proportion of integrated ads increasing after 1976. Chapko's analysis of the proportion of ads featuring 'relatively lighter' Black models reveals a truly substantial decline, from a high of 75 per cent in 1964, to a low of 54.6 per cent in 1974. Chapko allows the possibility that ads reflect the desires of the customer; thus, he concludes that Blacks were rejecting Whites as individuals to emulate (Chapko, 1976, p. 178). Leslie frames the more recent return to what he calls 'Eurocentric norms' as evidence of the failure of Afrocentric values to overcome the influence of the dominant culture.

Bowen and Schmid (1997) have provided an updated analysis of minorities in mainstream magazines. Arguing that mainstream magazines have had to adjust to the new competitive circumstances represented by the creation of new magazines targeted to narrow, more precise market segments, they suggest that the direction of this adjustment was toward greater inclusiveness that should be reflected in the advertising copy and images used. They assumed that minority groups excluded in the past – Asians and Hispanics – would be the beneficiaries of this expanded vision. Their examination of nine magazines, including *Esquire, Fortune, Sports Illustrated*, and *Time* identified nearly 2,000 ads with racially identifiable individuals. Their analysis revealed an increase in the use of Blacks between 1987 and 1992, with the presence of Asians and Hispanics low or even declining. This finding was incompatible with a view that suggests ads should reflect readership, given the fairly high readership by members of minority groups. They also noted a continuation of a tendency to use minority group persons more often in public service or government-funded advertisements than for consumer goods. Indeed, many of the ads placed by traditional advertisers that included minorities were 'public service' rather than consumption-oriented. They suggest that these ads do not seem to be based on target marketing. Instead, they are being used to establish a company position or a positive image. The consumer is led to believe that since the company cares about minorities and their problems we should feel good about the company and show our support by buying its products. At the same time, the message that minorities are in need of some assistance from the larger community is consistently reinforced. (1997, p. 143)

A somewhat different approach to the analysis of advertisements is provided by Ellen Seiter (1990). Seiter's analysis focuses on the differences between the roles and representations of White children in comparison with those of Black children. She suggests that White children are frequently represented by a type she labels the 'go-getter.' She suggests that the 'go-getter' is not a stereotype available for use with Black children in ads. Her explanation for this difference implies a set of assumptions on the part of advertisers about the interpretive limits within the mainstream culture that mark some stereotypes as inappropriate. Black children behaving similarly would be labeled 'pushy' rather than the more positive label, 'assertive' or 'self-confident', she sees being reserved for Whites. Seiter concludes that these ads express a 'hierarchy of race relations. White children are always the stars, African-American children the bit players' (p. 39).

When Black children do appear in ads, Seiter suggests that they are most often in ads defined by music or sports. These are now privileged relations for Blacks. She argues further that there is a more subtle message in these ads. In her view, Black youngsters are not being associated with music and sports as a reflection of strengths internal to their culture, but because these are talents they are born with. This is a reflection of an identification of race with genetic determination.

We note, however, that the Black athlete has in recent years become an extremely popular, and highly rewarded, component in the marketing of consumer goods. An early example of the successful use of a Black male athlete is the Coke commercial featuring a football player known professionally as 'Mean Joe' Greene (Davis, 1987). This 60-second morality play involving a White youngster and a Black superhero was an exceptionally popular commercial. The creater of the ad, Scott Miller, suggests that what this kid and his hero really 'have in common is Coke' (Blumenthal, 1983). People so fundamentally different in size, shape, color, and temperament can at least share their appreciation of a commodity, and do so through an exchange of valuables . . . the Coke for the athlete's sweatshirt. The ad not only won several advertising awards for its creativity, and millions in sales for Coca-Cola, but it also became the model for Coke ads around the globe. In Thailand, the athlete becomes 'Mean Joe' Niwat, a famous soccer player, 'Mean Joe' Zico in Brazil, and 'Mean Joe' Maradona in Argentina. The adaptation of the fundamental theme to different cultural contexts has been minimal (Englade, 1987).

While sports figures are often associated with fast foods, drink, and sports apparel, many advertisements are for products that are used to overcome or erase shortcomings or 'stigmas,' such as flaws in appearance. Davis (1987) hypothesized that Black actors would not be used in stigma-oriented commercials, unless these ads were in programs that were targeted to African Americans. Contrary to his expectations, Davis found that Black actors were actually very popular choices for these commercials. Indeed, he found that nearly half of the commercials featuring minority performers were of this type. Minority performers actually appeared in this kind of commercial at a higher rate than White performers. Davis suggests that minority status may provide some special claim on expertise in the management of 'spoiled identity.' Another interpretation might suggest that Blacks are more acceptable in the traditional role of service provider, of which this sort of personal advice is a part.

Some criticism of advertising is directed not primarily at the use of stereotypes but at the fact that racial and ethnic identity is used to promote controversial products such as alcohol and tobacco (Hacker *et al.*, 1987). In 1992, a new high-potency malt liquor was introduced. Named 'Crazy Horse', after a famous Oglala Sioux leader, the bottle was packaged to look like a liquor bottle, included a picture of the chief, and made graphic allusions to the Old West and Native American cultural traditions (Anon., 1992). Marketing alcohol to African Americans through targeted ads that included the appropriation of cultural signs had long been a practice of the advertising industry (Hacker *et al.*, 1987). It is in ads for alcohol that one finds evidence of the market's recognition of class-based variation within the African American population. Segmentation by class can be seen in the placement of ads for malt liquor almost exclusively on billboards in inner-city neighborhoods. These ads are especially offensive in their suggestion to Black males that not only will the beverage succeed in getting you high, but it will also help you achieve and enjoy a sexual conquest. Even in magazines directed at the Black middle class, however, the emphasis on sexual conquest is common. An ad for Seagram's gin promoted the product's aphrodisiac properties with the suggestion that it 'could turn a "maybe" into "again"' (Hacker *et al.*, 1987, p. 28).

African Americans were identified as a unique target market for the promotion of cigarettes and other goods as early as 1950. An analysis of *Ebony* and *Life* magazines between 1950 and 1965 revealed a shift toward using Black models almost exclusively in *Ebony*, and almost exclusively White models in *Life* during this period (Pollay *et al.*, 1992). The ads targeted to Blacks were more likely to use 'celebrity' endorsements, and athletes were among the most frequently used class of endorsers. Athletes endorsed cigarettes nearly five times more often in *Ebony* than they did in *Life* magazine. The cynical exploitation of ethnic pride and the athlete's image of good health exemplifies the ways in which knowledge of Black culture has been used in marketing with consequences that are far more than the simple by-products identified by Wilson and Gutíerrez (1995, p. 137).

More interpretive approaches to the study of minority images in advertising have emphasized the ways in which a racist ideology that permeates the advertising industry is reflected in the ways in which minorities, especially African Americans, are represented in commercial messages. An interpretive analysis of television commercials broadcast by the major television networks in March of 1994 identified six ideological themes that were likely to be present in ads that featured African Americans (Bristor *et al.*, 1995).

Although the proportional representation of African Americans in television commercials has recently come to exceed their proportion in the population, or even in the audiences for much of the network programming, a dominant racial ideology can be understood to have produced an emphasis on the Black athlete. One can easily read the emphasis on Black athleticism as a reinforcement of a belief that Black prowess reflects a genetic endowment. The concentration on Black athletes reinforces the distinction between brains and brawn that has long been part of a racist construction of the difference between Blacks and Whites.

The role of African Americans in the service industry is also reflected in ads for fast food and retail services. Good-natured Black youth offer friendly service to White customers in commercial after commercial. Although they did not claim that their sample was representative, Bristor (1995) and her colleagues noted that in the 208 commercials they reviewed Whites who were shown working in these low-status jobs were never shown serving Black customers. They also noted the relative absence of African American families in these commercials, although, in what may be an effort to counter the stereotype of the absent Black father, several ads did include African American fathers playing with their sons.

The charge of tokenism is based on the relative absence of commercials in which all the actors are Black, even though more than half of the ads had only White actors. The proportion of ads in which Blacks appear is high, in part because Black actors have been given token roles. A more troublesome reflection of a racist ideology that shares much in common with patriarchical views is what these authors refer to as *objectification*. An actor is objectified to the extent that his individuality has been denied. Such denials are produced when facial features, especially the eyes, are hidden or even purposely obliterated. This technique is clear in an example of a 'headless' athlete who is portrayed as being able to perform impossible athletic feats. Black individuals become identified solely by what they *do*, not by who they *are*. Objectification is akin to trivialization or marginalization which is accomplished through camera angle, position within the frame, or through association with the least important aspects of the 'story' of the commercial. Bristor and her colleagues (1995) summarize these techniques and outcomes in terms of their effect on the relative 'screen presence' of African Americans in television commercials.

Bristor's interpretive critique ends by focusing on the ways in which contemporary ads make strategic use of cultural cues to highlight or to subordinate aspects of Blackness. The use of light-skinned models is seen as taking advantage of the still powerful influence of the hierarchically ordered status system that is graded by color. Overall, Bristor and her colleagues found few examples of the kinds of blatantly racist representations that the Frito Bandito exemplified. Yet the more subtle aspects of a racial ideology that scholars have labeled 'modern racism' are easy to identify within television commercials.

These evaluations of media performance reflect both the perspective and the purpose of the observers. This chapter has privileged the assessment of critical scholars who have objected to the ways in which the media have represented the life and character of racial and ethnic groups and their members. The representations have varied over time, across media, and in response to shifts in markets and social forms. Content analyses have enabled us to take note of stability and change in the representation of the links between race, class, caste, and chance. Shifts in these relations have been examined at the manifest surface level and in more subtle ways as analysts have moved closer to the text. Although the underlying assumption behind the critical assessment of media performance is that misrepresentation produces harm, the nature of that harm, or evidence that it actually occurs, has not been detailed. These duties and concerns have been reserved for the next chapter.

5

Reproduction and change

According to media sociologist Charles Wright, functional analysis is 'concerned with examining those consequences of social phenomena which affect the normal operation, adaptation, or adjustment of a given system: individuals, subgroups, social and cultural systems' (1964, p. 94). The mass media are readily identified as a social phenomenon worthy of study in terms of the basic communication functions that may be performed by, or with the assistance of, information systems organized industrially, and financed through advertising. The assumption underlying such an analysis is that the consequences for society will vary as a function of the particular means through which basic requirements are met. To bring this analytical frame more closely in line with our concerns with matters of race, we might ask what the consequences are for the self-esteem of individuals, if the dominant representations of members of their racial group are negative stereotypes. If we believed that the self-esteem of members of one group depends in part on the comparisons they make between their group and other groups, we might be especially interested in knowing what difference it might make if their experience with members of other groups has been limited almost entirely to their use of mass media.

We might pursue this issue in another way by asking what the consequences might be for the level of trust and political involvement within the society as a whole if each citizen's understanding of political issues has been affected by their beliefs about who benefits and who pays for the implementation of particular social policies (such as those designed to overcome the burdens of racial discrimination). An individual's position on matters of public importance can be influenced by her sense of herself as well as her sense of others whom she believes are or are not like her. The ways in which knowledge of issues, participants, and the distribution of benefits can be shaped as a function of the performance of the news media is precisely the kind of question that communication scholars have been struggling to answer.

It should be clear by now that these are very difficult questions. The causal links between media use and social perceptions are not at all direct. Indeed, they are maddeningly complex and contradictory. Because of this complexity, almost any conclusions we might want to draw about causal determination will have to be tentative, and presented in terms of tendencies or suggested relationships. At the same time, however, the evidence that supports the existence of an important role for the mass media in the social construction of race and race relations is so extensive that it cannot be ignored.

Uncertainty about the relations between communication and race continues to exist not only because communication and race have changed before our eyes, but this uncertainty may have even expanded because the ways in which we make sense of these changes have also been transformed by the struggles being waged among intellectuals, activists, and officials. The ways in which we might understand the nature of this struggle, including who is winning, or even who is losing, will depend almost entirely upon where we choose to look.

As we have noted, there have been dramatic shifts in the gaze of scholars and policy actors which have influenced how we understand the world. The same kinds of periodic shifts that take place in markets and political systems also seem to take place in the development of theoretical systems, and these shifts are not at all well understood. Theorists who have pursued these concerns from the perspective of the 'sociology of knowledge' have tended to focus on influences internal to particular scientific or theoretical discourses (Kuhn, 1970), but this work has not been especially helpful in revealing some of the systemic influences that actually bring about 'paradigm shifts.' Influences from outside a particular scholarly discourse would appear to be at least as important as the internal responses to problems, conflicts, and contradictions.

For example, the approach of neoclassical economics and its focus on rational behavior in a variety of 'markets' has become so successful in moving beyond its traditional disciplinary boundaries that some observers refer to it as 'economic imperialism' (Radnitzky and Bernholz, 1987). Although many have noted, and quite a few have decried, the ways in which a *marketplace logic* has displaced moral and ethical considerations in the determination of government policy, few have attempted to explain this success. Among the more productive insights into this process is the notion of an 'epistemic community' (Haas, 1992).

Knowledge-based expertise that is shared and cultivated within a definable network has been recognized as an important influence on the development of a policy response to a host of critical problems. Epistemic communities may vary, but they are believed to share several things in common: (1) normative beliefs that aid the development of a value-based rationale for proposals, (2) causal beliefs derived from analyses of core problems or issues, (3) notions of validity, or criteria for evaluating knowledge claims, (4) policy-related practices reflecting professional competence (Haas, 1992, p. 3). The postmodern critique of the modernist Enlightenment project seems to have some of these attributes, but it seems unlikely at the moment that as an intellectual project postmodernism will achieve the level of epistemic influence that economic rationalism has (Best and Kellner, 1991; Laclau and Mouffe, 1985). In the review of the literature on media effects that will be explored in this chapter, postmodernist thinking figures hardly at all.

If we confine our investigation to the studies published in what are identified as the 'major' communication journals published in the United States, then we might conclude that the social science paradigm is the current winner. While the 'interpretive paradigm' accounts for about 34 per cent of the studies published in eight of these journals, studies identified as 'critical' represent only a fraction. Only about 6 per cent of the papers published between 1965 and 1989 take a critical stance, and are likely to provide a critical insight (Potter *et al.*, 1993). A very different result would obtain if we included commmunication journals published in Europe, Asia, or Australia where critical scholarship enjoys a more comfortable position within the academy. Even greater differences in perspective and insight would be found if we included journals that publish work from the many other disciplines that have claimed the right to comment on communications phenomena. Our assessment of what we know about the impact of communication on matters of race has been influenced by a variety of sources, but the influence of mainstream communication research published in American journals is substantial. You should bear this in mind.

What we believe about the nature of the world necessarily reflects what we feel about our sources of knowledge about that world. For many of us, our knowledge of much of the world depends upon acts of faith, because critical aspects of the world are beyond our capacity to observe directly, or to understand fully.

Historically, the Enlightenment project broke with dependence upon religious authority and acts of faith, and sought comfort in the human capacity for reason (Garnham, 1990). Consensus and common understanding, such as might be arrived at through the process of scholarly debate over evidence and logical argument, is the way in which the Enlightenment project is linked to the development of the human sciences as well as the public sphere. 'This Enlightenment project is also operative in the American, French, and other democratic revolutions which attempted to overturn the feudal world and to produce a just and egalitarian social order that would embody reason and social progress' (Best and Kellner, 1991, p. 2). We continue to differ, however, in the extent to which we believe that it is in fact possible to know the social world, and to understand it with the precision and confidence usually reserved for the natural sciences.

If scientific knowledge rather than knowledge *claims* is the goal of our efforts, some would argue that the phenomena to be studied must be stable, pancultural, and ahistorical (Cappella, 1991). This is not the social world we inhabit! Indeed, an increasingly popular ontological view is one that suggests that the social world is not only incredibly complex, but it is also continually being transformed. Such a world becomes difficult, if not impossible, to pin down with *any* theoretical or empirical certainty, in part because of the way that social theory becomes the raw material of emerging social facts.

Part of the struggle between modernist or Enlightenment theorists and those informed by the new wave of postmodern sensibilities is based in the confounded nature of relations between theories of being, or *ontology*, and theories of knowing, or *epistemology* (Best and Kellner, 1991). In postmodernist discussions of similar issues, theory itself has become suspect because we recognize (perhaps reluctantly) that our theories cannot be separated from the influence of their historical origins. Because knowledge and theory is based on an anchorless and unstable system of organizing facts and assessing relations, postmodernists deny that we have any objective, independent basis for determining the accuracy or truth of claims regarding social facts. Indeed, the ideals of truth, the search for meaning, and an understanding of causality are set outside the regions of worthwhile engagement for many postmodern theorists (Best and Kellner, 1991, p. 256).

There is not much utility to be gained by trying to justify taking a stand or choosing sides between empiricist and rationalist epistemologies. While theories about the relations between communication, race, and social structure can and should be tested empirically, we ought not to delude ourselves into thinking that our empirical methods can ever escape their basis in theory and socially constructed fact.

The contemporary emphasis on media consumption is the product of a more general shift in attention from the sources to the receivers of messages. Theorists associated with the 'uses and gratifications' tradition in mass communications research argued that 'it was not what media do to people, but what people do with media' (Blumler and Katz, 1974). Scholars within this tradition focused on the audience, rather than the media, and from a perspective that privileged psychological rather than social or structural explanations. For them, answers to important questions about mass communication were to be found in the cognitive sphere, and in theories about motivation and other functionalist notions of goal-directed behavior. The uses and gratifications tradition provided support for conceptualizations of an 'active audience' that would become far more central to the cultural studies paradigm than it had traditionally been in the more sociological field of media studies.

There are, of course, theoretically based, metaphoric constructions of media use which leave space for an active audience as well as powerful media. This is a perspective that asks us to recognize and then seek to understand that which is obvious upon reflection, despite the fact that it is fashionable to deny its theoretical implications. Robert Kubey is one who challenges us to reflect openly on the nature of media power:

> Although it is true that moviegoers or television viewers come to the same film or television program with different backgrounds, needs, and expectations, these media are often powerful enough that once involved in an effectively produced drama, say, a suspense plot, most viewers will care at exactly the same time whether the hero survives, whether a victim is rescued, and whether the villain is vanquished . . . . And, to be sure, audiences for comedic and tragic fare typically laugh or cry at the same time. (Kubey, 1996, p. 197)

While it is undoubtedly true that members of these audiences who might be classified by race, or even racial identity, might differ in the strength of their engagement with and response to these media cues, one has to grant their existence before a research effort can be expected to specify their character.

Attention paid to the study of communication and race by social psychologists has waxed and waned over time. We have seen a shift in emphasis away from the focus of early work which sought to measure racial attitudes, and to begin to define the nature of racial and ethnic prejudice (Dovidio and Gaertner, 1986). The 1950s was a period that was dominated by an emphasis on attitude change. Scholars hoped that their research might actually lead toward success in reducing or eliminating racial prejudice. Although this work was displaced somewhat by the more dramatic social and political upheavals of the 1960s, racial concerns re-emerged on the scholarly agenda in the 1970s. Much of the recent research on prejudice has tended to set aside some of the traditional concerns with social relations and public policy, focusing more intently on the cognitive processes involved in prejudiced thinking, and less on the social origins or consequences of such thinking. At the same time, because of the demands within science for theoretical progress based on the experimental control of variables, the troublesome and unstable definition of race, and the problematic measurement of racial identity, studies of prejudice that focus primarily on race have actually been demoted to second-class status within the field of social psychology (Dovidio and Gaertner, 1986, p. 15).

An emphasis on race in media studies emerged in part in response to the urban riots embodied in the report of the Kerner Commission (Kerner, 1968). Within the sphere of media studies, the question of race has been of such marginal import that the framework has been determined primarily from outside the field. Economists and economic theory have influenced the way we have thought about race primarily in terms of the ways we understand discrimination as irrational behavior (Becker, 1971). Political scientists have also been an important source of the ways in which we have understood the place of race in the framing of political debates (Carmines and Stimson, 1989).

Cultivation and mainstreaming

Despite the distressingly narrow body of empirical work examining the relations between communication and race there is still much that can be said about the matter. By extending the broad and general concepts of media effects at the heart of the Cultural Indicators project associated with George Gerbner, Larry Gross and others (Signorielli and Morgan, 1990), it is possible to organize an assessment of the major consequences that flow from media use to the reproduction and transformation of racialized social relations. Cultivation refers more generally to the process through which consumption of media messages cultivates a particular world view or social outlook. As will be discussed, that outlook includes impressions and assessments of oneself in relation to others. Cultivation is readily understood as a structurational process, through which the mediated experience of communication overcomes the direct material influence of concrete social relations. This is a process which is cumulative, and is to be distinguished from a tradition of media effects scholarship which is concerned with an immediate, and perhaps short-term, impact of exposure.

Cultivation analysis is traditionally combined with content analysis of prime-time television in order to establish the dominant patterns which help to specify the 'television answer.' Because of the early support for the project from the Surgeon General's Advisory Commission, perceptions about the nature of the world as a mean and dangerous place and the extent to which people can be trusted helped to provide early support for the cultivation hypothesis. A more recent adjustment to the cultivation hypothesis called 'mainstreaming' introduced a theoretical insight which improves the usefulness of this research paradigm as a companion to critical perspectives on the ideological effect of media (Tapper, 1995). The failure of most scholars working from within the cultivation perspective to specify in advance what the nature of the effect will be for particular subgroups underscores the absence of a well-developed understanding of the underlying processes that generate these different 'effects' (Morgan and Signorielli, 1990, p. 26).

Mainstreaming takes into account the influence of concrete social experience on the development of social perceptions that reflects the social class or other indicators of the social location of individuals. The ideological effect of television is realized to the extent that individuals, whose perceptions of the world ought to differ as a function of their different social locations, actually come to share social perceptions because of their common experience in the world of television (Gerbner et al., 1994; Morgan and Signorielli, 1990). The concept of 'resonance' is less satisfactory as a means of disentangling the influence of television use from the influence of other forces in society. Resonance suggests that the experiences or relationships or outcomes that are represented in television fiction may resonate with similar features of the viewer's immediate environment. Thus, they receive a 'double dose' and, as a result, heavy television viewers in this subgroup differ substantially from other heavy television viewers.

The limitations of the cultivation hypothesis are associated with an absence of experimental control. Because viewers rather than experimenters choose the level of their exposure to media content, it is impossible to eliminate the influence of 'third variables' as the cause of both exposure and social perceptions. The difficulties observed in demonstrating the impact of cultivation are reflections of a more general problem of specification that plagues media research more generally.

Media use or exposure

Part of the difficulty faced by mass communications researchers is the extent to which the various processes being theorized can in fact be reliably measured. Within the empiricist tradition, causal models generally involve the specification of variables that represent theoretical constructs. Can we measure, or even estimate, the metaphorical equivalent of the number of calories or the grams of sodium that we take in when we watch an hour of network news? Far too often, media scholars have tended to talk about these variables as though there was perfect agreement about what they meant, and how they were best measured. In fact, as fundamental a concept as 'television viewing' has been shown to have a range of divergent meanings within the field of media studies (Solomon and Cohen, 1978).

While concern with audience choice is central to many perspectives on media effects, some have argued that, in fact, television viewing is habitual, rather than reflecting informed choice. Empirical evidence suggests that, with some limited exceptions, the proportion of the audience who will watch the same program they viewed the previous week is predictable within a relatively narrow range (Barwise *et al.*, 1982). Others will counter that there is always audience choice, even if it is not a consciously made decision. This is evident in the observation that people are engaged in a great variety of activities while they are supposedly 'watching television' (Kubey and Csikszentmihalyi, 1990). From this perspective, audiences must choose, at some level of awareness, how much of their attention they will devote to the action on the screen from moment to moment.

Research which focuses on a viewer's choice to view or not to view is frequently associated with the related view of the consequences that accompany exposure, or viewing. The focus of this research is similar to a related view which emphasizes the features of the content being consumed. However, this view also assumes that the content is received and processed or *understood* without difficulty. This is a view which assumes a very high correlation between exposure and its consequences. This is an increasingly minority view.

Another perspective argues that television content is a coded text which must be interpreted, or decoded. These scholars assume that there will always be some difference in the ways in which those messages are decoded or understood by different individuals, or even by the same individual at different times (or upon reflection). Variations in decoding might be seen as reflecting differential skill or competence, or merely the result of a relatively open code which is subject to a great variety of interpretations or readings (Wolfe, 1992).

By example or argument, interpretive theorists claimed that audiences in fact had a capacity to produce a variety of *readings* that were greatly at variance with the readings 'intended' by producers or other controllers of media (Seamon, 1992). The demonstration that audiences were not subject to the control of media producers, but were free to read the media text any way they wished, was an assertion of audience power or agency. Although researchers in this tradition tend not to make statistical claims, the 'preferred' reading of their analyses would suggest that oppositional readings were commonplace, rather than exceptional (Evans, 1990).

On the basis of their use of one of these or other underlying conceptualizations of television viewing, different media scholars would have to develop critically different operational definitions of the exposure variable. For example, in relation to their work on cultivation, Gerbner and his colleagues assume that there is actually very little difference between programs or even genres in terms of what they convey regarding the important cultural facts about society. Thus, for the study of media cultivation, exposure to specific programs is not a particularly important concern. Instead, television exposure is measured solely in terms of the number of hours viewed on the average day (Gerbner *et al.*, 1986).

However, for those researchers who believe that media effects reflect differential attention to different content, and who argue further that such differences reflect individual goals and expectations, it makes sense to evaluate the *quality* of exposure to specific kinds of content within specific programs (Reeves *et al.*, 1986). Unfortunately, the kinds of generalizations that we would be able to make, on the basis of the kinds of controls we are likely to be able to establish within the confines of an experiment, are not likely to be very interesting because:

Television as a psychological stimulus is too complex; it is viewed in too many different situations, for too many different reasons, in combination with too many other activities to ever represent a stimulus located precisely in one category and never in the other. (Reeves *et al.*, 1986, p. 273)

However it is measured, media use varies considerably among individuals. Whether it is by reading, viewing, or listening, or merely being bombarded by the commercial messages that have spread over the surfaces of buildings, as well as the backs and pocket flaps of the shirts of the passengers on our train, we spend a substantial share of our waking hours consuming, processing, and making sense of mass mediated messages (Lull, 1995).

Media scholars and industry planners alike are very interested in understanding which factors help to determine just how much time individuals will spend with what particular medium, and with which types of content. Audience studies suggest that the variation in media use is 'systematically related to structural, positional and individual characteristics ranging from type of society to social position' (Rosengren, 1994, p. 21). Media use varies by age, race, gender, and class, but it also reflects individual differences in attitudes, values, tastes, and opinions. These observers also suggest that mass media, at first primarily music, but increasingly even television, film, and magazines, have come to serve as resources which help young people to define their individual lifestyle and cultural identity. A poor match between the cultural features of any program and the racial or ethnic identity of the audience may explain some of the differences in the kinds of insights or understandings that people 'take away' from their experience with the medium.

There are also important choices made and differences to be noted with regard to the circumstances or the contexts in which media are consumed. David Morley's studies of family viewing recognize that the social context of television viewing varies dramatically from home to home. Morley has noted, however, the existence of some common aspects of the viewing experience which are related to gender. These observed similarities have to do with the extent to which women actually choose, rather than merely agree, to view particular programs to please spouses, partners, or even children (Morley, 1992). This is a view that had been articulated most clearly by James Lull (1980). Lull had demonstrated that television viewing served different instrumental purposes for different members of the family.

The increasing popularity of ethnographic or field research methods among media scholars reflects a recognition of the problem of *ecological validity* that is created when traditional investigative formats and contexts are used to study audience behavior. The experimental conditions used in Morley's initial study of the *Nationwide* audience were not at all like the conditions in which most viewers were likely to view and respond to the program in their homes. Indeed, it seems likely that the Black participants in his study who were, according to Morley, 'unable' to make sense of the program when asked, probably would not have bothered to watch them in the first place. One of the Black participants in Morley's study offered the opinion that '*Nationwide* is so boring, it's not interesting at all. I don't see how anybody could watch it . . . all of BBC is definitely boring . . . . I go to sleep when things like that are on . . . it should be banned – it's so boring' (Morley, 1992, p. 107).

Despite this catalog of problems and limitations, there is still a broad consensus that there is the possibility of learning something meaningful about the relations between media use and a variety of individual, relational, and societal consequences that are implicated in the association between race and life chances.

Consequences

First, we should recognize the necessity of thinking of media effects as occurring at several different levels (McLeod and Reeves, 1981). While the primary focus of mass communications researchers has been on individual effects, it is also possible for us to think about the ways in which media affect social relationships, as in the interaction between people from different racial or ethnic groups. It is also possible to consider the effects of media consumption at the level of the society, where we might focus on relations between groups and between nations. We are certain that the mass media can have effects at the level of the society as a whole – effects that we think about as cultural. We are not in agreement about whether we can or even should attempt to separate out the effects as occurring independently at any of these levels.

Although we have not found it easy to describe the underlying process through which cultural change occurs, we think that an enormously popular television program such as *The Cosby Show* has helped to shift the ways in which mainstream culture organizes its thinking about race. This shift is somehow more than and different from the cumulation of individual level changes in our understanding of the details of African American family life.

Historically, the wealth of resources invested in communications research has been for the purpose of improving the management and control of people. This is what we have identified, somewhat pejoratively, as 'administrative research.' Because of this focus we know relatively little about the higher order and system level effects of media use. There is a similar limitation on what we know about the *nature of* these effects, although the reasons are not exactly the same. The impact of media can be understood in terms of its impact on knowledge, or attitudes, or behavior. While the disparity is not as great as it is with regard to the structural levels of media effects, we still know far more about the impact of media use on knowledge than we do about its impact on attitudes or behavior (Figure 5.1).

A recent shift in the focus of researchers within the traditions of social psychology away from attitudes and toward cognitions as part of an 'information processing paradigm' might be expected to increase this

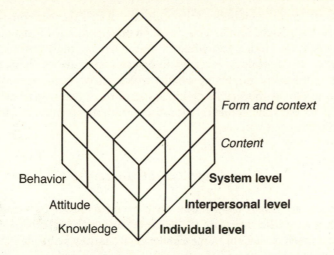

Figure 5.1 Structure of knowledge of media effects

disparity. Beniger and Gusek (1995) identify this paradigm shift as marking the end of a 15-year dry spell in scholarship on public opinion that began after Joseph Klapper's assertion that the effects of media were extremely limited (1960), and Bernard Bereleson's premature report of the discipline's demise (1959).

Because of the instrumental and bureaucratic concerns that guided much of the early research into media effects, outcomes or consequences had been traditionally defined in terms of changes or alteration of one's knowledge and opinion. Critical scholars, on the other hand, believed that ideological function of a mass media system was not the production of attitude change, but the maintenance or *reproduction* of particular views of the world. Although the emerging cognitive perspective as it was interpreted in agenda setting, spiral-of-silence, and even cultivation analysis research, side-stepped or avoided direct measurement of persuasion, conversion, or other demonstrable *change* in attitudes or cognitions, we still know far more about change than we do about the reproduction and reinforcement or strengthing of dominant perspectives.

Although, as we have noted, there is increasing attention being paid to the context within which media are consumed, and the nature of media systems, including its changing technical forms, the dominant causal model is one which focuses on content as the critical determinant of media effects.

Business and government have not, until quite recently, recognized the instrumental utility of knowing very much about the effects of the mass media in the area of race. Without retreating toward the level of surrender that is common to some versions of postmodern theory (Best and Kellner, 1991), it *is* important to recognize that the effects of media exposure are not the same for all members of the audience. While there is some research which emphasizes the direct effects of media behavior consistent with a stimulus-response model, and while in some quarters there still seems to be a preference for biological over sociological explanations, it is generally agreed that the most important challenge for theory and research within the field of media studies is the specification of the 'conditional' factors that modify the direct, one-to-one relationship between exposure and impact on individuals.

Context and conditions

Among the conditional factors that have been identified as modifying the direct effect of media exposure is the extent to which the representation is perceived as being *realistic*. One challenge to earlier published studies of television violence (Gerbner *et al.*, 1979) is a failure to distinguish between cartoons, or humorous representations, and the realistic violence in action-adventure programs, or in the theatrical films which are distributed by premium cable television services. Whether researchers make use of a objective measure of realism, or rely upon a self-reported assessment of perceived realism, the assumption and the usual findings are that realism increases the impact of media consumption or exposure (Messaris, 1994). Assessments of the reality of media portrayals are bound to vary as a function of race, class, and gender, because those assessments will be based on comparisons with the structured repertoire of impressions and schemata that vary with social position. Communications scholars have rarely been motivated to pursue such distinctions in perceived reality.

The concern with the realism of television portrayals also includes a concern about the reasonable expectation that the impact of representations within fictional programs (or even theatrical film) must be different from the impact from exposure to representations within the news. While both representations take advantage of, or at least rely upon, common experience in interpreting the visual (Moriarty, 1996), there are likely to be important differences in the ways in which news and fictional images are stored in memory, and then made available for use in developing generalizations or assessments of social reality (Shapiro and Lang, 1991).

While some theorists have argued that important preconditions for media effects are established quite early, such as predispositions that are characteristic of individuals with different personality types (Wober, 1986), others have argued that the more important preconditions are those which are determined by social location, indicated principally by social class (Bourdieu, 1989; Morley, 1992, pp. 73–130). It is only quite recently that scholars have examined racial group identity as an important conditional factor that might predict or explain specific media effects (Gandy and Matabane, 1989).

If, as the cultivation hypothesis suggests, individuals develop an under-standing of the social world, including not only how violent it is, but also how the distribution of victimization reflects dominant systems of power, we need to know something about how the viewer actually produces these estimates. At the moment there seem to be at least two likely explanations: (1) viewers keep a running account and, when asked, are able to produce an estimate of the relative frequencies of events and outcomes, or (2) because the underlying structure of representations is so similar, viewers estimate probabilities and relationships from the most recent programs or messages they have consumed. The first theoretical possibility is referred to as 'frequency estimation,' while the second is termed 'prototype extraction' (Shapiro and Lang, 1991). The jury is still out.

What we apparently require in order to make the right estimates is some way to avoid 'source confusion' (Mares, 1996). Some theorists suggest that success in arriving at accurate assessments is the presence of contextual markers that provide cues about which of the events we have stored in memory should be used for any particular assessment (Shapiro, 1991). Racial and ethnic differences in meaning structures make predictions about responses to cues generally unreliable. The fact that cognitive theorists seek general models means that there is little chance that such differences will be reported in the literature, however.

It may also be that the differences between memories derived from 'real' programs may be overwhelmed by those from fictional representations because the number of fictional exposures is so much greater. We are also unsure about the nature of coding, and the routines used for accessing the different memory 'stores' that would automatically label some images as inappropriate, simply because they came from a 'realistic' rather than a 'real' exposure. Mares' (1996) analysis of the relationship between the tendency to confuse or fail to remember accurately whether the 'facts' a person recalls came from news or from fiction, suggests that persons who made more fiction-to-fact confusions were also more likely to have esti-mates of social reality that have been influenced by television viewing. That is, fiction-to-news confusions appear to strengthen the cultivation effect (p. 295).

We do not know, of course, whether such confusions are common, whether they vary with the nature of the events remembered, or whether they vary as a function of other unrelated events. The tendency to make erroneous attributions is another 'individual difference' which challenges our ability to make generalizations about the nature of media effects. Here again, the search for cognitive universals means that individual differences are treated as noise, rather than important avenues worth pursuing.

Another set of conditional factors are those which describe the cognitive and emotional status of the audience member prior to or during exposure to the message. This is a bit different from the attitudinal predispositions that we believe are the result of a long-term process of socialization. For example, early experimental work on the effects of exposure to violent material determined that the impact of such exposure was greater if the subject was angered (Bandura, 1973) or, as later understood, aroused by a variety of means (Zillman, 1982).

Other prior conditions mediating the impact of media exposure on an individual audience member includes their orientation toward the medium. The literature on media orientations includes contradictory evidence suggesting that Blacks were less trusting, and more dissatisfied or critical, but more active consumers of mass media than members of other social groups (Gandy and Matabane, 1989). The expectations that viewers bring to the television experience have been demonstrated to explain at least some of the differences in the knowledge that is retained from each exposure (Gunter, 1987).

Measurement and inference

Experimental designs are valued for their ability to generate confidence in the conclusions about the nature of communicative processes. If well designed and executed, the experiment provides us with a basis for making claims about the nature of causal relations. This is not to say that all experiments are well done. There are a great many threats to the validity of experimental designs (Campbell and Stanley, 1963), and we can be sure that the literature is filled with reports of errors that we mistakenly take as truth. But that is not our point. Good experiments, done well, provide us with aid to understanding.

However, experimental designs are often quite limited in terms of the inferences that can be drawn about relationships outside the laboratory. The world outside the laboratory is far more complicated, and researchers are not equipped with their magical cloaking device, *randomization*, which when done well helps to ensure that individual differences do not interact with the stimulus materials in any systematic way. It makes little sense to try to determine which of the many departures from the ideal conditions of the experiment we should treat as the greatest threats to our confidence that we really understand what the effects of media are, or how they come to be.

Among the limitations of the experimental paradigm is its preference for the security of its *ceteris paribus* assumption. Randomization allows the experimental researcher to assume (although some also estimate the effectiveness of randomization) that experimental and treatment conditions have experimental subjects who can be assumed to be equal on all *other* relevant dimensions. By treating respondents as the same, the experiment makes it less likely that differences between types of people will be observed. The favored analytical model, based on the analysis of variance between and within randomized groups, also treats people as the same. It compares means or other measures of central tendency. Conclusions are usually based on the extent of the differences between these measures.

Such an analytical approach does not emphasize the number or percentage of people who are affected; rather it describes the overall effect on the constructed group. Thus, experiments generally tell us little about the proportion of people in the population who are likely to be affected by exposure to stereotypes. Instead, they tell us that 'on the average' people who have been exposed are likely to differ from those who have not. Other analytical designs, such as those based on correlation, provide estimates of the direction and the strength of the relationship between exposure and effect. A statistical hypothesis about the relationship between the frequency of exposure and the strength of the response is what we usually see evaluated.

Experimental designs are also extremely limited in their ability to tell us much about changes that are cumulative, especially those which take place over long periods of time. Field surveys attempt to capture the effect of time by including people who may have had greater exposure to media by virtue of their age. But, as we know from the previous chapter, media content has changed quite a bit over time, so that what teenagers were exposed to in 1960 is very different from what teenagers in 1996 are likely to be exposed to. Thus today's adults are bound to be different from the adults that today's teenagers will become. While these *cross-sectional* designs are limited in this important way, *longitudinal* designs which would follow today's teenagers throughout their lives as media users are far too expensive to be used extensively in the study of media effects.

Some media scholars have responded to the criticism of traditional surveys by turning to extended group interviews as a means of coming closer to what they believe is the fundamental character of the meanings that people derive from their exposure to media. After coming to the conclusion that it would be impossible to design a study that could, in any straightforward way, measure the *effect* of *The Cosby Show* on attitudes toward race, Jhally and Lewis (1992) decided to treat the comments of the people they talked with as akin to the 'evidence' and 'testimony' that jurors must weigh in coming to a decision about guilt or innocence. Their important study is an example of an attempt to combine empirical research methods with critical goals in the study of communication and race.

Self-image

We are complex, multidimensional creations of nature. The importance of race as a component of our self-concept is determined by a unspecified, but undoubtedly complex, set of influences, some direct, but most indirect (Figure 5.2). If we define identification as the desire to imitate, to 'be like' some role model, there is evidence that race is an important component of

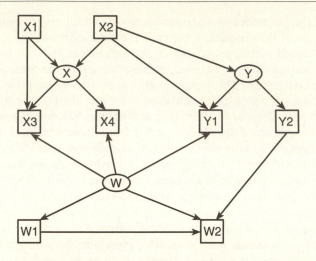

Figure 5.2 Structure of influence

our choice of model. That is, when given sufficient choice, both White and Black youngsters tend to identify with *same race* characters in television programs.

There are differences, however, that reveal the impact of the existence of racial hierarchies that constrain these choices still further. While the differences between White and Black youngsters' desire to be like a range of White television characters was not significant overall, the differences between Whites and Blacks was much greater when the characters were Black (Greenberg and Atkin, 1982). While Black youngsters apparently found it easy to set aside race in their selection of characters to identify with, it was apparently impossible for some White youngsters to do so. This may reflect the importance of ascribed social status in the selection of reference groups. Members of subordinate groups are perceived as inappropriate role models or resources for identity formation for members of dominant social groups, unless the potential models have extraordinary qualities, such as those common to the athletic superstars that have become idols for White as well as Black youngsters.

Part of an individual's self-concept may include an assessment of the individual's own racial group. Studies reported by Kenneth Clark in 1947 helped to establish the concept of racial esteem through the oft-demonstrated tendency for Black youngsters to select the White doll as the 'nice' one, while ignoring the Black one (Clark and Clark, 1947). Numerous studies reported after this classic study add additional evidence that Black youngsters had lower self-esteem than White youngsters, and this was the result of their absorbing the images of a racist ideology. This work is not without controversy, however, and counter-positions include a challenge to the fundamental assumption that own-group bias is necessarily healthy or proper (Penn *et al.*, 1993). Many of the critiques have been methodological, challenging the validity of the demonstration of choice behavior (Smith, 1995).

Challenges to the assumption that own-group preference is normal, perhaps because that is the behavior demonstrated most often by Whites, include studies which demonstrate that the pattern is not universal. Studies of Chinese and Chicano children did not find an own-group preference; nor was such a preference found among Native American youngsters prior to the age of five. More complicated critiques suggest that such preferences ought not to be viewed as a unitary concept, but should be allowed to vary as a reflection of different moments in the development of an individual's identity. Such a view is common to Black psychologists, such as Cross, who have developed stage-theoretic models of Black identity formation (Cross, 1995).

Although correlations cannot provide evidence of a causal influence of television viewing, a negative correlation between viewing and self-esteem is at least consistent with that conclusion (Tan and Tan, 1979). By the use of statistical techniques that remove the influence of age and other potential influences on self-esteem, the relatively high negative correlation between television viewing and self-esteem supports an interpretation that repeated exposure to programs 'which depict blacks in low status social roles causes low self-esteem in black audiences' (Tan and Tan, 1979, p. 134). Such an analysis must assume that own-race group identification is widespread.

These findings have been replicated in part in a study by Allen and Hatchett (1986) which concluded that even exposure to 'Black-oriented' television programs had a negative influence on self-esteem. A somewhat contradictory finding in this study was the association of a high-level of exposure to such programs and various forms of identification with Black groups. Allen and Hatchett had assumed that exposure to the negative portrayals of African Americans that were common in the situation comedies being broadcast in the 1970s would result in the cultivation of negative impressions in this group. Those who watched more of these programs were more likely to agree with negative stereotypes about Blacks, but they were also more likely to identify with mainstream and non-mainstream groups of Blacks, as well as to reflect what was identified as a 'black separatist perspective.' No compelling explanation for this puzzling result was provided, although Smith (1995, p. 90) suggests that 'personal feelings of self-worth and group identification are empirically separable phenomena.'

Jhally and Lewis (1992) argue that popular television programs like *The Cosby Show* reduce the number of choices available for Black youngsters to develop a positive self-image. The cultural critique of television mobilized by American Blacks has helped to minimize the negative images of Black life presented by television. As a result, however, television's focus on the upper middle class has eliminated positive images of lower and working-class Black life. If working-class Blacks accept television's image of economic reality, they have only their own immediate experience to compare it with. The comparison is painful, and one possible solution is to define their own experience as atypical.

Within the cultural studies paradigm, engagement with the question of media influence on self-image tends to be framed in terms of opposition and resistance. In part, this emphasis is one which seeks to deny the power of media, or the power of those who control media. As part of a political project that seeks to develop and reproduce the capacity for resistance, many studies pursued from this perspective seek to provide examples of success in the production of oppositional readings of media texts. What these analyses *should* provide is a greater understanding of the variety of *ways* in which people generate meanings that have potential for emancipatory social action (Verstraeten, 1996). There is little doubt that at least *some* of these meanings will contribute to what Giddens refers to as the 'distancing of commitment to a legitimate order' (Giddens, 1981, pp. 67–8). It also seems important for such studies to examine elite as well as subordinate populations for evidence of resistance. If cultural resistance is to have a truly transformative potential, it cannot be limited to those at the bottom of the well (Bell, 1992).

As we have noted, the primary criticism of the approach of cultural studies is its relative lack of interest or concern with generalizability (Ang, 1996b, p. 170). What we usually find in these publications are extended case studies in which a limited number of observations are made among an often specialized population. Some of these studies demonstrate the ways in which *oppositional readings* of media texts can be produced. A small number of these provide examples of the oppositional readings that are made by members of minority racial and ethnic groups. For example, Jacqueline Bobo (1995) provides a representation of some of the ways that a group of Black women have produced oppositional readings of popular films as members of an *interpretive community*. Bobo argues that the fact that many Black women actually responded favorably to Steven Spielberg's production of Alice Walker's *The Color Purple* ought not be seen as merely another example of manipulation by dominant cultural forces.

Bobo finds resistance in the fact that the Black women in her focus groups articulated well-developed reasons for liking the film, at the same time that they rejected the guidance of the mainstream critics who had suggested that Black people should not like this film (Bobo, 1995, pp. 91–2). Bobo suggests that the fact that the Black women of her interpretive community were able to resist the dominant perspective of the film, while at the same time being able to 'extract progressive meanings' by 'reading against the grain' is something to be valued (pp. 89–90). Of course, Bobo's interpretive assessment points to the part of the underlying limitation of the approach. It is not at all clear just exactly which source of domination is being opposed, or exactly which version of a polysemic text is being read.

There is the film, and then there is the reading of the film that White critics (and some Black ones as well) produce. Many of Bobo's Black viewers found some 'middle ground' at which they were able to feel good about enjoying this film. They were able to incorporate what might under other circumstances be distressing images into their progressive, Black feminist cognitive structures through a process otherwise recognized as rose-colored glasses.

The difficulty with the readings produced by Bobo, and those produced by Morley and countless others who seek to demonstrate and exemplify resistance, is the fact that the circumstances in which the readings were produced bear little relation to the circumstances of everyday, routine, media use. The data which Morley's group interviews produced for his study of the *Nationwide* audience were hardly measures of what people were 'able' to produce (Morley, 1992). At best, they were parts of impressions that people were willing to share. Indeed, the epistemological shortcomings of audience research are especially troubling in this regard because there is no way to determine if there is any relationship between the reactions generated in the context of a group viewing, which was organized at the behest of an elite educational institution, and the reactions that would be produced if the program had been viewed voluntarily at home.

It is also the case that the responses which people offer in the research context may also be examples of the kinds of 'readings' that people are *able* to produce upon request, especially when they have been cued to adopt the role of an intelligent viewer – one who is expected to be able to produce an intelligent, critical response. It is not at all clear that any such responses would be produced if they had not been requested and framed as such by the researchers.

It should be noted, however, that the problems of associating racial and other identities with the responses that media consumers in experiments, focus groups, or even in the more 'natural' environment of the ethnographic observations are not easily overcome. Social constructivists emphasize the possibility that identities may be seen by respondents as 'resources' which they can enact, accomplish, or bring into being in the context of responding to interviewer requests. Citing recent analyses of the responses of news viewers to relatively unstructured interviews, Dickerson concluded that respondents may engage in 'impression management' and may choose to 'produce a picture which is a self-conscious distortion in an effort to create an impression of being an "ideal" (or critically aware) news viewer' (Dickerson, 1996, p. 58). It is Dickerson's view that such strategic motives are not the only factors that may produce variations in the constructions of self that may emerge in the context of audience research. Dickerson concludes that 'audiences who talk about their consumption of the news [or other content, we should assume] can be understood as producing a constructed version of their activity, one for which many equally plausible alternatives may be available' (p. 78).

Shohat and Stam (1994, p. 354) suggest that there is a need to temper the 'euphoric' claims of cultural studies scholars like Fiske who assume, and occasionally provide examples of, the kinds of 'subversive' readings that members of oppressed minorities produce when they consume mainstream media. Instead, they suggest that 'while disempowered communities can decode dominant programming through a resistant perspective, they can do so only to the extent that their collective life and historical memory have provided an alternative framework for understanding.' It is not at all clear what social experiences would provide the kinds of cultural competence they refer to, and it is even less clear what the *distribution* of those experiences in the population might actually be. It seems logical, however, that if this competence were well distributed then the level of acceptance of the social conditions Fiske and others have described would be more actively opposed.

Ignorance and bliss

Among the most important effects of the mass media in the reproduction of a racialized system would have to be the reproduction and transformation of beliefs about members of racial and ethnic minority groups. As we have discussed more generally in Chapter 2, racism is multidimensional. It includes a tendency to hold negative beliefs about the personal qualities of minority groups. It also includes associational dimensions, perhaps reflecting the extent to which one feels threatened by, or is made uncomfortable by, contact with members of minority groups. Racial prejudice is often considered to be a combination of cognitive and affective responses to members of another racial group (Dovidio and Gaertner, 1986). Racism also involves attitudes and opinions regarding rights and responsibilities, and their formal representation in laws.

Hagendoorn (1993) distinguishes between different forms of contemporary racisms, and includes one form, identified as 'aversive racism', which is defined as the active avoidance of ethnic groups without explicit justification. The 'avoiders' are somehow characterized by emotional uneasiness and uncertainty regarding outgroups, and it is managed by keeping one's social distance.

Over time, Whites' attitudes toward Blacks have apparently become less negative, both in terms of beliefs about Blacks, as well as in terms of acceptance of social contact and willingness to support the extension of basic civil rights. Dovidio and Gaertner (1986) have reported that not only has the association of negative stereotypes with Blacks been reduced over time, but the stereotypes associated with Whites have become more negative, with the surprising result that there has been an increase in the amount of overlap between the stereotypes that Whites now assign to both Whites and Blacks.

If we grant that the measures of racial beliefs and opinions actually reflect a reduction of racism (and, as we have noted, this is not a conclusion that everyone is willing to reach), then we would like to be able to determine what the role of the mass media has been in bringing about or reinforcing this change.

A second question also presents itself. Although it appears that we have made substantial progress in modifying racist attitudes and beliefs, it is also clear that we have not come as far as we might in eliminating race as a factor in the distribution of life chances. Contemporary observers like Andrew Hacker (1992) still define the social reality of the United States in stark terms: 'two nations: black and white, separate, hostile, unequal.' Does the mass media share any responsibility for the continued existence of racism and social disparity, or does it merely reflect the conditions as they are?

The structural perspective that we have developed in this book assumes that racist beliefs are part of a complex structure that changes in identifiable ways in response to a number of complementary forces. Some of the difficulties that scholars have encountered in describing these emergent forms have to do with the ways in which these structures are measured, as well as the ways in which they interact.

For example, if the components of the belief structure which theorists have called variously 'modern, symbolic or subtle racism' involve a belief that racism is bad and that discrimination no longer exists, as well as a belief that minorities are making unfair demands on society, especially because they (Blacks in particular) already get more benefits and more special treatment than they deserve (Dovidio and Gaertner, 1986, p, 21; Kinder and Sanders, 1996, pp. 291–4), then we would need to determine what role the mass media played in the development of this system of belief.

This was the primary focus of one of the cornerstone studies of communication and race. Paul Hartman and Charles Husband (1974) set out to understand the role of the mass media in the formation of White beliefs and attitudes in Britain. They suggested that 'the negative symbolism and meaning surrounding blackness, with its deep historical roots in British culture, forms the interpretive framework within which the interracial situations are perceived in Britain' (p. 205). This racialized perspective operated to reduce the visibility of the injustice and exploitation experienced by Blacks and other minorities in England.

At the same time, because our conception of racial groups is so multi-dimensional, we believe that it is more resistant to change. As we discussed in the introduction, structures are understood in terms of the linkages between elements. Race is connected to several dimensions that define social relations: socioeconomic status, residence, language, and a host of cultural values linked to the consumption of commodities. That is, we think we can identify or define a person as Black in part on the basis of where they live, how they speak, what they wear, what kind of work they do, and what they have for dinner. The mass media are involved in reinforcing, or helping to change, the strengths of those links and the accuracy of the racial classifications that we might make on the basis of that information.

We might think about the structural aspects of racial classification by means of a variant of the input-output matrix that is used to describe the structure of an economy. Rather than describing inter-industry flows, we might simply indicate the strength of the linkage in terms of the probability that we could identify the race of a person on the basis of information we have from the other dimensions of the matrix. Think about the dimensions along which different racial and ethnic groups might be seen to differ. Hagendoorn (1993, p. 27) suggests that for most people racial and ethnic groups are believed to vary in their 'verbal and nonverbal codes, in their expression of status, authority, honour and guilt, in their rules for hygiene, sexual and marital behavior, or their valuation of time, labor, family and religion.' Think about the ways these differences might be evaluated from your own perspective, or from the perspective of others of different racial or ethnic groups. Think about how these differences might be used to rank order racial or ethnic groups. Finally, think about how images from the mass media might be used to assign the values and the eventual ranks for these groups. This ranking, based on stereotypes distributed by the mass media, helps to reproduce the racial or ethnic hierarchies that we can observe in any given society (Figure 5.3).

Of course, we need not be reminded that the most reliable indicator of racial group membership is still visual inspection. While not perfect by any means, physical characteristics are still used confidently because of their ready availability, and the absence of contrary evidence that might lead us to question the reliability of our assessment. Research suggests that factors which increase the importance of distinctions between groups also tend to increase the amount of bias between groups (Dovidio and Gaertner, 1986). Thus, ironically, the tremendous success of African Americans in sports, which is amplified by the virtual explosion of commercial sports programming in the mass media, may work to heighten awareness of racial difference. This would not be the result if the representation of interracial contact by the mass media did not provide such readily accessible validation of group difference.

For example, in a survey of American adults, people were asked to provide their 'best guess' of what percentage of the United States population was African American. The mean estimate was 23.7 per cent, nearly twice the actual proportion estimated by the 1990 census. What might explain this overestimate? Theory suggests that mass media portrayals of African Americans may affect estimates in two ways: the mere presence of

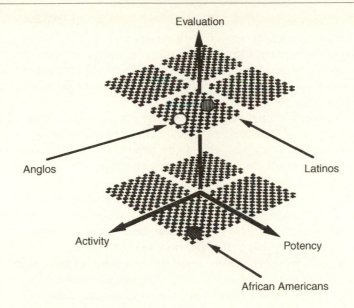

Figure 5.3 Structural influences on racial comparisons

Blacks in the media increases their salience in the minds of Whites and, as a consequence, increases their estimate of the proportion of Blacks in the population. Also, the *way* in which minority groups are presented in the media also influences their salience. That is, if minority groups are presented as threatening, they are likely to be seen as more numerous than they actually are (Nadeau *et al.*, 1993).

The primary emphasis of research associated with the cultivation hypothesis is the impact of exposure to television on social perception. The assumptions of the research paradigm are deceptively simple: the more time one spends in the 'world of television' the more one comes to see the world in television terms. These estimates of social reality are almost certain to be in error. These errors are not random, but reflect the systematic distortions in the structure of media representations. However, our acceptance of misrepresentations as true leads to a 'false consciousness' that is especially problematic if it also includes an agreement that what is 'normal' is also what is right and good.

In one of a small number of studies that have focused primarily on the role of television in the cultivation of social perceptions among African Americans, Matabane (1988) provides support for an interpretation of television's effect as ideological and hegemonic. After arguing that television fiction provided a positive portrayal of the benefits of integration in ways that either ignore or downplay the negatives (circa 1984), Matabane hypothesized that heavy viewers would be closer within the ideological 'mainstream' than those who watched less television. Matabane's test was primarily one of social estimation rather than evaluation. Three of the four items in her 'racial integration' scale were descriptive: 'Blacks are generally no different from whites in the way they act, dress, or socialize'; 'Most blacks have achieved middle-class status,' and 'Blacks and whites frequently socialize together.' The fourth was a bit more predictive: 'Blacks can easily fit into an all-white setting.'

Utilizing the traditional analysis of mainstreaming which relies on graphical and statistical assessments of difference between heavy and light television viewers, Matabane found the hypothesized differences by age, gender, church attendance, and community participation. The mainstreaming effect was higher among those with more education, higher income, and higher subjective social class. This is an important finding in that it suggests that it is not merely that Blacks who move into the upper classes shift toward the mainstream or dominant ideological view, but it is those who watch more television that are more likely to adopt that view.

From Matabane's perspective, the hegemonic effect of television 'seemed most effective in isolating pockets of black dissidence among the young and better-educated Afro-Americans.' She joined in the criticism of *The Cosby Show* because of the impact it seemed likely to have on Black political activism (Jhally and Lewis, 1992). She suggested that 'the illusion of well-being among the oppressed may lead to reduced political activity and less demand for social justice and equality' (p. 30).

A second study of the impact of television on the cultivation of social perceptions among African Americans uses a correlational rather than an analysis of variance model. As a result, it does not engage the hegemonic effect quite so directly (Allen and Hatchett, 1986). Instead, this study sought to place television within the context of other social and structural influences on social perception. The study also included measures of exposure to Black-oriented as well as mainstream media. Whereas exposure to television in general was associated with what might be interpreted as an integrationist perspective as in the study by Matabane (1988), Allen and Hatchett found that exposure to Black-oriented programming was linked to support for separatist positions.

Most analyses of the impact of television that proceed from within the paradigm of cultivation emphasize the contribution that television viewing makes to the construction of social reality. Cultural theorists have also suggested, however, that it is not only beliefs about the real world but mythical beliefs that play an important role in maintaining structures of domination within society (Sidanius *et al.*, 1992). Thus television and mass media may also play an important role in distributing the 'legitimizing myths' that help to justify the continuing relations between dominant and subordinate groups in society.

Legitimizing myths are parts of the structure of beliefs and values that help to explain why poverty exists, and why Blacks and Hispanics continue to occupy positions at the bottom of the status hierarchy. Cultivation analyses might, therefore, assess the extent to which exposure to television and other media is associated with accepting such myths as the explanations for continued disparity.

The most consistent criticism raised against the extremely popular *Cosby Show* has been that it helps to reproduce the myth of economic and social mobility – that anyone can make it in America (Jhally and Lewis, 1992). Jhally and Lewis suggest that US television fiction, by its overattention to the lives of the middle and upper classes, has actually helped to transform our understanding of social class. For them, 'the definition of what is normal no longer includes the working class' (1992, p. 133). The evidence from cultivation analysis studies of mainstreaming is supportive of this view. Heavy television viewers who are actually members of the lower or working classes by virtue of their objective social location tend to misidentify themselves as middle class (Gerbner *et al.*, 1982).

Jhally and Lewis (1992) suggest that by readjusting the 'rules' which normally define the boundaries of social class in order to produce a successful program about an African American family, television helped to make the realities of race incomprehensible to Whites (p. 135). When asked, most of the White respondents seemed unaware of the continued existence of structural limits to Black economic advancement. Whites understand that Blacks are, on the average, poorer than Whites, but they seem incapable of explaining the disparity, and their rejection of affirmative action can be interpreted as flowing naturally from their ignorance. Justin Lewis suggests that *The Cosby Show* can be implicated in perpetuating this ignorance (Lewis, 1991), although he and Jhally recognize that no single program, no matter how extensively viewed, can be the only source of such widespread ignorance and confusion.

Even though the Huxtables were a fictional family, the prominent role they had come to play in the lives and in the cognitive representation of race for many White viewers was one that would make opposition to affirmative action quite logical. The prominent example of the Huxtables demonstrated that there was no longer any need for government action, as it was obvious that Blacks had done well as a result of state-supported improvements in education and employment opportunity. The fact that the benefits of affirmative action had not trickled down very far into the Black class structure escaped the notice of a great many of the Whites in the *Cosby* audience. For those Whites that were aware of the substantial inequality that still exists, the success of the Huxtables helped to support the conclusion that the Blacks who had not 'made it' were either stupid or lazy.

Lewis (1991) claims that a unique form of 'deracination' had been produced by the *Cosby* experience. Whites who watched the show easily came to the conclusion that at least some Blacks were *just like them*. Some of these viewers felt that the show would be basically the same if the characters had been White. They did not categorize *The Cosby Show* with any of the other Black sitcoms on television at the time. The viewers seem to have incorporated an almost postmodern understanding of race:

> The assumption behind these judgements is that 'blackness' is a social construction, a collection of cultural indicators that can be freed from the physical actuality of being black. Consequentially, when you have what one respondent described as a 'black family in a white atmosphere,' it is possible to forget that the family on the TV screen is a different race. (Lewis, 1991, p. 175)

However, Lewis found that the more overtly racist among White viewers had more difficulty in making a distinction between 'blackness' as a physical attribute and 'blackness' as a cultural category. This would suggest the existence of stronger links between the elements of the construct of race that easily overcome the weaker links that might be cued by references to the markers of social class.

Black viewers of the program reportedly 'saw' an identifiably different program. Many of the aspects of 'Blackness' that were intentionally included in the settings and in the situations by the show's producers were largely invisible to White viewers. Black viewers, on the other hand, readily identified examples of racial signification. The 'background' features moved to the foreground for the Black viewers (Lewis, 1991, p. 195). The availability of these cultural markers may have helped to reduce the significance of the class markers for Black viewers. The Huxtables were more 'Black' than middle class for many of these viewers.

Selective exposure is frequently offered as an explanation for the frequently observed variations in responses to exposures to the same film or television programs. Selective exposure, or selective attention, refers to the tendency for audience attention to be easily distracted, or for differences in orientation and expectation to lead some members of the audience to attend more closely to some features of a program than to others. Selective exposure has been used as an explanation for the different responses to programs whose racial content was understood differently by different groups within the audience. Most important among these have been the studies of audience responses to *All in the Family* and *Roots* (Hur, 1978; Vidmar and Rokeach, 1974). A recent analysis of selective exposure and selective perception of the controversial series *In Living Color* concluded that the use of traditional stereotypes, especially in the context of 'inside jokes' or efforts at delivering critical comment through parody, is an ineffective strategy because audiences fail to make the distinction between 'realistic and parodic depictions' (Cooks and Orbe, 1993, p. 227). They see the result as a net increase in the strength of negative racial stereotypes. The economic realities of television which require an integrated audience to succeed would seem to argue against the use of traditional racist stereotypes, even for the purpose of reflexive social comment.

However, as the media marketplace continues to expand, and the need to avoid disturbing or confusing White audiences is diminished somewhat, because content providers are able to target their programs toward more racially and ethnically homogeneous audiences, we also have to consider the possibility that the media-based reproduction of the dominant mythology will either become less successful, or it will take on different forms (Neuman, 1991; Wilson and Gutiérrez, 1995).

Old-fashioned, modern, and symbolic racism

As we discussed in Chapter 2, our ideas about Black people, and other racial and ethnic minorities who have become the focus of public debate, are organized within a cognitive structure that also includes our underlying political ideology and world view. This world view also includes our system of moral and ethical values. Some scholars have suggested that new forms of racism have evolved and that an earlier emphasis on biologically determined incapacity that assigned Blacks and other subordinate groups to their despised or pitiable position has been replaced by an emphasis on traditional values and culture. The resulting assignments of these groups to their positions in the status and value hierarchy are similar, but the justifications appear to have changed. These are changes that many observers associate with media coverage and elite framing of the issues.

While racial feelings are a powerful influence on our policy preferences, they are not independent of our larger ideological orientation. This orientation is itself complex, including those aspects of political thinking that assign people along the continuum from liberal to conservative. These labels primarily reflect a person's opinions regarding what they see as the appropriate role of the government. They may also involve what we typically recognize as moral and ethical views about social justice as they relate to fairness. These notions of fairness include expectations regarding responsible action, expressed in part by the demand that people must do their fair share. These beliefs about values and persons have been discussed in terms of schemas, and the relations between them have been discussed in terms of a systematically ordered set that we have called an ideology.

Political scientists have responded to the ways in which social policy has become confounded with racial attitudes by creating a new construct which further confounds rather than overcomes the distinctions between perceptions of racial groups, and attitudes about what they deserve as a matter of legal rights or entitlements. This is an unsettled question at the heart of the concept of *modern racism* that attempts to understand the orientation of Whites toward a race-based policy like affirmative action. For many Whites, the failure of Blacks to achieve equality can be attributed to their failure to work hard and to improve themselves in ways that adherence to traditional values would suggest. The alleged failure of Blacks to behave responsibly can then be used as a pretext for denying public benefits without triggering the charge that the denial is racist in its motivation. This model of policy thinking suggests that expressed opposition to policies designed to reduce inequality need not be linked automatically to traditional racist beliefs or opinions. Is it the case that the expression of stereotypical beliefs about minorities has been suppressed because their expression has become unpopular, or socially unacceptable, but opposition to public policies can still be seen as legitimate (Sniderman *et al.*, 1991, pp. 245–6)?

Or is it the case, as van Dijk (1992) suggests, that the *denial of racism* is part of a defensive strategy which actually enhances ingroup preservation through positive self-presentation? Through the influence of elite opinion, reproduced and redistributed through the mass media, the denial of racism becomes so routine that making the charge of racism, or raising the possibility of its influence on social outcomes, becomes a serious social infraction, perhaps more serious than displaying overtly racist attitudes or behavior. Blaming the victim of racism, by focusing on negative aspects of outgroup behavior or values as an explanation for their subordinate status, is seen to be just one means of achieving ingroup preservation through the denial of racism.

The conservative attack against affirmative action includes an attack against what has been characterized by some as 'the culture of poverty.' It is the system of values that is reflected in, and reproduced by, popular cultural materials that celebrate the lifestyle of the ghetto. It is the assumed values of ghetto residents that are used to explain the continued subordinate status of Blacks and Latinos. Some of the debate surrounding the concept of 'Afrocentricity' is also focused on the distinction between aspects of African American culture, the culture of Blacks in the African diaspora, and the cultural heritage that survives from the African past (Asante, 1987; 1990; 1993).

Political scientists have used a number of different strategies in their effort to understand the relationship between racial attitudes and beliefs and the more fundamental social values that appear to be linked closely with traditional measures of political ideology. Political conservatism has traditionally been associated with opposition to egalitarian public policies. We would assume that racists would also oppose those policies if the policies would provide assistance to Blacks or other racial minorities. It may also be the case that racists are also politically conservative. The problem is one of determining how much of the opposition to egalitarian policies is determined by political ideology, and how much is determined by racism; and, further, how influential is the mass media in bringing the two together.

While a conservative would, all other things being equal, oppose any policy that provides government assistance, they should not, on the basis of political ideology, care whether the intended recipient is White or Black. A racist, however, would be more likely to oppose benefits for a Black person. According to one definition, 'racism . . . consists in a double standard – one standard of what is right and fair for whites, another and harsher standard for blacks' (Sniderman *et al.*, 1991, p. 248).

The debate about the best ways to define and measure the kinds of racism that operate in different societies is unlikely to be brought to a satisfactory close any time soon (Wood, 1994). At the heart of the debate is a disagreement about the motives which govern the expression of preferences for political candidates or public policy initiatives. How do we determine if the preference reflects racist, rather than politically conservative, anti-state motives? Is it in fact correct for us to discuss racism in terms of motives at all? If so, what kinds of motives are racist?

Experimental techniques have been used with limited success to separate racism from other forms of ideological constraint. Using what they called the 'laid-off worker' experiment, Sniderman and his colleagues told different respondents a story about a worker who had been laid off from the job. The experimental groups differed in terms of the attributes that were associated with the worker. They systematically varied age, gender, race, and marital status in order to see if there would be differences in responses about 'how much help in finding a new job the government should give.' Respondents were identified according to race and political ideology. The power of the experimental manipulation was immediately evident. Liberals were less generous when it came to White males than they were in the case of White females who were laid off. Race seemed not to matter to liberals. But, contrary to the expectations of the new racism thesis, conservatives actually were more generous toward the Black worker than the White worker. Even a manipulation which provided cues which would evoke an image of the dominant stereotype of a Black single parent still found self-identified conservatives responding more favorably toward Black single parents than toward White single parents.

A further experimental manipulation provided Sniderman and his colleagues with a basis for interpreting these results. They characterized the laid-off workers in terms of their 'dependability.' This manipulation had little effect on the recommendations of liberals, but conservatives now only wanted to provide support for the Black worker if they could assume that he had been dependable. It is in this final experiment that we find an explanation that links an orientation to a race-linked policy to perceptions of social reality that may be produced and reinforced by the mass media. 'Because conservatives expect blacks in general to be unreliable and untrustworthy, they tend to see a black who is dependable as an exception. "This one," they say to themselves, "is not like the others; he is really trying"' (Sniderman *et al.*, 1991, p. 253). Because they see him as an *exception*, they actually want to do more to reward him for his demonstration of personal responsibility.

We should not misinterpret the results of this research to mean that racists do not exist. What Sniderman and his colleagues have suggested is that the policy preferences of conservatives are not necessarily motivated by racial hatred. The fact that conservatives also tend to hold more negative stereotypes about Blacks is consistent with a racial interpretation of policy preferences that the experimental results challenge (Hartman and Husband, 1974, p. 45). However, because of the way Blacks are portrayed in the mass media, it is not only conservatives that hold such views. Nearly half of the Whites who identify themselves as liberal apparently accept the primary feature of the cultural stereotype of Blacks as lazy. That is, they also tended to agree that 'Most blacks on welfare could get a job if they really tried.' However, because social policies are not designed for individuals, but instead are designed for a group defined by race, the traditional opposition of conservatives toward public assistance combines with their stereotyped images of irresponsible Blacks to produce a strongly held opposition to programs like affirmative action which are targeted for this population.

While Sniderman and his colleagues (1991) offer an interpretion of the logic that produces the more generous treatment of unemployed Blacks, it is possible to offer other creative conjectures that could produce the same result, but might be understood as having been motivated by racist views. Wood (1994, p. 681) suggests, for example, that ingroup bias might lead Whites to overvalue 'hard work' *because* it is an attribute which they believe their own group excels in. A negative impression of Blacks could be combined with a traditional value scheme and still produce the results which Sniderman observed. Indeed, given what we know about the multi-dimensional nature of stereotypes and the construction of outgroup images, perceived group values are central features of our representations of social groups.

Unfortunately, political scientists have paid relatively little attention to the influence of media on the development of the social perceptions which are at the heart of racially sensitive public policy (Kluegal and Smith, 1986; Sigelman and Welch, 1991). This is a blind spot within the literature that is impossible to ignore. Public understanding of the problems and issues that become the focus of electoral campaign debates and political commercials are, to a great extent, dependent upon mass media representations. Public opinion about social problems is based on an understanding of the nature of the problem – how great is the suffering, who are the victims, who is responsible, and what is the likelihood that intervention will be success-ful.

Social problems can be seen as competing for position in the press and in public awareness as the most important problem of the day. The agenda-setting tradition of mass communication research has provided convincing evidence that coverage in the press influences the extent to which the public feels an isssue is serious (Protess and McCombs, 1991). Ray Funkhouser (1973) studied the links between press coverage and public assessment of what they thought was 'the most important problem facing America' during the 1960s. Not surprisingly, the most important issue was the Vietnam War, but the second most important issue, both in the press and in the public's perception, was race relations, and the urban riots that were seen as an index or consequence of those relations.

Winter and Eyal (1981) examined agenda setting in relation to the civil rights issue by comparing front page coverage in the *New York Times* with the public's assessment of issue importance as measured by 27 Gallup polls administered between 1954 and 1976. While their primary purpose was to determine the optimal time span between press coverage and public agenda measurement, their data did indicate a strong positive impact of press coverage on the perceived salience of civil rights. The association was highest ($r = 0.71$) when the assessment of the press's agenda was based on the month immediately prior to the measurement of the public's agenda. This lag of a month between the high point of media coverage and the high point of the issue in the public agenda may reflect the influence of interpersonal conversation about issues which have been in the press.

Both the dominant ideology and the interpretation of media information in ways that reinforce and reproduce that ideology take place in the context of conversations among family, friends, and coworkers. Conversation serves to activate and establish additional links to the kinds of confirming observations that day-to-day interactions among colleagues and associates provide (Allen and Kuo, 1991). Although communication researchers have not made much of an effort to determine what the differences in lag times are for different kinds of issues, it seems clear that the lengths vary as a function of the public's familiarity with the issue. It is believed, for example, that it took so long for the public to become concerned about the Watergate break-in, and its connection with the Nixon White House, because the public had little experience with, and therefore little reason to take seriously, claims that an American president could be involved in criminal activities of this sort (Lang and Lang, 1981). Events such as the 1992 riots in Los Angeles and the trials of O. J. Simpson are just a few of the many stories that have maintained the salience of race on the public agenda in recent years.

Public opinion and social policy

Observers of the political environment in the United States generally agree that 'considerations of race are now deeply imbedded in the strategy and tactics of politics, in competing concepts of the functioning of government, and in each voter's conceptual structure and moral partisan identity' (Edsall and Edsall, 1991, p. 53). The expanded role of the government in pursuing civil rights and social welfare goals has meant that state action is increasingly associated with achieving goals identified with specific racial and ethnic groups. However, the contemporary approach toward racial matters reflects a curve which has reached its maximum, and seems poised to begin its descent.

Despite the fact that the influence of race on the distribution of life chances has not been erased, the emphasis on the racial dimensions of public policy seems poised for replacement by an emphasis on economics and culture, or values.

This historical shift in the focus of politics away from race relations, which we might see as a moral concern, to what were explicitly race-conscious economic policies, like affirmative action, reflected a change in the ways in which racial thinking affected the framing of policy issues. The consequences of this discursive sleight of hand is expected to have important social and political consequences as it shifts once again. As one observer of the recent move away from race notes:

> The move away from racial preferences in policy and the increasing use of code words and imagery that disguise race in contemporary discursive practices are significant and disturbing developments in American politics. The movement away from explicit identifications of racial issues at the same time that race is an increasingly pervasive and ubiquitous dimension of social problems is likely to increase rather than ease racial tensions between those groups directly competing for resources. (Takagi, 1992, pp. 190–1).

There are other public policy issues that vary slightly in their salience, but they also seem to have a well-established link to race. Concern about crime has a well-established link to popular constructions of race. The mass media, both news and entertainment, have been seen to play a critical role in the images we construct of crime, criminals, and victims (Kidd-Hewitt and Osborne, 1995).

Contemporary discussions about the problems of race are taking place in the context of a significant decline in the economic status of Blacks, Latinos, and many Asian immigrants. This economic decline introduces a critical complication into the discussion of social policy, in that White opinions about Blacks seem to be declining at the same time as the economic and social conditions of Black life are in decline (Katz and Taylor, 1988). This creates an extremely 'vicious circle.' Recent efforts to 'reform' welfare or otherwise adjust the social safety net seem likely to demonstrate the truth of the warnings about 'two nations divided' that Gunnar Myrdal provided back in 1944. The next section examines the ways in which the mass media have been involved in the formation of public opinion regarding these racially sensitive issues.

Elite discourse and public opinion

Elites may participate in the formation of public opinion through their contribution to the sense-making process. At the heart of most public policy debates are struggles over both ideas and resources. Opinion leaders play a critical role in shaping these debates by helping to characterize the issues as well as the participants. A powerful ideological role played by elites is the identification of the bounds of legitimate discourse. Opponents can be marginalized by defining them as being on the lunatic fringe, not like the rest of 'us' because their ideas are radical and therefore outside the mainstream. Elites help to define the boundaries of commonsense in which the preferred positions in debates are defined as self-evident truths, and other positions become the targets of ridicule, as when the right-wing British press refers to the anti-racist left as 'loony' (van Dijk, 1992, p. 105). Through the press, elites provide the dominant *frames* that become the resources citizens use in the formation of their opinions and preferences regarding public policy.

William Gamson (1992) has devoted much of his scholarly career to the study of social movements. His recent work has contributed to our understanding of the role social movements play in sponsoring particular ways of seeing public issues. He calls these 'collective action frames.' With Gamson's help, we might come to understand ideological struggle as a form of active competition among interests to determine which *frames* dominate our thinking about the world.

Critical scholars have explained the dominance of particular frames as a reflection of unequal resources, differences in communicative competence, and the added burden of swimming against the ideological tide that keeps oppositional frames in their subordinate position (Gandy, 1982). Gamson provides only a thumbnail sketch of the 'affirmative action frames' that dominated media discourse in the 1970s. He characterized this discourse as one which changed rapidly, but generally as being composed primarily of 'injustice frames' which offered a number of different targets for moral indignation. Sometimes the targets were clear and explicit, as with unions that were denying Blacks access to construction jobs, and later the targets were more diffuse, as the dominant frames spoke of 'institutional racism.' The frames shifted once again during the Reagan administration, but now there were two distinct camps of victims, one White, the other Black (Gamson, 1992, pp. 43–5). Through his analysis of the discussions of contemporary issues among 188 people in some 37 groups that he brought together, Gamson identifies mass media discourse as just one of the many resources that people use in making sense and forming opinions about the issues of the day.

Gamson's concern is not primarily the demonstration of media effects. Indeed, from his perspective, the media do not produce perspectives. Rather the media are resources that people can use in developing their own understanding of issues. However, Gamson still talks about media influence, but in a sense that we are influenced by a source if we use it, or even come to rely on it for the concepts that become part of our cognitive structure. He suggests that 'when they use elements from media discourse to make a conversational point on an issue, we are directly observing a media effect' (p. 180). And, although his references are made with respect to people in the context of group discussions, Gamson suggests that people who use what he calls 'cultural strategies' to understand an issue are 'heavily influenced by the relative prominence of media frames. Their attitudes and beliefs are relatively unstable and subject to change as media discourse changes' (Gamson, 1992, p. 180). He suggests that people who use 'personal strategies' are 'relatively immune to media effects.'

The effect of media can be seen in terms of the resources that they make available for people to use in making sense of the world. The cultivation hypothesis would suggest that people who spend more time in the world of television will have had greater exposure to media frames, and are therefore more likely to use those frames. The use of the frames in conversation is likely to be more important in cognitive structuring than merely hearing these frames used by another person, but the influence of interpersonal discussion has been recognized as important in the process of creation, modification, and reinforcement of conceptual frames.

Gamson's discussion of the impact of different frames also underscores the influence of cultural context. Some frames, symbols, or metaphors tended to 'work well' within the context of a group discussion. Gamson referred to these examples as evidence of *cultural resonance*. We would like to think of this kind of resonance as a commonly shared structure of meaning that is readily and consistently evoked. Gamson suggests, 'when the resonances of widely used popular wisdom on an issue are the same resonances invoked by a media frame, it is easy for people to make a connection between this frame and popular wisdom' (Gamson, 1992, p. 143). Often common cultural themes are linked with counter or oppositional themes. Both may be evoked or activated by the use of terms, or symbols, or exemplars in conversation, or in the mass media. When the issue is about race, there are also likely to be cultural themes that resonate with both media frames and social discourse, but these themes are likely to be very different for Whites and for Blacks. These differences help to explain why conversations about race between Whites and Blacks are so difficult, and tend to be avoided (Gamson, 1992, p. 150).

We cannot assume that all elites are equally successful in having their frames accepted, amplified, and distributed by the press. Sometimes statements by movement leaders or intellectuals are actually used by the press and other policy elites to damage the interests of the movements those statements were intended to help. Although it has not been studied extensively by media scholars, the strategic use of Black scholars as unwitting sponsors of hegemonic frames has been the subject of critical comment and reflection. Steinberg (1995) charges both Cornel West and William Július Wilson with providing the raw material, or even ammunition, that would subsequently be used by opponents of affirmative action. For example, Steinberg suggests that Wilson (1980; 1987), perhaps the best-known of contemporary African American sociologists, has provided an analysis of poverty which all but denied the influence of race:

> This view is predicated on a blanket denial of complex ways that racism prevents blacks from acquiring the requisite education and skills, as well as the persistence of old-fashioned racism that affects even blacks who *have* education and skills. Totally absent from Wilson's analysis of black unemployment is any consideration of racism in occupational and labor markets. (p. 151)

By emphasizing the emergence of a Black middle class, Wilson's analysis overlooked the ways in which class-based tensions emerged between Blacks at the same time that racial discrimination operated to actually worsen the circumstances of the ghetto poor.

In the view of Steinberg and others, Wilson had accepted the 'culture of poverty' arguments made by the conservative right. Although Wilson resisted the language of pathology in favor of structural forces associated with a movement toward a service economy, Wilson's highly visible analyses became part of the 'package' of alternatives to affirmative action frames that emphasized the development of 'color-blind' policies more compatible with the preference for equality of opportunity (Winant, 1994, p. 128). In his most recent book, Wilson (1996) has reconsidered his earlier analysis, and now argues that a modified program of affirmative action that takes both race and condition of need into account will be necessary to overcome the legacy of American racism.

Cornel West's position is characterized by Steinberg as a new form of victim blaming:

> The practical implication of West's position is to substitute a vapid and utterly inconsequential 'politics of conversion' for a genuine political solution – one that would call upon the power and resources of the national government for what is at bottom a national problem and a national disgrace. (Steinberg, 1995, p. 132)

Academics are somewhat different from politicians and movement leaders. They may be more susceptible to strategic reframing of their comments than elites more focused on the public sphere. Because, whenever politicians speak, they are considered to be speaking in public, and therefore 'on the record,' they are usually more careful than other elites in their discussion of sensitive issues. This 'political' speech is therefore a very specialized form of discourse that may serve as a map or a guidebook to the boundaries of acceptable talk about race at any moment in time.

Metz and Tate (1995) have examined the ways in which political candidates make a racial appeal, or use 'the race card' as part of their electoral strategy. We might consider these candidates as the 'sponsors' of the racial frames that get reproduced and distributed by the news media and may or may not become part of the discussions of voters that ultimately decide elections. By studying newspaper coverage of 16 elections in which the two major candidates were Black and White, Metz and Tate hoped to be able to assess candidate strategy. They defined a campaign as having become 'racialized' if either of the candidates make explicit appeals to members of their own racial group, or if they limit their campaign appearances to their own group, or if they raise issues in the campaign that can be reliably identified as racial. They observed that White candidates have used explicitly racial campaigns less and less over time. They suggest that it may be the case that this kind of behavior is less acceptable from White candidates.

An alternative explanation rests in the fact that White candidate strategies, as compared with Black strategies, tended to be more negative, and voters over time have come to resent and to punish candidates for negative campaigns. It is also noted that Black candidates tend to avoid racial appeals if the proportion of Blacks in the electorate is relatively small. When the Black population is near a majority, the campaign is far more likely to become racialized through the initiative of the Black candidate's appealing to the interests of Black constituents. Metz and Tate's analysis underscores the linkage between communication and structure: 'because it becomes strategic for black and white politicians, under certain conditions, to engage in racial politics, racial group identities are strengthened in the process. And as long as it remains strategic, politicians will continue to cast issues as racial ones. Thus, race politics is how the game is played in the United States' (pp. 273–4).

Debates in the US Congress or in European parliaments about immigration and social welfare policy are always, at some level, debates about race. Because of their social role, the primary reference group for the politician is the nation. Other nations can therefore become the outgroups that can be criticized as a means of enhancing the self-image of the reference group. Other nations are racist, or place little value on human rights, whereas our nation has historically been 'the most liberal, freedom-loving, democratic, etc. in the world' (van Dijk, 1992, p. 110). Other nations can be criticized for political oppression, fiscal mismanagement, or other actions that are responsible for the 'washing up' of illegal immigrants on our shores. These politicians are not talking to the peoples of those 'other nations,' however: these are speeches designed for consumption at home.

Theda Skocpol (1995) has provided a historical review of changes in the ways in which African Americans have been linked historically with government efforts to provide services to the poor. Her analysis makes it possible to understand that the contemporary construction of welfare as a racial problem reflects the strategic reconstruction of the issue by conservative elites. While we have come to think of welfare reform as a policy perspective developed within the framework of 'symbolic racism' as a way of reducing the distribution of unjust benefits to Blacks, Skocpol demonstrates that in earlier moments of America's history of social welfare Blacks were far from the primary beneficiaries. Indeed, when the New Deal programs of the 1930s were introduced, Blacks were actually largely excluded from the benefits of Social Security because two-thirds of African Americans who were employed were in domestic service and agriculture – both categories of employment that were excluded from this new social insurance program (p. 142).

Ironically, the welfare programs which *did* provide support for some Blacks who were faced with hard times suffered the tarnishment that a distinction between the 'earned' and 'unearned' benefits allowed. Policy elites helped to sharpen these distinctions over time through their public statements. The fact that Blacks and Hispanics did benefit substantially from the expansion of the social safety net between 1965 and 1975 meant that they would also suffer the public indignities and insults that the Republican backlash would help to generate. Later, another shift in social security policy would serve to divide the legitimate from the illegitimate beneficiaries when 'worthy widows' were incorporated into the social security program, while the increasing number of Black and Latino mothers continued to receive similar benefits under the Aid to Families with Dependent Children (AFDC) program.

The role played by the mass media in helping to construct the ruling 'images of welfare' in Britain has been examined by Golding and Middleton (1982). They describe the involvement of the media in the framing of the debate by means of its unique ability to organize and structure our understanding in particularly limited and limiting ways:

> The reassertion of basic values of national unity, the work ethic, self-help, traditional family life, anti-welfarism and moral rectitude at times of crisis for the prevailing social order has brought in from the wings those social types now rampant in center stage . . . . Anti-welfarism is difficult to resist against a backlash so solidly based in the dramatic types of folk memory and the real privations of current recession. (p. 239)

Earlier analyses of the British press and its representation of economic life in the UK led Hartman and Husband (1974, pp. 206–7) to charge the British press with enabling erroneous perceptions of social reality to persist. 'Racism permits those who are alienated in their labor . . . to blow off steam . . . through scapegoating pariah groups . . . . Resentment is dissipated against the wrong groups and symptoms become mistaken for the real problems.' As we will see when we examine more recent studies, media-generated resentment continues to be a powerful influence in the structure of racist opinion.

Inequality

James Kleugel and Eliot Smith (1986) suggest that we can really only begin to understand changes in the level of support for affirmative action in relation to changes of the public's perception of the extent of inequality. This understanding includes not only an estimate of the extent of inequality, but it also includes a set of competing explanations of the *causes* of economic and social disparity. This explanatory framework is shaped in powerful ways by the system of beliefs that we have referred to as the dominant ideology. Among other things, this ideology is one which privileges individualism, and tends to associate economic success with individual effort. Because this dominant ideology also suggests that the nation is best characterized in terms of *equality of opportunity* and an absence of discriminatory barriers to success, individuals and groups who have not succeeded have simply not worked hard enough. Whatever people have in life is, more or less, what they deserve.

Kleugel's analysis of the stability of White public opinion over a ten-year period (1990) leads to a similar conclusion in that 'we seem to have reached an era of stable, comfortable acceptance by whites of the black-white economic gap' because Whites assign the responsibility for failure to Blacks themselves. For example, if Whites believe that the route one must take to a good job is through higher education, and if Whites doubt that racial discrimination stands in the way of Blacks gaining the education they need (and nine out of ten Whites questioned in 1989 denied there was any such discrimination), then a lack of education is not an excuse, but *evidence* to support the conclusion that Black poverty is justly deserved.

While it is easy to accept the influence of the dominant ideology on the level of one's acceptance or rejection of public policies that seem at variance with one's value system, it is a bit more difficult to understand how differences in perception of social reality are produced and maintained. That is, the long-term gap between White and Black support for public policies like affirmative action and school busing (Page and Shapiro, 1992) can be readily understood in terms of an acceptance or rejection of the dominant ideology that breaks down along racial lines. However, a similar difference between Whites and Blacks in terms of their estimates of the *extent* of inequality has no logical basis in commitment to ideology, except for the cognitive pressures toward consistency that may affect processing of mass media information about inequality (Sigelman and Welch, 1991).

Although Gerbner and his colleagues have tended to treat all television content as essentially the same, researchers who have distinguished between television news and prime-time television fiction have found that exposure to news predicts quite different social perceptions from exposure to television fiction (Armstrong *et al.*, 1992). Exposure to fictional television is generally associated with more positive assessments of the social status of African Americans, while exposure to television news is more closely associated with a negative assessment of the economic well-being of Blacks.

Although their study was not accompanied by an analysis of television programming, other published analyses (Entman, 1990; 1992) provided the basis for the assumption that the reality orientation of the news would provide more images of 'blacks in predominantly lower status contexts, and their association with stories concerning protest, poverty, welfare, crime, and unemployment' that would 'reinforce beliefs in a large economic gap' (Armstrong *et al.*, 1992, p. 157).

The orientation of Whites toward policies designed to reduce inequality also reflects their estimates of *how much* inequality is acceptable within a democratic system that proclaims a commitment to equality of opportunity (Verba and Orren, 1985). The concept of equality of opportunity is divided sharply along ideological lines, although the balance point appears to have shifted over time (Jencks, 1988). One point of division between liberals and conservatives is over whether advantages accumulated early in life can be carried over into the competitions one faces later in life and whether that competition can still be called an equal opportunity, or a competition which takes place on a 'level playing field.'

The distinctions between liberals and conservatives revolve around their assessment of the competitive advantages and disadvantages that class position, parental involvement, motivation, religious beliefs, and ethical and moral principles introduce into the day-to-day choices people make. It is clear that these experiences and influences generate orientations, competencies, and formal records of failure and accomplishment that affect the calculus of future choices. One can readily identify the kinds of advantages and disadvantages that accumulate rapidly depending upon whether one is born Black or White in any society in which the distribution of life chances is structured along racial lines that begin to diverge at birth (Dahrendorf, 1979).

Christopher Jencks (1988) illustrates the differences in the dominant variants of contemporary views on equality of opportunity by describing five ways in which a hypothetical teacher might ensure the provision of educational opportunity to her class. His examples readily evoke aspects of elite discussions of affirmative action in the media, and each reflects different values, different assumptions about human nature, and different theories about how social systems evolve. Because of the fundamental incompatibility between these commitments to equality, it is easy to see how different people can be genuinely committed to equality of opportunity, but disagree violently about the best way to ensure it. Elite opinion is a primary source of competing theories about how one ought to ensure equality of opportunity. Conservative theorists have been increasingly successful in presenting their analyses and recommendations as the logical expressions of the national ideology. The press plays an active role in organizing and distributing the views of leading contenders in ways that help to frame the dominant understanding of racial policy issues.

Although the tensions between Blacks and Asians did not erupt into violence at the University of California, the ways in which the press reported the debate over affirmative action in admissions helped to set the stage for the articulation of a more conservative White perspective on the issue: 'Neoconservative intellectuals and politicians folded discrimination against Asians into a trope of broader disaffection for liberalism in higher education. The end product was the most trenchant neoconservative critique of affirmative action yet' (Takagi, 1992, p. 113). Conservatives were able to use the image of Asians as victims of racial discrimination, and by means of this rhetorical strategy they were able to transform what had previously been designed as the antidote to discrimination into a form of poison that had to be eliminated for the good of the educational system.

Group interest and perceived threat

Political scientists have offered yet another perspective on the relationship between social perception and social policy preference in the area of race. The aspect of symbolic racism that involved an unwillingness to provide 'special' opportunities to members of minority racial or ethnic groups could be interpreted as a selfish, rather than a moralistic, stance. Prejudice against immigrants, or opposition to busing or affirmative action could be understood in terms of a perceived threat to one's own economic interests. It could also be considered an indirect threat to those interests if it was thought about in terms of threats to the well-being of one's reference or identity group.

Donald Kinder and David Sears (1981) sought to provide an empirical test of the theoretical perspective which came to be known as 'realistic group conflict theory' in the 1970s as an alternative to a theory of symbolic racism. Group conflict theory emphasizes the 'tangible threats blacks pose to whites' private lives' while symbolic racism emphasizes 'abstract, moralistic resentments of blacks traceable to preadult socialization' (p. 414). The competing theories were tested on the basis of interviews with White suburbanites in Los Angeles during the 1969 and 1973 elections for mayor. A White conservative incumbent (Sam Yorty) was being challenged by a liberal Black city councilman (Thomas Bradley). Respondents were asked to estimate the likelihood that a particular threat would actually materialize (e.g., a Black family would move into their neighborhood). According to other research available at the time, White opposition to equal opportunity for Blacks had all but disappeared, and few Whites believed (or would say they believed) that Blacks were less intelligent than Whites. They concluded that the political consequences (voting intentions) were 'carried by symbolic resentments, not by tangible threats' (p. 427). An earlier study also concluded that symbolic attitudes, that is, racial intolerance and politial conservatism, were more influential in determining White opposition to the symbolic threat of busing *any* White child, when compared with the 'real' threat of having one's *own child* bused. What was perceived of as threatening was not travel by bus, which many children do all the time, but the racial mixing that school busing for the purposes of integration actually implied. Sears and his colleagues (1979) concluded that 'it seems likely that whites' perceptions of the hazards of "busing" are generally based more on what it symbolizes than on what it actually is' (p. 383).

A recent European study (Quillian, 1995) explores the relationship between perceived threat to group interest and associated expressions of group prejudice among citizens of 12 EEC countries. Prejudice was defined as a 'response to a perceived threat' which varies with the size of the subordinate group (p. 591). The coding of the instrument enabled Quillian to make a distinction between anti-immigrant prejudice and racial prejudice. While the data were measures of individual responses, measures of the economic status of the respondent's nation, as well as estimates of the relations between dominant and subordinate groups, produced strong evidence of system level influences on the expression of prejudiced views. In discussing the implications of his findings, Quillian suggests that prejudice against African Americans may have been greater than that demonstrated against Asian Americans, in part because of the greater number of African Americans. This conclusion would, of course, have serious implications for the future of relations with Latinos in the United States. This population segment is expected to grow until it exceeds the Black population by the year 2013 (Wilson and Gutiérrez, 1995, p. 13). The conclusion that 'prejudice is largely a function of group position' and reflects perceived threat to groups more than individuals (p. 60) finds unexpected support in another study reported by Kinder and Sanders in 1996.

In a re-examination of National Election Studies of 1986, 1988, and 1992, Kinder and Sanders report the familiar gaps between Whites and Blacks in their support for those social policies believed to benefit Blacks. Examining these differences within groups divided by social class leads Kinder and Sanders to the conclusion that the differences are fundamentally racial, rather than class-based differences in policy preference (1996, p. 31). The question still becomes one of determining whether it is self-interest or group interest that explains this racial divide.

An additional question, and a question which is of central concern to communications scholars, is determining the role of the mass media in creating and maintaining these differences. Kinder and Sanders suggest that the perception of threat is influenced by the ways in which the story is framed in the press. They suggest that elite opinion makers provide the press with the frames that they reproduce and distribute to the public. Unfortunately, Kinder and Sears do not provide us with evidence from content analysis about the prevalence of a particular frame in the press;

they merely test whether particular frames, as reflected in the *questions* that people are asked, will be associated with particular answers.

In one sense, Kinder and Sears are merely telling us what we already know from what we have learned about cognitive structures and *priming*: that frames influence responses. This fact has been demonstrated repeatedly in laboratory and field experiments. In defense of their project, however, Kinder and Sears criticize this previous research for being too narrowly focused, even parochial in its pursuit of the confidence that a well-designed experiment can produce. 'From this perspective, social science research devoted to racial attitudes amounts to little more than an encyclopedia, in which each explanation has its own page. Which explanations are powerful and which are weak? We cannot say' (p. 40). Theirs was a call for a more complex integration of these influences as might be provided by a multi-variate analytical design. They attempted to gain some of the benefits of experimental control by randomizing their survey respondents' exposure to different frames in the *questions* they are asked.

Questions which explicitly framed a public policy in terms of threats that Whites would experience directly were associated with opposition to those policies. Thus, there was some support for self-interest as a determinant. More consistent support, however, was found for those frames that suggested that threats to Whites as a group would result from the implementation of a race-based policy. The influence of collective self-interest has been relabeled by Kinder and Sanders as a form of *racial resentment*. They suggest that elites have considerable influence over the ways in which issues of public policy are expressed in ways that evoke resentment of Blacks.

In each of their framing experiments, 'the prominence of racial resentment in white public opinion was shown to be contingent on how the issue was framed' (p. 284). Two critical components of a causal model are missing in their study, and in their analysis: (1) we do not know how racial policy discourse is framed in the press; and (2) we do not know how particular framings become dominant in the cognitive constructions of individuals. Their focus on the impact of framing on White opinion does not tell us how the differences between White and Black opinion come to be. They suggest that the 'racial divide' in opinion widens in part because Whites and Blacks do not talk to each other, but they ignore the fact that Whites and Blacks read the same newspapers and watch the same network news. They fail to understand how the cognitive structures that the social experience of Black life produces encourages a very different reading of the stories in the news. They do suggest, however, that 'black and white Americans have taken possession of distinct paradigms. In the extreme, blacks and whites look upon the social and political world in fundamentally different and mutually unintelligible ways' (p. 288). They experience different realities, different truths. An understanding of the media's role in this great divide remains just out of reach.

6

A critical research agenda

We have begun our exploration of the terrain that is defined by the intersection of communication and race. We have noted that quite a bit has changed, while much has remained the same. We must agree with the postmodernists that the world has become increasingly complex, in part because of the ways in which communications have affected the impact of time, space, and distance on the character of social, cognitive, and ideological structures. We accept that the role that identity plays in our lives has become much more uncertain as routine interactions with a great many 'others' have transformed, by making less reliable, the traditional guidelines and criteria we have used in the past to determine group membership, and to decide which of our identities ought to guide our actions.

We have little doubt that the mass media of communication play a central role in this transformation. We are also certain that the influence of the media is not unidirectional. The relations are far more complex. We have seen the ways in which the images of people of color have changed in patterns that reflect changes in the estimates of the economic value of racially and ethnically homogeneous audiences. These shifts in evaluation have been influenced by shifts in population that have been influenced in quite complex ways by shifts in the global political economy. The effects of violent political repression on patterns of ethnic migration clearly cannot be ignored.

We have also recognized the importance of elite opinion and intellectual leadership. By their introduction of framing structures into the discourse on social problems, elites enable the reproduction of dominant ideological structures that make it likely that people will understand inequality as the product of individual rather than structural inadequacies. At the same time, intellectual elites, including those on our campuses, have assumed positions of leadership in social movements committed to the elimination of racism's structural force.

But does this knowledge we share actually meet the requirements that we have established for it? Does our knowledge of communication and race provide us with insights we can use to eliminate the continuing influence of race in the distribution of life chances? What more do we need to know?

There are approaches to social theory which reject the pessimism of postmodernism, and begin to reveal the underlying systematic and structuring character of communicative interactions (Latané and Fink, 1996). They should be pursued further. We should not allow the mantra of 'complex overdetermination' cloud our vision. There *are* patterns in social systems. The patterns are the reflections of social structure. And these social structures are the product of the interactions which take place within structured social systems. These structures are multidimensional and dynamic, but they appear to have the kind of superordinate regularity that invites both the effort to express this regularity in theoretical terms, and efforts to use this knowledge to enhance the emergence of patterns that we value, and suppress the emergence of those we despise.

What we need is to begin the development of an epistemic community that understands, and helps to enable others to understand, that *race* need not be a determinant of the evaluative structures that organize the distribution of life chances. Institutions seem driven toward using a greater complex of attributes of persons and groups to govern interactions. These interactions will influence the development of still other governing structures. There will always be structures and structuration, but race need not continue to play the same kind of role that it has played in the past. Indeed the 'social dominance' perspective developed by Sidanius and Pratto (1993) suggests that even if 'African Americans suddenly ceased to function as America's "negative reference group," they would only be replaced by some other group serving the same role, perhaps undocumented workers or the "homeless"' (p. 206). Theirs is a pessimistic view which suggests that social policies aimed at reducing inequality 'will not only fail to achieve their publicly stated goals, but the efforts themselves will be ultimately unsustainable.' We need not agree.

Scholarship which is directed toward finding patterns, and revealing the relations between these patterns and the structures that they reflect, is what we need to support. Patterns are not likely to be revealed by scholarship that is focused almost entirely at the level of individuals. A focus on individual persons, television programs, films, records, songs, or other communicative acts will not help us see the patterns through which structural influence is revealed. This means that very little of the interpretive work that has emerged so centrally within cultural studies will help us describe the links between pattern and structure that reflect the continued use of race as a index of individual and collective qualities.

This means that we have to push forward, rather than retreating from, the problems of specification and measurement. For critical scholarship to make any progress in theory and social practice there needs to be a higher level of precision and agreement about the meanings we assign to the important concepts that are the raw materials of our theories. Theoretical progress requires a common code that enables the processes of challenge and test and critique to do their work in the process of building knowledge.

Of course, we do have to ask the question: what knowledge, for what purposes, is to be used by which social actors? It should be clear that not all information is knowledge, and not all knowledge provides the basis for wise decisions for all of us. It is also true that knowledge can be used for purposes other than those for which it was initially pursued. The aims of knowledge production can be easily subverted. If knowledge developed for the purpose of social control is transformed into insights that have an emancipatory result, we would see this as a good thing. That this would always happen is perhaps a naive hope. It is equally if not more likely that insights developed with revolutionary intent have been transformed into mundane market goods. Lee Thayer suggests that most of the research that has transformed our material world has been done with profit in mind (1983). Critical research directed toward social goals faces an uphill struggle. Those willing to pursue it must work against the grain. They must struggle harder over access to smaller pools of resources because the profit in their work is harder for sponsors to see. More importantly, those who would benefit most directly from their work are unable to afford to pay for it. More importantly still, these intended beneficiaries are, with good reason, also unwilling to pay for, or even to participate in, our research projects because they have come to mistrust the institutions with which we are identified.

As we noted initially, the purpose of understanding the world is to change it. But we recognize that we cannot change everything at once. Our understanding of the problem may or may not include an understanding about which actors, or which relationships, have the greatest potential for transforming the larger structure. We are no longer as confident as we once were that we could identify the 'primary contradictions' within the capitalist system. We know that racism is one of its critical flaws, but we also understand that racism exists because it serves some actors quite well. Does this mean that the focus of our energies ought to be those who are oppressed, or those who oppress, or those who are unaware of the ways in which they are affected by racism? Is it revolution or enlightened self-interest that has the greatest potential for reducing the significance of race? I do not pretend to have the answer.

Like Derek Bell (1992), who speaks of the permanence of racism, we have to declare that despair is an unacceptable response. We have to believe that by knowing more about communication, race, and racial disparity we will discover how to bring about its demise.

The place of race in identity

Among the more important subjects we need to engage within a critical research agenda is the way in which changing constructions of race diffuse throughout the population. As Garnham has suggested with regard to capitalism's not being the same in every place at the same time (1990), the construct of race and racial identity also varies greatly in time and place.

While the debates about race and hybridity have become intense and almost arcane within the academic community, the meaning of race and racial identity for the mass of people is of a far less uncertain or contested nature. There is great value, however, in understanding more about how race is understood by people who occupy different social locations in different nations or regions of the world.

It is quite clear, from a number of perspectives, that the perceptions of academics, scientists, and professionals are often at great variance from the perceptions of what we refer to as 'ordinary folks.' It is these ordinary folks who are guided by commonsense. Despite its error, and perhaps its irrationality, this commonsense forms the basis for the kinds of routine actions that reproduce racist structures. There is value, therefore, in attempting a periodic assessment of public conceptions of race, including the extent to which these conceptions privilege biological rather than cultural and historical determinations. We are not only interested in assessing the extent to which there has been a shift in the dominant view away from biological constructions, but we would also want to understand the ways in which differences in social position are also associated with attachment to particular views.

It seems that it ought to be possible to tease out the racial aspects of popular constructions of ethnicity and their combination into racial hierarchies. In the past, such work has focused primarily on the opinions of Whites. The migrations of peoples of color in Europe, the United States, Australia, and other parts of the globe have changed the differential calculus of race. It will also be important to describe, and then to understand, the ways in which different minorities characterize each other, especially as the creation of political coalitions among minority groups depends upon the recognition of a common identity – one that no longer seems likely to emerge on the basis of class alone (Stinchcombe, 1990).

This work would help us clarify some of the confusion about whether racism has declined, or merely been transformed like some dangerous virus that continues to evolve.

This work might also allow us to assess the impact of progressive interventions such as the radical efforts to destroy the advantages associated with Whiteness. The 'new abolitionists' and 'race traitors' are committed to 'e-racing' society by beginning with themselves, even as they run the risk of degrading the values that racialized minorities have constructed for themselves in opposition to Whiteness (Powell, 1997).

It would also help us to understand and assess the influence of a growing pool of Black and other minority conservatives who are helping to articulate an ideology of color-blindness in opposition to affirmative action and other race-based public policies (Conti and Stetson, 1993). This work would also help clarify the ways in which class consciousness among African Americans (Dennis, 1995) and other racially identified groups is associated with the development of a unique form of ideological identity we might refer to as a racial class.

The place of race in communication

We really have only the most primitive understanding of the ways in which racial identity operates as an organizing and orienting influence on our communications behavior. Much of the work which has been published of late has been limited by a failure to recognize that, if we have 'identities', they are multidimensional and they are influenced substantially by the environmental, contextual, or situational cues that suggest which aspects of our complex identity is most relevant to the task at hand. What progress we have made may be found in our understanding that aspects of our identity, including that which we have explored as race, class, and gender 'consciousness', can be triggered or 'primed,' or otherwise made more central to our assessments of particular options in particular circumstances.

The efforts by social scientists to assess the influence of different forms or aspects of identity, and ways in which they operate as a constraint, have developed a variety of measures that have some degree of measurement reliability and predictive validity. We have not made very much progress, however, in developing and testing the utility of different measures of racial identity. Survey forms generally treat this identity as a discrete nominal category. You are Black, or you are something else. This is inadequate and we know it.

While we do need to be concerned about the consequences that flow from the reification of some particular construction of racial identity to the exclusion of others, this concern ought not lead us to discontinue our search. There is far more to be gained from the development of a reliable measure of racial identity than continuing on in our work without one. Standardized measures of ideological self-identification are a commonplace in social research. Similar measures of racial identity should be developed and implemented in large-scale studies designed to understand shifts and patterns in public opinion and social behavior. Work in developing such measures has to include a concept of Whiteness which is not defined entirely in relation to Blackness.

Our pursuit of an operational definition of racial identity should engage the distinctions between forms of identity associated with consumption and those forms more closely identified with political action. These are distinctions akin to those made between Marxian and Weberian concepts of social class. It should be clear that communications media, linked so closely with and so dependent upon commercial finance, are likely to emphasize and heighten the salience of Weberian aspects of identity. The magazine racks, billboards, and television ads that call out to individuals on the basis of their racialized identities do so on the basis of a common experience in consumption, rather than on the basis of a common experience of oppression. Indeed, commercial media, with rare exceptions, seek to avoid activation of those unpleasant, conflictual aspects of identity and group consciousness common to those Marxian or neo-Marxian constructions that emphasize relations of power.

A critical engagement with the place of racial identity would require an examination of the role of minority-owned advertising and public relations firms whose survival depends upon the continued existence of a distinct sociocultural racial identity. Turow (1997) notes that owners and executives of African American agencies have protested the refusal of White agencies to hire African Americans at the same time that White advertising executives were arguing that Blacks could be reached as effectively through mainstream media as they could through targeted media. Black advertising executives understandably disagreed because their survival depends upon their ability to demonstrate that Black people are different and have to be approached differently, if they are to be reached as consumers. While the same communications professionals are using many of the same models and techniques to inform politicians about how to reach and influence racially identified segments of the electorate, this overall effort is minuscule in comparison with the expenditures directed toward reaching consumers. We might benefit, however, from noting what differences emerge when minority agencies advise commercial clients and when they advise political actors.

Critical scholars must begin in earnest to determine the extent to which, and the process through which, the construction of a racial identity is dominated by consumption, and the communications resources directed towards that goal. Dawson's construction of African American identity as a measure of 'linked fate' (1994, p. 77), and as measured by responses to the question 'Do you think what happens generally to black people in this country will have something to do with what happens in your life?', should be examined in the context of attitudes and behaviors that involve consumption as well as those that involve political action. To date, this essentially political measure has been used exclusively in studies of public opinion and politics. How would we begin to explore the links between racial identity and membership in 'taste publics,' 'fans,' and 'committed consumers' of particular kinds of goods and services?

The place of race in the media system

It also seems clear that we have not moved very far toward being able to provide a detailed answer to the question asked by Muriel Cantor (1980) and others: 'Will more minorities make a difference?' Certainly the answer to the question has to be *yes*, but we are a long way from being able to specify precisely what kinds of differences it will make. We want to be able to answer that question because we want to know whether it makes sense to participate in and lend support to demands for minority set asides, affirmative action, boycotts, strategic buying, or other race-based efforts to affect the democratic character of the media system. We want to know whether increasing minority participation is a good thing overall, or whether we should privilege and target particular kinds of participation.

First of all, we have to be clear about what we mean when we say 'more minorities.' Assuming that we take into account the differences in racial identity that we have just discussed, we will also need to specify which roles, and with what authority and power or resources are commonly available to persons in those roles. We believe that ownership is important because of the amount of power and influence that owners exercise over media organizations. However, we also recognize that the power of owners is diffused as a function of organizational size, as well as a function of the 'closeness' of the organizational structure, in geographic or other terms. The number of minority owners of media organizations is still remarkably small, but there are enough for us to begin to assess what the relationship between ownership and performance has been. It will be important, however, for us to recognize that the power and autonomy of any minority owner is also constrained by the economic realities of the market in which he or she operates. The reality of those markets includes not only an assessment of the extent of competition, but it also includes an assessment of the racial composition of the audience, and the willingness of advertisers or other interests to pay for access to that audience.

For example, Tait and Barber (1996) note that 60 per cent of the audience for Black Entertainment Television (BET) is non-Black. This percentage is likely to grow as BET can already claim 90 per cent of African Americans who have cable, and Bob Johnson and his investors depend upon his ability to continue growing, rather than to level out and stagnate. His growth depends upon his ability to attract more White or at least more non-Black subscribers. Tait and Barber express some concern about Johnson's social responsibility and his commitment to acting in the best interests of African Americans. They are concerned not only because of his dependence on 're-runs' and music videos but, as others note, by his willingness to advertise troublesome commodities like alcohol and hair products that privilege Eurocentric ideals of beauty. They conclude that 'BET's programming strategies and lucrative business practices have not made it a strong

African American voice in America's media forum.' They suggest that Johnson is becoming an increasingly powerful force within the US and international media industry. Yet, 'He is doing this not by providing an Afrocentric channel through which the African American community can voice its feelings and aspirations but by managing a successful capitalistic vehicle for reaching the African American consumer' (Tait and Barber, 1996, pp. 193–4).

This assessment of Bob Johnson and BET is only a limited case study of the performance of a single media owner. We need to expand this line of research so as to understand how the tension between a capitalist logic and a racialized social responsibility is being worked out in different countries and different media markets.

In similar ways, we need to assess the extent to which increases in minority presence among the media's management and professional staffs affect the character of the images and representations of race and race relations. Such studies should explore the concept of 'critical mass' in order to determine if the identifiable influence of minority presence changes noticeably when the number of minorities achieves a level beyond which individuals are less cautious about challenging the racist frames that would otherwise be introduced into media products. Achieving such a critical mass does not always mean that the outcomes will be favorable. The *resentment* which has been identified as the dominant feature of contemporary racial feeling has also been identified among White journalists. Richard Shafer's interviews with Black and Hispanic journalists reveal the existence of a twin-edged sword: 'white journalists who believe that their careers are threatened by policies of favoritism in hiring and promoting minorities' and minority journalists 'who see themselves as stigmatized by the perception that they are benefiting from such favoritism' (1993, p. 198).

As with media ownership, however, we should recognize that the influence of staff on content will reflect the influence of the market in which the organization operates (Gandy, 1996a). Particularly troublesome methodological problems will have to be overcome in order to identify the 'tipping points' at which shifts in structural orientation and status begin to be reflected in changed behavior. This is largely a problem of gathering sufficient data across longer time periods that will support the kinds of time series analyses that allow changes in content to be associated with changes in employment participation as well as with changes in the racial composition of the market.

The place of race in social action

The importance of race in national debates about public policy can hardly be overestimated, despite the efforts of many to disguise the racial character of their comments by using coded speech. We are just beginning to under-stand the importance of media frames – those in the news and those in what we consume as entertainment – in the construction of social reality.

We have not paid particular attention to the relative importance of news frames and fictional television and film frames in the shaping of social perceptions, in part because of the tremendous amount of time that such comparative analysis requires. The availability of sophisticated programs for the computer analysis of text will undoubtedly reduce the expense of coding text available in digital form. The problem of coding visual materials will not be so readily overcome and, as we have noted, quite distinct and powerful comments about race are provided by images as well as with words.

Some of the more important work toward understanding differences in perception across racial lines (Kinder and Sanders, 1996; Sigelman and Welch, 1991) has largely ignored the influence of media, or has merely assumed the nature of its dominant frames. We have to reduce the cost of describing the information environment in which political insights are constructed by different audiences.

We need to find a way to pool our resources and work collectively to develop archives of media content analysis that would allow for assessment of the relations between dominant frames in different media and shifts in public opinion over time. The project in International Cultural Indicators that George Gerbner announced in 1970 has been realized to a certain extent in projects such as those mounted in Sweden (Rosengren, 1981). What we need is for such studies to pay more attention to matters of race and ethnicity.

The availability of assessments of content, along with measures of media use, will allow us to assess more confidently the relationship between media framing and public opinion. This is not to suggest that the problems with understanding media effects is solely a problem of insufficient data. Clearly there is more to it than that. As we have suggested in the previous chapter, there is a whole host of contingent conditions that cannot merely be assumed away. There is also the most vexing problem of public wariness of opinion surveys. Part of this measurement fatigue is the result of a massive increase in survey research in support of marketing; part is a more general concern about privacy and social control (Gandy, 1996b). There are also the problems associated with social desirability, and the unwillingness of people to reveal their views on racial issues because they do not want to be thought of as racist or narrow-minded. While technology may reduce the costs of processing information, the costs of accessing public attitudes and opinions on political issues may rise dramatically.

Beyond race and communication

Among all the issues and concerns we have examined, the most important thing for us to understand and then to engage is the role that racial identity and its social construction play in the reproduction of racism. Samuel Gaertner and his colleagues (1997, p. 168) have demonstrated that even White Americans who are committed to egalitarian values, who support a liberal political agenda, and who firmly believe that they are not prejudiced against Blacks and other minorities, still do, and are likely to, discriminate against members of these groups in important ways. From their perspective, it is not so much that these Whites are anti-Black, but that they are pro-White. Richard McAdams (1995) has emphasized the great power that racial group identity represents, because this identity is linked so closely with the production and reproduction of social status. As though social status were a zero-sum game, in which one group's gain is another group's loss, maintenance of one's own status often seems to require the derogation of the status of another group. While there may be 'free riders,' in this process, all members of racially identified groups participate to some degree in the process of status production, even radical race traitors. The level of involvement reflects the salience of each group's racialized status at a particular point in time, as well as the willingness of politicians and other social actors to increase that salience through the manipulation of the press.

Howard Winant suggests that the social construction of Whiteness has taken on an increased salience in recent times, in part because of a belief that the status of Whites is at risk. Despite the absence of any credible evidence to support it, the mass media have helped to generate a widespread belief among Whites that Whiteness has become a *disadvantage*. This position may be held most strongly by White males, who have been led to interpret affirmative action as a direct assault on their historically dominant position. The *resentment* that this belief maintains has become a kind of 'cultural and political "glue" that holds together a wide variety of reactionary racial politics' (Winant, 1997, p. 42).

The response of Whites to this perceived threat to group status varies across the political spectrum. Winant has identified five 'racial projects' that span the distance from those on the far right to the radical 'new abolitionists.' He associates the neoconservative position with the desire to deny the existence of racial difference, in part through an emphasis on ethnicity, or culture. This appeal to 'color-blindness' as an alternative to divisive 'race-thinking' is on one hand attractive because of its inherently egalitarian and democratic tilt. However, it loses its appeal rapidly because its use in the public debate emerges primarily in the context of demands for the elimination of programs that would actually move toward the realization of egalitarian and democratic ideals. The neoliberal position is similar with regard to its position on color-blind policy making, but adherents are more willing to invite government action on the basis of other, presumably less troublesome, systems of classification.

From Winant's perspective, the neoliberal project does not go far enough, in that in focusing on disadvantage it fails to consider privilege, especially the privilege based on Whiteness. While color-blindness is a liberal ideal, its pursuit ought not to begin at the bottom of the status and power hierarchy, where the benefits are few, but at the top, where the benefits are substantial.

It seems that it is only the new abolitionists who seem to be actively engaged in a process which, if successful, might sever the links between racial identity and status and other material advantages by beginning at the top. Is this a project that is worthy of support? Is it a project that has any hope of success?

The question that critical scholars of communication need to engage is one which seems ironically administrative on the face of it. At the same time that our increased scholarly attention to the relationships between communications and the distribution of life chances will help us understand the reproduction of racism, we also need to examine and evaluate what appear to be the most promising ways to use communication to sever the links between race, class, and status. How might a social movement, like that of the new abolitionists, be popularized? Are there lessons to be drawn, and shared, about other social movements that might be applied to this racial project? What do we know about movements that call for self-denial? Are these only religious movements? Is there some basis other than guilt that makes the rejection of racial privilege satisfying? Is it akin to breaking the smoking habit? In the United States, smoking has experienced a rather dramatic loss of status. It has not only become illegal in many public places, but smokers have been socially ostracized, and millions have quit voluntarily.

While communications scholars and other social scientists are just beginning to reflect on the social processes that have been involved in shifting public sentiments away from behaviors like smoking (Baumgartner and Jones, 1993), it seems clear that quite substantial resources have been devoted toward affecting these shifts. While governments have traditionally been involved through the support of limited interventions in the past, real movement seems to occur when larger capitalist interests, such as those represented by insurance companies and large employers, become involved. Foundations very frequently have played an important intermediary role in support of various movements concerned with shifting public attitudes and behavior. Are critical scholars ready to approach foundations, government agencies, and other potential funders to begin a national, and then a global movement to separate, once and for all, the benefits that derive from racial identity, by beginning where the benefits are the greatest?

I certainly hope so.

Bibliography

Abelmann, N. and J. Lie, 1995: *Blue dreams: Korean Americans and the Los Angeles riots of 1992.* Cambridge, MA: Harvard University Press.

Adelson, A., 1997: Minority voice fading for broadcast owners. *New York Times,* 19 May 1997, D9.

Adorno, T. and M. Horkheimer, 1979: The culture industry: Enlightenment as mass deception. In J. Curran, M. Gurevitch, and J. Woollacott (eds), *Mass communication and society.* Beverly Hills, CA: Sage, pp. 349–383.

Allen, R. L. and S. Hatchett, 1986: The media and social reality effects. Self and system orientations of blacks. *Communication Research* 13 (1), 97–123.

Allen, R. L. and C. Kuo, 1991: Communication and beliefs about racial equality. *Discourse and Society* 2 (3), 259–279.

Allen, R. L., M. C. Dawson and R. Brown, 1989: A schema-based approach to modeling an African-American racial belief system. *American Political Science Review* 83 (2), 421–441.

Allen, W., 1994: The dilemma persists: Race, class and inequality in American life. In P. Ratcliffe (ed.), *Race, ethnicity and nation: international perspectives on social conflict.* London: UCL Press, pp. 44–67.

Althusser, L., 1971: *Lenin and philosophy and other essays.* London: New Left Books.

Andersen, R., 1995: *Consumer culture and tv programming.* Boulder, CO: Westview.

Anderson, J. A., 1996: The pragmatics of audience in research and theory. In J. Hay, L. Grossberg and E. Wartella (eds), *The audience and its landscape.* Boulder, CO: Westview Press.

Anderson, R., T. Bikson, S. Law, and B. Mitchell, 1995: *Universal access to e-mail. Feasibility and societal implications.* Santa Monica, CA: RAND.

Ang, I., 1991: *Desperately seeking the audience.* London and New York: Routledge.

Ang, I., 1996a: Ethnography and radical contextualism in audience studies. In J. Hay, L. Grossberg, and E. Wartella (eds), *The audience and its landscape.* Boulder, CO: Westview, pp. 247–262.

Ang, I., 1996b: *Living room wars: Rethinking media audiences for a postmodern world.* London and New York: Routledge.

Anon., 1992: 'Crazy Horse' malt liquor an insult to Native Americans. *Alcoholism and Drug Abuse Week* 4, 4.

Anon., 1996: Jordan is top sports pitchman; Projected to earn $38 million in endorsements. *Jet*, 16 September 1996, 46.

Anthias F. and N. Yuval-Davis, 1992: *Racialized boundaries: Race, nation, gender, colour and the anti-racist struggle.* London and New York: Routledge.

Apte, M., 1987: Ethnic humor versus 'sense of humor': An American sociocultural dilemma. *American Behavioral Scientist* 30, 27–41.

Armour, J. D., 1994: Race Ipsa Loquitur: Of reasonable racists, intelligent Bayesians, and involuntary negrophobes. *Stanford Law Review* 46, 781–816.

Armstrong, G. B., K. Neundorf and J. Brentar, 1992: Tv entertainment, news, and racial perceptions of college students. *Journal of Communication* 42 (3), 153–176.

Asante, M. K., 1980: *Afrocentricity. The theory of social change.* Buffalo, NY: Amulefi Publishing.

Asante, M. K., 1987: *The Afrocentric idea.* Philadelphia, PA: Temple University Press.

Asante, M. K., 1990: *Kemet, Afrocentricity and knowledge.* Trenton, NJ: Africa World Press.

Asante, M. K., 1993: *Malcolm X as culture hero and other Afrocentric essays.* Trenton, NJ: Africa World Press.

Asante, M. K. and W. B. Gudykunst (eds), 1989: *Handbook of international and intercultural communication.* Newbury Park, CA: Sage.

Astroff, R., 1988–9: Spanish gold: Stereotypes, ideology, and the construction of a U.S. Latino market. *The Howard Journal of Communications* 1, 155–173.

Atkin, D. and M. Fife, 1993–4: The role of race and gender as determinants of local tv news coverage. *The Howard Journal of Communications* 5, 123–137.

Atwater, T. and N. Weerakkody, 1994: A portrait of urban conflict: the *L. A. Times* coverage of the Los Angeles Riots. *Temple University Conference on the Press and the City.*

Austin, B., 1989: *Immediate seating: A look at movie audiences.* Belmont, CA: Wadsworth.

Baker, C. E., 1994a: *Advertising and a democratic press.* Princeton, NJ: Princeton University Press.

Baker, C. E., 1994b: *Ownership of newspapers: The view from positivistic social science.* Cambridge, MA: Harvard University, John F. Kennedy School of Government.

Baldwin, T., D. S. McVoy, and C. Steinfield, 1996: *Convergence: Integrating media, information and communication.* Thousand Oaks, CA: Sage.

Balibar, E. and I. Wallerstein (eds), 1991: *Race, nation, class: Ambiguous identities.* New York: Verso.

Ball-Rokeach, S., M. Rokeach, and J. W. Grube, 1984: *The great American values test.* New York: The Free Press.

Bandura, A., 1973: *Aggression: A social learning analysis.* Englewood Cliffs, NJ: Prentice-Hall.

Banton, M., 1977: *The idea of race.* Boulder, CO: Westview.

Banton, M., 1987: *Racial theories.* Cambridge: Cambridge University Press.

Baptista-Fernandez, P. and B. Greenberg, 1980: The context, characteristics and communication behaviors of blacks on television. In B. Greenberg (ed.), *Life on television. Content analyses of U.S. tv drama.* Norwood, NJ: Ablex, pp. 13–21.

Barber, J. and O. Gandy, 1990: Press portrayals of African American and white United States Representatives. *The Howard Journal of Communications* 2 (2), 213–225.

Barlow, W., 1987: Community radio in the United States: Creating a new culture. In O. Gandy (ed.), *Communications, a key to economic and political change.* Washington, DC: Howard University, Center for Communications Research, pp. 85–95.

Barnet, R. and J. Cavanagh, 1994: *Global dreams: Imperial corporations and the new world order.* New York: Simon and Schuster.

Bartlett, R., 1989: *Economics and power: An inquiry into human relationships and markets.* New York: Cambridge University Press.

Barwise, T. P., A. S. C. Ehrenberg, and G. J. Goodhardt, 1982: Glued to the box?: Patterns of tv repeat-viewing. *Journal of Communication* 31, 22–29.

Bates, S., 1995: *Realigning journalism with democracy: The Hutchins Commission, its times, and ours.* Washington, DC: The Washington Annenberg Program in Communication Policy Studies.

Bauman, Z., 1989: Legislators and interpretors: Culture as ideology of intellectuals. In H. Haferkamp (ed.), *Social structure and culture.* New York: de Gruyter, pp. 313–332.

Baumgartner, F. and B. Jones, 1993: *Agendas and instability in American politics.* Chicago: University of Chicago Press.

Bayles, M., 1994: *Hole in our soul: The loss of beauty and meaning in American popular music.* New York: The Free Press.

Becker, G. S., 1971: *The economics of discrimination.* Chicago: University of Chicago Press.

Becker, G. S., 1976: *The economic approach to human behavior.* Chicago: University of Chicago Press.

Becker, G. S., 1979: Economic analysis and human behavior. In L. Lévy Barboua (ed.), *Sociological economics.* London and Beverly Hills, CA: Sage, pp. 7–24.

Belay, G., 1996: The (re)construction and negotiation of cultural identities in the age of globalization. In H. B. Mokros (ed.), *Interaction and identity. Information and Behavior*, vol. 5. New Brunswick, NJ: Transaction, pp. 319–345.

Bell, D., 1992: *Faces at the bottom of the well: The permanence of racism.* New York: Basic Books.

Bem, D., 1970: *Beliefs, attitudes, and values.* Monterey, CA: Brooks/Cole.

Beniger, J., 1986: *The control revolution: Technological and economic origins of the information society.* Cambridge, MA: Harvard University Press.

Beniger, J. and J. Gusek, 1995: The cognitive revolution in public opinion and communication research. In T. Glasser and C. Salmon (eds), *Public opinion and the communication of consent.* New York: Guilford, pp. 217–248.

Benjamin, I., 1995: *The Black press in Britain.* Staffordshire, UK: Trentham Books.

Bennett, T., 1996: Figuring audiences and readers. In J. Hay, L. Grossberg, and E. Wartella (eds), *The audience and its landscape.* Boulder, CO: Westview, pp. 145–159.

Benzon, W. L., 1993: The United States of the blues: On the crossing of African and

European cultures in the 20th century. *Journal of Social and Evolutionary Systems* **16** (4), 401–438.

Berelson, B., 1959: The state of communication research. *Public Opinion Quarterly* **23**, 1–6.

Berg, C. R., 1990: Stereotyping in films in general and of the Hispanic in particular. *The Howard Journal of Communications* **2** (3), 286–300.

Berger, P. and T. Luckmann, 1966: *The social construction of reality. A treatise in the sociology of knowledge*. New York: Doubleday.

Best, S. and D. Kellner, 1991: *Postmodern theory. Critical interrogations*. New York: Guilford Press.

Béteille, A., 1967: Race and descent as social categories in India. *Daedalus* **96**, 444–463.

Beville, H., 1985: *Audience ratings. Radio, television, cable*. Hillsdale, NJ: Lawrence Erlbaum.

Bikson, T. and C. Panis, 1995: Computers and connectivity: Current trends. In R. Anderson, T. Bikson, S. Law and B. Mitchell, *Universal access to e-mail. Feasibility and societal implications*. Santa Monica, CA: RAND.

Blalock, H. M. J., 1982: *Conceptualization and measurement in the social sciences*. Beverly Hills, CA: Sage.

Blumenthal, S., 1983: Statecraft as spacecraft: John Glenn's media campaign is John Glenn's campaign. *The New Republic* **189**, 15.

Blumler, J. and E. Katz (eds), 1974: *The uses of mass communications. Current perspectives on gratifications research*. Beverly Hills, CA: Sage.

Bobo, J., 1995: *Black women as cultural readers*. New York: Columbia University Press.

Bodenhausen, G. V. and R. S. Wyer, 1985: Effects of stereotypes on decision making and information-processing strategies. *Journal of Personality and Social Psychology* **48** (2), 267–282.

Bogart, L., 1991: *Preserving the press: How daily newspapers mobilized to keep their readers*. New York: Columbia University Press.

Bogle, D., 1974: *Toms, coons, mulattoes, mammies and bucks*. New York: Bantam Books.

Boskin, J. and J. Dorinson, 1985: Ethnic humor: Subversion and survival. *American Quarterly* **7** (1), 81–97.

Bottomore, T., 1975: Structure and history. In P. Blau (ed.), *Approaches to the study of social structure*. New York: The Free Press.

Boudon, R., 1989: Subjective rationality and the theory of ideology. In H. Haferkamp (ed.), *Social structure and culture*. New York: de Gruyter, pp. 269–287.

Bourdieu, P., 1977: *Outline of a theory of practice*. Cambridge: Cambridge University Press.

Bourdieu, P., 1989: Social space and symbolic power. *Sociological Theory* **7** (1) 14–25.

Bourdieu, P. and J. Passeron, 1990: *Reproduction in education, society and culture*. London and Newbury Park, CA: Sage.

Bourdieu, P. and L. Wacquant, 1992: *An invitation to reflexive sociology*. Chicago: University of Chicago Press.

Bowen, L. and J. Schmid, 1997: Minority presence and portrayal in mainstream magazine advertising: An update. *Journalism and Mass Communication Quarterly* **41** (1), 134.

Bowles, S. and H. Gintis, 1992: The political economy of contested exchange. In T. E. Wartenbert (ed.), *Rethinking power.* Albany, NY: State University of New York Press.

Boyd-Barrett, O., 1982: Cultural dependency and the mass media. In M. Gurevitch, T. Bennett, J. Curran, and J. Woolacott (eds), *Culture, society and the media.* New York: Methuen.

Boyenton, W., 1965: The Negro turns to advertising. *Journalism Quarterly,* Spring, 227–235.

Bradley, G. (ed.), 1980: *Life on television. Content analyses of U.S. tv drama.* Norwood, NJ: Ablex.

Bristor, J., R. G. Lee and M. Hunt, 1995: Race and ideology: African-American images in television advertising. *Journal of Public Policy and Marketing* **14** (1), 48.

Brooks, D., 1995: In their own words: Advertiser's construction of an African American consumer market, the World War II era. *The Howard Journal of Communications* **6** (1–2), 32–52.

Brouwer, M., 1964: Mass communication and the social sciences: Some neglected areas. In Dexter, L. and D. White (eds), *People, society, and mass communications.* New York: The Free Press.

Brown, C. M., 1995: Writing a new chapter in book publishing. *Black Enterprise,* 28 February 1995, 108.

Burns, B., 1996: *Nitty gritty: A white editor in black journalism.* Jackson, MS: University Press of Mississippi.

Bush, A. and M. Martin, 1996: The FCC's minority ownership policies from broadcasting to PCs. *Federal Communications Law Journal* **48** (3), 423–445.

Busterna, J., 1989: Concentration in the industrial organization model. In Picard, R., J. Winter, M. McCombs and S. Lacy (eds), *Press concentration and monopoly.* Norwood, NJ: Ablex, pp. 35–53.

Calhoun, C., E. LiPuma, and M. Postone (eds), 1993: *Bourdieu: Critical perspectives.* Chicago: University of Chicago Press.

Campbell, C. P., 1995: *Race, myth and the news.* Thousand Oaks, CA: Sage.

Campbell, D., 1996: *Failure of marxism: Concept of inversion in Marx's critique of capitalism.* Brookfield, VT: Dartmouth Publishing.

Campbell, D. and J. Stanley, 1963: *Experimental and quasi-experimental designs for research.* Chicago, IL: Rand McNally.

Cantor, M., 1980: *Prime-time television: Content and control.* Beverly Hills, CA: Sage.

Cappella, J., 1991: The biological origins of automated patterns of human interaction. *Communication Theory* **1**, 4–35.

Carmines, E. and J. Stimson, 1989: *Issue evolution. Race and the transformation of American politics.* Princeton, NJ: Princeton University Press.

Chapko, M., 1976: Black ads are getting blacker. *Journal of Communication* **26** (4), 175–178.

Chévez, R., 1996: The Mexican Americans. In Lester, P. M. (ed.), *Images that injure: Pictorial stereotypes in the media.* Westport, CT: Greenwood Publishers, pp. 27–33.

Clark, K. and M. P. Clark, 1947: Racial identification and preference in Negro children. In Newcomb, T. M. and E. L. Hartley (eds), *Readings in social psychology*. New York: Holt, Rinehart and Winston, pp. 169–178.

Classen, S., 1994: Standing on unstable grounds: A reexamination of the WLBT-TV case. *Critical Studies in Mass Communication* 11, 73–91.

Cloud, D. L., 1996: Hegemony of concordance? The rhetoric of tokenism in 'Oprah' Winfrey's rags-to-riches biography. *Critical Studies in Mass Communication* 16, 115–137.

Cohen, S., 1994: Identity, place and the 'Liverpool Sound'. In Stokes, M. (ed.), *Ethnicity, identity and music. The musical construction of place*. Oxford and Providence, RI: Berg Publishers, pp. 117–134.

Combs, B. and P. Slovic, 1979: Newspaper coverage of causes of death. *Journalism Quarterly* 56, 837–843, 849.

Commission on the Freedom of the Press, 1947: *A free and responsible press. A general report on mass communication. Newspapers, radio, motion pictures, magazines, books*. Chicago: University of Chicago Press.

Comstock, G. and E. Rubinstein, 1972: *Television and social behavior. Report of the Surgeon General's Scientific Advisory Committee on Television and Social Behavior*. Rockville, MD: National Institute of Mental Health.

Conti, J. and B. Stetson, 1993: *Challenging the civil rights establishment. Profiles of a new black vanguard*. Westport, CT: Praeger.

Converse, P. E., 1964: The nature of belief systems in mass publics. In D. E. Apter (ed.), *Ideology and discontent*. New York: The Free Press, pp. 206–261.

Cook, F. and W. Skogan, 1991: Convergent and divergent voice models of the rise and fall of policy issues. In D. Protess and M. McCombs (eds), *Agenda setting. Readings on media, public opinion and policymaking*. Hillsdale, NJ: Lawrence Erlbaum.

Cooks, L. and M. Orbe, 1993: Beyond the satire: Selective exposure and selective perception in 'In Living Color'. *The Howard Journal of Communications* 4 (3), 217–233.

Cose, E., 1993: *The rage of a privileged class*. New York: HarperCollins.

Crab, I., 1992: *Anthony Giddens*. New York: Routledge.

Cripps, T., 1990: Film. In J. Dates and W. Barlow (eds), *Split image. African Americans in the mass media*. Washington, DC: Howard University Press, pp. 125–172.

Cross, W. E., 1995: Oppositional identity and African American youth: Issues and prospects. In W. Hawley and A. Jackson (eds), *Toward a common destiny: Improving race and ethnic relations in America*. San Francisco: Jossey-Bass, pp. 185–203.

Culley, J. and R. Bennett, 1976: Selling women, selling blacks. *Journal of Communication*, Autumn, 160–174.

Curran, J., 1990: The new revisionism in mass communication research: A reappraisal. *European Journal of Communication* 5, 135–164.

Curran, J., 1992: The new broadcasting order in Western Europe: A British perspective. In H. Kang (ed.), *Changing international order in North-East Asia and communications policies*. Seoul: NANAM Publishing House, pp. 75–100.

Dahrendorf, R., 1979: *Life chances*. Chicago: University of Chicago Press.

Dates, J., 1990: Advertising. In J. Dates, and W. Barlow (eds), *Split image. African Americans in the mass media*. Washington, DC: Howard University Press, pp. 421–453.

Dates, J. and W. Barlow (eds), 1990: *Split image. African Americans in the mass media*. Washington, DC: Howard University Press.

Dates, J. and W. Barlow, 1993: Introduction: A war of images. In J. Dates and W. Barlow (eds), *Split image. African Americans in the mass media*, 2nd edn, pp. 1–21.

Davis, C. N., 1996: Anglo American stereotypes. In P. M. Lester (ed.), *Images that Injure. Pictorial stereotypes in the media*. Westport, CT: Greenwood Publishing.

Davis, F. J., 1991: *Who is black? One nation's definition*. University Park, PA: Pennsylvania State University Press.

Davis, R. A., 1987: Television commercials and the management of spoiled identity. *Western Journal of Black Studies* **11** (2), 59–63.

Dawson, M. C., 1994: *Behind the mule. Race and class in African-American politics*. Princeton: Princeton University Press.

Dawson, M. E., 1993: *Reflecting Black. African-American Cultural Criticism*. Minneapolis: University of Minnesota Press.

DeFleur, M. and S. Ball-Rokeach, 1982: *Theories of mass communication*. New York: Longman.

Delgado, F., 1993–94: Richard Rodriguez and the culture wars: The politics of (mis)representation. *The Howard Journal of Communications* **5**, 1–17.

Delgado, R. (ed.), 1995: *Critical race theory: The cutting edge*. Philadelphia, PA: Temple University Press.

Demott, B., 1996: Sure, we're all just one big happy family. *New York Times*, 7 January 1996, 2, 1.

Dennis, R., 1995: Introduction: The black middle class as a racial class. In R. Dennis (ed.), *Research in race and ethnic relations*, vol. 8. Greenwich, CT: JAI Press, pp. 1–17.

Devine, P., 1989: Stereotypes and prejudice: Their automatic and controlled components. *Journal of Personality and Social Psychology* **56** (1), 5–18.

Devine, P., 1996: *Human diversity and the culture wars: A philosophical perspective on contemporary cultural conflict*. Westport, CT: Praeger.

Dickerson, P., 1996: Let me tell us who I am. The discursive construction of viewer identity. *European Journal of Communication* **11** (1), 57–82.

Dominick, J., 1987: Film economics and film content: 1964–1983. In B. Austin (ed.), *Current research in film: Audiences, economics and law*, vol. 3. Norwood, NJ: Ablex, pp. 136–53.

Donohue, G., P. Tichenor, and C. Olien, 1972: Gatekeeping: Mass media systems and information control. In F. Kline and P. Tichenor (eds), *Current perspectives in mass communication research*, vol. 1. Beverly Hills, CA: Sage, pp. 41–69.

Donohue, G., P. Tichenor, and C. Olien, 1985: Reporting conflict by pluralism, newspaper type and ownership. *Journalism Quarterly* **62**, 489–499, 507.

Dorfman, A. and A. Mattelart, 1975: *How to read Donald Duck. Imperialist ideology in the Disney comic*. New York: International General.

Dovidio, J. F. and S. Gaertner (eds) 1986: *Prejudice, discrimination and racism*. Orlando, FL: Academic Press.

Downing, J., 1990: Ethnic minority radio in the United States. *The Howard Journal of Communications* **2**, 135–148.

Duckitt, J., 1992: Psychology and prejudice. A historical analysis and integrative framework. *American Psychologist* **47**, 1182–1193.

During, S., 1994: Introduction. In S. During (ed.), *The cultural studies reader.* London and New York: Routledge.

Duster, T., 1990: *Backdoor to eugenics.* New York: Routledge.

Dyson, M. E., 1993: *Reflecting black. African-American cultural criticism.* Minneapolis, MN: University of Minnesota Press.

Eaman, R. A., 1994: *Channels of influence: CBC audience research and the Canadian public.* Toronto: University of Toronto Press.

Eder, K., 1993: *The new politics of class: Social movements and cultural dynamics in advanced societies.* London and New York: Sage.

Edsall, T. and M. Edsall, 1991: Race. *The Atlantic Monthly,* May, 53–86.

Ehrenreich, B., 1992: The challenge for the left. In P. Berman (ed.), *Debating P.C.: the controversy over political correctness on college campuses.* New York: Dell Publishing, pp. 333–338.

Eisenstein, Z., 1996: *Hatréds: Racialized and sexualized conflicts in the 21st century.* New York: Routledge.

Ellul, J., 1965: *Propaganda. The formation of men's attitudes.* New York: Knopf.

Englade, K., 1987: 'Mean Joe' Niwat has universal commercial appeal. *Business Atlanta* 16, 80.

Entman, R., 1990: Modern racism and the images of blacks in local television news. *Critical Studies in Mass Communication* 7, 332–345.

Entman, R., 1992: Blacks in the news: Television, modern racism and cultural change. *Journalism Quarterly* **69** (2), 341–361.

Erickson, E. H., 1968: *Identity: Youth and crisis.* New York: W. W. Norton.

Essed, P., 1991: *Understanding everyday racism: An interdisciplinary theory.* Newbury Park, CA: Sage.

Ettema, J., 1990: Press rites and race relations: A study of mass-mediated ritual. *Critical Studies in Mass Communication* 7 (4), 309–331.

Evans, W., 1990: The interpretive turn in media research: Innovation, iteration, or illusion? *Critical Studies in Mass Communication* 7, 147–168.

Ewan, S., 1972: *Captains of consciousness: Advertising and the social roots of consumer culture.* New York: McGraw-Hill.

Favell, A. and D. Tambini, 1995: Great Britain. Clear blue water between 'us' and 'Europe'? In B. Baumgartl and A. Favell (eds), *New xenophobia in Europe.* London: Kluwer Law International, pp. 148–163.

Federal Communications Commission, 1994: *Implementation of Commission's equal opportunity rules.* MM Docket no. 94–34, 5 October.

Fenster, M., 1995: Understanding and incorporating rap: The articulation of alternative popular musical practices within dominant cultural practices and institutions. *The Howard Journal of Communications* 5 (3), 223–244.

Ferretti, F., 1970: The white captivity of black radio. *Columbia Journalism Review,* Summer, 35–39.

Fife, M., 1987a: The impact of minority ownership on minority images in local news. In O. H. Gandy (ed.), *Communications, a key to economic and political change.* Washington, DC: Howard University, Center for Communications Research, pp. 99–125.

Fife, M., 1987b: Promoting racial diversity in US broadcasting: Federal policies versus social realities. *Media, Culture and Society* **9**, 481–514.

Fishman, M., 1980: *Manufacturing the news.* Austin, TX: University of Texas Press.

Fiske, J., 1996: *Media matters: race and gender in US politics*. Minneapolis: University of Minnesota Press.

Fiske, S., 1984: *Social cognition*. Reading, MA: Addison-Wesley.

Fitzgerald, T. K., 1992: Media, ethnicity, and identity. In P. Scannell, P. Schlesinger, C. Sparks (eds), *Culture and power: Media, culture and society reader*. London: Sage, pp. 112–33.

Flynn, J., P. Slovic and C. K. Mertz, 1994: Gender, race, and perception of environmental health risks. *Risk Analysis* 14, 1105.

Foucault, M., 1973: *The order of things: An archeology of the human sciences*. New York: Vintage Books.

Foucault M., 1979: *Discipline and punish. The birth of the prison*. New York: Random House.

Fox-Genevese, E., 1995: A Kafkaesque trip. *Academe*, May–June, 8–14.

Frank, R. E. and M. G. Greenberg, 1980: *The public's use of television: Who watches and why*. Beverly Hills, CA: Sage.

Franzwa, H., 1977: *Window dressing on the set: Women and minorities in television. A report of the United States Commission on Civil Rights*. Washington, DC: US Commission on Civil Rights.

Frederick, H., 1993: *Global communication and international relations*. Belmont, CA: Wadsworth.

Friedman, M. and J. Narveson, 1995: *Political correctness: For and against*. Lanham, MD: Rowman and Littlefield.

Fry, W., 1987: Humor and paradox. *American Behavioral Scientist* 30 (1), 42–71.

Funkhouser, G. R., 1973: The issues of the sixties: An exploratory study in the dynamics of public opinion. *Public Opinion Quarterly* 37, 62–75.

Gabriel, J., 1994: *Racism, culture, markets*. London and New York: Routledge.

Gaertner, S., J. Dovidio, B. Banker, M. Rust, J. Nier, G. Mottola and C. Ward, 1997: Does white racism necessarily means antiblackness? Aversive racism and prowhiteness. In M. Fine *et al.* (eds), *Off white: Readings on society, race and culture*. New York: Routledge, pp. 167–178.

Gamson, W. A., 1992: *Talking politics*. New York: Cambridge University Press.

Gamson, W. A. and A. Modigliani, 1987: The changing culture of affirmative action. In R. Braungart (ed.), *Research in political sociology*, vol. 3. Greenwich, CT: JA1 Press, pp. 137–177.

Gandy, O. H., 1981a: Toward the production of minority audience characteristics. In H. Myrick and C. Keegan (eds), *In search of diversity. Symposium on minority audiences and programming research: Approaches and applications*. Washington, DC: Corporation for Public Broadcasting, pp. 111–129.

Gandy, O. H., 1981b: Is that all there is to love?: Values and program preference. In S. Thomas (ed.), *Studies in communication*, vol. 1. Norwood, NJ: Ablex, pp. 207–219.

Gandy, O. H., 1982: *Beyond agenda setting. Information subsidies and public policy*. Norwood, NJ: Ablex.

Gandy, O. H., 1988: The political economy of communications competence. In V. Mosco and J. Wasko (eds), *The political economy of information*. Madison, WI: University of Wisconsin Press, pp. 108–124.

Gandy, O. H., 1992: The political economy approach: A critical challenge. *Journal of Media Economics* 5 (2), 23–42.

Gandy, O. H., 1993: *The political economy of personal information*. Boulder, CO: Westview.

Gandy, O. H., 1995: Tracking the audience: Personal information and privacy. In J. Downing, A. Mahammadi, and Sreberny-Mohammadi (eds), *Questioning the media. A critical introduction* 2nd edn. Thousand Oaks, CA: Sage, pp. 221–237.

Gandy, O. H., 1996a: If it weren't for bad luck. Framing stories of racially comparative risk. In V. Berry and C. Manning-Miller (eds), *Mediated messages and African-American culture: Contemporary issues*. Thousand Oaks, CA: Sage.

Gandy, O. H., 1996b: Legitimate business interest. No end in sight? An inquiry into the status of privacy in cyberspace. *University of Chicago Legal Forum*, 77–137.

Gandy, O. H. and P. Matabane, 1989: Television and social perceptions among African Americans and Hispanics. In M. Asante and W. Gudykunst (eds), *Handbook of international and intercultural communication*. Newbury Park, CA: Sage, pp. 318–348.

Gandy, O. H. and N. Signorielli, 1981: Audience production functions: A technical approach to programming. *Journalism Quarterly* 58, 232–240.

Garnham, N., 1988: Raymond Williams, 1921–1988: A cultural analyst, a distinctive tradition. *Journal of Communication* 38 (4), 123–131.

Garnham, N., 1990: *Capitalism and communication. Global culture and the economics of information*. London and Newbury Park, CA: Sage.

Garnham, N., 1995: Political economy and cultural studies: Reconciliation or divorce? *Critical Studies in Mass Communication* 12, 62–71.

Garst, D., 1985: Wallerstein and his critics. *Theory and Society* 14, 445–468.

Gellner, E., 1995: Nationalism and xenophobia. In B. Baumgartl and A. Favell (eds), *New xenophobia In Europe*. London: Kluwer, pp. 6–9.

Gerbner, G., 1973: Cultural indicators: The third voice. In G. Gerbner, L. Gross and W. Melody (eds), *Communication technology and social policy*. New York: Wiley, pp. 555–573.

Gerbner, G., 1983a: The importance of being critical – In one's own fashion. *Journal of Communication* 33, 359.

Gerbner, G., 1983b: Ferment in the field. *Journal of Communication* 33, 3.

Gerbner, G., L. Gross, M. Morgan and N. Signorielli, 1982: Charting the mainstream: Television's contributions to political orientations. *Journal of Communication* 32 (2), 100–127.

Gerbner, G., L. Gross, M. Morgan and N. Signorielli, 1986: Living with television: The dynamics of the cultivation process. In B. Jennings and D. Zillman (eds), *Perspectives on media effects*. Hillsdale, NJ: Lawrence Erlbaum.

Gerbner, G., L. Gross, M. Morgan and N. Signorielli, 1994: Growing up with television: The cultivation perspective. In J. Bryant and D. Zillman (eds), *Media effects. Advances in theory and research*. Hillsdale, NJ: Lawrence Erlbaum.

Gerbner, G., L. Gross, N. Signorielli, M. Morgan and M. Jackson-Beeck, 1979: The demonstration of power: Violence profile no. 10. *Journal of Communication* 29 (3), 177–196.

Gergen, K., 1967: The significance of skin color in human relations. *Daedalus*, Spring, 390–406.

Gibson, D. P., 1969: *The $30 billion Negro*. New York: Macmillan.

Giddens, A., 1981: *A contemporary critique of historical materialism*, vol. 1: *Power, property and the state*. Berkeley, CA: University of California Press.

Giddens, A., 1984: *The constitution of society. Outline of the theory of structuration*. Cambridge: Polity Press.

Giddens, A., 1990: Structuration theory and sociological analysis. In J. Clark, C. Mogdil, and S. Modgil (eds), *Anthony Giddens. Consensus and controversy*. London: Falmer Press.

Gilens, M., 1996: Race and poverty in America. Public misperceptions and the American news media. *Public Opinion Quarterly* 60 (4), 515–541.

Gillespie, M., 1995: *Television, ethnicity and cultural change*. London: Routledge.

Gilroy, P., 1987: *There ain't no black in the Union Jack: The cultural politics of race and nation*. London: Hutchinson.

Gilroy, P., 1991: It ain't where you're from, it's where you're at: The dialectics of diasporic identification. *Third Text* 13, 3–16.

Gilroy, P., 1993: *The Black Atlantic: Modernity and double consciousness*. Cambridge, MA: Harvard University Press.

Gitlin, T., 1985: *Inside prime-time*. New York: Pantheon.

Glasser, T. L. and C. T. Salmon (eds), 1995: *Public opinion and the communication of consent*. New York: Guilford.

Golding, P. and S. Middleton, 1982: *Images of welfare. Press and public attitudes to poverty*. Oxford: Martin Robertson.

Goldstein, J., 1976: Theoretical notes on humor. *Journal of Communication*, Summer, 104–112.

Gomery, D., 1989: Media economics: Terms of analysis. *Critical Studies in Mass Communication* 6, 43–60.

Goshorn, K. and O. H. Gandy, 1995: Race, risk and responsibility: Editorial constraint in the framing of inequality. *Journal of Communication* 45 (2), 133–151.

Gould, S. J., 1992: Life in a punctuation. *Natural History* 101, 10–21.

Graber, D., 1984: *Processing the news. How people tame the information tide*. New York: Longman.

Graubard, S., 1996: An American dilemma revisited. In O. Clayton (ed.), *An America dilemma revisited: Race relations in a changing world*. New York: Russell Sage Foundation.

Gray, H., 1986: Television and the new black man: Black male images in prime-time situation comedy. *Media, Culture and Society* 8, 223–242.

Gray, H., 1989: Television, black Americans, and the American dream. *Critical Studies in Mass Communication* 6 (4) 376–386.

Gray, H., 1993: The endless slide of difference: Critical television studies, television and the question of race. *Critical Studies in Mass Communication* 10 (2), 190–197.

Gray, H., 1995: *Watching race. Television and the struggle for 'blackness'*. Minneapolis, MN: University of Minnesota Press.

Greenberg, B., 1986: Minorities and the mass media. In J. Bryant and D. Zillmann (eds), *Perspectives on media effects*. Hillsdale, NJ: Lawrence Erlbaum Associates.

Greenberg, B. and C. Atkin, 1982: Learning about minorities from television: A research agenda. In G. Berry and C. Mitchell-Kernan (eds), *Television and the socialization of the minority child*. New York: Academic Press, pp. 215–243.

Greenberg, B. and P. Baptista-Fernandez, 1980: Hispanic-Americans: The new minority on television. In B. Greenberg (ed.), *Life on television. Content analyses of U.S. tv drama.* Norwood, NJ: Ablex, pp. 3–12.

Greenberg, B. and K. Neuendorf, 1980: Black family interactions on television. In B. Greenberg (ed.), *Life on television. Content analyses of U.S. tv drama.* Norwood, NJ: Ablex, pp. 173–181.

Greenberg, B., M. Burgoon, J. Burgoon and F. Korzenny (eds), 1983: *Mexican Americans and the mass media.* Norwood, NJ: Ablex.

Gregory, R. L., 1966: *Eye and brain. The psychology of seeing.* New York: McGraw-Hill.

Grossberg, L., 1993: Cultural studies and/in new worlds. *Critical Studies in Mass Communication* 10 (1), 1–22.

Grossberg, L., 1995: Cultural studies vs political economy: Is anybody else bored with this debate? *Critical Studies in Mass Communication* 12, 72–81.

Grossberg, L., 1996: Identity and cultural studies: Is that all there is? In S. Hall and P. du Gay (eds), *Questions of cultural identity.* Thousand Oaks, CA: Sage, pp. 87–107.

Guback, T., 1969: *The international film industry: Western Europe and America since 1945.* Bloomington, IN: Indiana University Press.

Guerrero, E., 1993: *Framing blackness. The African American image in film.* Philadelphia, PA: Temple University Press.

Gunter, B., 1987: *Poor reception. Misunderstanding and forgetting broadcast news.* Hillsdale, NJ: Lawrence Erlbaum.

Gutiérrez, F., 1990: Advertising and growth of minority markets and media. *Journal of Communication Inquiry* 14 (1), 6–16.

Gutiérrez, F. and J. R. Schement, 1981: Problems of ownership and control of Spanish-language media in the United States: National and international policy concerns. In E. McAnany, J. Schnitman and N. Janus (eds), *Communication and social structure. Critical studies in mass media research.* New York: Praeger, pp. 181–203.

Gutman, H. G., 1975: *Slavery and the numbers game. A critique of Time on the Cross.* Urbana, IL: University of Illinois Press.

Haas, P., 1992: Introduction: Epistemic communities and international policy coordination. *International Organization* 46, 1–35.

Habermas, J., 1987: *Theory of communicative action.* Boston, MA: Beacon Press.

Habermas, J., 1989: *The structural transformation of the public sphere. An inquiry into a category of bourgeois society.* Cambridge, MA: MIT Press.

Hacker A., 1992: *Two nations: Black and white, separate, hostile, unequal.* New York: Charles Scribner's Sons.

Hacker, G., R. Collins, and M. Jacobson, May, 1987: *Marketing booze to blacks.* Washington, DC: Center for Science in the Public Interest.

Hagendoorn, L., 1993: Ethnic categorization and outgroup exclusion: Cultural values and social stereotypes in the construction of racial hierarchies. *Ethnic and Racial Studies* 16 (1), 26–51.

Hall, S., 1982: The rediscovery of 'ideology': Return of the repressed in media studies. In M. Gurevitch, T. Bennet, J. Curran and J. Woollacott (eds), *Culture, society and the media.* London and New York: Methuen, pp. 56–90.

Hall, S., 1986: Gramsci's relevance for the study of race and ethnicity. *Journal of Communication Inquiry* 10 (2), 5–27.

Hall, S., 1992: Cultural studies and its theoretical legacies. In L. Grossberg, C. Nelson and P. Treichler (eds), *Cultural Studies*. New York: Routledge, pp. 277–294.

Hall, S., 1996: New ethnicities. In D. Morley and K. Chen (eds), *Stuart Hall. Critical dialogues in cultural studies*. London and New York: Routledge.

Halloran, J. D., 1977: Introduction. In S. A. C. United Nations Educational, *Ethnicity and the media. An analysis of media reporting in the United Kingdom, Canada and Ireland*. Paris: UNESCO, pp. 9–24.

Hamamoto, D., 1994: *Monitored peril: Asian Americans and the politics of tv representation*. Minneapolis, MN: University of Minnesota Press.

Hamilton, D. and T. Trolier, 1986: Stereotypes and stereotyping: an overview of the cognitive approach. In J. Dovidio and S. Gaertner (eds), *Prejudice, discrimination, and racism*. New York: Academic Press, pp. 127–163.

Haney López, I. F., 1996: *White by law. The legal construction of race*. New York: New York University Press.

Hardt, H., 1992: *Critical communication studies. Communication, history, and theory in America*. London and New York: Routledge.

Hardt, H., 1993: Authenticity, communication, and critical theory. *Critical Studies in Mass Communication* 10, 61.

Hartman, P. and C. Husband, 1974: *Racism and the media. A study of the role of the mass media in the formation of white beliefs and attitudes in Britain*. Totowa, NJ: Rowman and Littlefield.

Head, S., 1976: *Broadcasting in America. A survey of television and radio*. Boston, MA: Houghton Mifflin.

Hebdige, D., 1979: Reggae, rastas and rudies. In J. Curran, M. Gurevitch and J. Woollacott (eds), *Mass communication and society*. Beverly Hills, CA: Sage, pp. 426–439.

Hecht, M., M. J. Collier and S. Ribeu, 1993: *African American communication. Ethnic identity and cultural interpretation*. Newbury Park, CA: Sage.

Herman, E. S., 1995: *Triumph of the market: Essays on economics, politics and the media* Boston, MA: South End Press.

Higginbotham, A. L., A. Francois and L. Yueh, 1997: The O. J. Simpson trial: Who was improperly 'playing the race card'? In T. Morrison and C. Lacour (eds), *Birth of a nationhood: Gaze, script, and spectacle in the O. J. Simpson case*. New York: Pantheon, pp. 31–56.

Hilger, M., 1995: *From savage to nobleman. Images of Native Americans in film*. Lanham, MD: Scarecrow Press.

Hilton, J. and von Hippel, W., 1996: Stereotypes. *Annual Review of Psychology* 47, 237–271.

Honig, D., 1983: Relationships among EEO, program service, and minority ownership in broadcast regulation. In O. Gandy, P. Espinosa and J. Ordover (eds), *Proceedings from the tenth annual telecommunications policy research conference*. Norwood, NJ: Ablex, pp. 85–91.

hooks, b. and C. West, 1991: *Breaking bread. Insurgent black intellectual life*. Boston: South End Press.

Howe, G. and A. Sica, 1980: Political economy, imperialism, and the problems of world system theory. *Perspectives in Social Theory* 1, 235–286.

Howells, W. W., 1960: The distribution of man. *Scientific American* 48, 112–120.

Hughes, M. and D. H. Demo, 1989: Self-perceptions of Black Americans: Self-esteem and personal efficacy. *American Journal of Sociology* 95 (1), 132–159.

Hunt, A., 1997: Tiger joins with Michael in some very rare air. *Wall Street Journal*, 2 May 1997, B6.

Hur, K., 1978: Impact of 'Roots' on black and white teenagers. *Journal of Broadcasting* 22, 289–298.

Hurst, C. E., 1972: Race, class, and consciousness. *American Sociological Review* 37, 658–670.

Husband, C., 1994: *A richer vision: The development of ethnic minority media in Western democracies*. Paris: UNESCO.

Hutchinson, E. O., 1996: *Beyond O. J.: Race, sex, and class lessons for America*. Los Angeles: Middle Passage Press.

Inglehart, R., 1977: *The silent revolution*, Princeton, NJ: Princeton University Press.

Inglis, C., 1994: Race and ethnic relations in Australia: Theory, methods and substance. In P. Ratcliffe (ed.), *Race, ethnicity and nation: International perspectives on social conflict*. London: UCL Press, pp. 68–87.

Issacs, H. R., 1967: Group identity and political change: The role of color and physical characteristics. *Daedalus*, Spring, 353–375.

Iyengar, S., 1991: *Is anyone responsible? How television frames political issues*. Chicago: University of Chicago Press.

Jackson, J. W., 1993: Realistic group conflict theory: A review and evaluation of the theoretical and empirical literature. *The Psychological Record* 43, 395–414.

Jacoby, R. and N. Glauberman, 1995: *The bell curve debate: History, documents, opinions*. New York: Random House.

Jeffres, L., 1983: Media use for personal identification: Linking uses and gratifications to culturally significant goals. *Mass Communications Review*, Fall, 6–12, 22.

Jencks, C., 1988: What must be equal for opportunity to be equal? In N. E. Bowie (ed.), *Equal opportunity*. Boulder, CO: Westview Press.

Jenkins, A. H., 1995: *Turning corners: The psychology of African Americans*. Needham Heights, MA: Allyn and Bacon.

Jhally, S., 1990: *The codes of advertising: Fetishism and the political economy of meaning in the consumer society*. New York: Routledge.

Jhally, S. and J. Lewis, 1992: *Enlightened racism. The Cosby Show, audiences and the myth of the American dream*. Boulder, CO: Westview.

Jhally, S. and B. Livant, 1986: Watching as working: The valorization of audience consciousness. *Journal of Communication*, Summer, 124–143.

Jones, J. C., 1986: *The image reflected by mass media: stereotypes*. Paris: UNESCO International Commission for the Study of Communication Problems.

Jones, S., 1993: Crossover culture: Popular music and the politics of 'race'. *Stanford Humanities Review* 3 (2), 103–118.

Jowett, G. and V. O'Donnell, 1986: *Propaganda and persuasion*. Newbury Park, CA: Sage.

Jowett, G. and V. O'Donnell, 1992: *Propaganda and persuasion*. 2nd edn.

Kahn, J. S., 1995: *Culture, multiculture, postculture*. London: Sage.

Katz, P. A. and D. Taylor 1988: Introduction. In P. A. Katz and D. Taylor (eds), *Eliminating racism: Profiles in controversy*. New York: Plenum Press.

Kellner, D., 1990: *Television and the crisis of democracy*. Boulder, CO: Westview.

Kerner, O., 1968: *Report of the National Advisory Commission on Civil Disorders.* Washington, DC: US Government Printing Office.

Kern-Foxworth, M., 1994: *Aunt Jemima, Uncle Ben, and Rastus: Blacks in advertising, yesterday, today, and tomorrow.* Westport, CT: Greenwood Publishing Group.

Kessler, L., 1984: *The dissident press. Alternative journalism in American history.* Beverly Hills, CA: Sage.

Kidd-Hewett, D. and R. Osborne, 1995: *Crime and the media: The postmodern spectacle.* East Haven, CT: Pluto Press.

Kim, Y. Y., 1996: Identity development: From cultural to intercultural. In H. Mokros (ed.), *Interaction and identity: Information and behavior*, vol. 5. New Brunswick, NJ: Transaction Publishers.

Kinder, D. R. and L. M. Sanders, 1996: *Divided by color. Racial politics and democratic ideals.* Chicago and London: University of Chicago Press.

Kinder, D. R. and D. O. Sears, 1981: Prejudice and politics: Symbolic racism versus racial threats to the good life. *Journal of Personality and Social Psychology* 40 (3), 414–431.

Kinnon, J. B., 1997: Why Black male stars are sizzling in Hollywood. *Ebony*, January, 32.

Kitano, H. H. L., 1991: *Race relations.* Englewood Cliffs, NJ: Prentice-Hall.

Klapper, J., 1960: *The effects of mass communication.* The Free Press.

Kleiman, H., 1991: Content diversity and the FCC's minority and gender licensing policies. *Journal of Broadcasting and Electronic Media* 35 (4), 411–429.

Kleindorfer, P., Kunreuther, H. and P. Schoemaker, 1993: *Decision sciences: An integrative perspective.* New York: Cambridge University Press.

Kleinknecht, A., E. Mandel and I. Wallerstein, 1992: *New findings in long-wave research.* New York: St Martin's Press.

Kleugel, J., 1990: Trends in whites' explanations of the black-white gap in socioeconomic status, 1977–1989. *American Sociological Review* 55, 512–525.

Kleugel, J. and E. Smith, 1986: *Beliefs about inequality.* New York: Aldine de Gruyter.

Knox, P. and J. Agnew, 1994: *The geography of the world economy. An introduction to economic geography.* New York: Edward Arnold.

Korzenny, F., K. Neuendorf, M. Burgoon, J. Burgoon and B. Greenberg, 1983: Cultural identification as a predictor of content preferences of Hispanics. *Journalism Quarterly* 60, 677–685, 770.

Krippendorff, K., 1989: Content analysis. In E. Barnouw (ed.), *International Encyclopedia of Communications.* New York: Oxford University Press, pp. 403–407.

Krippendorff, K., 1995: Undoing power. *Critical Studies in Mass Communication* 12, 101–132.

Kubey, R., 1986: Television use in everyday life: Coping with unstructured time. *Journal of Communication*, Summer, 108–123.

Kubey, R., 1996: On not finding media effects: Conceptual problems in the notion of an 'active' audience (with a reply to Elihu Katz). In J. Hay, L. Grossberg and E. Wartella (eds), *The audience and its landscape.* Boulder, CO: Westview, pp. 187–205.

Kubey, R. and M. Csikszentmihalyi, 1990: *Television and the quality of life: How viewing shapes everyday experience.* Hillsdale, NJ: Lawrence Erlbaum.

Kuhn, T., 1970: *The structure of scientific revolutions*. Chicago: University of Chicago Press.

Kuklinski, J. H., R. C. Luskin and J. Bolland, 1991: Where is the schema? Going beyond the 'S' word in political psychology. *American Political Science Review* 85 (4), 1342–1355.

La Fave, L. and R. Mannell, 1976: Does ethnic humor serve prejudice? *Journal of Communication*, Summer, 116–123.

Laclau, E. and C. Mouffe, 1985: *Hegemony and socialist strategy: Toward a radical democratic politics*. London: Verso.

Lancaster, K. J., 1971: *Consumer demand. A new approach*. New York: Columbia University Press.

Lane, R., 1996: Nice guys finish first. *Forbes*, December, 236.

Lang, G. and K. Lang, 1981: Watergate: An exploration of the agenda-building process. In G. C. Wilhoit and H. de Bock (eds), *Mass communication review yearbook 2*. Beverly Hills, CA: Sage, pp. 447–468.

Lasswell, H., N. Leites and Associates, 1949: *Language of politics. Studies in quantitative semantics*. Cambridge, MA: MIT Press.

Latané, B. and E. L. Fink, 1996: Symposium: Dynamic social impact theory and communication. *Journal of Communication* 46 (4), 4–77.

Legum, C., 1967: Color and power in the South African situation. *Daedalus*, Summer, 483–495.

Leong, W., 1989: The culture of the state: National tourism and the state manufacture of cultures. In M. Raboy and P. Bruck (eds), *Communication for and against democracy*. Montreal: Black Rose Books, pp. 75–93.

Leslie, M., 1995: Slow fade to?: Advertising in *Ebony* magazine, 1957–1989. *Journalism and Mass Communication Quarterly* 72 (2), 426–435.

Lewis, J., 1991: *The ideological octopus. An exploration of television and its audience*. New York and London: Routledge.

Lewis, P., 1987: Joke and anti-joke: Three Jews and a blindfold. *Journal of Popular Culture* 21 (1), 63–73.

Lichter, R., L. Lichter and S. Rothman, with the assistance of Daniel Amundson, 1994: *Prime time*. Washington, DC: Regency Publishing.

Lieb, T., 1988: Protest at the *Post*: Coverage of Blacks in the *Washington Post Magazine*. *Mass Communications Review* 15 (2–3), 61–67.

Lieberman, L., R. Hampton, A. Littlefield and G. Hallead, 1992: Race in biology and anthropology: A study of college texts and professors. *Journal of Research in Science Teaching* 29 (3), 301–321.

Liebler, C., 1988: Beyond Kerner: Ethnic diversity and minority journalists. *Mass. Comm. Review* 15 (2,3), 32–44.

Lincoln, C. E., 1967: Color and group identity in the United States. *Daedalus*, Spring, 527–541.

Litman, B., 1985: Economic methods of broadcasting research. In J. Dominick and J. Fletcher (eds), *Broadcasting research methods*. Boston, MA: Allyn and Bacon.

Litman, B., 1988: Microeconomic foundations. In R. Picard, M. McCombs, J. Winter and S. Lacy (eds), *Press concentration and monopoly. New perspectives on newspaper ownership and operation*. Norwood, NJ: Ablex, pp. 3–34.

Litman, B. and S. Sochay, 1994: The emerging mass media environment. In R. Babe (ed.), *Information and communication in economics*. Norwell, MA: Kluwer Academic, pp. 233–268.

Lodge, M. and K. McGraw, 1991: Where is the schema? Critiques. *American Political Science Review* 85 (4), 1357–1364.

Lowery, S. and M. DeFleur, 1983: *Milestones in mass communication research*. New York: Longman.

Lule, J., 1995: The rape of Mike Tyson: Race, the press and symbolic types. *Critical Studies in Mass Communication* 12 (2), 176–195.

Lull, J., 1980: The social uses of television. *Human Communication Research* 6, 197–209.

Lull, J., 1995: *Media, communication, culture: A global approach*. New York: Columbia University Press.

MacDonald, J. F., 1992: *Blacks and White tv. African Americans in television since 1948*. Chicago, IL: Nelson-Hall.

Magowan, F., 1994: 'The land is our *Märr* (Essence), it stays forever': The *Yothu-Yindi* relationship in Australian Aboriginal traditional music and popular music. In M. Stokes (ed.), Stokes, *Ethnicity, identity and music. The musical construction of place*. Oxford and Providence, RI: Berg Publishers, pp. 135–155.

Maharey, S., 1990: Understanding the mass media. In P. Spoonley and W. Hirsh (eds), *Between the lines. Racism and the New Zealand media*. Auckland, NZ: Heinemann Reed, pp. 13–25.

Mansfield, E., 1970: *Micro-economics. Theory and applications*. New York: W. W. Norton.

Marable, M., 1994: The divided mind of Black America: race, ideology and politics in the post Civil Rights era. *Race and Class* 36 (1), 61–72.

Marable, M., 1995: *Beyond black and white: Rethinking race in American politics and society*. London: Verso.

Mares, M., 1996: The role of source confusions in television's cultivation of social reality judgements. *Human Communication Research* 23, 2.

Markus, A., 1988: Australian governments and the concept of race: An historical perspective. In M. de Lepervanche and G. Bottomly (eds), *The cultural construction of race*. Sydney: The Sydney Association for Studies in Society and Culture, pp. 46–59.

Martindale, C., 1986: *The white press and Black America*. Westport, CN: Greenwood Press.

Martindale, C., 1996: Newspaper stereotypes of African Americans. In P. M. Lester (ed.), *Images that injure. Pictorial stereotypes in the media*. Westport, CN: Greenwood Publishing, pp. 21–25.

Mastin, T., 1996: *Essence*: Advertising and editorial content. *The Howard Journal of Communications* 7, 221–229.

Matabane, P. W., 1988: Television and the black audience: Cultivating moderate perspectives on racial integration. *Journal of Communication* 38 (4), 21–31.

Maxwell, R., 1988: The Chicano movement, the broadcast reform movement, and the sociology of 'minorities and media': A study of cultural hegemony in the United States. *Confluencia: Revista Hispanica de Cultura y Literatura* 3 (2), 89–102.

McAdams, R., 1995: Cooperation and conflict. The economics of group status production and race discrimination. *Harvard Law Review* 108, 1003–1084.

McChesney, R., 1993: *Telecommunications. Mass media and democracy: The battle for control of U.S. broadcasting.* New York Oxford University Press.

McChesney, R., 1996: Is there any hope for cultural studies? *Monthly Review* **47** (10), 1.

McDaniel, A., 1996: The dynamic racial composition of the United States. In O. Clayton (ed.), *An American Dilemma revisited: Race relations in a changing world.* New York: Russell Sage Foundation.

McLeod, J., 1981: On the nature of media effects. In G. C. Wilhoit and H. deBock (eds), *Mass communication review yearbook 2.* Beverly Hills, CA: Sage, pp. 245–282.

McLeod, J., Z. Pan and D. Rucinski, 1995: Levels of analysis in public opinion research. In T. Glasser and C. Salmon (eds), *Public opinion and the communication of consent.* New York: Guilford, pp. 55–85.

McManus, J. H., 1994: *Market-driven journalism. Let the citizen beware?* Thousand Oaks, CA: Sage.

McNamara, J., 1991: *The economics of innovation in the telecommunications industry.* New York: Quorum Books.

McQuail, D., 1992: *Media performance. Mass communication and the public interest.* London and Newbury Park, CA: Sage.

McRobbie, A., 1994: *Postmodernism and popular culture.* New York and London: Routledge.

Meehan, E., 1993: Commodity audience, actual audience: The blindspot debate. In J. Wasko, V. Mosco and M. Pendakur (eds), *Illuminating the blindspots. Essays honoring Dallas W. Smythe.* Norwood, NJ: Ablex, pp. 378–397.

Merelman, R., 1994: Racial conflict and cultural politics in the United States. *Journal of Politics* **56** (1), 1–20.

Merton, R., 1975: Structural analysis in sociology. In P. Blau (ed.), *Approaches to the study of social structure.* New York: The Free Press, pp. 21–52.

Messaris, P., 1994: *Visual literacy: Image, mind, and reality.* Boulder, CO: Westview.

Metz, D. H. and K. Tate, 1995: The color of urban campaigns. In P. E. Peterson (ed.), *Classifying by race.* Princeton, NJ: Princeton University Press.

Middleton, R., 1990: *Studying popular music.* Buckingham, UK and Bristol, PA: Open University Press.

Miles, J., 1992: Blacks vs browns. The struggle for the bottom rung. *The Atlantic Monthly,* October, 41–68.

Miles, R., 1988: Beyond the 'race' concept: The reproduction of racism in England. In M. De Lepervanche and B. Gillian (eds), *The cultural construction of race.* Sydney: Sydney Association for Studies in Society and Culture, pp. 7–31.

Miller, D. C., 1991: *Handbook of research design and social measurement.* Newbury Park, CA: Sage.

Miller, T., 1993: *The well-tempered self: Citizenship, culture, and the postmodern subject.* Baltimore, MD: Johns Hopkins University Press.

Molnar, H., 1990: Aboriginal broadcasting in Australia: Challenges and promises. *Howard Journal of Communications* **2** (2), 149–169.

Montgomery, K., 1989: *Target: Prime time: Advocacy groups and the struggle over entertainment television.* New York: Oxford University Press.

Moriarty, S. E., 1996: Abduction: A theory of visual interpretation. *Communication Theory* **6** (2), 167–187.

Morley, D., 1992: *Television, audiences and cultural studies*. New York: Routledge.

Morris, N., 1995: *Puerto Rico: Culture, politics, and identity*. Westport, CT: Praeger.

Mosco, V., 1996: *The political economy of communication*. London: Sage.

Mouritsen, P., 1995: The Agonies of innocence. In B. Baumgartl and A. Favell (eds), *New xenophobia in Europe*. London: Kluwer Law International, pp. 88–105.

Mulgan, G. J., 1991: *Communication and control. Networks and the new economies of communication*. New York: The Guilford Press.

Murdock, G., 1982: Large corporations and the control of communication industries. In M. Gurevitch, T. Benett, J. Curran and J. Woollacott (eds), *Culture, society and the media*. New York: Methuen, pp. 118–150.

Murdock, G. and P. Golding, 1979: Capitalism, communication and class relations. In J. Curran, M. Gurevitch and J. Wollacott (eds), *Mass communication and society*. Beverly Hills, CA: Sage, 14–23.

Murgatroyd, L., 1989: Only half the story: Some blinkering effects of 'malestream' sociology. In D. Held and J. Thompson (eds), *Social theory and modern societies. Anthony Giddens and his critics*. New York: Cambridge University Press, 147–161.

Myers, G., 1960: *History of bigotry in the United States*. New York: Capricorn Books.

Myrdal, G., 1944: *An American dilemma: The Negro problem and modern democracy*. New York: Harper.

Myrick, H. and C. Keegan, 1981: *Review of 1980 CPB communication research findings*. Washington, DC: Corporation for Public Broadcasting.

Nadeau, R., R. Niemi and J. Levine, 1993: Innumeracy about minority populations. *Public Opinion Quarterly* 57, 332–347.

National Analysis, 1981: *Attracting minority audiences to public television*. Washington, DC: Corporation for Public Broadcasting, Office of Communications Research.

Neuman, W. R., 1991: *The future of the mass audience*. New York: Cambridge University Press.

Noam E. M. and R. A. Kramer, 1994: Telecommunications strategies in the developed world. A hundred flowers blooming or old wine in new bottles? In C. Steinfield, J. Bauer and L. Caby (eds) *Telecommunications in transition. Policies, services and technologies in the European Community*. Thousand Oaks, CA: Sage.

Nordenstreng, K., 1993: New information order and communication scholarship: Reflections on a delicate relationship. In J. Wasko, V. Mosco and M. Pendakur (eds), *Illuminating the blindspots. Essays honoring Dallas W. Smythe*. Norwood, NJ: Ablex; pp. 251–273.

Nordenstreng, K. and T. Varis, 1974: *Television traffic: A one-way street?* Paris: UNESCO.

Omi, M., 1997: Racial identity and the state: The dilemmas of classification. *Law and Inequality* 15, 7–23.

Omi, M. and H. Winant, 1994: *Racial formation in the United States: From the 1960s to the 1990s*. New York and London: Routledge.

Osgood, C., G. Suci and P. Tannenbaum, 1957: *The measurement of meaning*. Urbana, IL: University of Illinois Press.

Owen, B. and S. Wildman, 1992: *Video economics*. Cambridge, MA: Harvard University Press.

Owens, R., 1996: Entering the twenty-first century. Oppression and the African American press. In V. Berry and C. Manning-Miller (eds), *Mediated messages and African-American culture. Contemporary issues*. Thousand Oaks, CA: Sage, pp. 96–116.

Page, B. and R. Shapiro, 1992: *The rational public. Fifty year trends in America's policy preferences*. Chicago: University of Chicago Press.

Parsons, T., 1975: Social structure and the symbolic media of interchange. In Blau, P. (ed.), *Approaches to the study of social structure*. New York: The Free Press, pp. 94–120.

Pearl, D., L. Bouthilet and J. Lazar, 1982: *Television and behavior. Ten years of scientific progress and implications for the eighties. Technical Reviews 2*. Rockville, MD: National Institute of Mental Health.

Penn, M., S. Gaines and L. Phillips, 1993: On the desirability of own-group preference. *Journal of Black Psychology* **19** (3), 303–321.

Peterson, R., 1994: Measured markets and unknown audiences: Case studies from the production and consumption of music. In J. Ettema and D. C. Whitney (eds), *Audiencemaking: How the media create the audience*. Thousand Oaks, CA: Sage.

Peterson, T., 1964: From mass media to class media. In L. Dexter and D. M. White (eds), *People, society, and mass communications*. New York: The Free Press, pp. 250–260.

Petrovic, D., 1995: Bosnia-Herzegovina. Beyond xenophobia: Ethnic cleansing. In B. Baumgartl and A. Favell (eds), *New xenophobia in Europe*. London: Kluwer Law International, pp. 46–54.

Picard, R., 1989: *Media economics. Concepts and issues*. Newbury Park, CA: Sage.

Pickering, M., 1994: Race, gender and broadcast comedy: The case of the BBC's *Kentucky Minstrels. European Journal of Communication* **9**, 311–333.

Pillai, P., 1993: Rereading Stuart Hall's encoding/decoding model. *Communication Theory* **3**, 221–233.

Polic, J. and O. H. Gandy, 1991: The emergence of the marketplace standard. *Media Law and Practice* **12**, 55–64.

Polic, J. and O. H. Gandy, 1993: Regulatory responsibility and the emergence of the marketplace standard. In J. Wasko, V. Mosco and M. Pendakur (eds), *Illuminating the blindspots. Essays honoring Dallas W. Smythe*. Norwood, NJ: Ablex, pp. 222–247.

Pollay, R., J. Lee and D. Carter-Whitney, 1992: Separate but not equal: Racial segmentation in cigarette advertising. *Journal of Advertising* **21** (1), 45.

Popper, K. R., 1968: *Conjectures and refutations*. New York: Harper and Row.

Porat, M. U., 1982: *The information economy*. Washington, DC: US Department of Commerce.

Potter, W. J., R. Cooper and M. Dupagne, 1993: The three paradigms of mass media research in mainstream communication journals. *Communication Theory* **3** (4), 317–335.

Powell, J. A., 1997: The 'racing' of American society: Race functioning as a verb before signifying as a noun. *Law and Inequality* **15**, 99–125.

Powell, T., 1992: *The persistence of racism in America*. Lanham, MD: University Press of America.

Power, J. G., S. T. Murphy and G. Coover, 1996: Priming prejudice. How stereotypes and counter-stereotypes influence attributions of responsibility and credibility among ingroups and outgroups. *Human Communication Research* **23** (1), 36–58.

Pratt, S. B., 1996: Razzing: Ritualized uses of humor as a form of identification among American Indians. In Mokros, H. B. (ed.), *Interaction and identity*, vol. 5. New Brunswick, NJ: Transaction, pp. 237–255.

Pride, A. S., 1951: Negro newspapers: Yesterday, today and tomorrow. *Journalism Quarterly* **28**, 179–188.

Protess, D. and M. McCombs, 1991: *Agenda setting: Readings on media, public opinion, and policymaking*. Hillsdale, NJ: Lawrence Erlbaum.

Putnam, R., 1995a: Bowling alone, revisited. *The Responsive Community*, Spring, 18–33.

Putnam, R., 1995b: Tuning in, tuning out. The strange disappearance of social capital in America. Public lecture to the American Political Science Association.

Qualls, W. J. and D. J. Moore, 1990: Stereotyping effects on consumers' evaluation of advertising: Impact of racial differences between actors and viewers. *Psychology and Marketing* **7** (2), 135–151.

Quillian, L., 1995: Prejudice as a response to perceived group threat: Population composition and anti-immigrant and racial prejudice in Europe. *American Sociological Review* **60**, 586–611.

Rabinow, P., 1984: *The Foucault reader*. New York: Pantheon.

Raboy, M., 1990: *Missed opportunities. The story of Canada's broadcasting policy*. Montreal: McGill-Queen's University Press.

Radnitzky, G. and P. Bernholz, 1987: *Economic imperialism. The economic method applied outside the field of economics*. New York: Paragon Publishers.

Radway, J., 1984: *Reading the romance. Women, patriarchy and popular literature*. Chapel Hill, NC: University of North Carolina Press.

Radway, J., 1996: Identifying ideological seams: Mass culture, analytical method, and political practice. *Communication* **9**, 93–123.

Ramaprasad, J., 1996: How four newspapers covered the 1992 Los Angeles 'riots'. In V. Berry and C. Manning-Miller (eds), *Mediated messages and African-American culture. Contemporary issues*. Thousand Oaks, CA: Sage, pp. 76–95.

Ratcliffe, P., 1994: Conceptualizing 'race', ethnicity and nation: Towards a comparative perspective and 'Race' in Britain: Theory, methods and substance. In P. Ratcliffe (ed.), *Race, ethnicity and nation: International perspectives on social conflict*. London: UCL Press Limited.

Read, W. H., 1976: *America's mass media merchants*. Baltimore, MD: Johns Hopkins University Press.

Reeves, B., 1996: Hemispheres of scholarship. Psychological and other approaches to studying media audiences. In J. Hay, L. Grossberg and E. Wartella (eds), *The audience and its landscape*. Boulder, CO: Westview, pp. 265–279.

Reeves, B., E. Thorson and J. Schleuder, 1986: Attention to television: Psychological theories and chronometric measures. In B. Jennings and D. Zillman (eds), *Perspectives on media effects*. Hillsdale, NJ: Lawrence Erlbaum, pp. 251–279.

Reich, M., 1981: *Racial inequality. A political-economic analysis.* Princeton, NJ: Princeton University Press.

Reigel, K., 1975: Structure and transformation in intellectual history. In K. Reigel and G. Rosenwald (eds), *The origins of behavior. Structure and transformation,* 3. New York: John Wiley and Sons.

Reily, S. A., 1994: Macunamaíma's music: National identity and ethnomusicological research in Brazil. In M. Stokes (ed.), *Ethnicity, identity and music: The musical construction of place.* Oxford and Providence, RI: Berg Publishers.

Resnick, S and R. Wolff, 1987: *Knowledge and class. A marxian critique of political economy.* Chicago, IL: University of Chicago Press.

Rhines, J. A., 1996: *Black film/white money.* New Brunswick, NJ: Rutgers University Press.

Rifkin, J., 1995: *The end of work: The decline of the global labor force and the dawn of the post-market era.* New York: Putnam.

Riggins, S. H., 1992: The media imperative: Ethnic minority survival in the age of mass communication. In S. H. Riggins (ed.), *Ethnic minority media: An international perspective.* Newbury Park, CA: Sage, pp. 1–22.

Rios, D. and S. Gaines, 1997: Impact of gender and ethnic subgroup membership on Mexican Americans' use of mass media for cultural maintenance. *Howard Journal of Communications* 8 (2), 197–216.

Roach, C., 1993: Dallas Smythe and the New World information and communication order. In J. Wasko, V. Mosco and M. Pendakur (eds), *Illuminating the blindspots. Essays honoring Dallas W. Smythe.* Norwood, NJ: Ablex.

Robinson, D., E. Buck, M. Cuthbert and the International Communication and Youth Consortium, 1991: *Music at the margins. Popular music and global cultural diversity.* Newbury Park, CA: Sage.

Rodriguez, R., 1982: *Hunger of memory: The education of Richard Rodriguez.* New York: Bantam Books.

Roe, K., 1994: Young people and media use. In K. E. Rosengren (ed.), *Media effects and beyond: Culture, socialization and lifestyles.* London and New York: Routledge, pp. 183–204.

Rokeach, M. (ed.), 1960: *The open and closed mind. Investigations into the nature of belief systems, and personality systems.* New York: Basic Books.

Rokeach, M., 1968: *Beliefs, attitudes and values.* San Francisco, CA: Jossey-Bass.

Rokeach, M. and F. Restle, 1960: A fundamental distinction between open and closed systems. In M. Rokeach (ed.), *The open and closed mind. Investigations into the nature of belief systems, and personality systems.* New York: Basic Books.

Rosengren, K. E., 1981: *Advances in content analysis.* Beverly Hills, CA: Sage.

Rosengren, K. E., 1994: Culture, media and society: Agency and structure, continuity and change. In K. E. Rosengren (ed.), *Media effects and beyond: Culture, socialization and lifestyles.* New York: Routledge, p. 21.

Rosenwald, G., 1975: Epilogue: The universalism of structure. In K. Reigel and G. Rosenwald (eds), *The origins of behavior. Structure and transformation,* New York: John Wiley and Sons.

Ross, K., 1996: *Black and white media. Black images in popular film and television.* Cambridge, MA: Polity Press.

Rowland, W., 1982: The illusion of fulfillment: The broadcast reform movement. *Journalism Monographs* 79.

Sassoon, A. S., 1982: *Approaches to Gramsci*. London: Writers and Readers Publishing Cooperative Society Ltd.

Saussure, F. D., 1966: *A course in general linguistics*. New York: McGraw-Hill.

Scanlon, L., 1995: A victimless crime. *Academe*, May–June, 9–15.

Schement, J., 1994: Divergence amid convergence: The evolving information environment at home. In Institute for Information Studies, *Crossroads on the information highway. Convergence and diversity in communications technologies, 1995*. Queenstown, MD: Institute for Information Studies.

Schement, J. and T. Curtis, 1995: *Tendencies and tensions of the information age*. New Brunswick, NJ: Transaction Publishers.

Schement, J. and L. Singleton, 1981: The odds of minority ownership: FCC policy and Spanish-language radio. *Journal of Communication* 31, 78–83.

Schement, J., F. F. Gutiérrez, O. Gandy, T. Haight and M. E. Soriano, 1977: The anatomy of a license challenge. *Journal of Communication*, Winter, 89–94.

Scherer, F. M., 1970: *Industrial market structure and economic performance*. Chicago: Rand McNally.

Schiller, D., 1994: From culture to information and back again: Commoditization as a route to knowledge. *Critical Studies in Mass Communication* 11 (1), 92–115.

Schiller, D., 1996: *Theorizing communication. A history*. New York: Oxford University Press.

Schiller, H. I., 1969: *Mass communications and American empire*. New York: Augustus M. Kelley.

Schiller, H. I., 1976: *Communication and cultural domination*. White Plains, NY: M. E. Sharpe.

Schiller, H. I., 1989: *Culture, Inc*. New York: Oxford University Press.

Schiller, H. I. and A. Schiller, 1988: Libraries, public access to Information, and commerce. In V. Mosco and J. Wasko (eds), *The political economy of information*. Madison, WI: University of Wisconsin Press.

Seamon, W. R., 1992: Active audience theory: Pointless populism. *Media, Culture and Society* 14, 301–311.

Sears, D. O., C. P. Hensler and L. K. Speer, 1979: Whites' opposition to 'busing': Self-interest or symbolic politics? *American Political Science Review* 73, 369–384.

Seashore, S., 1954: *Group cohesiveness in the industrial work group*. Ann Arbor, MI: Institute for Social Research, University of Michigan.

Seiter, E., 1990: Different children, different dreams: Racial representation in advertising. *Journal of Communication Inquiry* 14 (1), 31–47.

Shafer, R., 1993: What minority journalists identify as constraints to full newsroom equality. *Howard Journal of Communications* 4 (3), 195–208.

Shah, H. and M. Thornton, 1994: Racial ideology in US mainstream news magazine coverage of Black-Latino interaction, 1980–1992. *Critical Studies in Mass Communication* 11, 142.

Shapiro, M., 1991: Memory and decision processes in the construction of social reality. *Communication Research* 18 (1), 3–24.

Shapiro, M. and A. Lang, 1991: Making television reality. Unconscious processes in the construction of social reality. *Communication Research* 18 (5), 685–705.

Shields, P. and R. Samarajiva, 1993: Competing frameworks for research on information-communication technologies and society: Toward a synthesis. In

S. A. Deetz (ed.), *Communication yearbook*, 16. Newbury Park, CA: Sage, pp. 349–380.

Shipp, E. R., 1994: OJ and the Black media; neither a typical hero nor a typical villain; he challenges typical coverage. *Columbia Journalism Review*, 33 (4), 39.

Shohat, E. and R. Stam, 1994: *Unthinking eurocentrism. Multiculturalism and the media*. London and New York: Routledge.

Sholle, D., 1988: Critical studies: From the theory of ideology to power/knowledge. *Critical Studies in Mass Communication* 5, 16–41.

Shy, O., 1995: *Industrial organization. Theory and applications*. Cambridge, MA: MIT Press.

Sidanius, J. and F. Pratto, 1993: The inevitability of oppression and the dynamics of social dominance. In P. Sniderman, P. Tetlock and E. Carmines (eds), *Prejudice, politics, and the American dilemma*. Stanford, CA: Stanford University Press, pp. 173–211.

Sidanius, J., E. Devereux and F. Pratto, 1992: A comparison of symbolic racism theory and social dominance theory as explanations for racial policy attitudes. *Journal of Social Psychology* **132** (3), 377–395.

Sigelman, L. and S. Welch, 1991: *Black Americans' views of racial inequality*. New York: Cambridge University Press.

Signorielli, N. and M. Morgan, 1990: *Cultivation analysis: New directions in media effects research*. Newbury Park, CA: Sage.

Simon, H., 1979: *Models of thought*. New Haven: Yale University Press.

Singleton, L. A., 1981: FCC minority ownership policy and non-entertainment programming in Black-oriented radio stations. *Journal of Broadcasting* **25**, 195–201.

Skocpol, T., 1995: African Americans in U.S. social policy. In P. E. Peterson (ed.), *Classifying by race*. Princeton, NJ: Princeton University Press.

Slack, J. D. and M. Allor, 1983: The political and epistemological constituents of critical communication research. *Journal of Communication* **33** (3), 208–218.

Smith A., 1991: *The age of behemoths. The globalization of mass media firms*. New York: Twentieth Century Fund.

Smith, B. C., 1996: Limits of correctness in computers. In R. Kling (ed.) *Computerization and controversy. Value conflicts and social choices*, 2nd edn. San Diego, CA: Academic Press, pp. 810–825.

Smith, E., 1994: *Transmitting race. The Los Angeles riot in television news*. Cambridge, MA: Harvard University, John F. Kennedy School of Government.

Smith, E. R., 1989: *The unchanging American voter*. Berkeley, CA: University of California Press.

Smith, R., 1986: Television addiction. In J. Bryant and D. Zillman (eds) *Perspectives on media effects*. Hillsdale, NJ: Lawrence Erlbaum.

Smith, R. C., 1978: The magazines' smoking habit. *Columbia Journalism Review*, February, 29–31.

Smith, R. C., 1995: *Racism in the post civil rights era: Now you see it, now you don't*. Albany, NY: State University of New York Press.

Smythe, D. W., 1977: Communications: Blindspot of Western marxism. *Canadian Journal of Political and Social Theory* **1** (3), 1–27.

Smythe, D. and Tran Van Dinh, 1983: On critical and administrative research: A new critical analysis. *Journal of Communication* **33** (3), 117–127.

Snead, J., 1994: *White screens/black images. Hollywood from the dark side* (ed. C. Maccabe and C. West). New York: Routledge.

Sniderman, P. and T. Piazza, 1996: The scar of race. In J. Arthur and A. Shapiro (eds), *Color, class, identity: The new politics of race.* Boulder, CO: Westview.

Sniderman, P. M., R. A. Brody and P. E. Tetlock, 1991: *Reasoning and choice. Explorations in political psychology.* New York: Cambridge University Press.

Snyder, R. J., J. Freeman and S. Condray, 1995: Magazine readership profiles and depictions of African Americans in magazine advertisements. *Howard Journal of Communications* 6, 1–11.

Solomon, G. and A. Cohen, 1978: On the meaning and validity of television viewing. *Human Communication Research* 4, 265–270.

Solomos, J. and L. Back, 1996: *Racism and society.* New York: St Martin's Press.

Somit, A. and S. Peterson, 1992: *The dynamics of evolution. The punctuated equilibrium debate in the natural and social sciences.* New York: Harcourt Brace Jovanovich.

Spencer, J. M., 1993: Trends of opposition to multiculturalism. *The Black Scholar* 23 (2), 2–5.

Spencer, M. E., 1994: Multiculturalism, 'political correctness,' and the politics of identity. *Sociological Forum* 9 (4), 547–567.

Splichal, S., 1992: Metro broadcasting v. FCC: Supreme Court upholds FCC minority preference policies, but affirmative action victory seems tenuous at best. *Howard Journal of Communications* 3, 281–298.

Spoonley, P. and W. Hirsh, 1990: *Between the lines. Racism and the New Zealand media.* Auckland, NZ: Heinemann Reed.

Steinberg, S., 1995: *Turning back. The retreat from racial justice in American thought and policy.* Boston: Beacon Press.

Steiner, L., 1988: Oppositional decoding as an act of resistance. *Critical Studies in Mass Communication* 5 (1), 1–15.

Steiner, L., 1992: The history and structure of women's alternative media. In L. F. Rakow (ed.), *Women making meaning.* New York and London: Routledge.

Stewart, S., 1996: My years with Betty. *Wall Street Journal*, 5 July 1996, A6.

Stinchcombe, A., 1990: *Information and organizations.* Berkeley, CA: University of California Press.

Stokes, M., 1994: Introduction: Ethnicity, identity and music. In M. Stokes (ed.), *Ethnicity, identity and music. The musical construction of place.* Oxford and Providence, RI: Berg Publishers, pp. 1–27.

Storm, J., 1996: Smaller networks trying to build audience with African American stars. Fall TV Season. *Philadelphia Inquirer*, 3.

Straubhaar, J., 1995: From PTT to private: Liberalization and privatization in Eastern Europe and the Third World. In B. Mody, J. Bauer and J. Straubhaar (eds), *Telecommunications politics. Ownership and control of the information highway in developing countries.* Mahwah, NJ: Lawrence Erlbaum, pp. 3–30.

Streeter, T., 1996: *Selling the air. A critique of the policy of commercial broadcasting in the United States.* Chicago: University of Chicago Press.

Stroman, C., B. Merritt and P. Matabane, 1989–90: Twenty years after Kerner: The portrayal of African Americans on prime-time television. *Howard Journal of Communications* 2 (1), 44–56.

Subervi-Velez, F. A., 1992: Republican and Democratic mass communication strategies: Targeting the Latino vote. In R. de la Garza and L. DeSipio (eds),

From rhetoric to reality. Latino politics in the 1988 elections. Boulder, CO: Westview, pp. 23–39.

Swanson, D., 1996: Audience research: Antimonies, intersections, and the prospect of comprehensive theory. In J. Hay, L. Grossberg and E. Wartella (eds), *The audience and its landscape.* Boulder, CO: Westview, pp. 53–62.

Tait, A. and J. Barber, 1996: Black Entertainment Television. Breaking new ground and accepting new responsibilities? In V. Berry and C. Manning-Miller (eds), *Mediated messages and African-American culture.* Thousand Oaks, CA: Sage, pp. 184–197.

Takagi, D. Y., 1992: *The retreat from race. Asian-American admissions and racial politics.* New Brunswick, NJ: Rutgers University Press.

Tan, A. and G. Tan, 1979: Television use and self-esteem of blacks. *Journal of Communication,* Winter, 129–135.

Tankard, J. and K. Pierce, 1982: Alcohol advertising and magazine editorial content. *Journalism Quarterly* 59, 302–305.

Tapper, J., 1995: The ecology of cultivation: A conceptual model for cultivation research. *Communication Theory* 5 (1), 36–57.

Taylor, D. and P. Katz, 1988: Conclusion. In P. Katz and D. Taylor (eds), *Eliminating racism. Profiles in controversy.* New York: Plenum.

Taylor, S. T., 1984: *Social cognition.* Reading, MA: Addison-Wesley.

Ter Wal, J., A. Verdun and K. Westerbeek, 1995: The Netherlands. Full or at the limit of tolerance. In B. Baumgartl and A. Favell (eds), *New xenophobia in Europe.* London: Kluwer Law International, pp. 228–246.

Thayer, L., 1983: On 'doing' research and 'explaining' things. *Journal of Communication* 33 (3), 80–91.

Thrift, R., 1977: How chain ownership affects editorial vigor of newspapers. *Journalism Quarterly* 54, 327–331.

Turner, J. C., 1991: *Social influence.* Pacific Grove, CA: Brooks Cole.

Turow, J., 1992: *Media systems in society.* New York: Longman.

Turow, J., 1997: *Breaking up America. Advertisers and the new media world.* Chicago: University of Chicago Press.

Ubbiali, G., 1995: France. Towards the institutionalisation of prejudice? In B. Baumgartl and A. Favell (eds), *New xenophobia in Europe.* London: Kluwer Law International, pp. 115–130.

Udick, R., 1993: The Hutchins paradox: Objectivity versus diversity. *Mass Communications Review* 20 (2–3), 148–157.

United States Bureau of the Census, 1979: *The social and economic status of the Black population in the United States: An historical view, 1790–1978.* Washington, DC: US Government Printing Office.

van Dijk, T. A., 1988: *News analysis. Case studies of international and national news in the press.* Hallsdale, NJ: Lawrence Erlbaum Associates.

van Dijk, T. A., 1991: *Racism and the press.* London and New York: Routledge.

van Dijk, T. A., 1992: Discourse and the denial of racism. *Discourse and Society* 3 (1), 87–118.

van Dijk, T. A., 1994: Discourse and cognition in society. In D. Crowley and D. Michell (eds), *Communication theory today.* Stanford, CA: Stanford University Press.

Vaughn, C., 1992: Simmon's rush for profits. *Black Enterprise,* December 67.

Veblen, T., 1953: *The theory of the leisure class.* New York: Mentor Books.

Verba, S. and G. Orren, 1985: *Equality in America. The view from the top.* Cambridge, MA: Harvard University Press.

Verstraeten, H., 1996: The media and the transformation of the public sphere. A contribution for a critical political economy of the public sphere. *European Journal of Communication* 11 (3), 347–370.

Vidmar, N. and M. Rokeach, 1974: Archie Bunker's bigotry: A study in selective perception and exposure. *Journal of Communication* 29, 36–47.

Wagatsuma, H., 1967: The social perception of skin color in Japan. *Daedalus,* Spring, 407–443.

Wallace, M., 1994: Negative images: Towards a black feminist cultural criticism. In S. During (ed.), *The cultural studies reader.* London and New York: Routledge, pp. 118–131.

Wallerstein, I., 1991: The construction of peoplehood: Racism, nationalism, ethnicity. In E. Balibar and I. Wallerstein (eds), *Race, nation, class: Ambiguous identities.* New York: Verso, pp. 71–85.

Walzer, M., 1983: *Spheres of justice. A defense of pluralism and equality.* New York: Basic Books.

Wänke, M., N. Schwarz and E. Noelle-Nuemann, 1995: Asking comparative questions. The impact of direction of comparison. *Public Opinion Quarterly* 59, 347–372.

Ward, E., 1980: Advocating the minority interest: Actors and cases. In B. Rubin (ed.), *Small voices and great trumpets. Minorities and the media.* New York: Praeger, pp. 247–290.

Wartenberg, T., 1992: Introduction. In T. Wartenberg (ed.), *Rethinking power.* Albany, NY: State University of New York Press, pp. xi–xxvi.

Wasko, J., 1994: *Hollywood in the information age.* Austin, TX: University of Texas Press.

Waterman, D. and E. Rogers 1994: The economics of television program production. *Journal of Communication* 44, 89–111.

Waxman, S., 1996: Hollywood reeling from article's accusation of racism. *Washington Post,* 12 March 1996, Style, D01.

Webber, A., 1990: The need for change: Responsibilities of the media. In P. Spoonley and W. Hirsh (eds), *Between the lines. Racism and the New Zealand media.* Auckland, NZ: Helnemann Reed, pp. 145–148.

Webster, F., 1995: *Theories of the information society.* New York: Routledge.

Webster, F. and K. Robins, 1986: *Information technology. A Luddite analysis.* Norwood, NJ: Ablex.

Webster, J. G., 1989: Television audience behavior: Patterns of exposure in the new media environment. In J. L. Salvaggio and J. Bryant (eds), *Media use in the information age: Emerging patterns of adoption and consumer use.* Hillsdale, NJ: Lawrence Erlbaum, pp. 197–216.

Webster, J. G. and L. W. Lichty, 1991: *Ratings analysis: Theory and practice.* Hillsdale, NJ: Lawrence Erlbaum.

Weiss, M., 1988: *The clustering of America.* New York: Harper and Row.

West, C., 1991: The dilemma of the black intellectual. In b. hooks and C. West (eds), *Breaking bread. Insurgent black intellectual life.* Boston: South End Press.

Weston, M. A., 1996: *Native Americans in the news. Images of Indians in the twentieth century press.* Westport, CT: Greenwood Press.

Whittler, T. E. and J. DiMeo, 1991: Viewers' reactions to racial cues in advertising stimuli. *Journal of Advertising Research*, December, 37–46.

Wilcox, C. and L. Williams, 1990: Taking stock of schema theory. *The Social Science Journal* 27 (4), 373–393.

Wildman, S., 1994: One way flows and the economics of audiencemaking. In J. Ettema and D. C. Whitney (eds), *Audiencemaking: How the media create the audience*. Thousand Oaks, CA: Sage, pp. 115–141.

Wildman, S. and S. E. Siwek, 1988: *International trade in films and television programs*. Washington, DC: American Enterprise Institute.

Williams J. (ed.), 1995: *PC wars: Politics and theory in the academy*. New York: Routledge.

Willis, J., 1994: *The age of multimedia and turbonews*. Westport, CT: Greenwood.

Wilson, C. C. I. and F. Gutíerrez, 1995: *Race, multiculturalism, and the media*. Thousand Oaks, CA: Sage.

Wilson, W. J., 1980: *The declining significance of race: Blacks and changing American institutions*. Chicago: University of Chicago Press.

Wilson, W. J., 1987: *The truly disadvantaged: The inner city, the underclass, and public policy*. Chicago: University of Chicago Press.

Wilson, W. J., 1996: *When work disappears*. New York: Knopf.

Wimmer, K. A., 1988: Deregulation and the future of pluralism in the mass media: The prospects for regulatory reform. *Mass Communications Review* 15 (2–3), 20–31.

Winant, H., 1994: *Racial conditions. Politics, theory, comparisons*. Minneapolis: University of Minneapolis Press.

Winant, H., 1997: Behind blue eyes: Whiteness and contemporary U.S. racial politics. In M. Fine, L. Powell, L. Weis and L. M. Wong (eds), *Off white: Readings on society, race, and culture*. New York: Routledge, pp. 41–51.

Winter, J. and C. Eyal, 1981: Agenda-setting for the civil rights issue. *Public Opinion Quarterly* 45, 376–383.

Wober, J. M., 1986: The lens of television and the prism of personality. In B. Jennings and D. Zillman (eds), *Perspectives on media effects*. Hillsdale, NJ: Lawrence Erlbaum, pp. 205–231.

Wolfe, A. S., 1992: Who's gotta have it?: The ownership of meaning and mass media texts. *Critical Studies in Mass Communication* 9 (3), 261–276.

Woll, A. and R. M. Miller, 1987: *Ethnic and racial images in American film and television*. New York and London: Garland Publishing.

Wolseley, R. E., 1990: *The Black press, U.S.A*. Ames, IA: Iowa State University Press.

Wood, J., 1994: Is 'symbolic racism' racism? A review informed by intergroup behavior. *Political Psychology* 15 (4), 673–686.

Wright, C., 1959: *Mass communication. A sociological perspective*. New York: Random House.

Wright, C., 1964: Functional analysis and mass communication. In L. Dexter and D. White (eds), *People, society, and mass communications*. New York: The Free Press.

Wright, E. O., 1982: Class boundaries and contradictory class locations. In A. Giddens and D. Held (eds), *Classes, power and conflict*. Berkeley, CA: University of California Press.

Wright, E. O., 1989: *The debate on classes.* London: Verso.

Wright, E. O. and L. Perrone, 1977: Marxist class categories and income inequality. *American Sociological Review* **42**, 32–55.

Wu, F., 1996: From black to white and black again. *Asian Law Journal* **3**, 185–214.

Wyatt, R. O., 1991: Free expression and the American public. A survey commemorating the 200th anniversary of the First Amendment. Murfreesboro, TN: Middle Tennessee State University for the American Society of Newspaper Editors.

Zaller, J., 1992: *The nature and orgins of mass opinion.* New York: Cambridge University Press.

Zheng, S., 1994: Music making in cultural displacement: The Chinese-American odyssey. *Diaspora* **3** (3), 273–288.

Zijderveld, A., 1983: The sociology of humor and laughter. *Current Sociology* **31** (3), 1–103.

Zillman, D., 1982: Television viewing and arousal. In D. Perl, L. Bouthilet and J. Lazar (eds), *Television and behavior. Ten years of scientific progress and implications for the eighties*, vol. II: *Technical Reviews.* Rockville, MD: National Institute of Mental Health, pp. 53–67.

Zimmerman, R., 1994: Issues of classification in environmental equity: How we manage is how we measure. *Fordham Urban Law Journal* **21**, 633.

Index